MAKING A HEAVEN OF HELL

Making a Heaven of Hell The Problem of the

Companionate Ideal in English Marriage Poetry, 1650–1800

WILLIAM C. HORNE

THE UNIVERSITY OF GEORGIA PRESS *Athens & London*

© 1993 by the University of Georgia Press
Athens, Georgia 30602
All rights reserved
Designed by Mary Mendell
Set in New Baskerville
by Tseng Information Systems, Inc.
Printed and bound by Thomson-Shore, Inc.
The paper in this book meets the guidelines for permanence
and durability of the Committee on Production Guidelines
for Book Longevity of the Council on Library Resources.
Printed in the United States of America
97 96 95 94 93   C   5 4 3 2 1
Library of Congress Cataloging in Publication Data
Horne, William C.
Making a heaven of hell : the problem of the companionate
ideal in English marriage poetry, 1650–1800 / William C.
Horne.
p. cm.
Includes bibliographical references and index.
ISBN 0-8203-1474-9 (alk. paper)
1. English poetry—18th century—History and criticism.
2. English poetry—Early modern, 1500–1700—History and criticism.
3. Marriage in literature. I. Title.
PR555.M29H67   1993
821'.509354—dc20   92-8814

British Library Cataloging in Publication Data available

Title page illustrations: top, from *Douce Ballads II*, folio 150r,
Bodleian Library, University of Oxford; bottom, from
Nuptial Elegies, third edition, Folger Shakespeare Library

For my wife, Susan—my reality principle

CONTENTS

Preface ix

Introduction: The Companionate Ideal and Its Problems 1

ONE *Polemic Poems* 32

TWO *The Rake in Fetters and the Pleasures of a Single Life* 54

THREE *Advice Poems* 99

FOUR *A Bargain Between Two Partners in a Trade* 129

FIVE *Evolving Types* 163

SIX *Real Bliss* 192

SEVEN *Dominion o'er the Breeches* 223

EIGHT *A Union Both of Sex and Mind* 270

NINE *What Comes After?* 284

Notes 297

Works Cited (Pre-1900) 316

Works Consulted (1900 and After) 318

Checklist of Marriage Poems, 1650–1800 326

Index 359

PREFACE

❦

DURING THE LONG EIGHTEENTH CENTURY IN England (1650–1800), marriage was a major topic of social discourse. The frequency with which it was addressed and debated in prose tracts, conduct books, legal cases, and the popular press as well as in drama, the novel, and poetry testifies to its immense sociological, legal, and theological ramifications. In the last twenty years, social historians such as Edward Shorter, Lawrence Stone, and Randolph Trumbach have examined evolving ideas of the family, sex, and marriage in the period, and their findings have aroused scholarly interest and stimulated feminist revision, especially from critics and historians such as Ellen Pollak, Mary Poovey, and Susan Staves. The approaches and controversies of the progressive historians and the feminist revisionists have been carried over into literary criticism. The topic of marriage has been examined in Restoration drama, particularly the plays of Dryden, Wycherley, and Behn; in the novel, specifically those by Defoe, Richardson, and the women novelists; in Johnson's writings; and, quite significantly for this study, in Milton's writings, especially *Paradise Lost*. Letters, diaries, legal and religious tracts, conduct books, and popular literature in general have also begun to be treated with some care.

Yet, in spite of the recent appearance of editions of poetry by women, no study has as yet focused exclusively on the topic of marriage in poetry. Perhaps this is because poetry as a genre depends heavily on form, convention, and myth. Critics treating marriage, sex, and the family in literature have followed the lead of the social historians and tend to use texts as documentation of social change. Generally speaking, they are not predisposed to pay attention to the ways in which formal, conventional, or mythical elements shape discourse in poetry.[1]

In the marriage verse of the long eighteenth century, the libertine and patriarchal ideologies of the canonical satirists, moralists, and celebrators are pervasive. Consequently, the literary period has achieved a special notoriety among feminist critics for the sexist, patriarchal attitudes of major figures such as Swift and Pope.[2] It also seems to have had an overabundance of didactic male versifiers, many of them clergymen, who were always willing to lecture wives on their duties or instruct them in obedience. Marriage poems by women, especially those expressing an antipatriarchal viewpoint, do appear in significant numbers. However, as interesting and culturally important as they are, poems by women are only a portion of the corpus of marriage poetry. Because of this and because many women poets do not move far beyond the formats, genres, and tropes of the canonical male writers, it would be narrow to use the women poets as the sole basis for a critique of marriage poetry. Though the growth of textual and biographical scholarship on women poets has made such an approach feasible, I have chosen to treat the poetry of the age in its full breadth. This allows me to consider how the predominant male discourse impacts on women and women's discourse.

My decision to pay attention to all marriage poetry is perhaps a controversial one that tacitly addresses the issue of canon revision (see, for example, Atlas). I do support expansion of the canon to include women writers. I posit however that attention to the way both canonical and noncanonical poets use or fail to use modes, types, formats, conventions, traditions, and myths can best help us understand the shifting ideologies of marriage and of the family and their problematic aspects.

Since many of the texts I treat are unknown to modern readers, even to students of the period, a portion of my effort has had to be descriptive and bibliographical. Before I could interpret ideology, I had to assemble the texts, a significant portion of which were available only in research libraries. Restoration and eighteenth-century poetry remains an iceberg; the top tenth has been examined with great care, but of the submerged portion we remain mostly ignorant. To make the work of future students of marriage poetry a little easier, I have provided a checklist keyed to the Wing *Short-Title Catalogue* and *The Eighteenth-Century Short Title Catalogue* (see Checklist). Entries indicate when the title is available in a modern edition or a reprint as well as on a microfilm series.

In treating the one hundred and fifty years of the long eighteenth century, I divide the period into two parts: the early part (the Restoration and early eighteenth century from about 1650 to 1740) and the later part (the middle and late eighteenth century from about 1740 to 1800). Though somewhat arbitrary, this division is roughly congruent with major shifts in mode and emphasis.

In completing the research and preparing this manuscript, I have been assisted by numerous groups and individuals. I would like to express my appreciation to the Salisbury State Foundation for four grants that supported the computer production of the manuscript and to the Fulton School of Liberal Arts at Salisbury State University for two grants to purchase computer access to *The Eighteenth-Century Short Title Catalogue*.

I am appreciative to many libraries for furnishing copies of poems and to the library staff who sent them to me along with helpful information. Specifically, I want to thank John Bidwell of the Clark Memorial Library, C. G. Cordeaux of the Bodleian, Joan M. Ogden of the Newberry, Melanie Wisner of the Houghton, Marjorie G. Wynne of the Beinecke, and the staff at the Folger Shakespeare Library. The librarians at Salisbury State University's Blackwell Library deserve special commendation for eleven years worth of assistance. In particular, I thank Lois Bromley, Kathryn Carson, Terry Daenzer, D. Andrews Reese, and Jim Thrash. I wish to acknowledge Joyce Fullard for sending me Checklist information and two graduate students—Laine Scott and Theresa Smith—for calling my attention to critics I had overlooked. I am most appreciative to colleagues, friends, and family who took the time to read the manuscript or parts of it and offer comments and corrections: David B. Ganoe, Ann Cline Kelly, Arthur Scouten, John Wenke, and especially my mother, Virginia Storrick Horne, who proofread the manuscript twice and my daughter, Shelley Watkins, who assisted with the index. For technical assistance with computers and programming, I am much indebted to Libby Collins, Suzanne Flanagan, Janice French, Marie Hearne, Linda May, John McNally, Shirley Perry, Theresa Pusey, Jane Trimmer, Wanda Yackley, and Linda Ziegler. For counsel and encouragement in times of stress and disillusionment, I am obligated to Steven Ackerman, Joseph Gilbert, the late Eric Molin, William Zak, and especially David B. Ganoe and my father, the Reverend Robert E. Horne.

Making a Heaven of Hell

INTRODUCTION

The Companionate Ideal and Its Problems

IN THE COURSE OF THE RESTORATION AND EIGHteenth century in England, as historians of the family have argued, a new model for marriage emerged. The companionate model fosters equality by emphasizing the importance of a couple's being matched in age, temperament, and background. Stressing as well their equality in expressing and sharing marital love, the model celebrates the husband and wife as affectionate friends, lovers, and parents. As such, it is the central feature in what marriage historians refer to as the emergence of the nuclear family and the rise of domesticity.[1]

Tracing the manifestation of this model in poetry, I examine the arguments of various personae to demonstrate how poetic discourse reinforces companionate ideology and myth.[2] Restating the arguments of personae to give them full expression is in one respect an implicit affirmation of that ideology, and my charting the emergence of it effectively amounts to such an affirmation. Yet while my methodology may support Stone, Shorter, and Trumbach in viewing the companionate model as progressive, I insist on the status of poetic discourse as ideology. This opens the way for a critique of the patriarchal bias of many of the pro-companionate arguments and for a consideration of challenges to the view that companionate ideology is always a liberalizing influence.

Such a critique may have an ideological basis in the protofeminist writings of the long eighteenth century, many of them from women's pens.

It is not coincidental that 1650 to 1800 is the first period when numbers of women who were not aristocrats or religious figures wrote poetry for publication. From the first to the last decade of the eighteenth century, women of letters whose verse was published increased fifteenfold (see Lonsdale xxi). The long eighteenth century is thus the first age of the woman professional poet.

Recent feminist criticism has viewed specific eighteenth-century women poets as critical of companionate ideology on issues such as dominion in marriage (see, for example, Williamson 94–100). Nevertheless, the majority of women poets, especially in the late eighteenth century, are pro-companionate and pro-domesticity. The question of how much modern feminist criticism in its various approaches and theories is indebted to eighteenth-century feminism is thus debatable (see Moi).

An underlying issue in current feminist theory by Teresa De Lauretis, Donna Haraway, Sandra Harding, Nancy Hartsock, Mary Poovey, and others is the argument over how much woman's biological nature does determine or should determine her sexuality and social identity. The unwillingness of revisionist critics to see companionate ideology and domesticity as progressive to any degree may stem from their opposition to the notion that biological gender should predetermine social role. Ideologies that glorify women as wives and mothers tend thus, ipso facto, to be judged patriarchal and reactionary. Even so, some historians of feminism, Jane Rendall and Alice Browne for example, see "modern feminism" as originating in the eighteenth century. It might be defined by the way in which women came "to associate together . . . and then to recognize and assert their common interests as women" (Rendall 1). Or it might be identified by its clear argument for "women's rationality, and for their duty to educate themselves, and to base their decisions, including the decision to obey a husband, on a rational understanding of life, not mindless submission to custom" (Browne 81).

To maintain the distinction between eighteenth-century women poets who argue for women's common cause and rationality, and twentieth-century feminists who view companionate ideology and domesticity as counterprogressive, I refer to the former as protofeminists. Though problematic, I suggest that protofeminism does make a positive contribution not just to women's consciousness and image in society but, over the long run, to women's socioeconomic progress as well. The late twentieth-century critique of domesticity does not arise ex nihilo, but evolves from the feminism of earlier centuries. Women needed to band together to create respect for their intellectual capabilities and for the dignity of their traditional roles before they could begin to compete as equals in professions and careers dominated by men. It is with this awareness that I draw on the work of Ellen Pollak, Mary Poovey, and Susan Staves, who counterpoint the progressive historians' argument that the emergence of companionate ideology is a step toward equality for women. Companionate ideology and domesticity, my study will argue, were an advance, though that advance is fraught with contradictions.

In chapters 1 and 2, I will demonstrate how companionate ideology developed in the polemic poems of the Restoration and early eighteenth century as an attack on the libertine ethos identified with the Stuart court. As chapters 3 and 4 show, the ideology gains power in advice poems that recommend unions in which the couple are compatible. It also is affirmed in satires that attack marriages for money and the grotesque mismatches they produce. In the evolution of poetic types seen in chapter 5, satire increasingly gives way to celebration as marriage poets adopt stances that allow for empathetic affirmation of the bliss of companionship. A concomitant of this affirmation, the secularization of the idea of bliss, brings with it, as chapter 6 reveals, a positive emphasis on marital affection and sexuality. At the same time, the secularization feeds the ideology of domesticity that, according to revisionist critics, turns wives into passive "women of sensibility" and sexual servants.

Revisionist challenges to the argument that companionate ideology is progressive focus on this contradiction and especially on the issue of dominion, which is treated in chapter 7. In this chapter and chapter 8, I will demonstrate that the broad pattern of evolution in the long eighteenth century involves a marked softening of the manner in which male dominion is affirmed. Although the early and mid-eighteenth century produce a number of spirited poetic attacks on husbandly tyranny, most of them from women poets, almost all marriage verse by the end of the century reinforces male dominion, though dominion softened by companionate ideology. Most women poets of the late eighteenth century affirm this ideology. Though revisionist criticism views such women as co-opted by a resurgent patriarchalism masked as egalitarianism, the fact that women poets embraced companionate ideology and found it attractive argues that they perceived it as beneficial to their interests. I share revisionist critics' reservations concerning domesticity and companionate ideology, especially on the dominion issue. Nevertheless, the widespread celebration of this ideology in late eighteenth-century marriage verse by both men and women obligates me to acknowledge its contemporary appeal and benefits as well as its weaknesses. In chapter 8, I will do this for the late eighteenth century, and in chapter 9 I will conclude with a glance forward at the separation of heaven from hell in the marriage poetry of the nineteenth and twentieth centuries.

To summarize, I posit that companionate ideology is revolutionary in markedly improving the image of women and their perceived social position. Yet as this ideology is judged by the ideologies of revisionist feminism, it may be seen in some respects as counterprogressive, especially as it reinforces patriarchy—not the overtly antifeminist patriarchy fostered by the traditional theological view of woman as willfully rebellious and consumed by lust but a "kinder and gentler" patriarchy that idealizes the complaisant wife who controls her husband by pleasing him, the wife of taste and sensibility who serves as her husband's dearest possession. Though I believe companionate ideology to be a clear-cut advance over the crude patriarchy and sexism of what Edward Shorter refers to as the "bad old days," the advance is fraught, as I said, with contradictions, contradictions that manifest themselves most blatantly in what Ellen Pollak calls "the myth of passive womanhood" and what Mary Poovey treats as the ideology of the "proper lady." In the arguments of Pollak, Poovey, and Staves, companionate ideology and domesticity are not seen as a direct route toward equality and independence for women. In fact, revisionist ideology views it unequivocally as a step backwards.

My study will pay attention to the contradictions implicit in companionate ideology. In idealizing marriage as a heaven and in rescuing marriage from the traditional satirists who portrayed it as a hell, many poets did not realize that heaven itself might become a hell, especially for the angelic wife who was idealized by the new mythos. In making a heaven of hell, poets increasingly failed to ballast their celebrations of companionship and domesticity with the satirical. My aim will be to analyze the discourse of poetry in which such problematic ideologies could flourish. Poetry examined in such a light is obviously being treated as cultural artifact. However, as my pairing of thematic and formal chapters indicates, I am interested in marriage verse not just as it documents social change but also as poetic formats and types give artistic shape to ideology and myth. I will be concerned not simply with abstracting ideology from its formal contexts but with understanding the ideological implications of a poet's choice of format, type, or mode of discourse.

Since poetic form in large measure is determined by tradition and fashion and since these are dominated in the long eighteenth century by male tastes, we can partially understand the formal evolution of marriage verse in terms of gender criticism. The shift from satiric to celebratory mode, which is central to the development of marriage poetry, can, for example, be seen as a "feminization" of that verse, the embodiment in poetry of qualities such as refinement, sensitivity, and affective emotionality that the ideology of the age attributed to women. Likewise, the choice of genres by both men and women poets has ideological implications, depending on the way a poet adopts, modifies, or rejects traditional male formats, types, and discourse.

The formal and ideological contradictions I will point to in the evolution of marriage poetry are obviously a reaction to the controversy within the social history of marriage itself.[3] To introduce the progressive/revisionist controversy as fairly as possible, I shall look first at the progressive historians' advocacy of four basic propositions. Immediately after, I shall consider revisionist challenges to these same propositions. Examining each proposition twice allows both positions to be voiced directly, and readers may see firsthand how differences of emphasis and significant oversights among the several (male) progressive historians open the way for the revisionist counterargument, a corrective that is salutary but at the same time oversimplified and one-sided in its insistence that companionate ideology is only counterprogressive. A final reconciliation of this gender-based controversy may not be possible since by nature all would-be reconcilers have gender. Even so, anyone aspiring to a balanced view should consider the arguments of both progressive historians and their revisionist critics, even if such arguments stand in contradiction. Arising out of this controversy will be my approach to marriage poetry—its topics, types, and formats.

My study will show that the shift from satire to celebration, from a male-centered attack on marriage as a hell to a feminized idealization of marriage as a heaven, strengthens woman's stature in the domestic sphere, although it effectively delays her acquisition of power in the legal and economic sphere. It increases respect for marriage and the family as social institutions; however, it does so by replacing traditional marriage theology with a secularized worship of woman in her roles as wife and mother. Though the secular glorification of domesticity may, over the short run, have bolstered the institution of marriage, secularization, over the long run, weakened the force of marriage theology even as it furthered woman's legal equality and personal freedom.

Historians of the family who view the emergence of companionate ideology as a progressive social force do not all focus on exactly the same phenomena, nor do all refer to it with the same terminology. Edward

Shorter discusses the displacement of the traditional extended family by the nuclear family and emphasizes the increasing importance of romance and sexuality in courtship and of mothering in marriage. Randolph Trumbach stresses the shift from patriarchal to an egalitarian or domestic system of household relationships, the emergence of an egalitarian idea of marriage among aristocrats, and an increased emphasis on the role of mother, even over that of wife.[4]

Lawrence Stone considers the emergence of the companionate model within his broader discussion of the rise of the closed domesticated nuclear family (1640–1800) from the restricted patriarchal nuclear family (1550–1700) and the open lineage family (1450–1650). Of nearly equal importance to the companionate model for Stone is the decline of patriarchal supervision of mating arrangements and the rise of affective individualism in the family and a "child-oriented, affectionate and permissive mode" in child rearing.

According to Stone, the companionate marriage develops progressively throughout the eighteenth century with the earliest and most significant adoption of its features among the lesser nobility, the squirearchy and gentry, and the professional and upper middle classes. Among the lower middle classes and the growing number of "labour aristocracy," marriage "often tended to be an economic partnership for productive work, although the higher levels of the urban lower middle class were increasingly seeking to elevate their status by choosing brides educated not for work but to display all the refinements of upper-class leisure activity." As with the squirearchy and upper middle classes, "affective bonding was often highly developed . . ." among this social group as well (Stone 292).

Though different historians of the family formulate the progressive argument with different emphases, it can be viewed as having at least four main propositions. The first is that the rise of domesticity and the glorification of romantic love produced an attack on libertinism and tended to discredit the double standard of fidelity in marriage, at least in its overt manifestations in polite society. Second, the emergence of companionate ideology produced a weakening of patriarchal control over mating arrangements. Third, the rise of domesticity and companionate ideology placed a salutary emphasis on expressions of marital affection and elevated the perceived importance of marital sexuality (and sexuality in general). Fourth, the rise of companionate ideology softened husbandly dominion and the traditional subordination of wives, or at least the blatant insistence on it.

Proposition: The Attack on Libertinism and the Double Standard

Glorification of the naturalness of the sex drive and of the freedom to pursue the pleasures of the body is fairly open in the urbane upper middle class and aristocratic culture of the early era (roughly 1660 to 1730). As Roy Porter points out, "these naturalistic and hedonistic assumptions—that Nature had made men to follow pleasure, that sex was pleasurable, and that it was natural to follow one's sexual urges—underpinned much Enlightenment thought about sexuality" (4). Porter finds manifestations of libertine attitudes in literate and popular printed culture, in the public area (e.g., in women's décolletage), and in the acceptance of the casual or promiscuous behavior on the part of gentlemen. Peter Wagner documents graphically in *Eros Revived* the burgeoning of erotica in print and visual media.

On the other hand, as Porter also points out, the acceptance of sexual urges as natural and good is "circumscribed" by several prominent forces in English society. One of these is the moralists and clergymen who inveigh against vice and immorality and dramatize its consequences in numerous tracts and sermons. This group draws on, but is certainly not exclusively a product of, England's strong Puritan tradition. Enlightenment permissiveness also does not extend deeply into village life, and the traditional mores and patriarchal family structures at this social level no doubt stifle it to a significant degree, as does lack of privacy. Finally, as Porter acknowledges, casual attitudes toward libertine behavior do not extend to women, at least not to respectable women, though Porter finds that Enlightenment thinking does not exclude women from the physical capability to enjoy sexuality as some Victorian moralists and physicians do.[5]

A few progressive historians of the family such as Randolph Trumbach and Keith Thomas treat the double standard of fidelity in the traditional family less as a function of Enlightenment libertinism than as an "institutionalization of men's desire to have an absolute property in women" (Trumbach 154). "Property in women was enshrined in the principles and actions of the law, and the most fundamental of these was that 'by marriage the very being or existence of a woman was suspended or at least it is incorporated into that of her husband, under whose wing, protection, and cover, she performs everything'" (154). The double standard is also manifested in such traditional customs as chivaris to mock cuckolded husbands and unwed mothers. While women's sexual misconduct elicited public derision, "the village turned a blind eye to male sexual abuses" and did not bother the husband who was unfaithful to his wife with another married woman (Shorter 220).

Whatever traditional social institutions reinforce the double standard, the chief force making it less openly tolerated in mid and late eighteenth-century polite society would seem to be the rise of companionate ideology with its celebration of affective bonding and romantic love. Porter discusses this ideology indirectly when he says that Romanticism rejected Enlightenment libertine attitudes as "gross and materialistic" and sought to idealize marital affection as well as the wife's role in spiritually elevating her husband above carnality. The Evangelical movement, specifically Methodism, also "sought to banish hedonism in general, and sexuality in particular, from the respectable consciousness and from public life" (Porter 21).

In contrast to Porter, Stone treats the increasing popularity of romantic love for the most part as separate from manifestations of the companionate model. He also does not discuss directly the attack on the double standard implicit in companionate ideology. Rather he sees the double standard as persisting throughout the period. For Stone, romantic love is essentially a literary phenomenon descending from the courtly tradition and popularized in the later half of the eighteenth century by the novel, especially the novels by women writers. "According to contemporaries, the growth of marriage for love in the eighteenth century was caused by the growing consumption of novels" (283). In contrast, the companionate model, for Stone, is more of a social phenomenon which "first developed as a norm among the more pious, often nonconformist, middle-class families of the late seventeenth century" (361); in the eighteenth century one increasingly finds examples of "affectionate couples" among the "upper squirarchy and nobility" as well as among the lower middle class and peasants (367).

Stone sees the double standard as a pattern among "the upper classes" throughout the Early Modern period (501). By this standard, women were expected to be virgins on the wedding night and were regarded by the husband as his property. The husband, in contrast, was expected to have some sexual experience before marriage, and the wife was encouraged to overlook his philandering after marriage especially if he was discreet about it. She on the other hand was to remain strictly faithful. Even in the late eighteenth century, according to Stone, the double standard prevails in upper-class marriages. In this respect England is unlike the continent, where chastity for women is enforced before marriage, but after marriage there is a tolerance of infidelity by both upper-class wives and husbands. While Stone does not directly credit companionate ideology with altering the double standard, he does acknowledge that, with the beginning of the nineteenth century, the resurgence of Puritanism and the drive for moral reform do make for a more repressive society in which hedonism and adultery are much less openly tolerated (673). Stone might have emphasized more strongly that companionate ideology, with its probable origins among the seventeenth-century Protestant middle class (predominantly composed of medium and small landowners, yeoman farmers, shopkeepers, and artisans) is fundamentally opposed to both male and female infidelity and becomes increasingly so when it was reinforced by the Evangelical movement of the late eighteenth and early nineteenth centuries.[6]

Proposition: The Weakening of Patriarchy in Mating Arrangements

The second proposition of the progressive historians is that the long eighteenth century sees a weakening of patriarchal control over mating arrangement. On this pattern historians are in greater agreement. Documenting his generalizations about the traditional family, mainly from France, Shorter finds that before "the nineteenth century the patriarchs of clan-like extended families would dispose of their marriageable daughters in the house's best interests" (139). The large majority of the French population did not, however, marry for money. Trumbach examines in detail the patterns of strict settlement by which fathers were able to control their eldest sons' choice of marriage partner for the economic benefit of the family and by which the father-in-law of the bride would negotiate for a marriage settlement that was to his financial advantage. Marriage settlements continue to be important in making a family's fortune throughout the eighteenth century, and negotiations between father, son, and father-in-law not only deal with the portion that the bride brought to her marriage (her dowry) but also the jointure settled on her in the form of yearly income (her pin money), a fund that would provide for her in case of her husband's death (82).

Stone finds that in the traditional family, before the end of the sixteenth century, "only a handful of children resisted parental dictation . . .

[in choice of mate], and their rebellion was soon crushed" (183). Patriarchal control continued strongly through the seventeenth century and "lasted longest in the richest and most aristocratic circles" (184). In the eighteenth century, especially in the later half, "public opinion in landed and bourgeois circles was turning decisively against parental dictation of a marriage partner" (289). The importance actually placed by parents on marrying for money varies according to the settlement that might be in question. Stone's evidence, mainly anecdotal, suggests that motives for marriage are most confused among the aristocracy (303). Be this as it may, Stone concludes that in the course of the eighteenth century the power of making decisions about mating arrangements is shifting from parents to children.

Other progressive historians of the family concur on this point. Trumbach finds that in the generation after 1720, "parents were increasingly inclined to allow their children to marry for love," though they still advise financial prudence (105). If romantic marriages are not wholeheartedly approved, "mercenary marriages" are forthrightly condemned. Marrying for love is tolerated initially more for sons than for daughters, since it is through the arrangement of a daughter's marriage that families seek to advance in society. Daughters of aristocrats are not permitted to marry out of their class even when romantic marriage is at its most popular (98).

Shorter finds a significant decline in class and status endogamy and an increase in age endogamy from the eighteenth century to the present. With the "infusion" of a romantic ideal into courtship, the couple distance themselves from community control (149). Though he does not directly mention the weakening of patriarchy in mating arrangements, Porter does note the Romantic movement's "idealization of love, particularly of woman" (20).

Proposition: The Increasing Emphasis on Bliss in Marriage

Several progressive historians of the family point to factors in the *traditional* family that inhibit the expression of affection and marital sexuality. Basing his generalizations mainly on peasant families in eighteenth-century France, Shorter paints a picture of traditional marriages as mostly loveless unions which were resented by husbands as a burden and by wives as an oppressive servitude. Husbands often regarded wives as property of the same order as livestock and showed little affection to them (58). In the absence of artificial means of contraception, wives bore large numbers of children, and after a number of pregnancies, the sex act for women no doubt became a threat rather than a pleasure. The lack of privacy in traditional households occupied by an extended family also must have inhibited enjoyment. As a "disincentive" to sexual pleasure, Stone mentions the pervasive lack of personal hygiene on the part of English men and women, even those of the upper class, and records several complaints by men that women were not accustomed to wash their private parts. Another "disincentive" was the lack of good health and the persistent threat of disease, especially venereal disease (485–91).

With the rise of affective individualism, Stone finds that "marriage ceases to be mainly an artificial but necessary constraint placed upon man's otherwise unbridled lust and becomes instead a prime source of pleasure, both emotional and sexual" (241). Central to the idealization of marital pleasure is what Trumbach calls "the ideal of domesticity," "that it was a woman's role in life to love her husband, bear his children, and remain at home to care for them" (166). In spite of the significant dangers to women of pregnancy and childbirth, the ideal glorifies woman's role as child bearer and the affection demonstrated between parent and child, especially mother and child. A number of progressive historians point to the new vogue for mothers, even upper-class mothers, to breast-feed children themselves instead of employing the services of a wet nurse (see Stone 426–32).

Shorter also emphasizes the rise of domesticity, "the family's awareness of itself as a precious emotional unit that must be protected with privacy and isolation from outside intrusion" (227). Once romantic love has freed the couple from supervision by parents and community, it is a logical step to idealize the home as a nest where maternal affection could flourish.

The role of sexual eroticism in companionate ideology, especially as it reinforces domesticity, is, as Shorter indicates, very difficult to document; progressive historians of the family are hesitant to generalize directly about it. Shorter points to the contradiction that though domesticity originates in the middle class, the lower classes are thought to be more lustful and animalistic in their behavior (248–89). Stone states at one point that mutual enjoyment of marital sexuality is an important emphasis in the new ideology among the squirearchy, professionals, and bourgeois classes and that increasingly the wife is expected to combine the role of wife and mistress (542–43). Even so, his anecdotal accounts of sexual behavior mainly document male extramarital sexual activity (see also Trumbach 281–82). Progressive historians seem generally not to address whether wives enjoyed sexual intimacy with their husbands, no doubt because there is little testimony on the topic. We can perhaps assume from the increasing incidence of poems celebrating the "connubial bliss" or the "blended bliss" of sexual consummation in marriage that the pleasures are seen as shared.[7] In these poems "heaven" may even be a code word for mutual sexual pleasure (see Spacks 39–40).

Although modesty no doubt inhibits women from speaking directly on the subject of sexual bliss in marriage, there are late eighteenth-century sociocultural indicators of their increasing concern with marital sexuality, especially as it might lead to improved fertility and more intelligent and beautiful offspring. One of these is the reported attendance by large numbers of women at waxworks of the female anatomy of reproduction (Stone 542–43). Another is the willingness of couples to patronize a dubious enterprise such as James Graham's celebrated Celestial Bed, which in 1780 appeared successively in several locations in London. Part of an elaborately contrived Temple of Health, Graham's exhibit reportedly cost £10,000 to set up. Couples paid Graham £50 a night to sleep in a bed twelve by nine feet with a "domed canopy 'supported' by forty pillars of brilliant glass of the most exquisite workmanship'" (Altick 82). Enhanced by perfumes, sculptured figures of Cupid, Psyche, and Hymen, a calliope of instruments providing celestial sounds, and the most elaborate contrivances of scientific quackery, Graham's bed worked to cure sterility by improving sensual enjoyment. As the phenomenon of Graham's bed illustrates, late eighteenth-century society increasingly celebrates marital sexuality in public contexts sanctioned by the ideology of domesticity.

Proposition: The Softening of Husbandly Dominion

Perhaps to set the stage for the argument that husbandly dominion becomes "kinder and gentler" as the long eighteenth century progresses, progressive historians of the family generally emphasize the repressiveness of patriarchal authority in the traditional family. Shorter focuses mainly on community pressure on the husband who fails to assert dominion over his wife or whose wife beats him. In old-regime France, chivaris were directed not only at cuckolds but also at husbands who allowed their wives to push them around, figuratively or literally. Wife beaters, on the other hand, were only mocked during May, which was "traditionally considered the women's month" (222–23). Stone sees a pattern of strengthening patriarchy in "husband-wife relations" in the sixteenth century. Reinforced by Protestant theologians and conduct book writers, patriarchal dogma insisted that the wife submit to a husband's authority and defer to him in the same way that children in the family were expected to defer. Upper- and middle-class wives in such traditional families had little independence, either financial or legal. This was also probably true of "wives of artisans, shopkeepers, smallholders, and unskilled labourers" (199). Though often participating directly in the family business or sharing the husband's labor, such wives possessed no more power or property rights than higher-class wives.

Trumbach argues that in the eighteenth century a new model for household organization emerges: patriarchy is gradually replaced by domesticity. Patriarchy is derived from a Biblical model and assumes that the husband is owner not only of things but of persons as well. "Women, like servants, entered contractually into patriarchal relations" (153). In defining domesticity, Trumbach draws on Shorter and Stone and their elaboration of companionate and affective models with their emphasis on "a pattern of close and loving association between husband and wife, and of doting care for children" (120).

Stone sees the emergence of the companionate model and domesticity as playing a central role in the weakening of kinship ties and the rise of the nuclear family. He views them essentially as egalitarian and progressive movements which gradually reverse the sixteenth-century trend toward stronger patriarchy. In the late seventeenth and eighteenth centuries, Stone finds that growth of affective individualism puts domestic patriarchy under attack within the family as did the emergence of feminist movements in society at large. Trumbach affirms Stone's qualification that domesticity could bolster rather than soften patriarchy, especially when it was intensified by Protestant religiosity, which made the household "the center of worship and affection" (121). As Trumbach puts it, "The new sexual roles that came with domesticity sometimes reinforced the old ones from patriarchy," and some men equated love with possession (151). Trumbach posits that "equality of men and women was accepted only with great difficulty" (150). He also finds that the "causes and consequences" of domesticity are more "problematical than he [Stone] realizes." Yet he admits that his explanations are "in many ways similar" to Stone's, and he seems finally to agree with him in viewing the companionate model and domesticity as progressive over the long run (121).

Revisionist feminist critiques of the rise of companionate ideology and domesticity often build on the qualifications and disagreements of progressive historians who, as we have just seen, sometimes find aspects of this new ideology to be problematic. Revisionists, however, usually challenge the progressive historians' overall evaluation and question their central assumption. That is, does the new ideology advance women's movement toward equality and independence, or does it enslave them in new or not so new ways? Some feminist historians suggest that women not only do not progress but that their sociopolitical position is effectively worsened.

A central assumption of revisionist criticism, one shared by this study, is that shifting attitudes toward marriage and women's role in it are governed by ideology, that is, "the prevailing system of values at any given historical moment" (Poovey xiii–xiv). According to Susan Staves, ideology is "the explicit public ideas . . . [people] have about human relationships, especially those ideas that serve to justify the power relationships between people, and to explain why it is right and good that different people should have different roles and different entitlements to power, wealth, and other social goods" (6). Ideology, as Mary Poovey defines it, governs "not just political and economic relations but social relations and psychological stresses" (xiv). It can be manifested in all aspects of a culture, even, for example, in literary style. As we examine each of four propositions of the progressive historians in light of revisionist challenges, we are made aware not only of eighteenth-century ideologies but also of the ideologies of the progressive historians *and* their revisionist critics.

Revisionist Critique: The Attack on Libertinism and the Double Standard

Revisionists do not appear to be especially critical of progressive historians' handling of this issue, possibly because the double standard is so obviously an inequity. Revisionists would agree with progressive historians that social toleration of infidelity by males and censure and punishment of women for the same act is clearly wrong.[8] Revisionists however see the eighteenth-century attack on the double standard as problematic for several reasons.

The celebration of companionate ideology and affective bonding may have made infidelity less fashionable. Yet, as Stone points out, the double standard persisted throughout the eighteenth century, especially among the upper classes. Men simply became more hypocritical. From the revisionist point of view, the eighteenth-century attack on the double standard cannot be taken seriously. A corollary reason revisionist criticism tends to discount this attack may be that the ideology that supports it is perceived as bourgeois and puritanical, restrictive of the behavior of both women and men.

This is no doubt why some feminist critics see a figure such as Aphra Behn as attractive. A poet and playwright who remained loyal to the Stuart court and its aristocratic libertine ethos, Behn, in her drama and verse, counters the male argument for freedom in love and sexuality with an equally strong female argument for the same (see Williamson 134ff). No doubt because they found companionate ideology attractive and perceived it as beneficial to women's interests, the majority of eighteenth-century women poets choose not to follow Behn's tack. They censure the male libertine argument by glorifying domesticity and sentimentalizing female victims of the double standard. By doing so, they buy into what Ellen Pollak calls "the myth of passive womanhood" with all its ideological baggage.

A central feature of this myth is the spiritualization of woman's role as wife and mother. Such an idealization can be seen as encouraging women to accept the injustice of the double standard since women are seen as morally superior to men and, consequently, have to guard themselves more strictly against any appearance of vice (see Poovey 8). "Women were advised that they had the power and responsibility to transform their adulterous husbands into models of chastity. If husbands' private conduct fell below the standards of decency, wives had only themselves to blame" (Staves 224). Quite obviously, if the progressive attack on the double standard becomes enmeshed in such ideology, it may simply perpetuate the double standard in a more sinister form. Revisionist criticism offers an important caveat to the proposition of the progressive historians. If the attack on the double standard makes improvements in women's social image, arouses sympathy for the wife victimized by her husband's infidelity, and creates, at least superficially, a valuation of equality, we must at the same time be sensitive to ways in which such idealization of women may effectively weaken their socioeconomic position and limit their freedom.

Revisionist Critique: The Weakening of Patriarchy in Mating Arrangements

In response to the progressive historians' argument that the force of patriarchy in mating arrangements is effectively weakened, revisionists ask, is patriarchy actually weakened or does it persist in a more covert form? On this issue, the progressive historian Trumbach strikes the note on which revisionist historians improvise, often in discord with Trumbach's sanguine tone. Trumbach does point out that, in the later part of the eighteenth century, class endogamy, especially among aristocrats, is enforced not so much by parental fiat as by class expectations and advice to young people to be prudent in their choices. The passage of Lord Hardwicke's Marriage Act of 1753 required consent of parent or guardian for the marriage of persons under twenty-one. This would seem to be a strengthening of patriarchal control, but, Trumbach argues, it is in actuality an acceptance of the ideology of romantic love. Within this ideology, children are expected to marry for love within their own class, preferably at a later age, and are not to be brokered to the highest bidder as a means of making a fortune (109).

Revisionist critics treat the same tension between parental control and children's freedom to choose, but they see no significant liberalization. Pollak acknowledges in passing the attack on the "mercenary marriage," especially as it occurs in social satire of the period. However, she has serious reservations about how much freedom young people actually did have under the new companionate ideology. Suggesting that the new ideology is guilty of an Orwellian obfuscation, she inquires rhetorically whether leading young people to believe that they had freedom to choose their mates was not simply another way of controlling their choice (34–35)? Poovey also recognizes that mercenary marriages came to be "denounced as scandalous" (14), but she points to the plethora of "informal safeguards" that "continued to enforce the importance of economic considerations" (13). Throughout the eighteenth century conduct literature insists on the importance of children obeying their parents' will in choosing a marriage partner (14).

Revisionists imply or argue directly that romantic or companionate ideology comes to be used as a smoke screen for the economic and social aggrandizement of families. The tenfold to twentyfold increase in the dowry settled on husbands by a bride's father in the long eighteenth century shows that the bottom line in making marriages continues to be money and property. This is so in spite of the increasing popularity of romantic ideology. Furthermore, as Poovey points out, the increase in dowry amounts in relation to the jointure settled on the wife by the groom or the groom's father would indicate that the price of women in the marriage market effectively falls. That men had the upper hand at the bargaining table is dramatized in novels by the increased complacency "of male suitors," confident that they will prevail (13). Concerning the institution of jointure itself, Staves shows with intricate legal arguments that the replacement by jointure of a widow's traditional dower rights in common law to one third of her husband's estate is not necessarily to women's economic advantage. Staves's view challenges that traditionally held by legal historians.

Assessing the revisionist critiques of the second progressive argument —that patriarchal control was weakening—seems in the broadest sense a question of emphasis. Should one pay most attention to the growing ideology that celebrates romantic love and children's freedom to choose, or should one focus on the socioeconomic and legal evidence that full equality and power are not in fact being extended, especially to women? As ideologically polarized as it seems, the issue may actually be a semantic one and may depend to some extent on what one means by "patriarchal control." If children are being given more voice in the choice of a mate, that constitutes a diminution to a degree in the parents' role in determining who the mate should be. In that respect, the parent actively exercises less control. At the same time, the pressures of class or of a moralistic ideology can subtly or indirectly perpetuate the influence of fathers over their daughters or husbands over their wives. This is not "patriarchal control" in the narrow sense, although it can have the same effect.

For women, that "effect" may have been the failure to gain equality or the actual loss of power in the legal and economic sphere. Thus, both the progressive historians and their revisionist critics are right, and both are right because, as I will argue, the situation is contradictory. Children gain more voice in the choice of a mate, but female children do not effectively gain power in the legal and economic sphere, and, in some respects, they lose it.

REVISIONIST CRITIQUE: THE INCREASING EMPHASIS ON BLISS IN MARRIAGE

Progressive historians of the family, as we have seen, view the glorification of domesticity and affective bonding in marriage as an improvement over the loveless unions predominant in traditional marriages. Instead of the husband resenting marriage as a burden and a bondage, he is to find pleasure in marital companionship, a loving union with his wife and children. His wife in turn is to be fulfilled in the "bliss" of domesticity, especially in motherhood.

Feminists' critique of the ideology implicit in this view has been strong, not only just recently but beginning with Mary Wollstonecraft and continuing through the nineteenth and twentieth centuries. Protofeminists asked pointedly whether the sexualization of women's role in marriage is ultimately to her benefit. Mary Wollstonecraft's argument that the fashionable "woman of sensibility" is actually a sexual servant and an upper-middle-class possession sets the tone for nineteenth-century critiques, especially John Stuart Mill's argument in *The Subjection of Women* (1869) that the subjection of women is not natural: even though women are culturally conditioned to accept their subordinate role, it is still in fact enslavement.

Wollstonecraft is especially sensitive to the ways in which the romanticization of woman's role in marriage weakens her sociocultural image. The idealization of delicacy of sentiment in a woman makes her a victim of her passions and discourages her from pursuing a course of education that would strengthen her reason and thus lead her to dignified self-sufficiency. For Wollstonecraft, women, encouraged to be hothouse flowers, turn into clinging vines and shrinking violets. She says that women educated frivolously in the arts of pleasing a husband become "weak beings," "only fit for a seraglio" (Wollstonecraft 10). "Why must the female mind be tainted by coquettish arts to gratify the sensualist?" she asks (31). Sensibility leads to vanity and coquetry. Wollstonecraft even turns against the fashion of romanticizing the bliss of marital love: "A master and a mistress of a family ought not to continue to love each other with passion" (30).

Similar to Wollstonecraft, revisionist criticism sees a sexualization of women's role implicit in the idealization of modesty and propriety. This idealization was promulgated by moralists and conduct book writers because women were seen as more sexual by nature than men. If women's "voraciousness" were allowed full rein, the moralists argued, the male-dominated social order would be threatened. Women need to be celebrated as angels because at heart they are rakes. Poovey shows how the late eighteenth-century emphasis on complaisance and self-effacing behavior actually calls attention to women's sexual nature (22). Pollak reveals that in the sentimentalization of women's domestic role, women are culturally constructed "as an accessory to masculine desire" (53); as an ornamental or useless possession, a wife becomes "a sign or token of her husband's plentitude." A wife's piety is the source of her "erotic appeal"; by blessing him she creates his bliss (53).

On this issue, the views of the progressive historians and of the revisionists seem more at odds than on the previous one, though some of the progressive historians, Trumbach for example, do point to a few of the problematic aspects of the sexualization of women's role. In spite of the fact that the social change must have involved both gains and losses, revisionists focus almost exclusively on the problematic aspects.

It is not simplistic to conclude that the progress achieved was fraught with contradictions and that the views of both the progressive historians and the revisionists are required to give us the complete picture. Though the critical impasse between the two critical positions cannot be unraveled, it can perhaps be clarified by pointing out that progressive historians tend to look at the rise of domesticity and the sexualization of marriage from the vantage point of the traditional loveless marriage and see it as an improvement. Revisionists view the change from the perspective of the nineteenth and twentieth centuries. Because the late eighteenth century's idealization of marital affection led ideologically to the Victorian spiritualization of the wife's domestic role and the repressive confinement of women to that role, revisionists are unwilling to see the evolution within the long eighteenth century as a step forward in any but the most superficial sense. However, as an examination of marriage verse will demonstrate, it would be foolish to deny that companionate ideology was more supportive of women, especially in their roles as wives and mothers, than were libertine and other traditional anti-feminist ideologies. In the long eighteenth century, women did advance, though certainly not in the directions and for the distances modern feminists would wish.

Revisionist Critique: The Softening of Husbandly Dominion

On this issue, revisionists seem most at odds with the views of the progressive historians. The idea that the exercise of husbandly authority (or its image) is made "kinder and gentler" in the late eighteenth century is mainly ignored by revisionists who assail the inequality implicit in the very fact of male dominion, whatever its degree.[9] Indeed, the issue of male dominion seems *the* basic feminist issue: almost all feminist critics hit on it in one way or another. The issue is addressed not just in revisionist criticism but throughout the eighteenth century itself. Protofeminists vary, however, in how forcefully they challenge women's subordination.

In the eighteenth century, Mary Wollstonecraft offers perhaps the most outspoken attack, although she is certainly not the earliest or the only writer to do so. Wollstonecraft blasts male conduct writers who encourage women to be obedient and submissive (25–26). She finds the "whole tendency in women's education is to render women pleasing" to men (27). "How grossly do they insult us who thus advise us only to render ourselves gentle, domestic brutes! For instance, the winning softness so warmly, and frequently, recommended, that governs by obeying" (20). She disparages Rousseau who says that women should never feel independent (25), and she then retorts, "Do passive, indolent women make the best wives? If they are really rational creatures, let them not be slaves" (34).

At the *beginning* of the eighteenth century, Mary Astell, whom Bridget Hill calls the first English feminist, does not challenge male dominion directly, though she does say bluntly in *Some Reflections upon Marriage* (1700) that a woman who cannot accept male dominion unconditionally should not marry. She questions the social pressure on women to find a husband and inquires whether women cannot have higher designs than this (see *The First English Feminist*). After Astell and before Wollstonecraft, attacks on women's servitude in marriage are quite frequent and can be found in works as diverse as Defoe's *Roxana* (1724) and Laetitia Pilkington's *Memoirs* (1748–49) (Hill esp. 94–95; also Browne esp. 81–101).

Apart from remaining respectable and single, a state that inflicted its own oppressions on women, the only option for those who did not wish to be subject to the power of a husband was to be a kept woman or mistress, a position that carried with it a problematic measure of freedom and opportunity. As Antonia Fraser shows, this option for making one's way in the world was undertaken by a number of notable (or notorious) upper-class women in the late seventeenth century. By the later era, however, standards of middle-class propriety become more prevalent, and the status of a kept woman is viewed with greater opprobrium.

By the end of the eighteenth century, the issue of women's equality in marriage is very much in the air, perhaps because of challenges to the principle of subordination posed by the French Revolution (Poovey 31). Since the ideologies of domesticity and of companionate equality were both prominent at this time, a significant contemporary disagreement arose whether women's power lay most in her domestic and affective influence over her husband or in her efforts to achieve equality and socioeconomic independence.[10] This question was debated in women's writing of the time, and revisionist criticism has challenged the argument of several women writers of the 1790s that women's power lies in her moral, emotional, or sexual influence over her husband. Poovey, for example, examines with sympathetic skepticism Laetitia Hawkins's fears in *Letters on the Female Mind* (1793) that in gaining equality women will lose all their power. Similarly, Poovey treats with interest Hannah More's reservations concerning equality for women, though she seems ultimately to regard More as deluded. In encouraging women to support the traditional social order, More, in *Strictures on the Modern System of Female Education* (2nd ed., 1799), called on women to reinforce propriety by being obedient wives and loving mothers. Such an affirmation of "public morals" and "religious principle" would reactivate piety and would meet the French threat indirectly but effectively. Poovey views such an argument as the final step of the ideology of propriety toward the repressive Victorian idealization of "the angel in the house," the wife as a powerless moral exemplar (34–35).

Revisionist critics and historians see the argument for the power of domesticity as a setback for women. Susan Staves, for example, cites Susan Okin to the effect that "sentimental ideology 'acted rather as a reinforcement for the patriarchal relations between men and women which had temporarily been threatened by seventeenth-century individualism'" (226). According to Staves, "Women thus sentimentalized were seen to lack not only the rationality required for citizenship but also the rationality required for active management of property" (226). "Not only in the middle classes but also in the gentry and aristocracy, genteel femininity increasingly became dissociated from active personal involvement in household management and household production and increasingly became associated with the possession of leisure time for amusement, consumption, and travel away from home" (225).

The social ideology that the majority of women of fashion espoused glorified the companionate marriage and domesticity. For most middle- and upper-class women, the struggle for equality was directed not so much toward economic self-sufficiency or social and legal independence as toward the perceived freedom to find husbands with whom they were emotionally, intellectually, and socially compatible. The husband was not to be foisted upon the bride by a father who in effect sold her to the highest bidder or used her as a pawn to improve his socioeconomic standing. In addition, the husband was supposed to exercise his dominion with love and respect. Companionate ideology along with domesticity became the modish ideologies, and, especially in the later era, many women embraced them because they were romantically attractive and genteel rather than because they would lead to power and independence.

In the face of such revelations, the counterargument for the power of domesticity may seem little better than myth. Revisionist criticism debunks the ideological axioms that wives are the "power behind the throne" and that they rule their husbands by the force of moral and emotional suasion and by their sexual attractiveness.

The question still remains, however, how much power women do actually exercise in these spheres of influence and how much women of the late eighteenth century, given the restrictions of their society, should be denigrated for opting for such influence. Examining this question need not sanction the old argument that women do not need to attain power in the socioeconomic or legal spheres because they traditionally hold power in domesticity. It may in fact be a recognition that women can exercise power in both traditional and untraditional ways.

When a modern feminist disdains or denies women's power through domesticity or marital sexuality, one must determine the basis for the critic's attitude. Is it that opting for such traditional spheres of influence reinforces women's weakness, that is, her lack of political and socioeconomic clout? Or is it that such ways of exerting power are held in contempt, are perhaps seen as irrational or below human dignity? The argument of the revisionists would seem essentially that the rise of the ideology of domesticity glorifies female passivity and that women have remained weak politically and economically by relying on such spheres of influence.

It is certainly true that eighteenth-century women lacked power in the public sphere. As Lawrence Lipking succinctly puts it, "women had no political rights, were limited to a few lowly vocations as servants, nurses, governesses, and petty shopkeepers, and were legally nonpersons who lost their property to their husbands at marriage and were incapable of instituting an action in the courts of law."[11]

But does this necessarily mean that women lacked power in the absolute sense? The argument of at least one eighteenth-century protofeminist is that the power that women exercise in the domestic and sexual sphere can be all too tyrannical. According to Mary Wollstonecraft, women need to be educated so that they can be the equals of men in the "political and civil sense" (167). Ignorant women who are subject to the whims of their passions or vanities Wollstonecraft calls "slaves." Yet she is quick to acknowledge that the "power which vile and foolish women have had over wise men who possessed sensibility is notorious" (174). Such women can be dangerous fools.

If some women can exert considerable influence for bad in the domestic and sexual sphere, it may well be that revisionist criticism challenges the ideology of domesticity not simply because it perpetuates women's weakness in the public arena but it considers, ipso facto, power exerted through domesticity and sexuality demeaning or irrational. In the controversy over dominion that arises from eighteenth-century poetry, especially poetry by women, we will confront the paradoxical issue of women's power and the arguments for the advantages and disadvantages of traditional and untraditional spheres of influence. Turning now to the ideological and especially the theological bases upon which poets praise and censure women's power, we can perhaps better understand our deep-seated ambivalence as moderns toward the influence women exercise in traditional domestic and sexual roles.

Revisionist criticism has tended to view the Christian theological conception of marriage as the foundation on which patriarchy is built. It is the Pauline epistles that set up the husband as the head of the household who must be obeyed just as the church must be subservient to Christ. Justification of the husband's authority as Godlike is standard doctrine in sixteenth- and early seventeenth-century conduct books. In his dominion over his wife, the husband's position is analogous to that of a master over a servant or a prince over a subject (Schucking 32–33).

Similarly, it was the spiritual status of marriage as a sacrament—not in name but in legal effect—that prohibited civil divorce *a vinculo matrimonii*. In this respect, Anglican theology constituted a reactionary force blocking softening of patriarchal attitudes and practices. Up until the Divorce Act of 1857, wives could not procure a civil divorce *a vinculo* from an unfaithful or cruel husband and had to have recourse to a separation from bed and board in an ecclesiastical court. In the case of the Divorce Act, the weakening of the Church's spiritual authority over marriage can be hailed as a significant liberalization.

Though such changes most certainly contributed to the cause of equality and freedom for the individual, the secularization of the ideology of marriage, at the same time, can be said to have had detrimental contingencies. Many conservatives would argue that the ideals of self-control, self-sacrifice, and duty have declined among husbands and wives. The progressive liberalization of the divorce laws in the twentieth century may have paved the way for men and women to dissolve marriage for self-serving reasons such as boredom or the desire for a younger, more attractive partner. As divorces have become easier to procure, their numbers in England in the years after World War II have mushroomed (see Stone, *Road to Divorce*). For whatever reason it is granted, divorce, especially as it adversely affects children, may well be undermining the fundamental bonds of the polis.

In the late eighteenth century, as Lawrence Stone points out, husbands seeking a Parliamentary divorce often exploited the criminal conversation suit by collusion to free themselves from wives who may or may not have been unfaithful. Secularization of the ideology of marriage not only resulted in an increase in Parliamentary divorces initiated by men but also may have contributed to a sharp rise in the consistory courts in the number of judicial separations from bed and board applied for by suitors whose spouses were cruel or unfaithful. Suitors in church courts were traditionally women, "except in the late eighteenth century when female adultery seems to have become much more common."[12] As companionate ideology placed more emphasis on domestic and sexual happiness, it no doubt led to the dissolving of marriages that should have been terminated because the couples were irreconcilably incompatible or one or both were neglectful, cruel, or abusive. At the same time, it may have opened the door to the recent trend of divorce for flimsy or selfish pretexts.

In poetry, similarly, the weakening of the spiritual ideal of marriage finds issue in a loss of its symbolic significance, of its spiritual place in the natural, social, and cosmic order. As the portrayals of marriage as a heaven gain prominence, poetry tends to replace the theological ideal of a lifelong obligation made sacred by vows with a secular, sentimentalized image of marital happiness. Marriage poetry accordingly loses much of its spiritual and moral vitality (see Schucking 34, 45–47).

We need to understand the theological context in which such a literary loss takes place. The fundamental binary opposition between marriage as a heaven and as a hell derives in large measure from the tradition of exegesis of the Eden story in Genesis. As James Grantham Turner demonstrates in *One Flesh: Paradisal Marriage and Sexual Relations in the Age of Milton*, this tradition reaches back to St. Augustine and becomes especially rich and entangled in the mid-seventeenth century. Turner's central concern is with the seemingly irreconcilable dichotomy in attitudes toward sexuality in the Eden story.

On one hand, sexuality in Paradise before the fall, if indeed it existed in the physical sense, is seen as a beautiful and rapturous conjoining, a chaste bliss designed and blessed by God. On the other hand, fallen sexuality is viewed as a curse; man is tormented by the lusts of the flesh and must suffer the negative biological and psychological consequences of his own carnality. The union between the sexes is fraught with strife. In short, sexuality is seen as both heavenly and hellish.

Paradise Lost is an important expression of the satiric tradition which portrays marriage as hellish. Milton dramatizes the darker aspects of sexuality in our first parents' loss of innocence, their consequent feelings of guilt and shame, the emergence of "high passions" such as anger, hate, mistrust, suspicion, and discord, and their subjection to "sensual Appetite" (9.1129). As Turner points out, "Milton does not turn away from the uglier side of sexuality. He is not afraid to make Adam and Eve the first fornicators as well as the first couple locked in wedded love." Milton even presents Adam as a satirist when, after the fall, he berates Eve harshly for being the cause of his misfortune and directs embittered accusations at women and marriage (10.867ff). Adam accuses Eve of being in league with the serpent. He blames the mischief that befell him on the inferiority of woman's creation—"based on a rib/Crooked by nature." He disparages all attempts by men to find happiness in "strait conjunction with this sex" (10.898).

Adam's antifeminist and antimatrimonial complaints are, of course, not uncharacteristic of the Puritan and the Protestant ethos. Intensely aware of the many and devious forms evil can take in the world to disguise itself as good or beautiful, this ethos can lead us to see corruption where we least expect it. It is not surprising then that Adam's hostile attacks on women and marriage stimulate a number of later representations of marriage as a hell, mostly in the early era. After Juvenal and the patristic and clerical tradition of satire that drew on his work, Milton's antimatrimonial passages in *Paradise Lost* have the second greatest influence on this era's marriage satire. Grub Street antifeminist satires of the Restoration such as M. S.'s *The Great Birth of Man* (2nd ed., 1678) and *Mysogynus: or, A Satyr upon Women* (1682) are obvious imitations of satiric passages in *Paradise Lost*.

If negative attitudes toward marriage and sexuality in Milton and in seventeenth-century Protestantism prompt representations of marriage as hell, *Paradise Lost* and the affirmation of marriage and sexuality in this same Protestantism have a much more significant and lasting influence on the long eighteenth century's portrayal of marriage as heaven. According to Turner, Milton's presenting Adam and Eve as a "Fair couple linked in happy nuptial league" (4.339) goes a long way toward reclaiming paradisal marriage from the special pleading, rationalizations, and denigrations it had suffered at the hands of mid-century mystical revisionists, protoscientific skeptics, and libertines.

> By the time Milton was writing *Paradise Lost*, the interpretation and representation of Genesis had entered its terminal crisis. The standard Protestant reading, literalistic, coherent, and universalized, conflicted with the very realism it had helped to engender. The rational component of exegesis conflicted with the emotional, and imagination—declared "evil" by even the most fantastic commentators—came under renewed suspicion, eroded first by the spirit of scientific enquiry, and later also by the reaction against visionary "enthusiasm." These problems had been endemic in the Genesis tradition, especially when it embodied the Protestant urge to found a spiritual renewal on a fresh return to origins and fresh production of the Word. But the seventeenth century threw them into higher relief. (140–41)

Complicating this conflict is the emergence of a libertine tradition which eroticized the Garden of Eden story, either by coarse Rabelaisian wit or by suggestive Cavalier celebrations of primeval sexuality.

Turner views Milton's accomplishment in "reclaiming paradisal sexuality" in *Paradise Lost* as an original shift in poetry away from the traditional Christian view of sexuality as sinful and corrupt: "By filling Paradise with 'the spirit of love and amorous delight' and the 'enormous bliss' of consummated sexuality, Milton breaks away from the standard interpretation; but unlike the equally adventurous 'Artists' of the esoteric tradition, his imagination flies *towards* rather than away from 'the sphere of generation.' Indeed, when he calls marriage the 'prime institution' and highest state of mankind, or when he makes sexual delight the 'sum' of Adam's happiness, he even approaches a different kind of libertine principle—that 'there is no heaven save woman'" (171). Indeed, when Milton pays tribute to "wedded love" in book 4 of *Paradise Lost* (lines 750–75) as a "Perpetual fountain of domestic sweets,/Whose bed is undefiled and chaste pronounced," he becomes one of the first and most important articulators of the ideology of domesticity in its assault on the libertine ethos. Milton gives expression to the strongest argument for marriage and the family in the long eighteenth century, that it provides a wholesome, sheltered, socially regulated, and spiritually sanctioned structure for human sexuality.

Though Turner emphasizes Milton's originality in celebrating the paradise of marital sexuality, his accomplishment need not be seen as uncharacteristic of seventeenth-century Calvinist Protestantism. According to Edmund Leites, the Puritan tradition is world affirming. Within it, conscience is not unalterably in opposition to natural appetite, though sexuality within marriage must be subject to self-control and made steady and reliable. As Leites argues, Puritanism in the long eighteenth century domesticates sexuality and integrates it into marriage.

This process serves as the basis for the feminized readings of *Paradise Lost* that Joseph Wittreich discusses and which are pervasive in the celebration of domesticity in middle and late eighteenth-century poetry. In *Feminist Milton*, Wittreich locates a developing line of interpretation, especially by female readers, which stands in opposition to the misogynistic readings of Milton's epic based on the patriarchal ideology of Protestant theology. The *Paradise Lost* of the feminized tradition discovered by Wittreich is not the poem of the male moralists who emphasize Eve's disobedience and her consequent subjection to her husband's authority. This poem is replaced by a *Paradise Lost* that glorifies Adam and Eve's joyful partnership in paradise, particularly their open celebration of the "Rites/ Mysterious of connubial Love" (4.743). Especially for women readers of Milton, Eve becomes less a rebel against God's and her husband's dominion than a marital companion whose aspirations toward equality Milton treats with respect and affection. For these eighteenth-century readers, Milton's affirmations of an affective companionship count more than his patriarchal theology.

In the literary context provided by *Paradise Lost* and its affirmation of marital love, celebration, then, prevails over satire, the myth of marriage as a heaven over marriage as a hell. The remaking of the myth of marriage has pronounced gender associations; these become complicated by a kind of poetic "cross-dressing." The argument that marriage is a hell becomes identified by satirists and libertines as a male argument. Even so, a few female libertines such as Aphra Behn present their version of the argument, and protofeminist poets such as Lady Chudleigh pick up the trope in attacking the tyranny of the husband and the unhappiness of the arranged marriage. Conversely, the argument that marriage is a heaven becomes identified in the later era with the romantic aspirations of women for the domestic bliss of the companionate marriage or for the domestic privacy of (married) love in a cottage. Yet an examination of the male poets of the time shows that they nurture this fantasy just as much as, if not more than, the women. One might conceivably argue, along with revisionist critics, that the trope of marriage as heaven was less an attempt by women to feminize marriage than an imposition on women by male poets who wished to maintain patriarchy by making it more attractive.

If the hell-heaven opposition is central to the marriage poetry of the period, the chief effort of the critic must be a disentangling of its complicated evolution. The feminization of marriage poetry (and of poetry in general) is a leading manifestation of the outward refinement of culture in the period. Writing a dedicatory poem for the prose *An Essay in Defence of the Female Sex* (1696) by Judith Drake, her brother, James Drake, sets the tone for this shift throughout the next century when he hails the end of male tyrannic dominion in satire and when he says "with purer waves henceforth shall satyr flow." We will see a gradually evolving feminization in the poetry of both sexes as well as the problematic aspects of it.

The positive achievement of celebratory poetry is to establish the ideal of a marriage in which partners are equal in their ability to express and share affection, in their intellectual and physical experiences of marital love, and in their capacity to create and achieve happiness. Such pro-companionate ideology is generally strongly embraced, even by proto-feminist women poets, for implicit in it is an affective veneration of women's role in society.

A fairly typical illustration of women's support for the companionate ideal is offered in "To a Lady Lending Me Heliodorus Just before Her Marriage" (1724) by Elizabeth Tollet, the well-educated daughter of a commissioner of the Navy. Heliodorus was a writer of romance, thought to be Bishop of Tricca in Thessaly. The thrust of Tollet's poem is based on the situational irony that a bishop whose views might be expected to be misogynous and antimatrimonial actually wrote a romance celebrating love in marriage.

> See! Love, by scornful Nymphs esteem'd a Fault,
> Here by a venerable Prelate taught:

> The good old Man, with rigid Zeal at Strife,
> Devoutly preaches up a marry'd Life.
> But he, such wond'rous Prevalence obtains
> The fondling Offspring of an Author's Brains!
> To save his Book, his Bishoprick resign'd.
> He thought, perhaps, his Sermons might not bear
> The nice attention of a Lady's Ear.
> These Lectures, he presum'd, might stand the Test,
> Which all the World applies to Practice best.
>
> (51)

Theology, in the person of the former bishop, in this case does not denigrate marriage and praise celibacy but actually affirms domestic affection and the companionate ideal.

As the celebratory mode displaces satire in marriage poetry, it does so, then, in its attitude toward women's roles in general. Milton's sympathetic treatment of Eve broadens in the late eighteenth century into a reverential stance toward all women. This attitude is exemplified by a passage from "The Female Advocate" (1771) by William Woty, a law clerk who subsisted for some years as a Grub Street writer.

> Too long have authors, with inglorious views,
> Debas'd the sacred office of the muse,
> Too long preferr'd, in rank, ill-natur'd lays,
> The shaft of satire to the plume of praise;
> And turning vile apostates from the Nine
> With most unhallow'd touch profan'd that shrine,
> Which best deserv'd their reverence on earth,
> The brightest pattern of excelling worth:
> Woman, I mean—against whose sacred charms
> Satire hath op'd his magazine of arms;
> With malice unprovok'd his batt'ry play'd,
> And meanly triumph'd in the wounds he made.
>
> (3)

As "The Female Advocate" illustrates, it becomes fashionable in later era poetry to idealize women, especially in their domestic roles of wife and mother. As Leites explains, this idealization is based on what he calls a division of moral labor, which establishes a hierarchy of the sexes. Men, because they are considered more animallike in their appetites, embody the will to command, while women are to heed the demands of conscience and serve as guardians of moral purity. Given the pervasiveness of the libertine argument and the strength of the double standard in male ideology, one can understand why "the myth of the fair sex" develops as a counterposition. In response to the negative myth of woman as sexual devil or hellish nag, the arouser, manipulator, or quasher of male desires, eighteenth-century culture turns by its antithetical logic to the positive myth of woman as angel. Hence, poetry tends increasingly to celebrate marriages based on affective bonding and domesticity in which the wife incarnates heavenly virtues.

For all the positive achievements of the celebration of marriage as heaven, this shift, as my survey of revisionist criticism has already indicated, can be seen as highly problematic. Ellen Pollak argues persuasively that the eighteenth century exchanged one restrictive image of woman for another. Replacing the myth of woman as shrew or whore, the myth of the "fair sex" or, as Pollak calls it, of "passive womanhood," falsely spiritualized the wife's role and thus turned her into the husband's most precious asset (*The Poetics* 53). As the wife became the angel in the house, her effective sphere of activity in fact narrowed while her image was enhanced. This repressiveness was reinforced by the Evangelical movement of the early nineteenth century and reached its extreme in the Victorian era with its severe restrictions on women's selfhood and its elaborate biological and cultural justifications for limiting women to domestic roles (but see Rendall 72–107).

In poetry, the spiritualization of the wife's role is actually (and ironically) an expression of the secularization of the marriage ideal. Much of the later satirical poetry comes to focus rather shallowly on fashionable conduct and manners and loses contact with the myth of marriage as the sacramental ideal that stands behind some conservative Restoration satires. Celebratory poetry increasingly disregards its ideological roots, the rich complex of Protestant exegesis that underlies sixteenth- and seventeenth-century portrayals of paradisal marriage, most notably those of Spenser and Milton. As a result, the idea of marriage not only becomes more secular; it often seems spiritually two-dimensional. In a number of poems, the snake and sin have been removed from the paradise of the happy marriage. It is important for a culture sometimes to portray marriage as a hell since satire can present negative examples of marital conduct and thus provide practical moral guidelines. It can also serve as catharsis for those wounded by marriage and those who cannot find fulfillment in the relatively confining roles marriage imposes. When heaven is located in marital domesticity, men and women need the mythos of marriage as hell to account for the inevitable failures of the ideal. For women specifically, the late eighteenth century's de-emphasis of the negative mythos reinforced their confinement within domesticity.

In secularizing the ideal of bliss, poets underplay marriage's power conflicts and its substantial dissatisfactions. The heaven poets celebrate does not exist in a world where babies cry, bills come due, wives are abused and repressed, and husbands bored and unfaithful, a world in which the pursuit of the bliss of domesticity can pinch the soul. This is the negative mythos of marriage later era poets regularly ignore in making a "Heaven of Hell."

CHAPTER ONE
Polemic Poems

I N ITS SENSATIONALIZED ARRAY OF IMITATIVE FORmats and penchant for repeating a successful formula, even by outright plagiarism, the popular marriage poetry published in the Fleet Street area or in the neighborhood of St. Pauls between about 1670 and 1720 reminds us of the rock-and-roll industry in the 1950s. The analogy may, however, give too much dignity to the quality of the marriage verse. If we credit Swift, Pope, and other satirists of the witty and polite traditions, the Fleet district was a veritable sewer, the printing houses in that district producing a debased literature that was the figurative counterpart of the excrement, refuse, and offal in the Fleet Ditch itself. In the satirists' view, bad poetry was only to be expected from the Fleet, a conduit which, according to Pat Rogers, "linked virtually all the most wretched corners of the city" (149).[1] There are, however, good reasons for examining this literature. What one society calls refuse may be a later society's popular culture, a prime indicator of changes in cultural attitudes toward marriage.

If any one format predominates in the popular poetry, it is the polemical. Especially in the last decade of the seventeenth and the first decade of the eighteenth centuries, marriage poets employ such formats as the tract or treatise, the answer or the reply, the proposal, and the debate. This verse often articulates a pro position in one poem and answers soon after with a con position in a separately published sequel. With the beginning of the eighteenth century, there is a tendency for separately standing pro-and-con arguments to give way to debates. In these, the opposing positions can be made to stand in some relationship to one another, with one usually set up to prevail over the other. Later debates begin to be embedded in larger works, and the function of the debate in resolving contradiction may become subordinate to some higher poetic purpose, some stance or emotional attitude the author wishes to share with the reader.

Eric Rothstein has observed that poetry from 1660 to roughly the 1690s tends to "focus on the theme of power, and poetry from the 1690s to roughly the 1740s focuses not on a theme, but on an operating principle, that of interaction, interconnectedness. From the 1740s to 1780, finally, what is most distinctive is a focus on neither a theme nor on an operating principle but on [a posture or] an attitude, that of fellow-feeling" (xiii–xiv).

We can see how the evolution of polemical formats roughly embodies Rothstein's scheme.[2] Separate pro-and-con arguments on marriage are often assertions of a power conflict between a traditional antimatrimonial, usually an aristocratic libertine ideology, and a newer, more middle-class, pro-companionate ideology, one that reflects feminized interests in undercutting male arguments for sexual freedom. As they are placed together in a debate, their interconnectedness is established to a lesser or greater degree. Pro-and-con positions may be allowed to stand side by side on their own merits (a version of Rothstein's first stage), or the traditional position may be subordinated to the new under some overriding rationale or operating principle such as society's good, God's plan, or the companionate ideal (Rothstein's second stage). Debates embedded and subordinated to the higher poetic purpose of sharing an affective attitude toward marriage or affirming a pro-marriage sensibility obviously fit with the last stage in Rothstein's scheme. Polemical formats in popular poetry appear to move through these three stages as a pro-marriage ideology eventually gains precedence.

STAGE ONE

A number of prose tracts evidently stimulated the separately standing pro-and-con verse arguments that appear in such proliferation from about 1690 to 1710. Especially in the case of the pleasures-of-the-single-life format of the first decade of the eighteenth century, the arguments were probably fed by the moralistic polemics of the 1670s.[3] At least five important, interrelated prose tracts appear in this decade. We will look at these in some detail since their Protestant, antilibertine ideology is at the root of the pro-marriage argument.

The first tract—*An Account of Marriage or The Interests of Marriage Considered and Defended, against the Unjust Attacques of This Age. In a Letter to a Friend* (1672)—seems to stand as a prototype and stimulus for the other five. The avowed purpose of this moralist is to counter the same gallantry and loose behavior that the wits of the age celebrate. The author mentions derogatorily the "fantastical definitions of the Malmsbury Philosopher" (4) and later accuses the wits who degrade marriage as "triumphing in atheism" (60). A particular target of this tract is the "atheistical" philosophy of Hobbes, which was seen by the clergy as encouraging the experimentation with the life of the senses more or less attempted by a few of the court wits and libertine poets and aspired to by the "men of the town." More generally, the author, who is probably a cleric, attacks those who discredit the institution of marriage by their attitudes and actions.

The body of the argument is in support of marriage. The writer opens his defense by exegesis of the "Divine Declaration" in Gen. 2:18: "It is not good that the man should be alone." The main burden of his argument is built on ten points asserting the goodness of marriage; each of these is defended by an obviously Protestant if not Puritan rationale. The emphasis on the role of marriage in stabilizing and improving society in points 2, 3, 6, and 8 may be, as I will explain at the end of this section, Calvinist in emphasis. I cite the ten points mostly verbatim to lay the foundation for this hypothesis and because even the flimsy ones are taken up by later tract writers, both in prose and verse.

Marriage is good, argues the author, (1) "to perpetuate Generations, and the variety of Ages"; (2) "as a model of the after Governments of the World: the dominion of a Parent in his Family is a true representation of the government of a Vertuous Prince, who is the Father of his Country"; (3) "as it brought in the grand foundation of peace and quiet of Kingdomes"; (4) "to have the honour, and delight of a hopeful issue"; (5) "to perpetuate the memory and dignity of vertue"; (6) "to inlarge the Sphere and establish occasions of practical vertue. He that is married has more compass, and a larger field of action"; (7) "to have a mind vigorous, and constant in the circles of Marriage. Vertue loses it's [*sic*] lustre and strength, when it is loosened by various entertainments"; (8) "for the education of mankind"; (9) "to present the inconveniences and extravagancies of a rambling love"; (10) "to have the society of a Sex that shoul'd once be the passage of the Son of God into the World; and that was of a Virgin too."

Though some of the rationales such as 9 and 10 may give expression to a more progressive ideology, one somewhat sympathetic to the interests of women, the pro-marriage attitudes articulated in this early work seem mainly an expression of the writer's patriarchal Protestant ethos and his opposition to aristocratic libertinism. Point 2 is the standard Protestant justification for fatherly dominion within the family as it is analogous to the Prince's dominion within the State and ultimately to God's dominion over the earth.

The tract that follows *An Account of Marriage* is *Remarques on the Humours and Conversations of the Town. Written in a Letter to Sir T. L.* (1673). Only a fourteen-page section of this treats marriage, and that takes the form of an harangue against town attitudes toward the institution. These are delivered in a letter of advice to a young man living in the country but desiring to come up to London. The target here is the same libertine disdain of marriage as a form of bondage that was attacked in *An Account of Marriage*.

Reflexions on Marriage, and the Poetick Discipline. A Letter by the Author of the Remarques on the Town (1673) purports to be an enlargement of *Remarques on the Town*. According to the author, it was precipitated by a "disingenuous and ill bred" reply to his earlier work. *Reflexions on Marriage*, in actuality, is an enlargement of *An Account of Marriage*; most of the earlier work is incorporated in it verbatim. The second work lifts nine of the ten arguments intact from the first. It then uses the ninth point—"Marriage prevents the inconveniences and extravagancies of a rambling love"—as a launching pad for an inflated exploration of the fantastically exaggerated powers attributed to love by the poets. It is true, says the author, that love plays a part in marriage, but never in the fanciful ways in which the poets have portrayed it. In this tract and the previous one, the antilibertine argument is given special prominence, and a pro-marriage ideology is even more evident than in the first tract.

The next two tracts in the series are a pair. *Conjugium Conjurgium, or, Some Serious Considerations on Marriage* by William Seymar (1673) is replied to by *Marriage Asserted: In Answer to a Book Entituled Conjugium Conjurgium* (1674), also probably by William Seymar (evidently an anagram for Ramsey). These two more learned arguments are structured in parallel, each with similar formal division by member, section, subsection, and division. Both works have the manner of a scholastic debate. *Conjugium Conjurgium* speaks against marriage, pretending to be a letter of advice to Philogynus. *Marriage Asserted* then counters each argument offered by the first work, praising especially the delights of companionship as sanctioned by the Bible. Significant is the way Ramsey sets up the two pieces so that *Marriage Asserted* wins out over *Conjugium Conjurgium*. Not only is the order of publication of the two works indicative that he intended to argue for marriage. The disproportionate length of *Marriage Asserted* also adds weight to the judgment that Ramsey intended the pro-marriage ideology to be victorious.

Why Ramsey published these two arguments under separate titles with two different publishers is a puzzlement. Obviously, the two works belong together, but in 1673, evidently the vogue in publishing still favored separately standing polemical pieces. The combination of them into a debate was evidently not yet the fashion.

Though prose tracts that answer one another, that extrapolate on one another, or that appear in separately published pro-and-con pairs can be found throughout the long eighteenth century, the prose tracts of the 1670s illustrate such patterns quite neatly. In the polemical marriage verse of ten to forty years later, we find numerous poems that answer one another or that stand as pairs. These tract poems address, though in less intellectual detail, many of the issues concerning the advantages and disadvantages of marriage taken up in the earlier prose tracts. The fullest and most intriguing series of verse replies are those to *The Pleasures of a Single Life, or, The Miseries of Matrimony* (1701). Throughout this series, there is an opposition between traditional clerical or libertine stances and what purports to be a pro-marriage ideology.

Two other verse series involving apparently conflicting ideologies are similar in size and configuration to the pleasures-of-the-single-life series. The first sequence is initiated by *Love Giv'n O're* (1682) by Robert Gould, manservant turned poet (reprinted in *Three Satires on Women*). In this virulent and offensively antifeminist harangue evidently modeled on John Oldham's "A Satyr upon a Woman, Who by Her Falshood and Scorn Was the Death of My Friend. A Satyr" (1:139–48), Gould's speaker savages all women because his beloved Silvia has proved unfaithful. The *Love Giv'n O're* series is made up of replies to Gould's poem in which Silvia and womankind in general are effusively defended. There are also replies to replies in which they are cursed again. As Nussbaum posits in her informative discussion of this series in *The Brink of All We Hate*, the feminism of the defenders of women, especially in poems by Grub Street poet Richard Ames, is suspect since it is based essentially on a reversal of antifeminist myths of women as monsters and whores.[4] In the pro-and-con pattern, we do see, however, a conflict between traditional antifeminist discourse and pro-marriage discourse, even if the latter is not in the main authentically feminist as Nussbaum rightly argues.

The second series—the fifteen-format poems—appears in the early 1700s and is evidently modeled on a series of fifteen-format prose pieces that appeared in the 1680s.[5] Most fifteen-format poems tend to be short, somewhat realistic in detail, and rather crudely written. Drawing on a popular tradition of antifeminism and antimatrimonialism and perhaps serving as a middle-class, prudential warning against early marriages, many of the arguments in this series tend to be strongly ironic in their handling of the "pleasures" of marriage. For example, *The Fifteen Comforts of Matrimony. Or, A Looking Glass for All Those Who Have Enter'd in that Holy Comfortable State* (1706) enumerates as "comforts" the various tribulations that married men encounter. These include the man who marries the handsome young bride, "Keeps her Extravagantly, Fine and Gay," but then "catches her with some enamour'd Youth"; the husband, who after only three full moons, discovers "the vast Comforts of a Breeding Wife"; the man overburdened with "a num'rous Offspring"; and the man that weds a shrew—"One that will talk and wear the Breeches too" (2–4).

In reply to this piece is a similarly structured poem of about the same length, *The Batchelors and Maids Answer, to the Fifteen Comforts of Matrimony. Being Real Encouragements for All Single Persons of Both Sexes to Marry as Soon as Ever They Can Get Wives and Husbands, in order to Avoid the Danger of Leading Apes in Hell* [170?]. Each of the comforts enumerated answers point by point the mock comforts of the previous poem. For the most part, this poem offers "real encouragements" to marry. It praises the "Charming Bliss" (1) of the marriage bed. In response to the man with the handsome wife who is unfaithful, it says that man is right to adore his wife:

> No sorrow can lay hold of Man or Wife,
> Where Love and Virtue is the Rule of Life.
>
> (2)

Countering the earlier poet's disparaging remarks about the breeding wife, this poet says the earlier poet was monstrous "to rail at those to whom thy Life is due." Even the scolding wife is seen as valuable since she will "Man's Patience try,/And bring Repentance too, before he die" (4). Because this poem reaches rather far in order to knock down the earlier poet's arguments, it may not represent a fully realized pro-marriage ideology, but only the reversal of the earlier poet's irony, perhaps to create a further irony. In this respect, it is like the defenses of women in the *Love Giv'n O're* series.

Other replies in the fifteen-format sequence are more obviously ironic. Harshly ironic is the praise in *The Fifteen Comforts of a Wanton Wife: or, The Fool Well Fitted* (1706/7), presenting the bad wife's progression in wickedness from the wedding day on. The "comforts" include her practicing to gain control of her husband, her finding others to supply her lust, her cuckolding him with a "little bantling," and her giving him the clap, feigning remorse, and then spending all his money. We have also the crudely ironic piece, *The Fifteen Comforts of Whoring, or, The Pleasures of a Town Life* (1706) and its answer, *The Whores and Bawd's Answer to the Fifteen Comforts of Whoring* (1706). The latter purports to be a straightforward defense of prostitution but is even more grossly ironic in attacking it than the former.[6]

After 1707, the vogue for fifteen-format poems mercifully dies off. Though this vogue is an ephemeral one, it is significant to note how the poems in this series, like those in the first series, pair off polemically into pro-and-con arguments on the same topic. We see how ingenious booksellers and authors were in exploiting an extant format to produce a counterargument in order to sell another one- or two-penny poem. The ideology behind both series is traditional in its antifeminism and antimatrimonialism and seems, on the surface at least, to be a function of Grub Street economics.

For first-stage polemics, external evidence concerning the identity and background of authors is generally lacking. However, it is worth speculating on the deeper ideological sources of the antifeminist, antimarriage hostility as well as of the pro-marriage arguments that characterize many of them. In the seventeenth century, a primary literary source, as I will show in chapter 2, are the two forms of the libertine argument. The first draws on the aristocratic and skeptical ethos of the Stuart court and ultimately the courtly love tradition. The second is based broadly in a prudential middle-class ethos and is perhaps rooted in the arguments for celibacy of the pre-Reformation patristic and clerical tradition.

If one searches for sources of hostility against women and marriage that are more exclusively social (as opposed to literary), one may posit that such hostility is in part a straightforward expression of the concerns of moralists and clergy, especially those whose values are identifiable with the rising, broadly Protestant middle class, the group often called "the middling sort." According to Gillis, parents in this social class "worried about premature marriages and misalliances that would drain resources from the family economy and cause ruin to all concerned. To the emerging middling sort, matches not only with the propertyless proletariat, but with the smallholder class posed a threat to capital accumulation (86). Beyond the immediate family, improvident marriages by the poor were to be discouraged since they drained community resources through parish distribution of poor law relief.

Satiric hostility may thus derive partly from the middle-class effort to assert patriarchal control over the choice of marriage partner, to forestall the romantic inclinations of children who might marry below themselves, and to discourage children of the poor from marrying altogether so that they might not become a burden on the more prosperous in the community. It is worth noting that the proportion of those never marrying reached a high point in England in the late seventeenth century. Is it only a coincidence that this was also the time when satires against marriage were most virulent?

A corollary to the provident-warning explanation is the prolonged-adolescence theory. Under this explanation, hostile portrayals in satire of women and marriage can be seen as the expression of a proverbial wisdom and a ritual warning from the adult community to the younger people that they are undertaking serious responsibilities when they marry. As John Gillis points out, marriage in the villages and small towns among the middle class traditionally meant setting up a household with all the responsibilities to servants and retainers that were entailed. For this reason, marriages up until the mid-eighteenth century and later were usually postponed until the couple could be economically independent, for, as soon as they married, the full burdens of farm and business were upon them.

While waiting to be married, young men and women enjoyed a prolonged adolescence as apprentices, assistants, or servants, an adolescence in which the single life-style was reinforced by strong friendships with members of the same sex. Courtship, especially in its early stages, was a group activity, and marriage was subject to the public scrutiny implicit in the publication of the banns. When the young person gave up long-nourished friendships among his or her own sex for marriage, he or she was often subject to a form of peer group hazing. Within this context of values, we can understand how antimarriage polemics could also be a ritual warning with partially ironic force.

Probing for the source of antimarriage polemics, not in the social but in the psychological sphere, one can find it rooted as well in psychosexual conflict. Men and women tend to be hostile to one another because the opposite sex arouses emotions that are strong and difficult to control or that cause one to feel vulnerable. Women's psychological sense of weakness is often exacerbated by their traditional lack of power in the political, legal, and economic spheres. Encouraged by Christian moralists, men have prided themselves on their rationality and self-control. Accordingly, they may feel contempt for the yearning they experience in sexuality and attack women savagely for provoking it. Men may disown their deep emotionality and attribute it to women. This accounts for the unfortunate tendency of male marriage satirists to project typically male failings, such as lust or drunkenness, on females, a tendency to which defenders of women and marriage pointedly call attention.[7] Indeed, the growing recognition by both men and women satirists of the mechanism of projection contributes to the development of a pro-marriage ideology.

What other factors in seventeenth-century culture contribute to the ideological change that makes marriage into a heaven? The shift from satire to celebration in the polemical pairs and the engagement of traditional antimarriage discourse by a pro-marriage, even an ostensibly feminist discourse, opens the way for further dialogue and for a more sanguine attitude toward marriage.

One explanation why satire gives way to celebration of the pleasures of companionship and emotional sharing is that the traditional village pattern of prolonged adolescence and late marriage begins to break down in the later era. As young people leave the village for the city, they also escape the oversight of their courtships by parents, friends, and community. Since they also lose the stability these village associations give to their lives, it is understandable that they would turn to sexual liaisons and earlier marriages for emotional nourishment. This must have taken place especially among the dislocated agricultural laborers for whom the availability of work was the primary organizing principle in their lives.

In the introduction, I suggested that a literary ideology provided by *Paradise Lost* in particular and seventeenth-century Protestantism in general affirms marital love and that within that context celebration prevails over satire. In this section we discovered, from the antilibertine thrust of many of the pro-marriage arguments in early tract pieces, that affirmation of marriage can also be a sociopolitical stance, perhaps a manifestation of a middle-class, Protestant offensive against the immorality of the Stuart court and the nobility and gentry whose behavior was influenced by it.

As I posited earlier in this chapter, antimarriage hostility is no doubt partially rooted in middle-class, prudential concerns. One of the most interesting contradictions in the history of marriage is that the Protestant ideology of this same social stratum can be identified as the primary source for pro-marriage ideology (see Haller and Leites). As James Turner Johnson demonstrates by examining Puritan theological rationales for marriage in early seventeenth-century conduct books, companionship consistently stands higher than rationales that were traditionally offered by Roman Catholic theologians such as procreation, faithfulness (or restraint and remedy of sin), and sacrament (or symbolic stability). Johnson sees the emphasis on companionship reinforced by love and duty as the distinguishing feature of Puritan marriage doctrine. This emphasis pointedly contrasts with that of Aquinas and Catholic theologians and with conservative Anglican theologians for whom *proles* or the sacred process of transmitting human life effectively stands at the top of the list (J. T. Johnson 40–49, 114–15). For Puritans and Anglicans influenced by Calvinist doctrine, marriage was a covenant rather than a sacrament. Calvinism locates the value of marriage more in the social relationship between husband and wife and less in the mysterious God-given role of procreation. Perhaps because the Calvinist conception of marriage was from the start more socially focused, it was more vulnerable to secularization than a sacramentally focused one.

In seventeenth-century England, conflicts were rife between Calvinist ideology and the survival of the pre-Reformation Roman Catholic doctrine of marriage as a sacrament. Since Calvin considered marriage as the social covenant of a man and a woman bound together by God, he ceded jurisdiction over it to civil authorities. However, since the state was to be a theocracy, civil magistrates would have to "handle all suits strictly in accordance with the principles of the New Testament as interpreted by the divines of the reformed Church" (Bailey 175). As with the Geneva Church, Puritan church polity was "taken directly from the pages of God's word—'not the filthye canon lawe' but a structure of life for all the elect which would ensure their keeping of the terms of the covenant of grace in their personal and corporate lives" (J. T. Johnson 30).

Calvin affirmed the "general principle of indissolubility," but he concurred with Christ in Matt. 5:31–32 in allowing divorce (and remarriage) in cases of adultery. This right was extended to both husband and wife. In the Geneva Ordinances of 1561, divorce and remarriage are permitted also in cases of desertion (Winnett 7). In pointed disagreement with Calvinism was Roman Catholic doctrine as reasserted by the Council of Trent at its twenty-fourth session (1563). Since marriage is one of the seven sacraments, God confers grace on the couple by their sexual union to procreate; jurisdiction over marriage is maintained by "ecclesiastical authority" through canon law. Symbolizing the union between Christ and the Church, consummated wedlock is indissoluble, and only separation *a mensa et thoro* can be granted by Church authority (Bailey 179).

Between these two extreme positions and on a number of other disputed issues, Anglican theologians found much room for disagreement among themselves. The Anglican "Form of Solemnization of Matrimony" is technically not a sacrament, and the Church of England under Henry VIII had broken away from the jurisdiction of Rome. Yet the Anglican marriage service "followed without any significant deviation the medieval marriage rite—principally that of the Sarum Manual. The doctrine taught therein is that traditionally taught by the western [i.e., Roman Catholic] Church" (Bailey 183). Though the Anglican Church was ultimately subject to the power of the English sovereign in matters in which he or she chose to assert it, canon law continued in force, and the official position of the Church was that marriage was indissoluble and that remarriage was not permitted even in cases of adultery. As A. R. Winnett shows in detail, a significant number of influential theologians within the Church of England disagreed with this position and argued for remarriage for men only or for both men and women.

Theological controversy both outside and within the Anglican Church can thus be viewed as an important and contradictory source of both anti- and pro-marriage polemics. This is perhaps why the confrontation of the pro-and-con positions within the debate format is inevitable in the eighteenth century. As polemical poetry evolves, it is also inevitable that the theological sources that produced this confrontation should become progressively more secular and less identifiable as religious ideology (see Winnett 118).

STAGE TWO

From separately standing pro-and-con arguments to the debate format is not a big jump. Indeed, the debate format seems a perfectly logical extension of the paired polemical format in which one poem may argue against marriage and its answer argue for marriage. To combine both pro-and-con arguments in one poem is an innovation one would anticipate. Once there is sufficient disagreement, there is pressure to harmonize it, and the debate format takes the emphasis off controversy and puts it on resolution. Debate formats usually unbalance or contrive the debate so that one side will win. In order for marriage poets to use such a format, they have to be willing to begin to harmonize conflicting ideologies toward marriage under some overriding rationale or operating principle, not just let them stand.

I do not wish to suggest that previous to this the debate format had not been used in marriage poetry. The debate or dialogue has a sophisticated heritage in medieval and Renaissance prose and verse treating marriage.[8] In the Restoration, however, it takes some time before the popular debate with its hyperbolical polarizations supplants separately standing pro-and-con polemical arguments. A few poets in the tradition of learned wit employ it before it works its way down into the popular tradition. One of the earliest examples of learned wit impinging on the popular tradition is the marriage debate in *Hudibras* III.i. Not quite a fully realized illustration of Rothstein's second stage, Samuel Butler's marriage debate pits strongly polarized pro and con positions against each other, but the narrator of *Hudibras* offers little direct help in resolving the conflict. Rather, the reader of Butler's satire must rely on reason in an attempt to supply the harmonizing rationale.

In the early eighteenth century, as the vogue for polemical verse arguments fades, the debate format slowly begins to gain popularity. Ned Ward resolves his marriage debates by introducing a narrator who serves paternalistically as the voice of reason. Swift uses the embedded debate in several of his poems treating marriage, and if pro-and-con positions are resolved at all, it is by the narrator's humor or wit—in effect an appeal to good sense. The humor and wit softens the paternalism of Swift's stance. Lady Chudleigh turns a marriage debate over dominion into an argument for woman's intellectual dignity and in doing so relies on the forceful rationality of her mouthpiece character to undermine tyrannical paternalism. Her strategy, however, *approaches* Rothstein's third stage since she resolves debate almost as much by affirming an affective stance as by appealing to justice and reason. As we shall see when we move on to examples of Rothstein's third stage, debates over marriage in the later era are increasingly resolved by the poet's sharing his celebration of the companionate marriage with the reader and thus softening his paternalistic didacticism.

The marriage debate in *Hudibras* III.i.522–1052 does not appear until 1678 when *Hudibras. The Third and Last Part* is published. Though some complain of the falling off of Butler's powers in this part, the debate in the first canto does retain the liveliness and satiric ingenuity of the earlier parts of *Hudibras*. In constructing the debate, Butler works in the comic tradition of Rabelais in book three of *Gargantua and Pantagruel* (1522–24). With his hilarious back and forth between Pantagruel and Panurge over whether the latter should marry, Rabelais offers a prototype of Rothstein's second stage in which arguments for and against marriage are allowed to stand on their own merits and neither stands very tall. In *Hudibras* Butler adds a dramatic complexity to this pattern that captures in a rather maddening way the contradictions that the issue of marriage had acquired in middle and late seventeenth-century Protestant polemics and social history.

Butler's debate between the Presbyterian knight, Hudibras, and the outspoken, self-sufficient widow, whose jointure Hudibras lusts after, opposes the hell against the heaven of marriage in an open battle of the sexes. The debate in *Hudibras* III.i is much more than a simple pro-and-con interchange on marriage. Hudibras, who throughout Butler's poem is the perfect embodiment of Puritan hypocrisy and paternalism, for once offers arguments which *sound* convincing. Hudibras uses many of the points in defense of marriage which we have seen in prose marriage tracts of the 1670s.[9] Elsewhere in *Hudibras* the widow is almost always the touchstone of wit and good sense; she consistently shows up Hudibras's arguments as bogus. In the marriage debate, however, her wit and cynicism may be too intense and unrelieved. Speaking as a Restoration feminist, she runs the danger of being identified as a doctrinaire libertine and thus discrediting herself. She is a sort of enthusiast in the religion of coffee house cynicism. Hudibras himself realizes this when he says of her argument:

> these Reasons are but strains
> Of wanton, over-heated Brains,
> Which Ralliers in their Wit, or Drink,
> Do rather wheedle with than think.
> (III.i.757–60)

Did Butler want his readers to side with the Puritan Hudibras and his attack on the libertine position, or is Hudibras's defense of marriage compromised by his hypocrisy and paternalism? And if Hudibras's stance is compromised, is not the widow's as well? In his short poem "The Licentious Age of Charles the 2D," Butler attacks his era as

> a strange *Age* we've liv'd in, and a lewd
> As 'ere the Sun in all his Travels view'd;
> An *Age* as vile, as ever Justice urg'd,
> Like a fantastic *Letcher* to be scourg'd:
> (*Satires* 56)

Would the same Butler who savaged the libertine character of his times have condoned the modish cynicism of the widow? Describing the age's wariness toward marriage, the widow at one point almost seems to approve of a couple's living together as "French, and fashionable."

> For now the World is grown so wary,
> That few of either Sex dare marry,
> But rather trust, on tick, t'Amours
> The *Cross* and *Pile*, for *Bett'r* or *Worse;*
> A Mode, that is held honourable,
> As well as French, and fashionable,
> For when it falls out for the best,
> Where both are incommoded least;
> (III.i.677–84)

The widow's rationale for permissiveness seems too facile for Butler to approve wholeheartedly, but then it is difficult throughout this debate to determine where Butler himself stands. Neither the argument of Hudibras nor that of the widow seem finally to stand up very well, and the author's position cannot be identified readily with one or the other. The reader's difficulty in pinning down Butler's actual position is, I posit, a deliberate satiric strategy in his use of the debate form. Allowing each position to stand on its own (de)merits in opposition to the other, Butler mirrors the intellectual, social, and religious contradictions of marriage in the Restoration.

On one hand, the widow's cynical and possibly libertine denigration of marriage reduces it ultimately to a hell. Her argument is marked by an increasing profusion of debased, violent images in her speech that begins: "*Marriage is but a Beast,* some say,/That *carries double in a foul way*" (III.i.569–70). The vehicles of metaphoric figures include venereal disease ("Jealousie is but a kind/Of *Clap,* and *Grincam* of the mind"), siege warfare ("Finds all his *Having, and his Holding,*/Reduc'd t'Eternal *Noise,* and *Scolding,*/The *Conjugal Petard,* that tears/Down all *Portcullices* of Ears"), and animal behavior ("When only arm'd with Noise, and Nails/The Female Silkworms ride the Males" or "Like *Syrens* with their charming Notes:/Sweet as a Screech-Owl's *Serenade*"). The widow's speech reduces the relationship of the sexes in marriage to pathological sordidness, destructive mechanism, or noisy bestiality.

On the other hand, in opposition to the widow's hellish representation of marriage is Hudibras's romantic overidealization, an idealization that is reinforced by the Presbyterian knight's metaphysical conceits and courtly diction.

> And what security's too strong,
> To guard that gentle Heart from wrong,
> That to its Friend is glad to pass,
> It self away, and all it has:
> And, like an *Anchorite,* gives over
> This World, for th'Heaven of a Lover?
> (III.i.921–26)

Because Hudibras's celebration of marriage is compromised by his Puritan hypocrisy and tyrannic paternalism, the widow is right to suspect it, and with her characteristic cynicism she counters the knight's portrayal of marriage as a heaven:

> I grant (quoth she) there are some few
> Who take that course, and find it true:
> But Millions, whom the same does sentence
> To Heaven, b'another way, repentance.
> (III.i.927–40)

Butler does not step in as narrator and resolve the debate between Hudibras's marriage as heaven and the widow's marriage as hell. Yet the reader, drawing on the principle of reason and good sense that Butler implicitly endorses, may choose to side more with the widow, even though both her and Hudibras's positions are extremes.

Turning to three examples of marriage debates from the early eighteenth century, we see that authors tend more to resolve the contradictory arguments in favor of one of the contesting positions. More important, an overriding, secular harmonizing principle such as good sense or social justice is imposed on the debate, usually by the narrator. Who wins the debate is made to seem less important than is the operating principle involved in the resolution. The conflict will be reconciled, it is implied, if the narrator's (or author's) sense of things prevails, and his or her point of view should reasonably be the reader's as well. In these respects, the three poems all might be taken as examples of Rothstein's second stage.

In *Nuptial Dialogues and Debates* (1723) by Edward or Ned Ward, publican in Moorfields and twice-pilloried "humorist of 'low extraction,'" the operation of the stage-two pattern is simple and Ward's ideology rather traditionally patriarchal, though without any direct support from Protestant theology (*DNB*; see Troyer for an extensive biography). Many of Ward's dialogues or debates involve dramatic oppositions between antithetical types: "a surly husband and a condescending wife," "an extravagant husband and a prudent wife," "a wealthy niggard and his generous termagant," "a nice affected gentleman and his careless slatternly wife." Each dialogue dramatizes the conflicts between the couple and then concludes with "Moral Reflexions" which put the conflict in some perspective, often by reaffirming male dominion exercised wisely. The narrator intrudes, meting out blame and offering appropriate advice. Usually the dialogue has been weighted from the start on one side so that by the end of the dialogue the reader can anticipate the narrator's judgment. The expression of conflicting positions is not an end in itself, nor is it finally that important whether the husband or wife wins. What is significant is the author's ostensibly harmonizing patriarchal judgment, which prevails as an operating principle to resolve the conflict with apparent wisdom and justice.

Even in a poem as sophisticated as *Cadenus and Vanessa* (1726) by the Church of Ireland clergyman Jonathan Swift, the embedding of the marriage debate seems to follow a pattern that exemplifies Rothstein's second stage. *Cadenus and Vanessa* is not ostensibly a marriage poem, nor does the debate format persist throughout. Nevertheless, the opening of the poem does take the form of a debate or, to be more precise, a hearing in a court of law, and this hearing is resolved in the conclusion. Venus calls a council to adjudicate the rival claims of men and women against each other. The women charge that men have lost the art of (romantic) love and no longer pay allegiance to its power:

> Now Love is dwindled to Intrigue,
> And Marriage grown a Money-League.
> (Swift 2: 687; lines 12–14)

Shifting terms, the men counter with the defense that women of today are no longer moved by (platonic) love:

> That modern Love is no such Thing
> As what those antient Poets sing;
> A Fire celestial, chaste, refin'd,
> Conceiv'd and kindled in the Mind,
>   (lines 27–30)

Women today, the men maintain, only know "gross Desire"; their minds are preoccupied with trifles and "Female Toys":

> Hence we conclude, no Women's Hearts
> Are won by Virtue, Wit, and Parts;
>   (2: 688; lines 61–62)

In a significant sense, this interchange is a debate about marriage since it concerns not only the winning of a heart but the choice of a mate for life. The creation of Vanessa by Venus is in fact a bait to see whether the men of fashion will recognize and marry a woman of beauty and sense. To make the bait realistic in eighteenth-century terms, Vanessa is given a fortune of £5000.

Critics have suggested that Swift wrote *Cadenus and Vanessa* as a way to deflect Esther Vanhomrigh's romantic passion. Embarrassed or frightened by the intensity of her passion, and unwilling to end their relationship, he found an "outlet in penning *Cadenus and Vanessa* at Windsor during the autumn of 1712" (Swift 2: 684). This explanation may account for one of Swift's main purposes in writing the poem. However, it overlooks the strategic victory that clergyman Swift attempts to achieve in using the embedded marriage debate. The pro-and-con debate serves as the tactical battleground for the entire poem. Because the men of fashion do not recognize the merits of the beautiful *and* intelligent Vanessa, Venus resolves the debate by finding against the men.

> "She was at Lord knows what Expence,
> "To form a Nymph of Wit and Sense;
> "A Model for her Sex design'd,
> "Who never cou'd one Lover find.
> "She saw her Favour was misplac'd;
> "The Fellows had a wretched Taste;
> "She needs must tell them to their Face,
> "They were a senseless, stupid Race:
> "And were she to begin agen,
> "She'd study to reform the *Men*;
>   (2: 713–14; lines 864–72)

The resolution of the debate in the women's favor serves the function of flattering Vanessa and intelligent women in general. It also conveys, to Esther, Swift's fatherly judgment that those men who overlooked her attributes as a good marriage match are a "senseless, stupid Race."

In voicing this position, Swift, the Anglican cleric, may affirm a prudential version of the companionate ideal. Swift's awarding the women victory in the dispute, however, is less important than his strategic attempt to use the poem to cast his relationship with Esther into a light that would give him some fatherly control. Though Swift censures men for their failure to recognize Vanessa's merits, he presents himself as an unfit partner for her. He is middle-aged, "Declin'd in health," and inept at romance. Swift's flattery of Vanessa by finding against the men and his belittling of himself may be his attempt to fend off Esther and direct her toward a suitable marriage partner. It also somewhat ironically affirms a prudential companionate ideal since, though Swift and Esther may be intellectually compatible, they are not well matched in other ways.

The smaller debate may have been resolved, but the larger issue of Swift's relationship to Esther is left at "sixes and sevens" as Venus leaves the chaotic world under Cupid's control and flies up to heaven. Swift implies that heaven is the only place where lovers will find both justice and satisfaction. He laments the failure of society to provide suitable partners for intelligent women and looks, albeit pessimistically, toward the possibility of reform. As with Ward's poem, the embedded debate is subordinated to the purpose of conveying the author's good-sense resolution, except that in Swift's poem there is only the attempt at resolution or at the least an affirmation of his desire for it.[10]

An example of a second-stage debate that verges on Rothstein's third stage is *The Ladies Defence: or, The Bride-Woman's Counsellor Answer'd: A Poem in Dialogue between Sir John Brute, Sir William Loveall, Melissa, and a Parson* (1701) by Mary, Lady Chudleigh. Married to Sir George Chudleigh of Ashton in Devon, a baronet, Lady Chudleigh, an admirer of Mary Astell, evidently led a solitary life-style. In her protofeminist poem, the debate pits Melissa against the three men. Melissa is a spokesperson for Lady Chudleigh and for women in general, and the men are representatives of unjust male dominion in its various forms. The liveliness of the interchanges and the creation of three distinct male characters give the debate the appeal of a drama. The husband, Sir John Brute, is tyrannical and insensitive in asserting his patriarchal rights. Sir William Loveall, the young single man about town, at first pays high tribute to women but later is shown to be just as selfish and insensitive as the husband.

The Parson stands for the Rev. John Sprint. It is his sermon on women's duty to obey their husbands to which Lady Chudleigh's poem responds. More broadly, the Parson represents all those intellectuals and clergy who feed the fire of authoritarianism by evoking the rationales for male dominion in Protestantism. Sparks fly especially between the Parson and Melissa on several controversial topics: women's supposed intellectual inferiority to men, education for women, women's vocation in life, and women's duty to obey their husbands in all things.

As with other second-stage debates, the dialogue in Lady Chudleigh's poem is set up so that one side will emerge the victor. Because Melissa accedes, men win the debate over male sovereignty, but Lady Chudleigh intends that Melissa emerge from the poem with our sympathy and admiration. Almost as a final revenge against the men, Melissa the feminist martyr will become after death the Christian saint triumphant. Freed of their earthly "clay," women will inhabit a heaven in which they will possess mental (and physical) equality with men:

> In glorious Bodies we shall bask in Day,
> And with inlightned Minds new Scenes survey.
>
> (22)

If women cannot find heaven in marriage on earth, they will achieve the heaven of sexual equality in the afterlife. By imposing such a contrived resolution on the debate, the author through Melissa makes us sympathetically aware of the arbitrary pattern of male discrimination that prevails in society and in interpretation of Protestant doctrine. The author's status as a spokesperson for justice and as a resolver of debate actually allows her to continue to be an emotive advocate for women's dignity. As the voice of justice and good sense, the author would resolve the debate in the second-stage manner. As the articulator of an intensely affective stance that overwhelms rational debate as she shares it with the reader, Lady Chudleigh verges on Rothstein's third stage.

Stage Three

The Ladies Defence is remarkable in approaching Rothstein's third stage as early as it does. By the later era, the pattern becomes more common. In the anonymous *Matrimony, Pro and Con: or, the Resolve* (1745), Mary Collier's "The Happy Husband, and the Old Batchelor. A Dialogue" (1762), and Cowper's "Mutual Forbearance Necessary to the Happiness of the

Married State" (1782) we find clear-cut examples of the third stage in which opposing positions are not allowed to stand freely but are subordinated to a third overriding point of view. This ostensibly secular point of view is made to prevail by the speaker's emotional affirmation of it which he shares with the reader. The reader is not rationally convinced but converted, perhaps in the same way that one is converted to Methodism.

Using heroic couplets flexible enough to handle rapidly shifting dialogue, *Matrimony, Pro and Con* does not so much give us a debate between two opposing sides of equal strength as the emotional victory of the didactic and celebratory pro-marriage position over the satiric antimarriage position. Satire is incorporated in the antimarriage speeches of G, and as such it is not especially virulent:

> *Odio* will own he has a beauteous Mate,
> And Wealth enough to live genteel—or great;
> Yet mention Wedlock, and he'll mourn his Chain,
> And sudden Torture feel thro' ev'ry Vein.
>
> (2)

Since G is persuaded by J to embrace wedlock only a few lines later, the reader must assume that his opposition to it cannot have been deeply felt. Once G has been convinced to pursue marriage, he must of course be instructed in how to proceed.

For the remainder of the poem (from 4–12), J gives G advice on the qualities to seek in a wife and on how to pursue his courtship of his chosen, *Amata*. The character of this advice is neither witty nor outlandishly romantic, but mainly affirms in idealized terms the codes of the established society of that day. In this debate, the pro-marriage position takes the high middle ground of empathetic instruction, and the antimarriage position is converted to that of the eager student whose answers prompt further advice. Our sense of a debate is almost entirely lost as the student's answers harmonize with the instructor's advice in one grand chorus of affirmation. In the conclusion, the student celebrates his intention to propose to a "Sweet,—lovely Creature, and all over Charms!" He invokes heaven to favor him in his suit. Marriage, if he can achieve it, will be a heavenly consummation.

More resistant to conversion is the "Old Batchelor" in "The Happy Husband and the Old Batchelor. A Dialogue" by Mary Collier, the washerwoman poet of Petersfield in Hampshire. Before he yields to the justice of his friend's pro-marriage sentiments, the free-spirited, self-indulgent "Batchelor" must be assured that a virtuous, loving wife will be obliging and prudent, will not take away his freedom completely, will serve as a "faithful Friend in time of need," and will legitimize fatherhood. Collier's protofeminist point of view is evident in the husband's reply to the bachelor's skepticism about finding a wife so good. He answers justly that loving husbands who rule with kindness and set virtuous examples are difficult to find as well.

> But where strict virtue bears the Sway,
> That virtue cannot lead astray.
> When mild reproofs have little force
> To check a Husband's vicious course,
> A Wife provok'd, with rage and fear,
> May utter truth he hates to hear.
>
> (28)

When the bachelor is finally convinced by such telling arguments, he vows to leave behind his profligate single life.

> Altho' my bloom of life be past,
> I hope I shall reform at last.
> But first my care shall be apply'd
> To chuse a virtuous loving Bride,
> And so behave to her that we
> May live in love and unity,
>
> (40)

Collier dramatizes the bachelor's conversion to the companionate ideal much as other third-stage debates do, and even in her conclusion she emphasizes the husband's responsibility in making a marriage happy.

Broadly similar to the two earlier poems in its advice affirming marriage is Cowper's "Mutual Forbearance Necessary to the Happiness of the Married State" (1782). This piece begins with a near comic debate illustrating a communication breakdown between Sir Humphrey and his young wife. Sir Humphrey is somewhat deaf and mistakes his wife's complaint about antiquated hangings in some of the rooms as her request to dismiss a servant who rode her horse with "whip and spur" for a mile. The wife becomes irritated with the husband's hearing problem and, after screaming at him in exasperation, ends by saying in a low voice that it does not matter whether he hears or not. Cowper now steps in to terminate the debate, to moralize on the evils of domestic strife, and to affirm the importance of that "gentle, delicate, and kind" love which rises above the minor faults and frailties of a spouse. If we do not forbear to dwell on infirmities, which are common to all, then the harmony of the marriage state will be lost:

> Instead of Harmony, 'tis jar,
> And tumult, and intestine war.
> (Chalmers 18: 656)

Cowper concludes his poem praising love as a secularized force that overcomes discord and suffering.

> The love, that cheers life's latest stage,
> Proof against sickness and old age,
> Preserv'd by virtue from declension,
> Becomes not weary of attention;
> But lives, when that exterior grace
> Which first inspir'd the flame, decays.
> (18: 657)

Avoiding the excesses of many later era celebratory poets, Cowper affirms love warmly as an affective attitude that triumphs over the verbal conflicts and vicissitudes of married life. Debate is subsumed in the category of those negatives that love overcomes. In this poem of the 1780s, the controversy of Protestant polemics has almost completely disappeared and is displaced by a sympathetic, fatherly didacticism and the celebration of loving companionship, a feminized domesticity. This disappearance is widespread in many poems of the later era.

CHAPTER TWO

The Rake in Fetters and the Pleasures of a Single Life

WE SAW IN THE PRECEDING CHAPTER THAT the libertine argument is central to the polemics of marriage verse and to the pro-and-con debate over its pains and pleasures, the argument whether marriage is a hell or a heaven. As the rake's justification of libertine behavior is given expression in Restoration poetry, it is the search for "perfect freedom" that underlies his (or her) rationale.¹ For those bound by the restraints of civilization, such a search, though in some ways heroic, is bound to prove illusory. This is perhaps why Restoration libertinism, skeptical and even cynical by nature, takes several different forms, the argument for each involving a different idea of freedom. The argument for sexual freedom is usually that the pleasures of love cannot be institutionalized in marriage because what pleases us shifts from time to time. Consequently, people ought to be free to pursue the reality of bliss, not to feign it, force it, or do without it, as married men and women often do. A man can enjoy sex with a mistress or a prostitute without the lifetime enslavement that marriage imposes. A woman can take lovers rather than have a tyrannical husband.

In the courtly tradition and the libertine argument that stems from it, marrying for love stands as a contradiction in terms. Articulators of courtly doctrine from Andreas Capellanus onward repeatedly point out that since love in marriage is under a duty or necessity, the lady cannot exercise her free choice and thus "her love cannot . . . increase [her lover's] *probitas*" (Lewis 26). Additionally, as C. S. Lewis shows, some medieval theologians considered passionate or lustful love of one's own wife to be adultery.[2] At the least, a husband who approached his wife out of sexual passion rather than out of desire to procreate or to pay his marriage debt was committing a mortal sin. Even if marital intercourse were prompted by the right motives, the act was still seen as evil, though not a sin (15–16). In contrast, love in the courtly tradition was seen as ennobling or freeing the lovers, sometimes platonically uplifting them into a spiritual sphere.

A second and related argument is that the pleasures of the single life are preferable to the pleasures of marriage. A man or woman can find greater freedom in the wholesome activities of the celibate life: same-sex friendships, intellectual conversation, reading, drinking in moderation, country recreations.[3] In the second argument, the Edenic pleasures of celibacy are set off against the tribulations of matrimony: financial cares and worries, a nagging, domineering, insatiable, or unfaithful spouse, noisy children, jealousy, and domestic disharmony in general. The philosophical roots of this argument seem less in the courtly love tradition and more in the various clerical and patristic dissuasions from marriage designed to promote celibacy. The argument for celibacy, especially for clerics, is a longstanding one in Christian advice poetry, and it reaches back well before the Reformation.

In the case of the first form of the argument during the Restoration, the libertine exploration of will and how far it could carry one was bound to run up against limits; chief of these was the institution of marriage. No matter how unnatural the libertine might consider it, this institution is at the center of the religious, legal, economic, and cultural structures of society. Even if the libertine does not believe in marriage, he or she must inevitably live life in its presence. Often this meant marrying for appearance or for financial security.

The libertine ethos of the Restoration court wits is descended from the courtly love tradition, specifically the arguments of Cavalier poets such as Lovelace, Suckling, and Carew who celebrate the spontaneous pleasures of love for the moment. In Charles II's court, among the "mob of gentlemen who wrote with ease," these arguments are handled with cynicism, skepticism, even nihilism as poets such as Rochester experiment with the discourse of materialist or atheist philosophy. Such intellectual and artistic explorations within aristocratic court circles were bound to conflict with Christian morality, especially the Puritan-based morality of a significant portion of the English middle class. As this conflict persisted into the late Restoration, middle-class morality increasingly prevails. A watershed date may be 1688 when the Protestant, middle-class ethos of William III's reign displaces the aristocratic, libertine, French-inspired Stuart court. In the poetry of the 1790s (as with the drama), more and more rakes are "enlarged" into husbands, and their female counterparts "dwindle" into wives. By the eighteenth century, an argument begins to develop that men and women experience greater freedom in the trusting companionship of marriage.

Eric Rothstein's schemata can again be instructive. For Rothstein, we recall, the distinctive focus of poetry from the 1690s to the 1740s is "not on a theme but on an operating principle, that of interaction, interconnectedness" (xiii). "Forms that exalted individuals, . . . yield to those that locate individuals within God's dispensation, England's controlling needs, and the rules of society" (48). With the two main libertine arguments (for sexual freedom and for the freedom of celibacy or the single life), what occurs broadly, as we move from the Restoration into the early eighteenth century, is that celebrations of the untrammeled status of the libertine or single man to determine his own life-style are increasingly treated ironically or countered by moral arguments that appeal to religious ideals, to moral standards, or to reasonable norms for human interaction. Poems that employ the polarized modes of satire and celebration side by side might seem to offer a debate or a true power conflict; however, the polarization is always loaded in favor of one side. Thus the moral or normative position is calculated to assert itself. Within this position there is usually an appeal to some higher authority, God's or society's law. With increasing predictability, poets take the side of heaven against the devilish individual will of the rake.

Although a few women poets argue for a freedom comparable to the male rake's, the majority are antilibertine in their sentiments; most feel that marriage provides women with important social and legal protections. In the later era, the arguments for sexual freedom and for the freedom of celibacy can still be found, though increasingly they are checked, often emotionally, by the prevailing affirmation of a companionate marriage in which both partners find (perfect) bliss.

The Argument for Sexual Freedom: Early Era

The first argument that love should be free may be derived in large measure from Petrarchan love poetry, especially those Renaissance poems that perpetuate the courtly love myth in their rhetoric of passion (see de Rougemont 180–84). The argument for the freedom of celibacy seems more the property of the moralists, and its ultimate source may well be the antifeminism and antimatrimonialism of the pre-Reformation church. The patristic and clerical writers who expressed a hostility to women and marriage originally may have done so in order to glorify the celibate life and to recruit more men for the priesthood and holy orders. This antimatrimonialism evidently spilled over into secular literature and became a common feature of medieval and Renaissance satire.

Though both arguments may sometimes merge indistinguishably in a particular poem, they are usually readily identifiable. Expressions of the first argument can be found in the libertine philosophy in the 1660s and 1670s and in the songs and satires of the best poets such as Dryden and Rochester. These are the poets who are usually credited with giving expression to the most positive portrayals of the life of the rake. Dryden, especially as the author of *Marriage à la Mode* (1673), gained something of a contemporary reputation as the initiator of a new looser morality.[4] Rochester came to be seen as the archrake in the libertine court of Charles II, the wicked Lord Rochester of fact and legend. Yet, their reputations notwithstanding, the poetry, especially the satires of each on marriage, is not so easily stereotyped.

To find the stereotype fulfilled, we must turn to the imitators of Dryden and Rochester, especially to the poets of the 1680s and later who pick up the first argument and formularize it. It was after the Glorious Revolution that the French-influenced promiscuity of the Stuart court was replaced by the more middle-class Dutch mores encouraged by William III. Though William was evidently homosexual, his public behavior was more proper and not in direct conflict with English Protestant morality.[5] Significantly enough, it is in the 1690s that poetry using the first argument becomes formulaic to the point that the argument turns into a stereotype of itself. In some cases, this was a purposeful strategy as poets wished to satirize the libertine argument or to use the rake's confessions for didactic purposes. As the aristocratic, libertine ethos is displaced by middle-class Protestant, even nonconformist mores, the sophistication of the poetry also seems to decline as satire loses its multidimensional ironies, becomes formulaic, and then finally turns didactic in rigid and unhumorous ways.

For one of the earliest celebrations of the first argument, we can turn to the song with which the wife of the rake Rhodophil opens Dryden's *Marriage à la Mode*. Doralice's rationalization of marital infidelity is undercut by later events in the play. The would-be adultery is averted at the last minute, and the couples are reassigned to their proper partners. Taken by itself, however, Doralice's song can be read as an almost perfect expression, even an idealization of the first argument.

> Why should a foolish Marriage Vow
>   Which long ago was made,
> Oblige us to each other now
>   When Passion is decay'd?
> We lov'd, and we lov'd, as long as we cou'd,
>   Till our love was lov'd out in us both:
> But our Marriage is dead, when the Pleasure is fled:
>   'Twas Pleasure first made it an Oath.
>   (*Marriage à la Mode* 11; 1.4–11)

The song suggests that marriage binds its partners no more than the sexual attraction that led them to it; a marriage is no longer in force when it no longer gives pleasure. Such an argument, as attractive as some might find it, obviously runs up against all the religious, economic, and legal codes society has built to support marriage. Perhaps this is why in *Marriage à la Mode*, Dryden had to find some way, even a contrived one, to defeat it. In later poetry, Dryden seems more direct in satirizing the libertine life-style that he is sometimes credited with glorifying.[6]

In Rochester's poetry, the libertine argument is often qualified by dramatic irony or treated with skepticism or cynicism. On first glance, the sonnet "Against Marriage" (1675 or earlier) seems little more than a series of stock tropes denigrating marriage. These are set off by a candid description of instinctive sexuality. If we list the tenor of the tropes Rochester's speaker employs to denigrate marriage, we find respectively poison, disease, torture, and slave labor.

> Out of mere love and arrant devotion,
> Of marriage I'll give you this galloping notion.
>   It's the bane of all business, the end of all pleasure,
> The consumption of wit, youth, virtue, and treasure.

> It's the rack of our thoughts, the nightmare of sleep,
> That sets us to work before the day peep.
> It makes us make brick without stubble or straw,
> And a cunt has no sense of conscience or law.
>
> (159; lines 1–8)

In contrast, sex with a "generous wench" (not necessarily a prostitute) is characterized as "noble."

> If you need must have flesh, take the way that is noble
> In a generous wench there is nothing of trouble.
> You come on, you come off—say, do what you please—
> And the worst you can fear is but a disease,
> And diseases, you know, will admit of a cure,
> But the hell-fire of marriage none can endure.
>
> (lines 9–14)

A closer look at the poem suggests a conundrum rather than a simple harangue. Note the paradox, for example, in presenting venereal disease as preferable to the disease of marriage. Consider also the rather puzzling opening in which the speaker explains his motive for presenting such a negative idea of marriage as "mere love and arrant devotion." Is the speaker offering advice on marriage to a cherished bachelor friend, or are the unmitigated love and devotion to be understood as love and devotion in the abstract? In other words, it may be the force of love and devotion in a marriage that makes a man bridle at the restriction of marriage. If the bonds of love had no force at all in the speaker's consciousness, he would not rail at them.

If "Against Marriage" seems, on the surface at least, to celebrate natural sexuality over sexuality institutionalized in marriage, a second poem by Rochester, a "Fragment" of uncertain date, suggests that simple consummation of the sexual act is not by itself sufficient. This poem presents the speaker, a young woman of quality, as directly opposed to the pleasure ethic such as is expressed in the sonnet "Against Marriage." The speaker scorns the reduction of the entire courtship ritual to the act of sexual possession. In this "ill-bred age" women have

> Fall'n from the rights their sex and beauties gave
> To make men wish, despair, and humbly crave,
> Now 'twill suffice if they vouchsafe to *have*.
>
> (102; lines 5–7)

The speaker resents the way the young men about town choose marital partners as if they were buying a horse:

> T' th' Pall Mall, playhouse, and drawing room,
> Their women-fairs, those women-coursers come
> To chaffer, choose, and ride their bargains home.
> (lines 8–10)

The more open, natural climate of the age in which sexual liaisons are formed without courtly formalities works against the interests of women, says the speaker. Temporarily at least, Rochester seems to share his speaker's nostalgia for a more romantic past that she would dream about in a melancholy revery, perhaps a masturbatory one.

> Ere bear this scorn, I'd be shut up at home,
> Content with humoring myself alone;
> Force back the humble love of former days
> In pensive madrigals and ends of plays,
> When if my lady frowned, th'unhappy knight
> Was fain to fast and lie alone that night.
> (102–3; lines 21–26)

This brooding nostalgia for the old days has its romantic charm, yet with no explanatory transition Rochester shifts from the courtly image of a lady exercising dominion over her knight to a dominating wife image straight out of harsh antimarriage satire. The husband who would free himself from the tyranny of his wife puts himself in turn under the milder dominion of his whore. Out of the daydream, we are jolted back to present reality.

> But whilst th'insulting wife the breeches wore,
> The husband took her clothes to g[i]ve his —,
> Who now maintains it with a gentler art:
> Thus tyrannies to commonwealths convert.
> (103; lines 26–30)

The impact of this stark image of the tyrannical wife and whoring husband following hard on the heels of the softer romantic daydream is at first confusing. However, the reader soon should see that both images involve women in control: "my lady" *over* the "unhappy knight," then the "insulting wife" and the whore (to whom the wife's clothes are given) *over* the husband. Just as the romantic daydream of the knight's courtly subservience is undercut by the harsh satiric image of the tyrannical wife and whore, the female speaker's desire for more courtly formality in relations between the sexes is compromised by the base reality of instinctive sexuality: sexuality subjugates both men and women.

> Then, after all, you find, whate'er we say,
> Things must go on in their lewd natural way.
> Besides, the beastly men, we daily see,
> Can please themselves alone as well as we.
> Therefore, kind ladies of the town, to you
> For our stol'n ravished men we hereb[y] sue.
> (lines 26–30)

As both men and women can masturbate, so the behavior of both is a function of their sexual urges and the pressure of social institutions. It is not so much that romantic courtship patterns have been set aside in the present age; it is more that the romantic image of the relationship between the sexes was never a reality. People in earlier ages deluded themselves, while the poet, through his disillusioned female speaker, at least observes human behavior more honestly: "Things must go on in their own lewd natural way."

If Rochester can employ a female speaker as a more or less straightforward critic, his male speakers can be both critics of hypocrisy and embodiments of it. Sarah Wintle shows that Rochester's male speakers can entertain the idea that women should be as free as they to pursue pleasure; however, jealousy, possessiveness, selfishness, or an egotistical insistence on male prerogatives make them incapable of accepting it in specific instances (161). Coercion of freedom by (marital) partners who domineer or by selfish subjection to mechanistic sexual urges is the reality of the human condition Rochester dramatizes.

If the concluding sestet of "Against Marriage" presents the new style of pleasure-inspired sexuality as "noble" (though probably ironically so), the "Fragment" shows the present character of social relationships between the sexes as not at all "noble." By stereotype, Rochester was supposed to have been one of the chief exponents of the libertine argument. In the poems we have examined, we see Rochester treating it with notable skepticism and dramatic irony, even, at times, cynicism.

Turning again to the marriage debate in Butler's *Hudibras* (part III, 1678), we find a more thoroughly cynical, even jaundiced, portrayal of the effect of the argument for sexual freedom on courtship and marriage.

As the widow attacks marriage with a libertine-sounding wit, **Butler has** her represent the force of love on human behavior in vividly mechanistic images that show men as victims of their sexual urges, not as liberated by pursuing them. Love, says the widow, is

> but an ague that's reverst,
> Whose hot fit takes the Patient first,
> That after burns with cold as much,
> As Ir'n in *Greenland*, does the touch
> Melts in the Furnace of desire,
> Like Glass, that's but the Ice of Fire,
> (III.i.653–58)

Love may be a natural force, but it is a violent natural force that propels men back and forth between physical and emotional extremes. Under its power, men become sexual machines whose behavior is just as predictable as the firing of a gun:

> For when he's with Love-powder laden,
> And Prim'd, and Cock'd by *Miss* or *Madam*,
> The smallest sparkle of an Eye
> Gives Fire to his Artillery;
> And off the loud Oaths go, but while
> Th' are in the very Act, recoyl:
> (III.i.661–66)

Males in their sexual passions are notoriously inconstant, and the swearing of oaths by men in love is directly linked to the mechanism of male tumescence and detumescence. Butler finally takes a jaundiced stance toward the first argument as a rationale for behavior in courtship.

His assessment of the effect on marriage of the argument for sexual freedom is even more negative:

> Hence 'tis, so few dare take their chance
> Without a sep'rate maintenance,
> And Widdows, who have try'd one Lover,
> Trust none again, 'till th' have made over;
> Or if they do, before they marry,
> The Foxes weigh the Goose they Carry:
> . . . .
> For now the World is grown so wary,
> That few of either Sex dare marry,

> But rather trust, on tick, t'Amours
> The *Cross* and *Pile,* for *Bett'r* or *Worse;*
> A Mode, that is held honourable,
> As well as French, and fashionable.
>   (III.i.667–72, 677–82)

Men whose loyalty to their vows alters with the excited or unexcited state of their sexual organs do not make very trustworthy husbands. Butler shows the libertine ethos as undermining people's confidence in the institution of marriage. Women entering marriage protect themselves from exploitation by legalisms, or couples do not marry at all—just have love affairs. Although Butler may share some of the widow's libertine cynicism toward Hudibras's hypocritical defense of marriage, his underlying attitude toward the first argument is, if anything, even more negative than Rochester's.

From the rich, vivid, often skeptical or ironic treatments of the libertine argument in Dryden, Rochester, and Butler, it would seem a giant step down to poets who handle the first argument in a more rigid, formulaic way. This step need not seem quite so great if we consider in passing a few works by poets of the 1670s, 1680s, and 1690s who retain vitality and wit in the argument for sexual freedom.

No doubt the most interesting to modern readers is Aphra Behn whose *Poems Upon Several Occasions* (1684) contain several pieces in which she handles the male libertine argument from the female point of view. An avowed admirer of Rochester, she specifically imitates a number of his themes and formats.[7] In her fragmentary "Ode to Desire," Mrs. Behn is more forthright than women of her era dared to be in celebrating sexual desire and its natural effects on the body (see *Poems by Eminent Ladies* 1: 143–45). In one of her strongest poems, "The Golden Age," she creates a libertine paradise in which nature operates unconstrained by the corrupting force of social and religious codes; men and women are free to follow joy where it leads them. At the heart of this poem is her satiric denunciation of honor as a thief of women's sexual energy.

> Oh cursed Honour! thou who first didst damn,
>   A Woman to the Sin of shame;
>   Honour! that rob'st us of our Gust,
>   Honour! that hindred mankind first,
>   At Loves Eternal Spring to squench his amorous thirst.
>   Honour! who first taught lovely Eyes the art,

> To Wound, and not to cure the heart:
> With Love to invite, but to forbid with Awe,
> And to themselves prescribe a cruel Law;
>   (Behn 4: 141–42)

Though she does not attack marriage by name, she does satirize the tyranny of social forms which oppress men and women in their relationships: men as they are unnaturally denied sexual satisfaction by coquettes and women as they deprive themselves of pleasure in attempting to maintain their reputation. Behn is much attracted to the male libertine argument as it undercuts social hypocrisy and allows her to acknowledge that women feel sexual desire. Even so, as Angeline Goreau argues, she does not sanction predator sexuality that emphasizes conquest by whatever means. Rather than sexuality as a form of exploitation, she calls for "plain dealing" and equality through freedom and honesty in love. Ironically, middle-class society responded to Mrs. Behn's candor by regarding her as degraded and by labelling her a whore. "She had taken a position for sexual freedom, for women as well as for men, that would make her name a scandal to be reckoned with for three centuries" (Goreau 165).[8] Censuring the male poets' arguments for sexual freedom as licentious, society was even more willing to do so in the case of a woman poet. Male libertine ideology operating in a hypocritical society puts women in a double bind. It attacks women for their hypocritical modesty in refusing to acknowledge their sexuality. And when they do openly give voice to desire, men revert to judgment by conventional standards of moral decency.

Male poets of the 1670s, 1680s, and 1690s using the first argument usually lack the philosophical daring and problematic shading of Behn's challenge to society's restrictions on sexuality. In "To a Lady, an Advocate for Marriage" (published 1728–29), the dramatist William Wycherley argues in a seduction poem of some ingenuity that love offered in wedlock is not a generous or "free Gift" but a "mercenary Trade."

> That courteous Virgin most our Thanks demands,
> Who on no Wedlock-Terms precisely stands:
> And she who soonest, cheapest, grants her Love,
> Does the most honourable Mistress prove:
>   (4: 215)

Such "free, uncraving, willing Mistresses" "with a Grace their dearest Charms impart." In contrast stands the mercenary wife:

> Each she, in Wedlock, whorishly contrives
> To fix her self for Life at Bed and Board,
> And make a Keeper of her pinion'd Lord:
> Nay, makes him (more injurious is the Force!)
> To keep her too, *for better and worse.*
>
> (4: 216)

Respectable wives are whores, and mistresses are honorable women. The paradox is cleverly conceived, and the argument that love is best enjoyed when given or taken freely is an authentic statement of the first argument. Even so, the overall force of the plea to the lady is less witty than labored, the courtly love stance less charming than predictable.[9]

Poets of lesser ability than Wycherley tend often to coarsen the first argument and rigidify it into formula, though they can occasionally be charming or witty. Formulaic in its characterizations of marriage but clever and rollicking in its tropes and verse form is "The Batchelor's Song" by Thomas Flatman, a miniature painter and poet with legal training. This piece is followed immediately in Flatman's *Poems and Songs* (1674) by another song called "The Second Part." "The Batchelor's Song" offers a number of fairly predictable similes of entrapment to describe the plight of the married man. Yet the song has a kind of rough cleverness that is enhanced by the paradoxical concluding couplet.

> Like a Dog with a Bottle, fast ty'd to his tail,
>   Like a Vermin in a Trap, or a Thief in a Jail,
>   Like a *Tory* in a Bog,
>   Or an Ape with a Clog:
> Such is the man, who when he might go free,
>   Does his liberty loose,
>   For a Matrimony noose,
>   And sells himself into captivity.
> The Dog he do's howl, when the Bottle does jog,
> The Vermin, the Thief, and the *Tory* in vain
> Of the Trap, of the Jail, of the Quagmire complain.
> But welfare Poor *Pug*! for he plays with his Clog;
> And though he would be rid on't rather than his life,
> Yet he lugs it, and he hugs it, as a man does his Wife.
>
> (120–21)

The neat twist in the conclusion helps the poem rise above the stock libertine harangue and shows a man, like a monkey, embracing his captivity in marriage. The speaker is not suggesting that a man is dissimilar to all the animals in enjoying entrapment. Rather he *is* like at least one of the animals: the ridiculous ape.[10]

Even below Flatman in ability are a number of Grub Street poets who turned out verse on marriage in large quantities. Much of this was printed anonymously, and much of it adheres fairly rigidly to formulaic versions of the first argument. Tom Brown, the Tory pamphleteer and Grub Street hack "of facetious memory," is credited with a poem entitled "To a Lady, Whom He Refus'd to Marry, Because He Lov'd Her" (1707–8). Similar in its basic argument to Wycherley's poem, Brown's piece combines a stock harangue against marriage with an Edenic description of the golden age when marriage was unknown. Predictably, marriage is

> That damn'd Restraint to Pleasure and delight,
> Th' unlawful Curber of the Appetite.
>   (*Works* 1[2]:28)

In contrast, "Love," in the golden age, "was unadult'rate and true;/ Then we did unconfin'd Amours pursue." This stock mythical heaven-hell opposition is handled in rather carelessly arranged couplets and triplets (1[2]:28).

Treating the role of the rake is an anonymous piece called *The Rake in Fetters: or, The Marriage Mouse Trap* (17—). Like Flatman's "The Batchelor's Song" it uses animal entrapment similes, but without his saving satiric cleverness. *The Rake in Fetters* is a humorless lament enlightened only by its intense moroseness:

> I
>
> Of all the simple Things I know,
> To rub o'er a whimsical Life,
> There's ne'r a Folly half so true,
> As that very bad Bargain a Wife:
> 'Tis like a Mouse in a Trap,
> Or Vermin catcht in a Gin;
> We sweat, we fret, and strive to escape,
> Then curse the sad Hour we came in.
> . . . .
>
> III
>
> My darling Freedom crown'd my Joys,
> I never was vext in my Way:

> But now, if I cross her Will, her Voice
> Makes my Lodging too hot for my stay.
> Like a Fox that is hamper'd, in vain
> I gnaw out my Heart and my Soul,
> Run to and fro the Length of my Chain,
> Then forc'd to creep in to my Hole.
>
> (1)

In this formulaic poem, the stance of the rake has lost almost all philosophic shading and tonal complexity. Being a single man is a heavenly freedom, and marriage is a trap, a prison, and an earthly hell. The "Hole" the rake is forc'd to creep into (at the end of the poem) with its suggestions of stale marital sex may be the center of that hell.

If libertines in Grub Street poetry can find hell in marriage, they can also find heaven in repentance for their riotous and wasted lives. Morality in poetry at this level is not distinguished by its concern for nuances, and rakes often end their evil lives in death and damnation or, after an eleventh-hour conversion, in salvation. In *The Rake: or the Libertine's Religion, a Poem* (1693), attributed to Richard Ames, the "Libertine's" lifestyle leads him to death, but he achieves salvation because of a death-bed repentance.

In its form Ames's *The Rake* is like *The Rake in Fetters* a dramatic monologue. In the Preface, Ames describes the speaker as "a zealot or bigot in the religion of pleasure" and tells the readers that they will find this "Posthumous Piece the Product of a double Conception: The Libertine Begins, but the Penitent Concludes." Ames's sensational tone in the Preface seems to promise plenty of explicit descriptions of the narrator's wild debauches (before his inevitable repentance). However, what the reader is given are tame glimpses of the "Libertine's" "Levies" with his friends Jack Wildblood and Tom Ramble, drinking "a large Carouse" at the tavern, "scowring the Watch, or Roaring in the Streets," and contriving a "sweet Intrigue" with some "well dress'd Vizor Mask" at the playhouse. Because of the absence of detail, one has to have a lurid imagination to find such descriptions titillating.

What *The Rake* does provide with some realism are dramatizations of the thoughts and emotions of the rake as he descends toward self-destruction. Such a dramatization of the rake's sensibility anticipates the novel, and in this respect Ames's poem may be seen as the predecessor of the letters that Lovelace writes to Belford in Richardson's *Clarissa* (1747–

48). The reader is treated to the libertine's philosophical rationalizations for leading a life of pleasure; however, the speeches of Ames's "Libertine" are more blatantly didactic than the letters of Richardson's villain. Ames's speaker gives us a stock version of the first argument so that the reader can pass a stock moral judgment on his misguided thinking (see esp. 2–3 and 12).

Though Ames or whoever wrote this poem must have lived at some social distance from the circles in which libertines moved, he nevertheless has some sharply formed ideas about what rakes think and feel and some even more rigid ideas about how they are to be judged. In applying these ideas in *The Rake*, Ames is catering to the moral expectations of his readership, a readership that must have been to a large extent middle class or lower middle class and aggressively Protestant. Such readers with their hostility to the permissiveness of the Stuart court increasingly saw the rake and his libertine philosophy as a threat to moral decency and to the institution of marriage.

By the time the first argument is picked up by poets such as Ames, it has become a stock argument with little philosophical shading or tonal complexity. This is in line with the didactic intention of such poets. Unlike a poet such as Rochester who could use the satiric mode with freedom, skepticism, even cynicism to examine the philosophical and social implications of the argument for sexual freedom, Ames and moralistic poets of his ilk have purposely rigidified the first argument to create a negative moral example, a picture of the libertine suffering in the psychological and moral hell he has created for himself (see *The Rake* 15–16). During the early era, the movement of the first argument is clearly downward in social class as the poets employing it become less aristocratic and skeptical and more middle class and narrowly moralistic. Not only does the argument itself become formularized, but the poems using the argument decline in literary sophistication.

The Argument for the Freedom of Celibacy: Early Era

A substantial popular debate in verse over the advantages and disadvantages of the single life was initiated in 1701 with the publication of the anonymous Grub Street piece *The Pleasures of a Single Life, or, The Miseries of Matrimony*.[11] This composition hatched a whole brood of sensationalized verse replies that took various, usually opposing positions on the question whether the single life or marriage is freer and happier. Additional replies took up new but related issues. As an elicitor of replies, *The Pleasures of a Single Life* is a significant poem. The extreme polarization of its opposition between the hellish misery of marriage and the heavenly bliss of the single life becomes typical of almost all of the Grub Street pieces that reply to it or imitate its polemical format.

Several Restoration poems which precede *The Pleasures of a Single Life* employ roughly the same format and argue for the greater freedom and happiness of either the single life or marriage. These poems draw on a tradition of wit, do not use the Grub Street pleasures-of-the-single-life format, and do not offer as their central contrast a sharply polarized opposition between the hell of one state and the heaven of the other. The pre-1701 poems have more to them thematically than a simple heaven-hell opposition. After 1701 these more complex poems generally stopped appearing, and the formula poems with their polarized oppositions crowded the stage.

Though the Grub Street poems give the impression of a debate, they are actually polemical tracts that appeal, in Rothstein's terms, to the higher authority of God's or society's laws to resolve the apparent power struggle. As the eighteenth century progresses, the heaven of marriage prevails with increasing regularity. As the argument is finally resolved, it does not matter so much whether the single life is freer since God and society condone the happy state of matrimony. Growing out of the polarized hyperbole of the Grub Street polemical poems, a polarization that mirrors in exaggerated form the contradictory attitudes toward marriage within seventeenth-century Protestantism, the pro-marriage argument emerges as the feminized, progressive stance, the one that is clearly identifiable with women's aspirations in the era.

Although the pre-1701 poems do not use the Grub Street pleasures-of-the-single-life formula, some of them participate in a much older verse convention in which the pains of marriage are enumerated. This convention probably grows out of the medieval and Renaissance clerical tradition that draws on Juvenal and the patristic writers in attacking marriage and praising the celibate life.[12]

Pre-1701 poems show their indebtedness to this tradition in various ways. Sir John Denham's "Friendship and Single Life against Love and Marriage" (1668), an alternately celebratory and satiric piece in iambic tetrameter tercets, is both concerned with the destructive power of love and with the miseries of matrimony. An aristocratic poet who supported the

Royalist cause, Denham devotes several tercets specifically to the noble freedom of the single man and to the disadvantages of being married.

> Secure from low and private ends,
> His life, his zeal, his wealth attends
> His prince, his country, and his friends.
>
> Danger and honour are his joy;
> But a fond wife, or wanton boy,
> May all those generous thoughts destroy.
>
> Then he lays-by the public care,
> Thinks of providing for an heir;
> Learns how to get, and how to spare.
> (Chalmers 7: 246)

Denham seems to bear no particular animus against marriage. He simply offers observations about the priorities of the married and single man, observations that have an air of philosophical objectivity.[13] Denham's conclusion moves beyond the sphere of love and marriage to generalize about the purposeful viciousness of human behavior. Roughly similar in its final conceit to the controlling metaphor of Rochester's "Satyr against Reason and Mankind" (1679), Denham's poem transcends its initial contrast of friendship and the single life against love and marriage to introduce a higher thematic concern. Man can be more bestial than the beasts, Denham suggests, when he allows his behavior to be directed by irrational passions, especially love.

Denham's pre-1701 praise of the single life is finer and more philosophical than *The Pleasures of a Single Life, or, The Miseries of Matrimony*. Another pre-1701 poem, Charles Cotton's "The Joys of Marriage" (1689), is perhaps just as philosophical at root, though its surface tone and style is lighter. Cotton's ironic celebration of the joys of marriage depends on innovative repetition as the poet keeps adding variations to a basic verbal configuration. The playful accretion of variations is comic in a style suggestive of such early Renaissance writers as John Skelton or Rabelais. With each pattern, Cotton moves through at least twenty or so permutations.

> If fair she's subject to temptation,
> If foul her self's solicitation,
> If young and sweet she is too tender,
> If old and cross no man can mend her,

> If too too kind she's over clinging,
> If a true scold she's ever ringing,
>
> (319)

A wife is always running to contradictory extremes, Cotton tells us, and she never can achieve a mean. Nevertheless, though woman "still is mischief's mother," men cannot leave her alone:

> And yet cannot Man forbear,
> Though it cost him ne'er so dear.
>
> (320)

Cotton is unlike poets using the argument for the greater pleasure of sex outside marriage when he implies that pleasure is not a sufficient reason for marriage. If one marries for pleasure, Cotton suggests, then why marry at all; there are easier ways of finding satisfaction with women. He, however, leaves open the possibility that one may want to marry (and endure marriage's tribulations) for reasons other than (or higher than) pleasure.

Cotton gives a thorough comic-satiric enumeration of the joys (read "miseries") of matrimony. The satire by Cotton, who was a friend of Izaak Walton and a translator of Montaigne's *Essays*, is more good humored and tolerant, less selfish in rationalizing his personal pleasure than those using the first argument. As early articulators of the argument for the freedom of celibacy, both Denham and Cotton seem aligned in their stance with less hostile, more philosophical Renaissance satire, the sort that treats the tribulations of marriage along with the contradictory emotions men feel toward their wives. This stance is also clearly distinguishable from the first argument for sexual freedom offered by such Restoration poets as Rochester, Behn, Wycherley, Walsh, Brown, Flatman, and Ames.

One of the most notable praises of the celibate life is also in the higher, more philosophical Renaissance tradition represented by Denham and Cotton. In John Dryden's "To my Honour'd Kinsman, John Driden, of Chesterton" (1700), the persona's commendation of his cousin's single life-style at the beginning of this poem is unlike the earlier expressions of scorn for the marriage vow such as we encountered in Dryden's "Song" from *Marriage à la Mode*. The commendation in the former poem is part of its more general celebration of the cousin's peaceful and virtuous life in the country.

> Promoting Concord, and composing Strife,
> Lord of your self, uncumber'd with a Wife;
> Where, for a Year, a Month, perhaps a Night,
> Long Penitence succeeds a short Delight:
> Minds are so hardly match'd, that ev'n the first,
> Though pair'd by Heav'n, in Paradise, were curs'd.
> For Man and Woman, though in one they grow,
> Yet, first to last, return again to Two.
> He to God's Image, She to His was made;
> So farther from the Fount, the Stream at random stray'd.
> How cou'd He stand, when put to double Pain,
> He must a Weaker than himself sustain!
> Each might have stood perhaps; but each alone;
> Two Wrestlers help to pull each other down.
> Not that my Verse wou'd blemish all the Fair;
> But yet, if *some* Bad, 'tis Wisdom to beware;
> And better shun the Bait, than struggle in the Snare.
> Thus have you shunn'd, and shun the married State,
> Trusting as little as you can to Fate.
> (Dryden 606; lines 17–35)

Though some of Dryden's earlier wit in constructing the first libertine argument may be evident in his antifeminist playfulness with the creation story (see especially the double entendre in line 27), the overall tone of the passage is more suggestive of the patristic antimatrimonialism of a St. Jerome or the prudential wit of Andrew Marvell's celebration of the single life in "The Garden" (1681).

The first argument, we recall, emphasizes that marriage is a flawed institution that attempts to regulate the experience of a natural pleasure; one should maintain one's instinctual freedom by avoiding marriage. The basis for Dryden's advice in this second-argument poem is, in contrast, prudential; it is not based on the desire for sexual spontaneity. Many of the values linked with country life that Dryden's persona celebrates—concord, lack of strife, control of self—can be associated with the Roman Catholic apology for the celibate life and with the tradition of the Horatian country retreat poem (or country house poem). The poem expresses a disdain for marriage, especially for the view that marriage is primarily for pleasure of companionship rather than procreation. In contrast to those poems that celebrate the Edenic bliss of the marriage of well-matched partners, Dryden's poem praises instead the delights of the single life of country freedoms. This secular heaven he places in direct contrast to the conflicts that inevitably enslave men in marriage.

A Roman Catholic disdain for marriage is exhibited overtly in "A Virgin Life" (1688) by Jane Barker, daughter of a former Royalist soldier. This Catholic convert's praise of virginity goes beyond enumerating the advantages of celibacy to personifying the beauty of female chastity as "pure, celestial,/Thy thoughts divine, thy words Angelical" (Greer 361). Marriage, in contrast, would involve not only the loss of virginity; it would cause her to "fall into the power,/Of mans, allmost omnipotent amour" (360). Coloring Barker's religious ideology is a protofeminist awareness of the power that marriage gives a husband over his wife's emotions and body.

As with the other pre-1701 praises of the single life by Denham and Cotton, Barker's and Dryden's poems evoke a philosophical or religious rationale richer than the sensationalized oppositions of the Grub Street series treating the pleasures of a single life. The prototype for this series is *The Pleasures of a Single Life, or, The Miseries of Matrimony* (1701). Distinguished, as I said, by its hyperbolic polarizations, this piece alternately employs the satiric and the celebratory mode to reinforce the popular myth of the single life as heaven and marriage as hell. The poem opens with a curse of marriage and closes with an even stronger invective directed at woman. After the initial curse, the narrator paints a highly idealized picture of the heaven that was his life as a single man, when the world "seem'd Paradice." Employing an extended sailing metaphor, he describes how he coasted "in Pleasures-Bay" and "steer'd aright" through wholesome pleasures such as reading history and morality, walking in the fields and contemplating nature, and, at nights, indulging in "some inoffensive chat" over a bottle with a well-chosen friend—the sorts of activities usually mentioned in the argument for the freedom of celibacy. The speaker enjoys sleeping alone, and he dreams not of voluptuous women but of

> The Pleasure of the last precedent day,
> Thus whilst I singly liv'd, did I possess
> By Day and Night incessant Happiness,
> Content enjoy'd awak'd, and sleeping sound no less.
>
> (6)

How such a sexless man comes to be married is difficult to explain, but the author takes a hint from Milton and blames it on the Devil. Satan, it seems,

> Flung Woman, Faithless Woman in my way:
> Beauty she had, a seeming Modest Mein,
> All Charms without, but Devil all within,
> Which did not yet appear, but lurk'd, alas unseen.
>
> (6)

Naturally, the narrator cannot resist such "seraphick" attractions. Continuing his sailing metaphor in a passage suggestive of Rochester's "Satyr against Reason and Mankind," he explains how he is lured off course into marriage, and how by stages his marriage ends up on the rocks. As he shifts to describe it, the poem's celebratory mode progressively gives way to the satiric.

> By Beauty's *Ignis fatuus* led astray
> Bound for Content, I lost my happy way
> Of Reason's faithful Pilot now bereft,
> Was amongst Rocks and Shelves in danger left,
>
> (7)

Betrayed into the shipwreck of marriage, he is now condemned

> To the dull drudgery of a Marriage-Bed;
> That Paradise of Fools, a Sport for Boys
> Tiresome its Chains, and brutal are its Joys,
>
> (10)

Though the speaker's disdain for marital sex makes him sound like an advocate of sexual freedom, we soon realize that he is denigrating sexual activity in general. But his impotence or distaste for sex are not the causes of his marriage's failure. As we might expect within the antifeminist ideology of popular satire, it is his wife's unfaithfulness. She, whom he had earlier described as having a "Charm for Man in every State," is quick to cuckold him. He confronts her in her guilt, and she "made Essays to clear her Innocence." He forgives her and tries to treat her well, but she returns to adultery with a natural inevitability:

> Lust, which if once in Female fancy fix'd,
> Burns like Salt Petre, with dry Touchwood mix'd:
>
> (11)

He in turn resorts to harsher measures, but even the "Whip and Spur" do not subdue this hellcat, and she at last "turn'd both Libertine and Shrow [*sic*]," growing

> still more head strong, turbulent and Lewd
> Filling my Mansion with a spurious brood.
>
> (12)

He finally has no recourse but divorce:

> On these just Grounds for Divorce I su'd,
> At last that head-strong Tyrant wife subdu'd,
> Cancel'd the marriage-bonds, and basterdiz'd her brood.
>
> (12)

The poem concludes with a harsh curse of Woman—"thou worst of all Church-plagues"—and with a farewell to marriage:

> Farewell Church Juggle that enslav'd my life,
> But bless that Pow'r that rid me of my Wife.
>
> (12)

Reaffirming all the traditional antifeminist and antimatrimonial myths, the poem runs the gamut from idyllic celebration of celibacy to hostile invective against women suggestive of John Oldham, Robert Gould, and Richard Ames at their most severe.[14]

What distinguishes *The Pleasures of the Single Life* from pre-1701 praises of the single life is its hyperbole, the extreme nature of its modal oppositions. The poet's description of the pleasures of the single life is fantastically idealized, and the marriage the narrator enters into deteriorates archetypally. The contrast is nothing if not sensational. Here is little of the philosophical detachment of a Denham, the good humor in suffering of a Cotton, or the appeal to the integrity of the country life or the virtuous freedom of celibacy of a Dryden or a Barker. In *The Pleasures of a Single Life*, the mythical heaven of the single life is directly juxtaposed to the hell of marriage.

Since this is the first poem that so sharply contrasts the pleasures of the single life and the miseries of matrimony, it is difficult to account for its degree of hyperbole. The subtitle's stipulation that the poem was "Occasionally Writ upon the many Divorces lately granted by Parliament" suggests that the author is advocating civil control of divorces. Under the jurisdiction of the ecclesiastical courts, we recall, divorce *a vinculo matrimonii* did not in fact exist, and couples could only be granted a separation *a mensa et thoro*. Civil divorce had been granted only in a handful of cases to wealthy individuals such as Lord Roos who appealed for a specific act of Parliament to dissolve his marriage (see Haw part 2, chapter 1;

Fraser 291–310). Perhaps the author of this poem wished to extend this privilege to a larger group of people; the poem then might be seen as propagandist support for such legislation.

Although the hyperbole in *The Pleasures of a Single Life* may have somewhat hazy origins in Restoration legal history as well as in the contradictory tendency of seventeenth-century Protestantism both to affirm and fear the flesh, the sensationalized polarizations in the series of poems replying to *The Pleasures of a Single Life* are obviously a direct takeoff of the 1701 prototype. Consider, for example, *An Answer to the Pleasures of a Single Life: or, The Comforts of Marriage Confirm'd and Vindicated: With the Misery of Lying Alone, Prov'd and Asserted* (1701). Drawing on the Miltonic celebratory tradition, this piece uses the account of Eden in *Paradise Lost* as the basis for its argument that marriage was established by God to provide a companion for man in his loneliness:

> So the alwise Creator thought it best,
> That Man and Wife together might be blest:
> Appointed then immortal Bonds to tye,
> Two Hearts in one, with equal Amity;
> And so he than by his alwise Direction,
> Both Souls united with like affection;
> So very sweetly and with such delight,
> The swiftest Winged Minutes take their flight
> And thus Gods Love to Mankind did dispence
> The sacred Wedlock, which did then commence:
>
> (3)

An Answer to the Pleasures of a Single Life reverses the mythical polarization of the 1701 prototype poem. If married life is contrived by God to be "an Emblem of Eternal Love" and is the "Crown of Man and Wife's content," the single life conversely is a hellish state dominated by lust and envy:

> Thus single Sots, who Wedlock vainly slight,
> Are Slaves to Lust both Morning, Noon, and Night;
> Ruin their Health, their Honour and Estate,
> And buy Repentance at a curssed rate:
>
> (4)

Sounding suspiciously like a clergyman, the defender of marriage in this poem offers trenchant psychological insights into the motivations of marriage haters:

> The Hard Mouth Fops, a single Life applau'd,
> And hates a Woman, that woun't be a Baw'd:
> Nothing he values like a single Life,
> For tho he loves a Whore, he hates a Wife,
>
> (3)

Hyperbolic antitheses, as in the last line, are a stock-in-trade with this poet. The rhetorical opposition, in some instances, becomes extreme enough to be unintentionally comic.

> I'le with a Wife in lawful Wedlock sport,
> While you in Woods with Beastes of Prey resort:
>
> (4)

In another set of harsh antitheses, the poet is not above accusing a single man of making a "Sodom of himself" because he will inevitably have recourse to masturbation. With a surprisingly perceptive understanding of the phenomenon of repression, the poet accuses the male attacker of projecting his masturbation-induced self-loathing outward and besmirching women's reputation.

> Your bawdy Books, your silent Consort be,
> While happy Man and Wife in Love agree,
> And both unite in mutual Harmonie.
> *Sodom* for Sins like thine, by Fire was burn'd,
> And from a City to a Lake was turn'd;
> Even so, the shamless loathsome single Elff,
> Worse than the Beast makes *Sodom* of himself;
> And then to lessen those his hateful Crimes,
> He Rails at Wedlock in confused Rhimes,
> Calls Woman Faithless, 'cause she woun't consent,
> To humour what his Brutish Thoughts invent;
> No wonder then, if with his poisonous Breath,
> He strives to Blacken the Brightest thing on Earth:
>
> (4)

Giving us a portrait of male hostility that rises out of disappointed sexual fantasies and guilt, this poet offers acute psychological perceptions. Though distorted by hyperbole, the poet's opposition to the argument for the single life manages in a pre-Freudian analysis to locate some of the psychic bases of antifeminism and antimatrimonialism in the conflict between the male id and the superego.

Wedlock a Paradice, or, A Defence of Woman's Liberty Against Man's Tyranny. In Opposition to a Poem, Entitul'd, The Pleasures of a Single Life, &c (1701) concentrates more on idealizing women and marriage than on analyzing antimatrimonialism. The argument proceeds by contrasting the happy freedoms of marital companionship with the enslavements that the traditional activities of celibacy actually entail. First giving the reader a picture of his unhappy single life, the narrator tells how he took to the law, and "Immoderate Study stupifi'd my Brain" (2). He finds friendship with males undependable.

> When *Drunk*, of Friendship, Love and Freedom full;
> But *Sober*, strange, shy, negligent and dull,
>
> (4)

As a consequence, he turns away from such inconstant bottle companions. Bidding "adieu" "To that deceit, call'd *Friend*," the speaker now finds his stability in the goodness of women:

> *Woman,* I thought on Earth the only Good,
> And she alone my restless Soul pursu'd;
> Trusted in her, nor fear'd to be deceiv'd.
> The more I look'd, the more I still believ'd,
> In her sweet Conversation I should find,
> All that was Grateful, Generous and Kind;
>
> (4)

The discovery of the pleasures of feminine companionship has the force of a religious conversion; not unexpectedly, the speaker goes on to marry, a state which he finds to be nothing less than a perpetual heaven.

> Her Goodness never wanted some Device,
> To always make my *Home* a *Paradice.*
>
> (7)

Although *Wedlock a Paradice*, like the other post-1701 formula poems, is distorted by hyperbole, it nevertheless stands as an early expression of pro-companionate ideology. That the poet—whether male or female—expected such ideology to appeal to women readers is indicated by the celebration of female worthies that follows the opening narrative.

Women readers were obviously being drawn into the argument for the freedoms of celibacy. It is not at all surprising then that Juvenalian advice poems with a male narrator should be addressed to women, warning them against the folly of marriage and presenting a gallery of bad husbands. In a 1702 piece attributed to Defoe, we find just that in *Good Advice to the Ladies: Shewing That as the World Goes, and Is Like To Go, the Best Way for Them Is To Keep Unmarried*. Because pro-marriage ideology was becoming more attractive to women readers, it is also to be expected that advice poems not to marry would be quickly answered by defenses of matrimony. Such occurs also in 1702 in a piece that pointedly identifies itself as "Written by a Young Lady"—*Wedlock Vindicated: Or, The Ladies Answer, to the (Pretended) Good Advice to Them, Proving That a Married Life, Is the Best Way to Support the Reputation of Both Sexes, and a Single Life Scandalous, Dangerous, and Obnoxious Both to Men and Women; with Seasonable Cautions To Avoid It*. The "Lady" advises women to be wise and not to believe the "Marriage haters." Sounding a little like Robert Herrick in "To the Virgins, To Make Much of Time," she forthrightly counsels young women to indulge in the "sublime" joys of sex as soon as they can marry.

> Perform Love's Vows, as soon as e're you can,
> And taste that sweet and pleasant Creature, *Man*:
> For Wedlock Bands it takes away the Crime,
> And makes the Joys more pleasing and sublime:
> It lets all roving Mankind know their own,
> And makes him Vertuous who to Vice was prone:
> [3]

In contrast to such blissful marital sexuality is the chaotic and destructive life of those who live together in sin.

> But where the Marriage Knot it wants the tye,
> What strange Confusions in that House do lye:
> Disorders, Ruine, Plagues and endless Strife,
> With those who keep a Whore, and not a Wife:
> Besides uneasie restless thoughts within,
> When musing on the foulness of the Sin:
> [3]

Treating both the outward and inward hell of living together without benefit of clergy, this poem does not denounce the single life in the usual sense of the male living alone or with other men. However, the polarizations carry the same force as in the other formula poems. Even though the couple are bound in wedlock, the joys of marriage are "more pleasing and sublime," while those who just live together produce "Disorders, Ruine,

Plagues, and endless Strife." Most interesting is the "Lady's" candid celebration of sexuality in marriage, which may remind us of Aphra Behn's overtly libertine argument for sexual freedom. In this poem, however, the affirmation of marital sexuality for women runs directly counter to the earlier argument that society and social institutions restrict women's sexual energy.

Eric Rothstein has suggested that one of the fascinations of Restoration poetry is with the theme of power (xiii). In satire, this power is often exerted by a puritanical speaker who browbeats or lashes others into adopting his (moral) view. Or the speaker may be self-deluded, and his violent assertion of his point of view may show us through dramatic irony how wrong he and his values are. With the polarized oppositions of the pleasures-of-the-single-life formula poems, power conflicts occur in nearly pure form as poets with opposing attitudes toward marriage try to beat each other down with rhetorical hyperbole, either in the satiric or celebratory mode. Once the hyperbole has been raised to an excessive level, poets basically have two choices: (1) they may attempt to escalate it even more, or (2) they may attempt to bolster their stance by appealing to a higher authority such as God or society's law. With the pleasures-of-the-single-life formula poems, poets seem to be following both tacks at once, though the second option gradually emerges as the dominant one. Poets increasingly affirm the new myth of the companionate marriage that is supportive of women's equal role in marriage as a sharer of its tribulations and a partaker of its joys.

To be sure, in the early eighteenth century, some arguments for the freedom of the single life can still be found in which a rake persists in asserting his rebellion against God or his independence from the conventions of society. However, almost all of these tend to be more ironic than serious.[15]

A stance of rejection of marriage does become more frequent in poems with a protofeminist stance. Instead of males asserting the pleasures of the single life over those of marriage, we begin to encounter a few verses (some by women) that argue against marriage for women. The major reason brought to the bar is the misconduct of males in marriage. Poets represent husbands as unfaithful, possessive, jealous, miserly, and, worst of all, as tyrannical and abusive. Although these poems seem to argue for the freedom of the single life, they also may affirm the new pro-marriage ideology. Their argument is that many men's oppressive, coarse, brutish, or adulterous behavior disqualifies them for the companionate ideal.

In a Grub Street piece such as *Good Advice to the Ladies* (1702), the male poet satirizes negative types of husbands in order to celebrate the rare ideal of the good husband; the advice to women not to marry is mainly intended to make women more prudent in their choices. Somewhat different is Anne Finch, Countess of Winchilsea's "The Unequal Fetters" (written ca. 1700). Here the speaker's decision not to marry is a more serious moral protest against the double standard in marriage:

> Free as nature's first intention
>   Was to make us, I'll be found
> Nor by subtle man's invention
>   Yield to be in fetters bound
> By one that walks a freer round.
>
> Marriage does but slightly tie men
>   Whilst close prisoners we remain
> They the larger slaves of Hymen
>   Still are begging love again
> At the full length of their chain.
>   (Winchilsea 151)

Anne Finch's criticism of marriage may strike us as more sincere and autobiographical than the ironic counsel of the speaker in *Good Advice*. However, since this woman poet, who achieved recognition during her lifetime, married with longstanding and apparently happy results, the stance of her speaker may finally be like the speaker's in *Good Advice*, a dramatic, ironic one designed to make women more cautious—aware of male hypocrisy.

In her use of the collectlike refrain "Libera Nos," the speaker in Elizabeth Thomas's "A New Litany, Occasion'd by an Invitation to a Wedding" (1722) sounds as if she is rejecting marriage outright for the freedoms of a single life.

> From Marrying in haste, and Repenting at leisure;
> Not liking the Person, yet liking his Treasure:
>   *Libera nos.*
> From a Mind so disturb'd that each Look does reveal it;
> From Abhorring One's Choice, and not Sense to conceal it:
>   *Libera nos.*
> From a Husband to govern, and buy him his Wit;
> From a sullen ill-natur'd, and whimsical Citt:
>   *Libera nos.* (98)

Looking more closely, however, we see that Elizabeth Thomas, known as Corinna, is censuring abusive male dominion and marriage for money as she condemns unions not based on shared love and affection. Thomas herself had never experienced such a union since her father died when she was two, she was courted but never married, and she was chronically indigent, at one point confined to the Fleet for debt (Lonsdale 32–33).

Mehetable (or Hetty) Wright's "Wedlock. A Satire" (written ca. 1730) reminds us of the stock vituperative attacks on the enslavement of marriage employed in the first and second libertine arguments. We know, however, that Wright, the sister of John and Charles Wesley, as well educated as her brothers, had been personally disappointed by marriage. While having difficulties finding a husband whom she liked or of whom her father approved, she became pregnant and was forced by an exasperated father to marry William Wright, a plumber and glazier (Lonsdale 110). As we learn from her "Address to Her Husband," Wright was clearly not an equal to Hetty in intellect, education, and emotionality, and it was probably more the failure of companionship than the desire for sexual freedom that inspired the curses in her "Wedlock: A Satire."

> Thou scorpion with a double face,
> Thou lawful plague of human race,
> Thou bane of freedom, ease and mirth,
> Thou deep damnation upon earth,
> Thou serpent which the angels fly,
> Thou monster whom the beasts defy,
> . . . .
> That wretch, if such a wretch there be,
> Who hopes for happiness from thee,
> May search successfully as well
> For truth in whores and ease in hell.
> (publ. 1862; Lonsdale 114)

Although Wright's invective is reminiscent of Rochester's rodomontade *Against Marriage*, I would argue that it is not based in male, antimatrimonial ideology. As Michael Suarez suggests, it emerges from "the envisioned possibility of a marriage rooted in mutual respect and affection" (8).

The force of the three attacks by women on bad marriages is not to assert the primacy of the individual libido or to praise the freedoms of female celibacy but to raise women's and society's expectations for the behavior of husbands and for what marriage should aspire to be. These poems then are quite in tune with Rothstein's schemata for poetry from 1690 to 1740. They attempt to bring the power of the individual more in conformance with equitable social standards and thus affirm a pro-marriage ideology.

Such is likewise the case with Elizabeth Thomas's pathetic monologue "The Forsaken Wife" (1722). In this piece the deserted woman's stinging indictment of her husband's perfidy evokes the reader's sympathetic moral indignation to censure the husband's mistreatment of women (see Lonsdale 44). Similarly, in Hetty Wright's remarkably candid "Address to Her Husband" (written ca. 1730), her sharply argued inquiries into her husband's neglect of her (to drink with "vile companions") forces him to examine his behavior in the light of common reason. Wright's persona whets the cutting edge of reason with sarcasm and pathos: Do you frequent, she asks plaintively, some "obscure, unclean retreat" because I have become unattractive? Have I stunned your ears with "loud complaints," with "matrimonial melody"? Have I not

> practised every art
> T'oblige, divert, and cheer thy heart,
> To make me pleasing in thine eyes,
> And turn thy house to paradise[?]
> (Lonsdale 113; lines 53–56)

Since the speaker's husband cannot answer in the negative to any of these questions, he evidently has no reasonable basis for shunning her "faithful arms." Consequently, she can only respond irrationally as well. She thus vows histrionically to die of grief, which shall

> To thee thy liberty restore
> To laugh when Hetty is no more.
> (Lonsdale 114–15)

A poet such as Hetty Wright creates a pathetic and humorous persona to convey her forceful attack on male libertine behavior and to affirm a pro-companionate ideology. Though revisionist critics blame such ideology for fostering the "myth of passive womanhood," Hetty's speaker cannot by any standard be characterized as retiring. She dramatizes her position as a victim, but in the process she asserts herself and achieves substantial rhetorical power. Eighteenth-century women poets frequently employ companionate ideology to bolster their attack on male libertine ideology, an ideology that fostered male behavior which women viewed as exploitive and self-indulgent.

If poems such as those we have just looked at subordinate the individual will to reason or society's law or to an ideal of equitable companionship, other poems employing a version of the argument for the freedom of celibacy show the willful self-indulgence of a rake brought in check by religion or morality. Similar in its moral thrust to Ames's *The Rake, or, The Libertine's Religion* (1693), *The Rake Reform'd* (1718) by A[braham] G[lanvill] is superior to Ames's poem in detailing the city life of debauch that the narrator pursued before his conversion to a virtuous, God-centered, celibate life in the country. Glanvill gives us as a narrator a willful libertine who is hardened in his self-indulgence.[16] The rake's day, filled with illusory blisses, hits rock bottom in the hell-like void of the jail cell. What jolts him out of his "Round of fancy'd Bliss" is the death of a friend and fellow libertine, who falls a victim to wine and women. The shock pushes the rake into a "sincere Repentance," and he "chang'd the City's Fogs for *Isis* healthy Air" (20).

At this point *The Rake Reform'd* presents its argument for the single life. Glanvill's rake does not repent on his deathbed as Ames's rake does. Rather he is converted to a celibate, rural life-style in which his chief friend is male. In the country the former rake possesses "substantial Happiness" and indulges in a wholesome set of truly pleasurable daily activities: rising with the sun, thanking God in his morning prayers for clothing him, wandering with delight through "adjacent Fields," and returning to "feed on wholsome Fare." Occasionally, he rides or walks to visit the parish priest, a true man of God, free from pride, ambition, and ostentation. As he shares a bottle with the priest and discusses theology, the narrator is brought to a love of Christ. The narrator thus gives up the delusory happiness of his former life for real bliss:

> For then alone is Bliss compleatly whole,
> When with the *Body* we advance the *Soul*.
>
> (32)

Like *The Pleasures of a Single Life* and its replies, *The Rake Reform'd* features a polarized, hyperbolic contrast: in this case between a debauched life in the city and the virtuous life in the country. What is different about *The Rake Reform'd* is the extent to which it emphasizes the narrator's surrender of his personal quest for pleasure to the idea that our greatest pleasure lies in Christ. As occurs increasingly with both the first and second libertine argument in the early era, individual will has clearly been subordinated to a higher authority.

The Argument for Sexual Freedom: Later Era

In the later era, the argument that men and women ought to be free to pursue the reality of pleasure outside marriage can still be found. Increasingly, however, it and the aristocratic ethos that nourish it are countered by a middle-class, pro-companionate ideology. This ideology becomes increasingly intolerant of literary celebrations of adulterous sentiments. Initially, in the late Restoration, as the antilibertine crusade is articulated by figures such as the Anglican nonjuror clergyman Jeremy Collier in his prose tract *The Short View of the Immorality and Prophaneness of the English Stage* (1698), the ethos underlying it might be identified as distinctively Protestant. However, as the century progresses, the gospel of middle-class respectability becomes even more widespread and heterogeneous. It broadens and secularizes to the point that it becomes part of aristocratic as well as working-class attitudes.

The ideology also stimulates the emergence of protofeminist writings that play a role in creating more outward respect for women, in making it less fashionable to celebrate openly the pleasure women might give as sex objects, and in softening manners and refining cultural attitudes. Even older literary texts, most significantly *Paradise Lost*, may be said to be feminized, reread in a new light more supportive of the progressive attitudes of the time.[17] Accompanying this is a growing wave of male gallantry toward the "fair sex," an idealization of women's strength in weakness.

One however may question, as revisionist criticism does, how much this new wave of adulation is due to respect for women's actual attributes and how much is the emergence of a new myth. In the popular imagination, as later era marriage verse exemplifies, women exchange one mythical role for another as they shift from being an object of contempt (the hellish wife, the whore, or the slut) to an object of adoration (the heaven-sent companion, the exemplar of the "fair sex," or the angel). Similarly, women shift from an object of libertine sexual desire to becoming the most valued property in the husband's middle-class inventory—the angel in his domestic heaven. In one respect, significant social progress does not occur since women are still held to be of a different order from men.

Instead of denigrating the unique vices of women, poets now turn to praise their unique virtues. Both stances unfortunately involve condescension and dehumanization, though more covert in the latter. Again, it is tempting to trace the tendency of poets to run to extremes—either to excoriate or idealize—back to contradictions implicit in seventeenth-century Protestant attitudes toward sexuality and marriage. Eve can be either a temptress, the corrupter of mankind, or a heaven-sent companion.

As we examine the way later era poets treat the argument for sexual freedom, we will discover a few poets who still handle the stock libertine argument for freedom with some sympathy or at least find it attractive poetic material, even if they do not condone it. Most poets, however, judge the argument reprehensible or advise against it in the didactic mode. In the limited number of poems in which the argument survives, it is sometimes weakened and transposed to women. At least one male poet celebrates not a male libertine but a female. In opposing the first argument, male didactic poets are often concerned with dampening the romantic expectations of women about to marry so that they do not think the excitement of courtship will continue in married life. Women poets themselves occasionally toy with a libertine stance, but most oppose it and affirm the companionate ideology, a position they evidently felt to be more in their interest. The dramatic monologue continues as a vehicle for discrediting the argument, but lighter satire and witty comedy tend to displace the sensationalized denunciations of heavy-handed moralistic narrators.

Two relatively early pieces done by Pope in 1717 exemplify contrasting attitudes toward the argument for sexual freedom, particularly as that argument draws from the courtly love tradition. Pope's apparently contradictory stances may be a manifestation of his ambivalence. Pope still finds the courtly argument attractive, yet he also has been influenced by pro-marriage ideology.

Of *Eloisa to Abelard* and the second of two choruses composed for the Duke of Buckingham's *Tragedy of Brutus*, the former is by far the greater (and longer) poem of the two. *Eloisa to Abelard* chooses to ignore the historical fact that the tragic pair were secretly married after the birth of their son. Pope presents Eloisa's praise of her illicit passion for Abelard in terms that are clearly those of the first libertine argument.

> How oft', when press'd to marriage, have I said,
> Curse on all laws but those which love has made!

> Love, free as air, at sight of human ties,
> Spreads his light wings, and in a moment flies.
> Let wealth, let honour, wait the wedded dame,
> August her deed, and sacred be her fame;
> Before true passion all those views remove,
> Fame, wealth, and honour! what are you to Love?
> (254; lines 73–80)

Eloisa's emphasis on the freedom of love and on its separateness from "fame," "wealth," and "honour" are traditional courtly attitudes that were absorbed into the first argument in Restoration poetry. Although defenses of adultery are increasingly avoided by eighteenth-century poets, Pope may have Eloisa take such a strong antimarriage stance because it makes her melancholy and longing for death all the more pathetic. Pope can present her defense sympathetically because he is working with characters from the twelfth century who suffered greatly for their love. Such poetical distance and pathos lend sanction to Eloisa's romantic passion.

In contrast, Pope could just as readily dramatize anticourtly love sentiments. In the second stanza of the second chorus from the *Tragedy of Brutus*, he expresses an opposition to the argument for sexual freedom and forthright support for marital love:

> Love's purer flames the Gods approve;
> The Gods, and *Brutus* bend to love:
> *Brutus* for absent Portia sighs,
> And sterner *Cassius* melts at *Junia's* eyes.
> What is loose love? a transient gust,
> Spent in sudden storm of lust,
> A vapour fed from wild desire,
> A wandring, self-consuming fire.
> But *Hymen's* kinder flames unite;
> And burn for ever one;
> Chaste as cold *Cynthia's* virgin light,
> Productive as the Sun.
> (297; lines 13–20)

This stanza enunciates the standard eighteenth-century condemnation of romantic love as lawless, ungovernable, and evanescent. It also affirms the Roman Catholic theological view of marital love as constant and productive, that is, leading to procreation. The representation of marital love as "Chaste as cold Cynthia's virgin light" may be Pope's unintentional denigration of marital love as lacking in passion, though he may have wanted to emphasize its purity in ensuring faithfulness. Although the marital love praised may be less poetically attractive than the romantic passion of Eloisa, Pope's celebration of it is more in line with the emerging antilibertine ideology.

Not too many mid-century poems preserve in untransposed and unmodified form the male argument for sexual freedom used in the Restoration. One that appears to do so is "Marriage à la Mode: or the Two Sparrows. A Fable" by the Hon. Nicholas Herbert, a member of Parliament and the younger son of an earl. Printed in Dodsley's *Miscellany* in 1758 (3.205–8), this piece, however, can be identified from its title as an adaptation of fable 21 from book 4 of Antoine Houdar De La Motte (1672–1731). The product of an earlier time and French culture, "Marriage à la Mode" may not reflect prevalent mid-century English progressive attitudes. On the other hand, Herbert's poetic representation of amorous sparrows who are loving and happy when free but angry and quarrelsome when caged may be more than a stock denigration of marriage as inimical to love. Since the sparrows' behavior is observed through the glass of allegorical narrative, the poet may intend the reader to ask why their confinement produces ill humor and strife. If the sparrows are loving and kind to each other when free, why, one wonders, can they not continue to be so when caged? Rather than simply disparaging the enslavement of marriage, Herbert may be holding up a critical mirror to stereotypical societal assumptions.

One form in which the argument for sexual freedom does survive is transposed by a male poet into the mouth of a female speaker. *The Female Rake: or, The Modern Fine Lady. An Epistle from Libertina to Sylvia* (1735) by Joseph Dorman adopts the fiction of a female letter writer as a sensationalizing device. By having a woman offer the standard male argument, Dorman makes her defense of tactful promiscuity provocative. His use of the character of Libertina not only involves a sexual transposition. Her philosophical defense of libertinism also amounts to a curious modification of the first argument. Libertina does not so much advocate that pleasure is greater when love is free and unconfined as that it is more reasonable to indulge in the pleasures of sex than to suffer the pain of self-denial. Libertina is less romantic than pragmatic. This is why she advises prudence in carrying out love affairs discreetly with well-chosen men. She does not reject the hypocrisy of those who would confine love to marriage. Rather she rationalizes the hypocrisy of covert promiscuity because all the world is hypocritical. Though Dorman might have been using dramatic irony in Libertina's monologue, it is more likely he wanted to make her argument vicariously attractive, especially to male readers who might fantasize about meeting such a woman. Coming from a man's mouth, the argument would probably have been found reprehensible in the 1730s.

I suspect a similar pattern of cross-dressing in "An Epithalamium" (1731), attributed anonymously to "A Lady" (see Lonsdale 116–17). The speaker purports to offer warning to young women to avoid the "False hopes and phantom joys" of marriage, but what the poem actually presents is a glorification of romantic passion outside marriage:

> He warm and active as the sun at noon,
> She gay and genial as the wanton June;
> They speak in raptures, and with transport move;
> They meet, they kiss, they press, they pant, they love.
>
> (Lonsdale 116)

While Aphra Behn wrote such poems in the 1680s, it is not likely that a woman would have in the 1730s.

The large majority of later era poems treating the argument for sexual freedom attempt to counter it in one way or another. Their mode is usually at base didactic. A number of pieces giving advice to young women about to marry work to dampen the romantic expectations of future wives, expectations that may have been nurtured by the quasi-libertine fantasies of romances and other literature drawing on the courtly tradition. In *Female Conduct* (2nd ed. 1759), Thomas Mariott adopts a paternalistic stance to make it clear to his women readers that a husband is not the same person as a lover:

> Think not, fair Pupil, when in Wedlock join'd,
> The Lover, in the Husband long to find;
> Then farewell Visions of Love's Paradise!
> Farewell the Raptures of the Lover's Bliss!
> The Stile of Wedlock differs far from this;
>
> (238)

Mariott takes a hard line in attempting to disenchant young women who expect marriage to be a continuation of the "Bliss" of courtship. Perhaps Mariott assumes that most brides-to-be commit themselves without check to romantic fantasy. He may conceive of them as Sheridan does Lydia

Languish in *The Rivals* (1775) or as Molière, Magdelon and Cathos in *Les Précieuses Ridicules* (1659). Instructing young women that the relationship between a husband and wife is of a different order than that of courting lovers, Mariott quashes a feminine version of a libertine fantasy: the single woman's dream of the deliciously romantic courtship in which one or more handsome beaux are solicitous to her every whim.

Though he is a little gentler in tone than Mariott, Edward Lovibond, scholar, gentleman, and man of means, makes a similar effort to bring down to reality the romantic expectations of a young bride. In "To Lady F———, on Her Marriage" (1785), Lovibond's speaker grants that "Light airs, and the rapture of youth" may belong to Hymen's "gay season," yet he attempts to subdue essentially the same courtship fantasies as Mariott.

> Farewell to the triumphs of beauty,
>   To the soft serenade at your bower,
> To the lover's idolatrous duty,
>   To his vigils in midnight's still hour.
>
> To your frowns darting amorous anguish,
>   To your smiles chasing every care,
> To the power of your eyes lively languish,
>   To each glance waking hope or despair.
>   (Chalmers 16: 298)

That the ingredients of young women's fantasies are drawn from the rituals and conventions of courtly romance is even more apparent in Lovibond's poem than in Mariott's. Lovibond, however, does not simply replace the romantic with the cold reality of subservience to a husband. Rather Lovibond's bride is advised to

>   welcome, in nature's own dress,
> Purest pleasures of a gentler kind;
> O! welcome the power to bless,
>   To redeem fortune's wrongs on mankind.
>
> Be a goddess indeed, while you borrow
>   From plenty's unlimited store,
> To gild the wan aspect of sorrow,
>   To cheer the meek eyes of the poor.
>   (16: 298)

For the quasi-libertine fantasy of the beautiful young woman worshipped by many admirers, Lovibond substitutes a more socially permissible aspiration for a late eighteenth-century married woman, the young wife as a "goddess" distributing charity among the poor. Because she will be doing something of benefit to mankind in this role, Stella will be remembered not just for her beauty but her goodness. At least that is how the script reads. Whether the poor receive her as Lady Bountiful or as a meddling rich woman is another question.

If some mid-century advice poems by males attempt to check women's romantic dreams, poems by women may sometimes indirectly entertain the fantasy of sexual or romantic freedom in love. Most women poets however oppose the argument as it might be used by either sex and affirm the bond of love marriage creates for both partners.

A number of women poets of the later era compose lovers' dialogues, laments, and celebrations in the covertly erotic pastoral mode. These do not express the argument for sexual freedom in any direct way, but marriage and conventions restricting women's behavior in society are not a part of the love-dominated world of such poems. In her odes, epistles, and songs influenced by Sappho and Ovid, Charlotte Lennox, the author of the novel *The Female Quixote* (1752), offers many verses in this vein.

Most women poets are critical of the argument for sexual freedom. In this respect, they take their place in the Protestant, middle-class, pro-marriage tradition of earlier attackers of aristocratic libertinism. In a witty treatment of mythological fable in "To Mrs. S———. An Epigram" (1740), Mrs. Sarah Dixon, identified as a widow living in Canterbury, attacks Mrs. S——— slyly but unmistakably for her unfaithfulness to her husband (see Lonsdale 174). Jupiter, Mrs. Dixon tells us in her ingeniously constructed insult, knew he could not seduce the mortal Alcmena in any of his usual disguises—a bull, a swan, or a golden shower. He thus approached her in the guise of her husband, Amphitryon, and was successful. With Mrs. S———, however, the case would be different.

> Love's Power's eternal! shou'd the God forego
> His Heaven a while, to be belov'd by you,
> With less Expence, he might his Passion own,
> In any Shape succeed,—if he your Husbands shun.
> (46)

The tone of the conclusion may empathize slightly with Mrs. S———'s aversion to her husband, but the poet's predominant attitude is sharply censorious.

Lady Dorothea DuBois was the eldest daughter of an Irish earl who declared her illegitimate and disinherited her when he repudiated his marriage with her mother and took up with a younger woman (Lonsdale 265–66). She uses the pastoral dialogue not to dramatize romantic fantasies but to show deftly how the male argument for sexual freedom can be countered by a female argument in kind. The way to resolve such a stalemate, the poem implies, is by marriage.

Philander opens "A Dialogue Song" (1764) with his argument:

> Prithee, Dear *Celia*,
> If I love *Delia*,
> Where's the Crime? for *Delia* is fair;
> 'Tis a Man's Duty,
> To adore Beauty,
> I'm to each Nymph, in Turn, sincere.
>   (122)

Celia counters with hers:

> Farewel, *Philander*,
> I'll to *Lysander*.
> He will prize, what's slighted by you;
> 'Thou art deceitful,
> False and ungrateful,
> Do therefore now your Scheme pursue.
>   (123)

Celia's argument brings Philander to ask her forgiveness, she grants it, and the poem concludes with the couple rejoicing in unison in their newfound (marital) relationship.

> Truly contented,
> Our Love cemented,
> Now unchang'd, for ever shall last;
> Happy and fonder,
> Ne'er will we wander
> Or ever think of Trifles past.
>   (124)

In "An Emblematic Tale" (1764), which no doubt has autobiographical significance, Lady Dorothea DuBois is more pragmatic in her approval of marriage. In this narrative, allegorical only in the characters' names, Snow takes up with a Pirate in a common-law marriage. But he turns to an affair with a leaky Brig. When he dies, Snow is forced to contest at law with the Brig to claim his property. Although marriage did put the wife in a position legally and economically subordinate to her husband, it did guarantee her rights to ownership of his property when he died.

As with Lady Dorothea DuBois's "A Dialogue Song," "Verses, Written to a Friend on His Marriage" (1755, 1766) by Catherine Jemmat, the destitute daughter of an English admiral, is also critical of the male argument for sexual freedom and supportive of the companionate marriage. The speaker inquires of a former Don Juan how he came to give up his "wild" and "roving" ways. The mocking questions conceal a good deal of partly ironic flattery so that the satire is not so harsh.

> What! has the heart, so wild, so roving,
> So prone to changing, sighing, loving,
> Which widows, maids, attack'd in vain,
> At last submitted to the chain?
> Who is this paragon, this matchless she,
> That fix'd a weather-cock like thee?
> (81)

A companion piece, "The Reply," presents the Don Juan as a convert, not only to the outward beauty but to the inner charm of his new wife.

> Nor is't my friend, her speaking face,
> Her shape, her youth, her winning grace,
> Mere outward charms, that pass away,
> But those that bloom when they decay,
> Have reach'd my heart, the fair one's mind,
> Bright as her eyes, yet soft and kind;
> (82–83)

The light satire of the first poem gives way to the celebratory mode of the second with its praise of the bride's virtues and the groom's happiness.

The first poem, with its seemingly double attitude toward the subject's former libertine behavior, is more interesting for this chapter. How this poem is to be understood depends on whether we take the questioner to be male or female. If the questioner is female, the mockery may conceal jealousy or deep regret that such a good catch has been snared by another woman. There may even be a touch of pathos to the questioner's barely concealed admiration of the subject. If however the speaker is male, which is more likely, then the mockery can be seen as good-humored derision of the "weather-cock" for finally consenting to be tied down. There is admiration in the questioner's tone for the heroism, so to speak, of the subject's former libertine lifestyle. But more than admiration, there is a satisfaction inspired by male envy: the "weather-cock" has finally been brought down a peg.

If the questioner is seen as male, this would help us make sense of "The Reply" as well. By gallantly acknowledging the charming power of the woman he surrendered to, the "weather-cock" silences his friend's laughter by showing him that he gained much more than he lost when he married. The groom is obviously much prouder of being married to Maria than of being a former sexual adventurer. The didactic force of this poem works by example as male readers are shown a former archlibertine who has been converted to the religion of female beauty and inner worth as discovered in a companionate marriage. Though the husband that Catherine Jemmat married impulsively turned out to be a debt-ridden drunkard, women readers were to imitate not her personal experience but that of her speaker who testifies to the force of companionate ideology. This poem works with a more subtle psychology and charm than the antilibertine poems by Dixon and DuBois.

Light and charming disparagements of male libertine behavior are also offered by male poets as in William Cowper's little epigram "If John Marries Mary, and Mary Alone":

> If John marries Mary and Mary alone,
> 'Tis a very good match between Mary and John.
> Should John wed a score, oh! the claws and the scratches!
> It can't be a match:—'tis a bundle of matches.
>
> (1: 232)

Though the ostensible subject of this comic-satiric poem is polygamy, the force of it is really directed against the male libertine fantasy of having many women and of moving with impunity from one to the other. Cowper's witty wordplay uncovers the social reality under the fantasy: he reminds men of the combativeness that would prevail in a polygamous marriage. A man may dream of having several women fighting over him; however, the actuality of such a marriage would not be harmonious companionship ("a match"), but a series of hostile flare-ups. Cowper's light epigrammatic wit is quite effective in disparaging the argument for sexual freedom.

By the late eighteenth century, this argument is widely held in social disapprobation, and both male and female poets use a light hand or enlist romantic sentiment in attacking it. Such is the case in "The Siller

Croun" (1790) by Susanna Blamire, Scots songwriter and musician who was educated at her village school. This dramatic monologue features a young Scots woman protesting in dialect that she had rather die before she consents to be a rich man's mistress and breaks her promise to marry Donald. Blamire's having her speaker refuse the libertine's offer "to walk in silk attire" or to have "a siller croun" makes her choice of virtuous though impoverished wedded love all the more touching.

The Argument for the Freedom of Celibacy: Later Era

Like the argument for sexual freedom, the argument for the freedoms and pleasures of the single life survives in the later era in weakened or modified form, where it survives at all. Usually, whenever the argument appears, it is overcome in debate or undermined by light satire.

The pleasures-of-the-single-life argument shows up in two pieces published previous to mid-century that are either translations or adaptations of classical materials: Parnell's "Hesiod: or, The Rise of Woman" (1726) and the anonymous *The Happy Marriage: An Eclogue. In Imitation of Virgil's Tityrus* (1733). As with a number of other translations or imitations of earlier satires on women or marriage, one suspects eighteenth-century poets use the imitation format to voice harsh antifeminist or antimatrimonial sentiments while hiding behind the mask of an older poet. As the courtly stance toward the "fair sex" becomes more fashionable, satirists sometimes resort to smoke screens.

This would seem to be the case with "Hesiod" by Thomas Parnell, Archdeacon of Clogher and a Scriblerian. In Parnell's adaptation of the Greek poet's version of the Pandora myth, man, before the creation of woman, lived in a "golden age."

> At first the creature man was fram'd alone,
> Lord of himself, and all the world his own.
> For him the Nymphs in green forsook the woods,
> For him the Nymphs in blue forsook the floods,
> . . . .
> No care destroy'd, no sick disorder prey'd,
> No bending age his sprightly form decay'd,
> No wars were known, no females heard to rage,
> And Poets tell us, 'twas a golden age.
>   (12–13)

In the satiric section of Parnell's poem (12–14), we find a fairly typical version of the second argument, albeit one adapted from a Greek poet. Though males in the "golden age" are free to be sexually promiscuous with the nymphs, Parnell places emphasis on their mastery of all creatures and the peacefulness of their life before the creation of women. Men are happy in Parnell's adaptation, especially because they are not made to feel vulnerable by the sexual desire women arouse.

In *The Happy Marriage*, the second adaptation of classical materials, we are given the second argument as part of the Virgilian dialogue between Moeris and Damon. Reminiscent of the pleasures-of-the-single-life poems, *The Happy Marriage* gives us Moeris whose praise of bachelorhood is not convincing:

> But we for Comfort to the Tavern fly,
> Where thirsty Souls the flowing Bumpers ply;
> Or else with Clowns to soggy Ale repair,
> And quite from the *Beau Monde* secluded
> These are the only social Joys for me,
> Whose Age no Offspring e'er can hope to see.
> Shall I then buckle with a youthful Bride,
> Whose spurious Breed my Fortune may divide?
> Hence jealous Discord and domestic Strife,
> And Wedlock then becomes the Bane of Life.
>
> (9)

Damon, who is happily married, offers not only a celebration of marital bliss but a correction of Moeris's earlier mistaken notions of marriage:

> That State, they Wedlock call, I foolish thought
> A Weight of Cares, but little Pleasure brought.
> That Wives, like Mistresses, were prone to tease,
> And, Mistress like, they must be brib'd to please.
> Thus Wives like Cats, their Mates like horned Deer,
> To my affrighted Fancy us'd to appear.
> But Marriage does the single Life excell,
> Beyond Compare or what the Tongue can tell.
>
> (5)

The dialogue between Damon and Moeris concludes as the former invites the latter to come and sup with him that night so that he can observe a happy marriage first hand. We leave the poem with the hope that Moeris will be more wholesomely entertained than he is accustomed with the "clowns" with whom he drinks his "soggy Ale." Like *The Answer to the Pleasures of a Single Life* (1701), *The Happy Marriage* presents the "pleasures" of bachelor life only to discredit them. This adaptation of Virgil's first eclogue uses the older poem not as a smoke screen for misogyny and antimatrimonialism but as a vehicle to counter them.

Though neither a translation or an adaptation, *Matrimony: Pro and Con: or, the Resolve* (1745) uses a dialogue format in roughly the same way *The Happy Marriage* does. *Matrimony: Pro and Con* employs a debate loaded on one side, a pattern quite reminiscent of the pleasures-of-the-single-life formula poems. The second argument does get briefly stated by G, but he is quickly converted to the pro-marriage position argued by J. G's position is comprised mainly of reservations and bad reports about marriage from friends. He even suspects one friend of praising wedlock out of spite in order to lure others into the same trap in which he has fallen. Though G offers a number of reasons for not marrying, his direct arguments in praise of the single life are meager:

>G. Single is bless'd, to wed is worse than vain,
>Since Change is possible from Bliss to Pain.
>   J. If giv'n to *Adam* to be bless'd alone,
>As good have wanted *Eve*, and kept his Bone.
>Woman, of all Creation last and best,
>Was made for Man, and made to make him bless'd.
>   G. When Life's best Joys to Liberty I owe,
>These for a Fair-One shall my Soul forego?
>   (3)

J has only to utter one more couplet asserting that liberty can exist in love, and G abruptly capitulates.

>   J. The same is Liberty on Earth;———Above;
>Its Sphere the same, and 'tis the Sphere of Love.
>   G. Enough,———my Bosom changes its Design;
>Scruples be gone, and Wedlock I am thine.
>   (3)

So much for the argument for the pleasures of the single life! By 1745, as is evident here, it could be disposed of very quickly.

That the argument had lost most of its vitality by mid-century is evident from the paucity of poems employing it after this time. One post-

1750 poem that does so transposes it ironically to a woman's experience. "A Ballad" (1765) by William Shenstone, gentleman-poet turned landscape gardener, satirizes the unwillingness of a young socialite to leave the pleasures of her single life in London. Mentioned specifically are the playhouse, French fashions, Ranelagh, Vauxhall Gardens, the "opera, the park, and the ball." A young squire from Lincoln attempts to bring her up to his seat as his wife, but she cannot bear to leave the town for the wholesome delights of the country.

> She might yield to resign the sweet singers of Ruckholt,
> Where the citizen-matron seduces her cuckold;
> But Ranelagh soon would her footsteps recall,
> And the music, the lamps, and the glare of Vauxhall.
> 					(Chalmers 13: 302)

In the last stanza we discover that the delights of the single life in London are not the only reason she refuses to marry "honest Harry." When a "coach with a coronet trail'd her to Tweed," we surmise that the socialite has agreed to elope to Scotland with a titled aristocrat. For this smart young thing, the freedom of her single life evidently included less innocent diversions than those she enumerates. The socialite's pleasures-of-the-single-life argument is discredited by her dishonesty and subterfuge.

By the late eighteenth century the second argument also seems to be vitiated. Satirists and didactic writers disparage the single life and praise marriage to the point that the single life carries little poetic appeal, even as an argument to be attacked or advised against. After the barrage of hyperbolic formula-poem attacks on the single life after 1701, the argument loses much of its vitality; lighter satire and witty comedy become more appropriate to treat it. When these play themselves out after midcentury, the argument effectively disappears. Bolstered by a secularized Protestant morality, the sentimentalization of domesticity, and the idealization of the "fair sex," the feminized pro-marriage argument effectively discredits both the first and second libertine arguments.

CHAPTER THREE

Advice Poems

↭

VIEWED BROADLY, ALMOST ALL THE MARRIAGE poems of the long eighteenth century could be said to be hortatory in some respect. Most of the modes employed by poets take on an advisory function in addition to the one proper to themselves. As we saw in chapters 1 and 2, polemical poems that argue for the pleasures of the single life and the miseries of marriage may in effect be warnings that the responsibilities of marriage should not be undertaken lightly. In the same way, satirical representations of the hell of marriage may be taken as counsel or warnings against its pitfalls. Conversely, praises of marriage may set up normative or idealized models of behavior for couples who are about to enter wedlock. Thus, celebratory poems may also perform an advisory function.

During the course of the long eighteenth century, the broad evolution of advice poems is from the satiric mode to the celebratory. Poets shift from warning readers against the hell into which marriage can fall to urging them to aspire to the heaven to which it can rise. As with polemical poems, this evolution loosely follows Rothstein's schemata but in a way that can be delineated within various categories of advice poems rather than by tracing the movement of advice poems as a block. In this chapter, we will follow the permutations of the shift from satire to celebration within the formats and narratorial stances of four categories of advice poems.

(1) Like polemical poems in Rothstein's first stage, poems in this cate-

gory advise the reader either to avoid marriage entirely or to embrace it wholeheartedly. Advice poems in this group seem strongly indebted to the model of Juvenal's sixth satire and to the patristic and clerical antimarriage satires of the Middle Ages and Renaissance influenced by Juvenal. Just as Juvenal counsels his friend Postumus not to marry, category one poems often use the fiction of addressing a friend who is about to marry and more often than not advise him against it. Category one poems sometimes recommend marriage, and as the eighteenth century progresses, the number of pro-marriage poems increases as does the prevalence of the ideology that supports them. In general, poems in the first category—both pro and con—appear most frequently in the early era.

(2) A second category of advice poems are those that give relatively detailed portraits of the types of husbands and wives to avoid. Broadly analogous to the work of prose character writers, these also draw on Juvenal as the model for their satiric galleries. Going beyond Juvenal, some poets, at the end of their galleries, describe, even celebrate, the normative or ideal mate. The simple satiric gallery poems generally appear earlier than those that include the norm or ideal at the end. In the positive portraits we often are given pro-companionate ideology that mixes humanistic with providential or class-conscious criteria. The imposition of an ideology to resolve contrast and opposition is perhaps illustrative of Rothstein's second stage. As the century progresses, the positive portraits tend to become more idealized and insubstantial. In the later era, the prudential and moralistic criteria applied in creating the satiric gallery may be masked or displaced by more romantic criteria as the myth of marriage as a heaven is emotionally affirmed. This pattern suggests Rothstein's third stage.

(3) Poems that might be called the verse counterparts of prose conduct books appear throughout the period. Category three poems—"conduct poems"—give prospective husbands and wives, as well as married couples, general counsel on the behavior and attitudes expected of them in stages of their courtship and marriage. This advice may be offered broadly, or it may be organized under headings such as how often to make love, how to handle verbal disputes, or what to do about a husband's drunkenness. During the course of the Restoration and eighteenth century, the substance of this advice becomes slightly more liberal. However, more markedly, it is the voice of the advisor that softens and becomes less patriarchal and more empathetic (à la Rothstein's third stage). Prescrip-

tiveness becomes less blatant, and the advisor, though still paternalistic, may employ entertaining fictions in attempting to make his advice palatable. This shift corresponds roughly to shifts that occur in prose conduct books, though, generally speaking, "conduct poems," more so than prose conduct books, tend to be something more than simple works of advice.

(4) A special sort of advice poem, the progress poem, is mainly satirical and paternalistic; it consequently tends to appear with greater frequency in the early era when satire is the vogue. Later didactic and celebratory marriage poems generally do not lend themselves to handling a progression through time, especially a negative one. In didactic poems of the late era, time tends to be presented in an eternal present or a prospective future when marital discord is always correctable. Celebratory poems likewise praise marriage either in an eternal present or a mythical future, comparable to the "happily ever after" of fairy tales. The affective, empathetic stances of the narrators in such poems again suggest Rothstein's third stage.

Category One: Advice Not to Marry or to Marry

Advice poems of the first sort are those that either counsel complete avoidance of marriage or that recommend it wholeheartedly. Especially in the early era, antimarriage advice poems may be an expression of a traditional Christian clerical hostility to marriage as opposed to celibacy, or they may voice a middle-class prudent concern that couples not marry improvidently or immaturely. For these advisors, marriage is a lifelong commitment that involves important socioeconomic considerations and responsibilities. If a young person chooses unwisely and ignores these considerations or if he or she marries too young and fails in these responsibilities, the person may become a burden to parents or the community.

An early example of an antimarriage advice poem is *A Satyr against Marriage* (1700) in which the speaker counsels his friend Frank to avoid the "Plague and Nonsense of a Wife." *An Essay upon Marriage in a Letter Address'd to a Friend* (1704) by William Forbes of Disblair (possibly a Professor of Law at Glasgow) warns his friend against marrying "*Belinda*, that fine Tawdrie thing," and follows with a thoroughly negative portrayal of all the tribulations of marriage. These include "Caterwau'ling, Bawling Titts," freakish and temperamental moods in a wife, not to mention her jealous, wheedling, treacherous behavior.

Good Advice to the Ladies: Shewing, That as the World Goes and Is Like to Go, the Best Way for Them Is to Keep Unmarried (1702) gives an equally if not a more negative picture of the range of behavior Lesbia may expect from a husband: from verbally abusing her to taking up with

> Some Kitchen-Wench, or filthy thing that's grown,
> The common talk and Scandal of the Town:
>
> (3)

Good Advice to Beaus and Batchelours (1705), which answers *Good Advice to the Ladies*, counsels Damon not to be imprudent and hasty in his choice of marriage partner. It follows with an entirely negative portrayal of the stages of marriage and all the trouble women create for men in each of them.

If category one poems are considered within the context of literary tradition, it is Juvenal's sixth satire that stands as the general model for almost all of them. Juvenal's advice to Postumus not to marry is such a rhetorically powerful prototype that no marriage poet in the period could match his satiric energy and tonal range. Although a poet might not rise to Juvenal's stature, he or she could adopt his format of giving advice to a friend and then sermonize or rant against marriage with varying amounts of satiric finesse. However a poet imitated it, Juvenal's sixth satire stands as the major influence on advice poems in the early era portraying marriage as hell.

The fact that many of the eighteenth-century poets had a serious hortatory concern, more serious probably than Juvenal himself, lends a somewhat more positive stance to certain category one poems. Only in one or two places in his overwhelmingly negative sixth satire does Juvenal give any consideration to the possibility of a good marriage or a good wife. And when he does entertain such a possibility, he rejects it out of hand.

> But is none worthy to be made a Wife
> In all this Town? Suppose her free from strife,
> Rich, Fair, and Fruitful: of Unblemish'd Life:
> Chast as the *Sabines*, whose prevailing Charms
> Dismiss'd their Husbands, and their Brothers Arms.
> Grant her, besides, of Noble Blood, that ran
> In Ancient Veins, e're Heraldry began:
> Suppose all these, and take a Poet's word,
> A Black Swan is not so Rare a Bird.

A Wife, so hung with Virtues, such a freight;
What Mortal Shoulders cou'd support the weight!
    (Dryden, *Works* 4: 162–63; lines 233–43)

In contrast to Juvenal, a category one poet who advises a friend against marriage may sometimes allow, especially in his or her introduction, preface, and conclusion, that there may be exceptions to the generally negative picture. In making such an allowance, a poet may be indicating that his or her antimarriage advice is partially ironic in force. In this respect, many antimarriage advice poems may be read as cautions against improvident choices and romantic immaturity. For example, William Forbes of Disblair states in the advertisement to *An Essay on Marriage in a Letter Adress'd to a Friend* that his poem was "never meant to Disobliege the Virtuous, and Best Natur'd of the Fair Sex, of Whom he believes, there's a competent number in the World." Forbes says he wrote the poem only to "Obliege his Friend who Earnestlie Solicited" the advice (2). In effect, Forbes's message to young men may well be not to avoid marriage but to keep a sharp eye out in choosing a wife.

Similarly, the author of *Good Advice to the Ladies* grudgingly allows that there may be "hardly half a score" of tolerably good husbands in the world, and he includes his *vir bonus*, Amintas, in that number. The poet in *Good Advice to Beaus and Batchelours* celebrates the happiness of the young man who does not rush headlong into marriage, who makes a "timely Cov'nant with his Eyes," so that "no false Pleasures can delude the Sence." In "Advice to a Widow" the poet says that if Celia after all must take a husband, he wishes her all happiness. Most category one poets advise strongly against marriage, yet many, unlike Juvenal, allow for the exceptional happy marriage or the good husband or wife. In doing so, they may point to the companionate ideal.

CATEGORY TWO: THE SATIRIC GALLERY

Category two poets describe in detail the sorts of husbands or wives to avoid and at the end of this satiric gallery sometimes draw the norm or ideal to be sought. Norms often mix humanistic with prudential concerns, and as satiric gallery poems evolve in the later era, they become more overt in romanticizing the ideal mate, disguising or softening patriarchal criteria in doing so. Similar to category one poems, the model of Juvenal is pervasive in this category as well. Juvenal's satiric gallery includes such notorious portraits as Hippia the senator's wife, who "loath'd her old Patrician Lord,/And left him for a Brother of the Sword" (116–17), and the wife of emperor Claudius, who paid to do a nightly stint in a low-class brothel:

> Still as one drops another takes his place,
> And baffled still succeeds to like disgrace.
>   (178–89)

Then there is the woman who sees a "Dancing-Master Capring high,/And Raves, and Pisses, with pure Extasie" (91–92). Juvenal gives the reader a "whole Hydra more" of drunkards, adulteresses, and poisoners and, as I said, offers no positive portrait or ideal.

The early era has given us a number of advice poems that are like Juvenal's sixth satire in offering only negative characters. In *A Satyr against Marriage* (1700) the poet warns his friend Frank against "the Noise, the Plagues and Nonsense of a Wife" (12). To dissuade Frank from marriage, the poet draws in his opening several portraits of the "Wretched Lover in all Forms": as a green young man, as a "Fluttring-Fop with Dance and Song," and as an old man who pursues love even "Tho Wrinkles Seventy Years have Plow'd his Face." His final portrait of the widower, who "half wreck'd before,/Ventures again, and leaves the happy shore" (7), does not deviate from the negative. Similarly offering a negative satiric gallery, *The Fifteen Comforts of Matrimony* (1706) crudely describes objectionable types of wives as it enumerates the "comforts" of marriage that men will encounter.

In *Marriage: A Satire* (1728) the poet exhibits a rich Juvenalian tonal range and rhetorical vigor as he gives us finely drawn negative portraits that seem to anticipate the types in Pope's *Epistle II. To a Lady* (1725). We have the wife inclined to wit:

> In deep Enquirys thus she spends her Life,
> And scorns the humble Dutys of a Wife;
>   (17)

Next there are the men

> Who, by unhappy Stars to Ruin led,
> Took each a gaming Fury to his Bed:
>   (19)

We are also shown the "sprightly Dame"

> Whose Wit and Cheeks enliv'ning Draughts inflame;
> In secret, with a Set of chosen Friends,
>
> (22)

Further portraits include the "fierce Bigotte, swell'd with her godly Pride," and "Some high bred Maiden of Patrician House" (22, 25). The last will scorn her husband and "honour more her Marmozet than you." The gallery's penultimate portrait is the hellish tale of a hellish wife whose only virtue is her thrift. She starves her husband to death, and, eating "her Scraps on hoarded Bags of Gold," her miserable life of avarice ends when she is stabbed by thieves (29). The poem concludes with equally negative portraits of a wife from a rich family and a poor family.

As *Marriage: A Satire* illustrates well, category two poets who offer a simple satiric gallery seem committed to imitating Juvenal more closely than those who add a portrait of a normative or ideal mate.[1] Though the antifeminist and antimatrimonial ideology of these poems may be rooted, as with category one poets, in clerical hostility to marriage and sexuality as well as in middle-class prudential concerns, satires of both types also tend to be an unthinking, self-perpetuating mode, imitating the stance and the style of earlier successful satires, especially Juvenal's.

In the positive portraits of eighteenth-century gallery poets, it is possible to isolate elements of a pro-companionate ideology. Most male advice poets tend to be paternalistic in their stance, and some female poets, maternalistic (a Dutch aunt, as it were). However, depending on the degree to which concerns about money and social class manifest themselves, their criteria for recommending a mate may range from the humanistic to the class-conscious and crass. These values may be confusingly intermixed. For example, in "To His Friend Inclined to Marry" (1702) by the Bedfordshire vicar John Pomfret, the speaker advises Strephon not to choose a mate

> From too exalted, or too mean a state;
> For in both these we may expect to find
> A creeping spirit, or a haughty mind.
> Who moves within the middle region, shares
> The least disquiets, and the smallest cares.
>
> (219)

For Pomfret, marrying a woman of the middle class or of the middling sort is equated with marrying a woman without personality extremes and with the fewest moral flaws. Women of the lower and higher classes are not only out of bounds socially; they exhibit bad human traits.

In *The Ladies Choice* (1702), the types of husbands Belinda advises against are proscribed out of a rationale that mixes humanistic concerns with class bias. Melissa is counseled against "*self-admiring Beaux,*" the "*Lewder Wits* o' th' Town," and aspiring courtiers—types who are undesirable because conceited, extravagant, or vainly ambitious respectively. Yet each of these three types also exhibits aristocratic excesses that mark him as socially out of bounds. Belinda also advises Melissa against marriage with a soldier or with a man of business. The former will be absent from her much of the time, and the latter will be married to his job and will be inattentive as a lover. More important, both are below the status of a gentleman, the ideal that Melissa is taught to prefer. This man, "not with a great, yet a good Estate," exhibits the middle-class virtues of good sense, modesty, and temperance. At the same time he is enough of an aristocrat to be generous and well-bred. The poet's pattern of imposing gentrified values on a middle-class prudential base is epitomized by his requirement that Melissa's husband should "Read *Poetry*" but "not write."

Pope's *Epistle II. To a Lady* (1725) is the finest category two poem treating women in the period. It is also a poem whose judgments are based on a deeply felt and metaphorically reinforced structure of values. The nature of these values has, however, recently been called in question, especially by feminist criticism.[2] Laura Brown, for example, reads Pope's attack on women's changeableness as an expression of his misogyny (see 101–7). This misogyny, Brown argues, does not "spring fully grown from his own personal antagonisms" (102). Rather, as Pope draws on the tradition of antifeminist satire stemming from Juvenal, "women come to embody for him the material consequences of commodification much more directly than men" (102). Because women become obvious consumers in a "commodity culture," Pope can attack them unequivocally as representations of the "acquisition, luxury, and accumulation of his age" (102).

As Brown suggests, Pope *is* hostile to the excesses of a "commodity culture." It is also true that in *To a Lady* he uses women as scapegoats as he draws on a conventionalized tradition of misogyny to attack that culture. Brown, however, underplays the importance of the exemplary portrait of Martha Blount at the end of the satiric gallery and dismisses the portrait as unreal. She finds that Pope presents Martha Blount either as a "'softer Man' or an androgyne, mingling the virtues of both sexes" (272). She further argues that there are no substantial women in *To a*

Lady. They are either ghosts of men or simply pictures of women from the walls of a portrait gallery. In *To a Lady*, "'Woman,'" Brown concludes, "is purely emblematic." She is a creation of the male fantasy, "a reified embodiment of an assertion of moral stability" (107).

The question of the reality of Pope's moral judgments in his portraits of women is an intriguing one. Certainly, one cannot expect of Pope's satire a minute, candid examination of women's characters as the product of social and natural forces such as one might find in nineteenth- and twentieth-century naturalistic fiction or twentieth-century "images of women" writing. Nor perhaps is it appropriate to compare, as Brown does, the stereotypical reality of Pope's portraits of women with his more contradictory, indeterminate "characters" of men in *Epistle to Cobham* (1734), a satire in which he begins "to acknowledge but ultimately refuse[s] to accept the division of private from public virtue" (104). *To a Lady* and *To Cobham* are in fact quite different poems. The portraits of women in *To a Lady* have at base a more conventionalized reality founded on the satiric and exemplary formulae the portraits employ and modify.

As in other category two poems, Pope alters the satiric gallery formulae to make his portraits more distinctive. Pope's characters of women take on a more vivid existence than in other category two poems because he draws his portraits in sharper detail with a broader range of tonal hues. He breathes life into them by the variety of stances the narrator adopts in his role as artist-satirist. Pope's narrator is by turns humble and egotistical, disengaged and intense, complaisantly cavalier and puritanically harsh. Pope's fine manipulation of technique and tone brings the role of the artist-satirist into the foreground almost as much as the portraits he draws.

Ultimately, the moral cosmography that infuses the characters is solidly based in the Christian didactic tradition of writings treating the behavior of women and wives. Though this tradition is patriarchal as well as conventionalized, it certainly has substance. Only if one denies the existence in western Europe of centuries of didactic writings on the conduct of women and wives can one say Pope's final exemplary portrait is empty. Pope's "final picture of an esteemable woman" contributes to his celebration of particularized virtues as his satiric portraits of hellish women do his satire of particularized vices.

If *To a Lady* is examined in the light of the format and attitudes of other advice poems on marriage, Pope's values appear no more misogynous than those of his contemporaries, even somewhat more progressive than most. *To a Lady* does not consistently present the types and individuals it satirizes as wives or prospective wives, nor does it generally offer advice on marriage. The fact that some of the portraits do treat married women could well be coincidental. Even so, *To a Lady* may stand in the tradition of eighteenth-century advice poems on marriage more than is at first obvious. At least four of Pope's major portraits—Papillia, Philomede, Simo's mate, and Atossa—treat women in their role as wives or mothers. In addition, like many advice poems on marriage, Pope's praise of the ideal woman emphasizes strongly her God-given ability to sway her husband by submitting to him.

> Oh! blest with Temper, whose unclouded ray
> Can make tomorrow cheerful as today;
> She, who can love a Sister's charms, or hear
> Sighs for a Daughter with unwounded ear;
> She, who ne'er answers till a Husband cools,
> Or, if she rules him, never shows she rules;
> Charms by accepting, by submitting sways,
> Yet has her humour most, when she obeys;
> Let Fops or Fortune fly which way they will;
> Disdains all loss of Tickets, or Codille;
> Spleen, Vapours, or Smallpox, above them all,
> And Mistress of herself, though China fall.
> (568–69; lines 257–68)

Martha Blount is the good woman or the good wife of seventeenth- and eighteenth-century conduct literature, an ideal Pope tries to humanize by his mock heroic tone and humor. Though Martha's main virtue is her submission in good humor to her husband and to life itself, this virtue helps to define her nature, not deny her "id/entity" as Pollak suggests (*The Poetics of Sexual Myth* 126).

Pope's women may be more types than individuals, yet this need not take away from the substance of the moral advice that stands behind them. In his role as painter, Pope pretends to be offering quick, light sketches knocked off in an odd moment.

> Pictures like these, dear Madam, to design,
> Asks no firm hand, and no unerring line;
> Some wandering touches, some reflected light,
> Some flying stroke alone can hit 'em right.
> (565; lines 151–54)

Yet, as we examine the poem with care, we can see how the metaphoric language creates a codified basis for his judgments—albeit one imbued in paternalistic discourse. The paradoxical picture of Philomede as "Chaste to her Husband, frank to all beside,/A teeming Mistress, but a barren Bride" shows an unnatural reversal of a God-given order. This picture and that of the angry Atossa as a childless mother are pictures of marriage become a hell on earth.

> Atossa, cursed with every granted prayer,
> Childless with all her Children, wants an Heir.
> To Heirs unknown descends th'unguarded store,
> Or wander, Heaven-directed, to the Poor.
> (565; lines 147–50)

Just as Philomede reverses the natural order, Atossa's God-given fertility and her love as a mother for her offspring are perverted by her rage. Instead of blessing her life, they curse it. In contrast, the ideal woman seems guided by heaven in her ability to deal with her subordinate position as wife and to accept the blows to her ego that life offers. She is "blest with Temper" which allows her, unlike Atossa, to control herself.

More so than other category two poets, Pope's advice to women reveals a humanized concern with moral conduct. He may have recourse to the conventional paternalistic advice that wives will conquer by stooping, but he gives this advice within the deeper context of a warning, not against domineering wives, but against the loss of self-control. Similarly, Pope does use the mythical heaven-hell contrast between the good woman and the bad woman, the good wife and the bad wife, but he resorts somewhat less to the stereotypical, hyperbolic praise and denigration of the popular marriage poets. Pope's satire is more solidly realistic than the others, and his celebration of the ideal woman to a large degree avoids the sentimentalized romanticizing of many later era advice poets. Pope's portraits may often have a sexist bias or a degree of metaphoric distortion, but at base they are founded on well-defined moral expectations about how people should limit their behavior.

If Pope's *To a Lady* can be considered a category two advice poem, it stands at the zenith of eighteenth-century marriage satire in its appeal to codified but substantial notions of moral realism. At the same time, Pope should be commended for exhibiting a hostility to the "outward signs of female falseness derived from a commodified culture" (Brown 102). Many satiric gallery poets previous to Pope, as we have seen, mix their traditional humanistic standards with more overtly class-conscious concerns about money and wealth. As the evolution of companionate ideology in category two poems continues, this pattern persists. In contrast to Pope, later era poets frequently sanction the values of the new bourgeois culture. In addition, most category two poets increasingly tend to idealize the mate they recommend. In these idealizations the satire of the gallery portraits gives way more and more to celebration, in some cases sentimentalized celebration which, unlike that in Pope's *To a Lady*, should be called insubstantial.

We see such idealization in the conclusion of *The Creation of Woman; A Poem* (1725), a satiric gallery poem that is adapted from "the remains of the old Greek Poet Simonides." It uses a version of the creation myth as a basis for offering crudely animalistic portraits of various female types and their appropriate mates. Man asks Jove for a wife, and Jove decides to punish him by creating women from various earthly creatures and compounds. From the "Swinish Herd" Jove creates slovenly women who are gluttons. These are married to fox hunters so that they might agree in "mutual filthiness" (2). From the fox itself, Jove creates a cunning, shifty woman who is married to a peaceful citizen in order to destroy his peace. Female gossips are made from the dog, and they are married to "th' ill-natur'd *Critick*." Each type of superficiality, ignorance, and passion finds her appropriate match (and punishment). The ideal woman, in contrast, is created from the bee. Her type does not just embody the middle-class virtue of diligence but also more humanistic virtues such as wisdom and good nature. Yet once he has created a woman with such admirable qualities, the poet cannot resist celebrating her effusively as a "treasure," a term indicative of the commodification of women.

> Blest is the man, blest as the heavenly train,
> Who shall th'inestimable treasure gain:
> No coyness, nor affected complaisance
> Shall lead him wandring through a mazy dance.
> (10)

The wittier, more Popean *Modern Matrimony. A Satire to a Young Nobleman* (1737) is a down-to-earth poem in its sharply drawn satiric portraits of various fools and coxcombs and the appropriately bad mates they choose. But even this poem in its conclusion is quite capable of idealizing the good wife and portraying marriage to her as a romanticized heaven on earth.

> And you, my Lord, shall know, in future Life,
> Heav'n gave its greatest Blessing in a Wife.
>
> (8)

A more overtly romanticized conclusion to a satiric gallery is offered in the third book of *The Nuptials* (1761) by Richard Shepherd, chaplain to a bishop and later Rector of Wetherden and Helmingham in Suffolk. Shepherd uses the periphrases and circumlocutions typical of Miltonic descriptive blank verse to offer clever satiric portraits of a fox hunter, a bookworm, and a beau or fop. In drawing his gallery, Shepherd seems less concerned with recommending humanized values in the choice of a mate than in helping women find a man who is not a socially objectionable type.

Shepherd does not follow this gallery with a picture of the ideal mate. Rather he concludes a tirade against marriage-become-a-trade with an epithalamium celebrating a happy rustic marriage that exists in the freedom of poverty. In this idealized wedding we find

> Joys pure,
> Without Alloy: not purchased at the Price
> Of Innocence; nor with the poisonous Sting
> Of dire Remorse attended. Hand in Hand,
> Home to their little Cot, that decent smiles,
> The Couple blithe proceed:
>
> (79; lines 224–29)

By the time that Shepherd writes, the sharpness and simplicity of the Juvenalian model has been diffused by the poet's adoption of the style of Miltonic descriptive verse. The satiric gallery is not at all at the center of his poem but has been subordinated to a small part of a larger didactic and celebratory scheme. Celebration predominates especially in the concluding epithalamia, which is sustained through five pages of antiphonal refrains. The poet's prudential concerns are masked by the romantic fiction of love-in-a-cottage.

Category two advice poems follow the pattern of much eighteenth-century marriage poetry in assimilating a companionate ideology. Patriarchal advice in the satiric and didactic modes, which often mixes humanistic and prudential concerns, tends to be displaced by celebratory poems that soften but do not eliminate the patriarchal stance; these tend often to become romantically idealized and insubstantial. Group three poems, as we will see, show a roughly similar movement.

Category Three: Conduct Poems

Poems in the third category are those that correspond roughly to prose conduct books, though "conduct poems" tend more so than their prose counterparts to soften their paternalistic didacticism with rhetorical ingenuity and elegance or with the use of a benevolent, empathetic narrator.[3] A pattern of trivialization of advice occurs as poets in the later era focus increasingly on social behavior and manners, especially the ways in which women may please men both before and after marriage. In looking briefly at the sorts of poems that give general advice on conduct before and after marriage, we will see that as the category evolves few poems remain "conduct poems" in a narrow prescriptive sense. In the later era especially, most poems are this and something more, such as an entertainment or a celebration.

Two early eighteenth-century poems that are paternalistic in a blunt and unvarnished way are Samuel Jackson's *The Duty of a Wife. A Poem* (1707) and the companion poem, *The Duty of a Husband: Or, the Lady's Answer to the Duty of a Wife* (1707). The first poem essentially counsels wives to be obedient to their husbands in all things. They are not supposed to quarrel with him if he is "in Drink," they are to order "Fire in's Room" if he comes home wet, and they are not to "scold or Brawl, nor no such thing;/For that will nothing but Disorder bring" (2). Jackson dresses his advice with a few mythological and Biblical allusions, but for the most part his paternalism is served up in undisguised form. The answer to *The Duty of a Wife*, which may be by Jackson as well, takes on something of a polemical, protofeminist cast as it attempts to teach husbands that they must be tolerant of their wives and that they have moral obligations in marriage as well. In a work that is slightly more tactful than *The Duty of a Wife*, husbands are advised to love their wives, to refrain from grieving their wives by "Beastly Actions" such as keeping a whore, and to avoid "Ill-grounded Projects & Romances" as well as "vain Expences." Husbands should by right be obeyed, but they must not be tyrannical. In the straightforward prescriptiveness with which *The Duty of a Wife* and *The Duty of a Husband* give their advice, they resemble many of the conduct books of the early and mid-seventeenth century, especially those identified by James Turner Johnson as being Puritan in their emphases.

As early as 1735, we have an example of a "conduct poem" that softens its prescriptiveness by several means. Francis Blyth's *Advice to a Friend on His Marriage, A Poem* employs a narrator with a more empathetic tone who hesitates to be dictatorial:

> Another Counsel I could add to This;
> Cou'd you e'er stand in Need of such Advice;
>
> (12).

Because his advice is offered to a particular friend, Drusus, and to an evidently wealthy one, the advisor mitigates his severity:

> Not with the Harshness of the clam'rous Drum,
> Nor the shrill Shriek of untun'd Fifes, I come,
> With mercenary Views Reward to claim:
> Calm, my Salute; and gen'rous is its Aim.
>
> (2)

Blyth tries to make his counsel not just instructive but charming as he adds anecdotes and entertaining figures of speech.

> Free from the Miser's Gulph, ah! never run
> On wild Profusions Rock, to be undone.
>
> (11)

Though published only thirty years after *The Duty of a Husband*, Blyth's poem is a distance away from its predecessor in its softer tone and literary tact.

Other poems in the thirties and forties demonstrate more significant movement away from prescriptiveness. For example, *The Woman's Labour* (1739) by the "Washerwoman Poet," Mary Collier, is not really a "conduct poem" in the strict sense at all. Rather than instructing a wife in her duties, this poem treats sympathetically from a woman's point of view the many exhausting jobs a lower-class woman is obligated to perform—in her own home, in the field, and as a washerwoman in the homes of gentry. Forthrightly protofeminist, Mary Collier's poem has a strong polemical cast since her piece was a reply to Stephen Duck's *The Thresher's Labour* (1731). Collier demonstrates in quasi-naturalistic detail the truth of the proverb that while a man's work may be from sun to sun, a woman's work is never done. She is less concerned with showing how working-class women should behave than with how they *must* behave.

John Armstrong's *The Oeconomy of Love. A Poetical Essay* (1736) and Robert Shiells's *Marriage: A Poetical Essay* (1748) are "conduct poems" in a broad sense. However, they might more accurately be called marriage manuals since both of them describe and celebrate such physiological processes as puberty, intercourse, childbirth, and death as these relate to courtship and marriage. In spite of this apparent scientific focus, the underlying concern in these Miltonic descriptive poems, especially Shiells's, is with moral behavior. The poets counsel readers to control nature, not just respond to it.

Several later era poems, which are more strictly "conduct poems" than the pieces by Collier, Armstrong, and Shiells, employ an obvious variety of fictive and narratorial devices to soften their prescriptiveness. The increasing tendency to focus on social behavior and manners is evident in many of these as well. Edward Moore and Henry Brooke's *Fables for the Female Sex* (1744) uses narratives, some with animal speakers, to instruct young women (unmarried and married) on various points of conduct. A wife, for example, is advised not to neglect her appearance after she marries. In this way she may maintain her conquest of her husband:

> 'Tis harder far (you'll find it true)
> To keep the conquest, than subdue;
> Admit us once behind the screen,
> What is there farther to be seen?
>
> (25)

Nathaniel Cotton's *Visions in Verse* (1751) uses satire in an allegorical narrative presented as a dream vision to make its instruction more entertaining. Thomas Mariott in *Female Conduct* (2nd ed., 1759) attempts to decorate his patriarchal ideology with rhetorical and tonal flourishes. He is quite direct in stating that he will teach wives the various arts to charm their husbands. The poet however offers archly ingenious parody and allusion as well as other learned wordplay in an overly clever effort to divert his female readers (see, for example, 229). One hopes that Mariott's readers were as charmed by his learned playfulness as he seems to be himself.

If Mariott attempts to cut his didacticism with cleverness and learned wit, *Precepts of Conjugal Happiness* (1767) by John Langhorne, tutor and Rector of Blagdon, Somerset, adopts an empathetic narrator who scarcely deigns to offer moral advice to his female auditor at all:

> Friend, sister, partner of that gentle heart
> Where my soul lives, and holds her dearest part;
> While love's soft raptures these gay hours employ,
> And time puts on the yellow robe of Joy;
> Will you, Maria, mark with patient ear
> The moral Muse, nor deem her song severe?
>
> (427)

Using allegorical personifications to highlight his sensitive, heartfelt tone, Langhorne goes out of his way to avoid the "severe" didacticism of earlier "conduct poems."

In spite of the softness of his narratorial stance, the poet does in fact offer throughout the body of his poem solid moral insights into the sources of marital unhappiness. For example:

> The source of half our anguish, half our tears,
> Is the wrong conduct of our hopes and fears;
> (427)

By the conclusion of his "song," the poet's softened didacticism is, however, drowned out by his rising chorus of celebration as he praises the ideal of companionship in which joy and sorrow are shared:

> O bliss beyond what lonely life can know,
> The soul-felt sympathy of joy and woe!
> That magic charm which makes e'en sorrow dear,
> And turns to pleasure the partaken tear!
> (428)

In some sections of *Precepts of Conjugal Happiness* the celebratory tone becomes so intense it effectively masks the poet's underlying didactic intent.

In "A Good Wife" (1761) by Francis Fawkes, a vicar and rector who was always indigent, the author's celebratory tone prevails over his didactic tone in not just a few passages, but throughout his entire poem. Embroidering the prose of Proverbs 21 with his homespun versification, the poet praises the qualities and abilities of the good wife.

> More precious far than rubies, who can find
> A wife embellished with a virtuous mind:
> In her securely, as his better part,
> Her happy husband cheerful rests his heart:
> (247)

Implicit in the celebration of the good wife is the moral imperative to imitate her. However, in spite of Fawkes's evident Christian orientation, he completely submerges his didactic intent in his celebratory stance. Although perhaps an extreme example, Fawkes does illustrate well the tendency of later era "conduct poets" to soften their patriarchal prescriptiveness by one means or another. In the case of Fawkes, prescriptiveness is not just softened but effectively muted. Didacticism in this poem takes a backseat to celebration of companionate ideology.

Category three "conduct poems," as with category two poems, tend generally to move away from harsh satire and unvarnished didacticism toward softened forms of advice. Use of entertaining fictions and an empathetic narrator are two of the primary ways that male poets deflect attention from their paternalism. These poets tend less to paint harsh pictures of negative conduct or to advise good conduct in authoritarian tones and more to counsel their readers sympathetically on how they can be more pleasing to their spouses or, if unmarried, more socially attractive.

Women poets who write conduct poems show a similar pattern of softening prescriptiveness and moving toward celebration, though the tones women adopt can be more obviously sympathetic to women's confinement in their roles as housewives. In "Advice to a Young Lady Lately Married" (1752) by Esther Lewis, the daughter of a Wiltshire clergyman, the speaker expresses solicitude to her correspondent, "Peggy." She also admits that her authority as an advisor might be challenged since she herself is unmarried. This however does not stop Lewis from offering Peggy conservative advice that emphasizes prudence, cleanliness and neatness, equanimity, submissiveness, and playing a "sympathising part" toward her husband (Lonsdale 232).

In contrast is Jane West's stance in "To a Friend on Her Marriage, 1784." A self-educated poet who lived essentially in seclusion, "engrossed" by domestic duties, West has her advisor express much more sympathy toward her friend's fall from "the glory of the stately belle" into the role of housewife.

> No more attentive Strephon flies,
> Awed by the lightning of your eyes;
> No longer, "Madam, hear my vows,"
> But "Mend this ragged wristband, spouse;
> I mean to call upon a friend,
> Do you your household cares attend."
>
> (Lonsdale 381)

West realizes many women too readily accept their confinement to the "household care" and become inured to the limitations of their small world.

> Our tables and our chairs, in fact,
> Possess perfections which attract,

> Till, like the snail, we gladly bear
> The constant weight of household care;
>
> (381)

Consequently, West's advisor recommends to her friend that she regard her duties as "trifles" that she should complete and move beyond for a more active life of social concern and charitable enterprise. Yet, perhaps in contradiction, the advisor also stresses the importance of a well-ordered household as it proves the wife's merit and "proclaims a regulating mind." After affirming women's pride in intellect, the advisor concludes by celebrating the companionate ideal of "Hymeneal friendship's placid calm" (282).

After mid-century, in conduct poems by both men and women, didacticism frequently gives way to celebration of a blissful ideal of marital happiness. Although this ideal is by its nature implicitly didactic, category-three poets, like category-two poets, mask their moralizations by use of the celebratory mode. The ultimate implications of this may be the idea that happiness in marriage is less a matter of right conduct in specific situations and more a psychological benefit of the marital state itself. Bliss in marriage is not something that comes from each partner's working hard at behaving well toward each other. Rather it is thought of more as an inherent attribute of the wedded state, even perhaps a benefit to which all are entitled.

Category Four: Progress Poems

As the checklist of Reginald Harvey Griffith has amply demonstrated, the progress poem is a special form of advice poem that has its vogue throughout the period (see also Swayne 84–92). Griffith defines the progress poem as "an imaginary tour of an allegorical abstraction." The idea of a forward movement is clearly implied, probably even in the sense of a gradual betterment over time. This often was handled ironically. The meaning of *progress* may also hark back to the royal tours marked by pomp and pageantry.

Swift's "Phillis, or, The Progress of Love" (written 1719, published 1727), his "The Progress of Marriage. Jany 1721–2" (1765), and the anonymous *The Progress of Matrimony* (1733) are the only marriage poems I have located which use *progress* in their titles. There are, however, many pieces which are progress poems in their format. The evolution (or devolution) they feature may take up an entire poem, or it may occupy only a small portion. Previous to Swift's progress poems, the format is used mainly in Grub Street poems. These tend in the main to be rather crude, repetitive, and formula bound. Swift's finely innovative achievement in the format may influence a few later poets, but none of them surpasses or even matches his accomplishment. After Swift, the format in marriage poetry dwindles, perhaps because he had exhausted its satiric possibilities.

Progress poems treating marriage come in two varieties: the man's or rake's progress, which usually treats the "progressive" degeneration of a libertine into vice and self-indulgence. The first sort often ends with the rake's death. The second focuses on the deterioration of a woman's or wife's behavior into rebellion and adultery. This devolution is usually treated in the context of the degeneration of a marriage; it may terminate in divorce.

Progress poems treating males need not always focus on rakes. Dryden, for example in "Prologue to a New Play, Call'd, *The Disappointment: or, The Mother in Fashion*" (1684), sketches the development of a spoiled young heir from overindulged infancy to foolish adulthood. The heir's chasing after actresses behind the scenes at the playhouse leads to his marriage to one. After his father dies, he brings her "in Triumph, with her Portion down" to his estate. Her portion, the poet tells us, is "A Twillet, Dressing-Box, and Half a Crown" (Dryden 321; line 49–50).

More typically, progress poems treating males focus on a rake's moral and physical degeneration. This can be handled in a brief account of his precipitous decline and death as it is toward the end of Hugh Newman's *A Poem in Praise of Marrying for Love* (1698).

> O'recharg'd at last with Debts and Sin,
> All Rags without, and Pox within;
> Bereft of Friends, th'unhappy Fool
> Becomes the Publick Ridicule;
> Unpittyd does his Fate Bewaile,
> In Ditch, or Hospital, or Gaole;
> Till thrust out by encroaching Fires,
> From her loath'd Cell his Soul retires,
> And Life's snuff in a stick Expires.
> (10)

The rake's progress can also be dramatized in lengthier pieces with an equally fatal outcome as it is in the first-person confessions of the young "zealot or bigot in the religion of pleasure" in Richard Ames's *The Rake, or, the Libertine's Religion* (1693). In a poem such as A[braham] G[lanville]'s *The Rake Reform'd* (1718), the confession can even be combined with an account of penitence and salvation. In a subtype of the rake's progress, accounts of the death of a young man are sometimes narrated in the grieving voice of a friend; the friend may be hostile to the prostitute who infected his friend and brought on his demise. In progress poems treating the deterioration of woman or wife, the speaker's hostility may be prompted by a friend's bad experience in marriage or by the narrator's own marital experiences.[4] In either case, the speaker is strongly wary of women's power to hurt men, either psychologically or physically. Even so, the antifeminism in these pieces seems in the main less gratuitous in motivation than prudential.

One of the earliest examples of a woman's "progress" is Robert Gould's "A Consolatory Epistle to a Friend Made Unhappy by Marriage: or, A Scourge for Ill Wives" (1688/9). Gould's poem, though not perhaps his best, is interesting not only for its early adaptation of the woman's progress format but also for its inventive and bawdy use of the related day-in-the-life convention. A few other poets on marriage offer a descriptive sequence in which a typical day's activities of a wife, often a rich wife, are detailed. These can range from the broadside ballad *The Married Mans Complaint* (1680) to Swift's richly innovative "The Journal of a Modern Lady" (1729) and "The Progress of Marriage" (1721–22).[5]

Gould's day-in-the-life sequence in "A Consolatory Epistle" is certainly not constrained by good taste. As soon as the wife wakes, she is eager to misspend her time in the pursuit of sin. Her footmen are called to help her dress, a practice the wife dignifies with the fashionable French phrase: "a Janty mode." Then her Hackney coach is summoned:

> *Hackney* is call'd, *Hackney* her dear *Alcove*,
> (Where Coachmen, for their Fare, enjoy her Love).
> *(Poems* 242)

Gould injects an "Encomium," which the wife sings while she enjoys the coachman's embrace as they bounce together over the stones. From this point on, the day can go only downhill. The wife sups and drinks with a lewd gang of females who almost manage to outdo Juvenal's frenzied devotees of Priapus in their gluttony and lust; these women however act out their passions not with slaves and water carriers but with one another. The wife concludes her day with her friends, sallying through the town in men's clothing. She

> Bounces, like Bell-men, against every door,
> And roars out a *good morrow* with Rogue and Whore.
> In all her walk no Window can escape,
> For mischief's her delight in every shape.
>
> *(Poems 244)*

In portraying the wife's unruly behavior, Gould indulges in a pattern of accusation used sometimes by authors of woman's progress poems and by male satirists in general. He transfers vices usually identified with male rakes to women. Male satirists typically displace male guilt by making women behave as men sometimes do.

Framing the particular sequence of the day-in-the-life is a broader wife's "progress" that encompasses almost the entire opening and closing. Using the advice-to-a-friend-about-to-marry format, Gould gives his friend a scenario for his wife's behavior throughout their marriage. She will progress rapidly from the charming virgin to the unfaithful wife. After the sizable day-in-the-life sequence, we see how the carousing wife degenerates into a pocky whore who keeps bullies with "five foot Swords to vindicate her Fame." Her final manifestation as a foul, deformed monster is even more repulsive:

> Bloated all o'er, her Hyde can hardly hold her,
> Neck shrunk, her Head does lean upon each shoulder,
> Her Face carbunkl'd, Nodes upon her Skin,
> Which shows there's rank Contagion lodg'd within.
>
> (246)

Showing the wife's progressive physical and moral degeneration throughout marriage, Gould misogynously affirms the self-serving linkage in the male imagination of female unattractiveness and moral turpitude. At the same time he sets a crude, bawdy model for later woman's progress poems. These include a number of rough-hewn popular pieces that precede Swift's "Phillis, or, The Progress of Love" and "The Progress of Marriage."

One of these pre-Swiftian pieces is *A Satyr against Love* (1703), which was probably revised and corrected by William Congreve (see Barnard). In this conventional antimatrimonial piece, a one-hundred-line section, heavily salted with verbal irony, cynically describes the stages of a young woman's development from pubescence to marriage and childbearing.

> And now begins the Drudgery of Life,
> Oh, the vast Comforts of a loving Wife!
> In three months time the Yoke uneasie grows,
> And in three more you're weary of your Spouse:
>
> (8)

In "The Character of a True-Born English-Woman," a section of the crudely written *Female Apostacy* (1705), there is a more extensive treatment of the same progression. Though the irony is less developed, the stages of life are extended to include infancy and old age. In her marriage the English woman's chief endeavor is typically to "govern what she cannot guide."

> Thus does she fright the poor mistaken Sot,
> To change his Breeches for a Pettycoat;
> While he bewilder'd in a mist of Blindness,
> Dreams on (poor wretch) and takes it all for kindness.
>
> (2)

"A True-Born English-Woman" gives us the conventional domineering, hellish wife of much popular antifeminist marriage satire; her character reappears in a number of Grub Street satires of this era that feature a bad wife's devolution from covert infidelity to brazen whoredom.[6]

Swift's "Phillis, or, The Progress of Love" (written 1719), "Corinna" (written 1711), and "The Progress of Marriage" (written 1721/2) stand obviously as more accomplished productions than the earlier Grub Street pieces. Though Swift's indebtedness to the earlier antifeminist portrayals is quite evident, Swift in his narratives is much more inventive. While the Grub Street pieces mainly give separate sketches of a woman's behavior in different stages of her premarital and marital life, Swift offers a connected story with enough plot complexity to engage our interest fully. Swift's "Phillis" centers around her wedding day elopement with John the Butler. This takes up most of the poem, but like the earlier poems, Swift also presents other stages in Phillis's life: her character as a hypocritical prude before her intended elopement, and her life with John after her elopement. The reader thus has a clear sense of Phillis's deterioration from an eligible young woman of class to a hostess and whore in a low-life tavern. At the same time, one sees a consistency in Phillis's character from her feigned prudishness in the beginning to her posing as a hostess in the end.

It is in the realistic character insights that Swift's satiric originality emerges. Contrast Phillis, for example, to *Female Apostacy* which gives us a somewhat cleverly drawn picture of the young woman in church preoccupied with the vanities of dress and social status:

> She goes to Church (as Men t'a Coffeehouse)
> To Paraphrase on all she sees and knows,
> O're all the Crowd she lets her fancy roam,
> Then ridicules 'em when she comes at home;
> Reflects on those that nodded in her Pew,
> And Madam such a one, was all in new;
> Whose gown with Silk and Stuff was intermix'd;
> She knows such trifles better than the Text;
>
> (2)

The accusation is a thoroughly conventional one, and the cleverness of the verse does not save it from being so. In contrast, Swift's portrayal of Phillis in church shows us that Phillis's attempt to worship God is quite confused with her effort to call attention to her "bare" bosom and attract male worshippers of her person (see Swift 1: 222; lines 9–18). Given Phillis's narcissistic character, it is no wonder that she is seduced by the romantic fantasy of an elopement with "a serving man of low degree."

Swift's stance in "Phillis," though indebted to the popular misogynous tradition, amounts to a significant understating of the hyperbolic denigration of earlier progress poems. Whereas earlier poets often rely heavily on sneering and heavy sarcasm, Swift employs less verbal irony than dramatic and situational irony. Phillis's letter to her father on her elopement is a splendid indicator of her romantic folly. Though it may parrot companionate ideology, her stock rationalization that "Marriages are made in Heaven" serves perfectly to foreshadow the hell she will create in her life. The narrator's seemingly neutral recounting of Phillis's behavior serves to satirize her much more effectively than heavier ridicule could do. In addition, the rapid pace of the narrative and the narrator's refusal to slow down to sermonize are in obvious contrast to the practice of earlier "progress" poets who do much ponderous moralizing.

Swift's use of a breathtaking narratorial pace to suggest the rapid certainty with which human action brings about moral consequences is one of his hallmarks. He uses it not only in "Phillis" but with devastating cruelty in "Corinna" (written 1711). "Corinna" contains a kind of progress poem in miniature as she moves from a "subtle Jade" at six, to a "Wit and a Coquette" at twelve, then becomes "half Whore, half Wife," and finally "Turns Auth'ress, and is *Curll's* for Life" (Swift 1: 150; lines 17–28). It is not just that Corinna's behavior has moral consequences (as is the case with Phillis), but her bad character has blossomed forth into a bad life and, by the satirist's logic, has made her a bad author. Swift is not trying to play fair with Mrs. Manley, and his use of the poisoned-well argument derived from the antifeminist logic of the progress poem makes his attack all the more malicious.[7] According to this logic, women only seem to progress; they actually remain what they always have been: coquettes, whores, monsters, and shrews.

"The Progress of Marriage" is structurally an even richer progress poem than "Phillis" or "Corinna." One of the main reasons is that Swift focuses on the behavior of both the dean and his bride as well as on the overall degeneration of their marriage. Basically, there are four stages in the "progress," though the second one is expanded greatly with fugue-like shifts between her routine activities and his. This section almost takes over the poem. In each stage increasingly we see the practical and moral consequences of the dean's ill-advised choice of a partner too young and worldly for him. Swift's poem is not only a progress poem but, in a sophisticated sense, an advice poem.

The first stage, the wedding day itself, is treated with a combination of mythological debunking and comic realism, especially in the description of the bridegroom with his "artificial Vigor." This section, however, is mainly static in plot movement, though it clearly establishes the disparity of the couple's ages and interests. This, as I indicated, is the chief reason for the eventual failure of their marriage.

Along with some snatches of conversation, the second section offers rapidly shifting contrasts of the dean and his wife's routine activities. Swift uses the day-in-the-life convention of cataloging the wife's daily activities: dressing, shopping, gossiping, riding in a coach or a sedan chair, going to a masquerade. However, he complicates the movement of this section by counterpointing her activities with her husband's: cheapening books, picking over his food, worrying over his accounts, calling the family to prayer.[8] When they cross paths, as they do several times, their life patterns are at odds, or, with symbolic appropriateness, they collide:

> If in her Coach she'll condescend
> To place him at the hinder End
> Her Hoop is hoist above his Nose,

> His odious Goun would soil her Cloaths,
> And drops him at the Church, to pray
> While she drives on to see the Play.
> He like an orderly Divine
> Comes home a quarter after nine,
> And meets her hasting to the Ball
> Her Chairmen push him from the Wall:
> (1: 292; lines 77–86)

The dean is repeatedly pushed to the side—both figuratively and literally—by the press of her affairs. "Progress" in the day-to-day life of this marriage tends to revolve around the wife. The husband exists as only a minor satellite. Since the marriage centers around the wife's entertainment and self-indulgence, the long-term "progress" of this marriage is predictable. It was obviously not based on a companionate equality from the start.

In the third section of the poem, we see the couple a year into the marriage. During this year Lady Jane has miscarried twelve times. The failure of the marriage to produce a child, which might give the marriage a positive direction, is emphasized by the repetition of more fruitless cycles, in this case the wife's monthly ones. The accusation of fruitlessness is compounded by the trifling diversions Lady Jane undertakes at Bath:

> His Money and her Time employs
> In musick, Raffling-room, and Toys,
> Or in the cross-bath seeks an Heir
> Since others oft have found one there;
> (1: 294; lines 125–28)

The economy of the arrangement between the couple is satirically perfect. Since the dean claims to have spent all his money before they go to Bath, she wastes her time (as well as his remaining money) when they get there. The suggestion that Lady Jane may not have relied just on the *waters* of the *cross-bath* to bring about conception is also appropriate since the dean at fifty-three is overspent, and a younger man might be more potent.

The last stage of the marriage's progress is the direst, yet Swift handles it (excuse the pun) most swiftly. As in "Phillis," there is little moralizing and even less pity at the dean's demise, a death that comes on with shocking suddenness. The narrator's tone is crisply understated; he seems almost bored by the predictability of the dean's death. Only in the last verse paragraph does the narrator's anger at the wife's behavior break through. In this paragraph, Swift borrows again from the arsenal of popular invective as he curses the "Widow."

> Oh, may I see her soon dispensing
> Her Favors to some broken Ensign
> Him let her Marry for his Face,
> And only Coat of tarnish'd Lace;
> To turn her Naked out of Doors,
> And spend her Joynture on his Whores:
> And for a parting Present leave her
> A rooted Pox to last for ever.
> 		(1:295; lines 159–66)

"The Progress of Marriage" opens in the high comic tradition. Swift caricatures the mismatched couple using burlesqued mythological allusion to lighten the tone and distance the narrator from his subjects:

> Her Parents and her Friends consent,
> The Couple to the Temple went:
> They first invite the Cyprian Queen
> 'Twas answered, she would not be seen
> The Graces next, and all the Muses
> Were bid in form, but sent Excuses:
> Juno attended at the Porch
> With farthing Candle for a Torch,
> While Mistress Iris held her Train,
> The faded Bow distilling Rain.
> Then Hebe came and took her Place
> But showed no more than half her Face
> Whate'er these dire fore-bodings meant,
> In Mirth the wedding-day was spent.
> 		(1:290; lines 5–18)

There is light satire in this mythological comedy: Venus, the graces, and the muses do not sanction such a mismatch, and Hebe, the goddess of youth, honors the bride only. Even the weather is not auspicious since Juno brings only a farthing candle (not the sun); Iris, the goddess of the rainbow, brings instead the rain. Swift in fact gives a comic paradigm of the companionate marriage and makes everything, even the weather, affirm the mismatch.

If Swift opens in comic refinement, his conclusion, as just seen, is harsh with invective quite typical of a vein of vitriolic antifeminist satire begun in the Restoration by Rochester and continued by Oldham and the Grub Street satirists Gould and Ames. By employing such invective, Swift reveals that his satiric roots are in the popular misogynous tradition. He asks that his reader's awareness of the "progress" of marriage move in such regressive directions—from the sophisticated to the basic, from the detached and coolly ironic to the harshly antifeminist in the vein of Oldham, Gould, and Ames.[9] Swift's paternalism is enlightened, but it is based on the Christian notion of the corruptibility of the flesh. Within Swift's discourse, women such as Lady Jane who allow their sexuality to lead them into imprudent behavior epitomize this corruptibility.

After Swift, a progress poem treating marriage appears in at least one other instance: a character portrait entitled "The Modern Fine Lady" (1751), elegantly done in Popean couplets by Soame Jenyns, miscellaneous writer and political essayist. This piece is more in the refined comic tradition employed by Swift than in the cruder Grub Street tradition on which he sometimes drew. What makes this "character" a progress poem is that Jenyns does not just lump together the typical qualities of a fashionable aristocrat. Rather, as with earlier progress poems, he offers a coherent narrative graphically descriptive of each stage of the lady's life: as a fifteen-year-old in high society ("wing'd with diversions"), as a young woman courted by a variety of fops and beaus ("th'embroider'd colonel" and the "cropt ensign"), and as an older single woman who has lost her "fortune, health, and reputation" and who marries a title-seeking country squire out of desperation. We see her next as a married woman, looking elsewhere for the "transports" that the bridal-bed does not provide—first with a menagerie of beaux, clowns, templars, captains, parsons, and rakes, and later in nightly rounds of gambling at cards.

Jenyns then presents her "in ruins frightful jaws." Due to her profligate life-style, she must pawn all her jewels, furniture, and plate and go into exile at her lonely country seat. He paints a plaintive picture of her forced departure from the town:

> Now rumbling o'er the stones of *Tyburn-road*,
> Ne'er press'd with a more griev'd or guilty load,
> She bids adieu to all the well-known streets,
> And envies every cinder-wench she meets;
> (Chalmers 17: 599)

Arriving at the "ruin'd hall," she is greeted by the curate, tradesmen, and "great coated tenants." Jenyns's final portrayal of the lady is "a peevish mistress and a sulky wife" in the "sad decline of Life." The end of the lady is sad indeed, though poetically appropriate to her misspent life.

> At length half dead, half mad, and quite confin'd
> Shunning, and shunn'd by all of human kind,
> Even robb'd of that last comfort of her life,
> Insulting the poor curate's callous wife,
> Pride, disappointed pride, now stops her breath,
> And with true scorpion's rage she stings herself to death.
>
> (17: 599)

Like Swift, Jenyns concludes not playfully but in a harsh antifeminist tone, one that exhibits no sympathy for the final "progress" of the woman who began life on such a fashionable high note. As with Swift's Phillis, the "modern fine lady" sows the seeds of her frivolity in her youth and reaps the poison and corruption of her self-indulgent life in her old age. In this sense, Jenyns, like Swift, suggests that (some) women do not progress but remain constant in their folly.

Both Jenyns and Swift stand high above the earlier Grub Street poets who use the progress poem format. Though Jenyns lacks Swift's masterful control of irony and his vividly counterpointed narrative structures, Jenyns does approach Swift in his ability to integrate realistic detail into an engrossing, novellike story line. Jenyns's verse may be more refined than Swift's, perhaps in a negative sense. His couplets sometimes achieve a Popean dramatic brilliance, as in his description of the lady's forced departure from town. Building on the achievements of Swift in "The Progress of Marriage" and in his other published progress poems, Jenyns perpetuates the antifeminist logic of the format.

Why poets such as Swift and Jenyns choose to focus on a woman's progress rather than a rake's progress is perhaps because the rake's progress had been overworked, and poets in the mid-eighteenth century, as with novelists such as Richardson, were finding it increasingly interesting to explore women's roles and women's voices in their works. As Jean Hagstrum has shown in *Sex and Sensibility*, a new consciousness was emerging in eighteenth-century literature and art, and the examination of the feminine sensibility was an important part of it. Though they are harshly unsympathetic to a woman's struggle for self-realization, especially if it may involve romantic frivolity and self-indulgence, Swift, Jenyns, and other woman's progress poets do certainly pay attention to women and, by their choice of focus, show that they are quite concerned with the moral consequences of women's behavior. As satirists and advice poets drawing on the antifeminist popular tradition, Swift and Jenyns do not usually explore objectively the psychological motivations of women who act immorally, nor are they especially sympathetic to the emotional logic of the female sensibility.

Much more sympathetic treatments of women's "progress" can be found in the English novel, especially in *Clarissa* (1747–48) and in novels by women writers working in the Richardsonian tradition.[10] Generally speaking, the novel is the genre that supplants satiric poetry in handling marriage realistically. Perhaps the novel is the main cause of the demise of the women's progress poem. Novelists treat a woman's devolution not as a subject for satire and moral advice but as an experience for empathy. In the novel, women become as much victims of social pressures as moral agents responsible for their own fate. Once one complicates the question of who is to blame for a woman's fall, the progress poem as such is no longer possible.

Though its evolution as a format is attenuated, the progress poem moves in the same direction as other advice poems. With polemic and advice formats—and, as we will see in chapter 5, with poetic types—the overall movement involves the softening of antifeminism, the development of more empathetic, less paternalistic narratorial stances, the displacement of the satiric with the celebratory mode, and the emergence of a pro-companionate ideology within a feminized, affective sensibility. Because formats are closer than traditional poetic types to prose, the emergence of this sensibility in formats tends to anticipate and parallel more closely the development of a feminized consciousness in the novel. Unfortunately, unlike the novel, the evolution of poetry is not toward increasing realism but toward lyrical effusiveness and romanticized celebration of marriage as a heaven. As we will see next, this vitiates the articulation of the companionate ideal and opens it to hypocrisy.

CHAPTER FOUR

A Bargain Between Two Partners in a Trade

AS THE PRECEDING CHAPTER SHOWS, THE PRIMARY topic of advice poets is the proper choice of mate; for poets of the long eighteenth century the chief cause of improper choice of marriage partners is the marriage of convenience or, more bluntly, marriage for money. The satiric attack on the marriage of convenience as a hellish or crass debasement of the sacrament or social bond of marriage occurs not just, as I showed in chapters 1 and 2, in hostile antimarriage polemical arguments drawing on libertine or prudential ideology. As we saw in chapter 3, it also is central to hortatory poems, and as such comes to develop a more normative pro-companionate thrust.

Satires on marriages made for money have a basis in the socioeconomics of the period. There are indications that more money was changing hands in marriage settlements and that marriage settlements were becoming increasingly important in making or rescuing the fortunes of families. Sir John Habakkuk, for example, argues that marriage "was the single most important factor in the 'rise of great estates'" (Bonfield 486). In the Restoration, in addition to responding to socioeconomic phenomena, the attack on marriages for money implies, within the mythology of the heaven-hell dichotomy, that marriage previously, perhaps before the Civil Wars, had been entered into for reasons other than financial aggrandizement and that marriage in the Restoration had fallen away from some spiritual ideal or religious standard. Unlike the Grub Street polemical poets whose hyperbolically polarized arguments for and against marriage may reflect the contradictory tendency of Calvinistic Protestant theology both to abhor and affirm sexuality, a few Restoration satirists from the tradition of wit who attack marriage for money have recourse to the myth of a golden age when marriages were sacred and uncorrupted by greed. This myth may reflect a conservative Anglican (and Tory) ethos that looks back to a sacramental ideal.

Though almost no Restoration marriage satire articulates this ideal fully, one can look to the Anglican marriage "form" and the vows contained in it for its complete statement. It is true, as John Gillis points out, that the connection between marriage and the Christian church is a relatively recent one in western European history; the involvement of the priesthood in the marriage ceremony began as late as the twelfth century. Yet by the sixteenth century "most people were bringing their vows to the church as the final step in the marriage process, . . . though they reserved for themselves the right to make their own betrothals" (Gillis 20). Both in historical fact and in the popular imagination, a church ceremony and its attendant vows must have been central to most persons' conception of marriage.

In official Anglican theology, marriage was a sacred and indissoluble union, sealed by the bride and groom in a religious vow before the altar of God. The union was mystical in nature and was in essence above the law of man: "What God hath joined together, let no man put asunder." For centuries marriage had found its spiritual sanction in the analogy between the union of the husband and wife and of Christ and the Church. It must be granted that since the time of Henry VIII's break with Rome, marriage was no longer an actual sacrament in which grace accompanies the couple's consent to join together. Yet marriage was in effect a sacrament in everything but name.[1]

It is a commonplace of intellectual history that the execution of Charles I gave a mortal blow not only to the king himself, but to the divine sanction of his right to rule. In a similar way the social and political turmoil of the Interregnum brought temporarily under challenge the Anglican church's spiritual authority over marriage that had prevailed in previous centuries. Especially since the time of Henry VIII, political and social forces and the pressure of Calvinist and Lutheran theology had always asserted some measure of secular influence on the church's spiritual control, but the Commonwealth broke abruptly with past practice. The Marriage Act of 1653 provided "for banns to be read and marriages to be contracted in the presence of civil magistrates in places other than the parish churches" (Haw 65). Although the Marriage Act of 1653 lapsed in 1660, its impact was significant, if only ideologically, for it marked a clear effort to establish marriage as a secular institution. The Act effectively wrested control of marriage from its lax administration by church officials and put it into the hands of civil officials who would enforce marriage regulations more rigorously.

The underlying motive for this change, as John Gillis suggests, was to control marriages between the poor so that they did not become a burden on the ratepayers in the parish. Even when the Marriage Act lapsed in 1660, couples wishing to marry were often screened by a vigilant parish "which asked for securities when paupers announced their intention to marry. Money," says Gillis, "was speaking with increased authority" (89).

The growth of the marriage market, especially the increase in the amount of money changing hands, is a striking manifestation of the secularization of marriage, especially in the upper and upper middle classes. As they were conceived at the beginning of the long eighteenth century, satires on marriages for money may in part be a response to the loss of a religious standard. However, as the ideology of satirists develops in more secular directions, the heaven that the predominantly male satirists idealize increasingly becomes a romantic, domesticated one, a heaven in which the husband is rewarded more by the blissful love of his bride than her dowry. Women poets join the attack on marriage for money, especially after 1700 when they modify satiric formats to admit an element of the sentimental or the romantic. Women poets usually reinforce their attacks with the antilibertine ideology they employ to quash the male argument for sexual freedom (and the double standard). In the later era, the ideology of both male and female satirists becomes strongly pro-companionate and their tonal stances more empathetic, even in places celebratory.

One of the major achievements of English literature of the late medieval period and the Renaissance, especially in the work of Chaucer, Spenser, Shakespeare, and Milton, was the softening of the opposition between love and marriage and the integration of courtly materials into a popular romantic tradition that celebrated what Alfred Harbage calls "monogamic idealism." In this tradition, forced marriages were portrayed negatively and romantic love as a basis for marriage was celebrated. Initially, however, conservative Restoration satires on marriage for money are less glorifications of monogamic idealism than pointed indictments of the materialism and greed of an aggressively corrupt and secular age, an age increasingly dominated by Whig interests. Later satires on marriage for money could be said in some ways to embrace these interests as they develop a secular and romantic pro-companionate ideology.

A secular ideology stands behind the prevalent concern with the mismatched hope, the substitution of money for youth. This attack becomes pervasive in the long eighteenth century and serves as the basis for satires of specific mismatches (as opposed to sweeping censure of the corruption of the institution of marriage). Both sorts of attacks occur throughout the period, but the former emerges as more poignant since it concerns society's willingness to repress healthy marital sexuality for profit. Satire treats young males without an inheritance who chose to marry widows for their estates and, more pitiful, young women in their prime forced by mercenary parents to marry older men who are unattractive, impotent, or both. Though it most frequently assumes a male voice, early era satire in its attack on marriage for money can be seen as essentially progressive, especially as it condemns woman's social victimization.

In the later era, the marriage market itself becomes more lucrative. Advice poetry intended for upper-middle-class youth in fact temporizes with this social reality when it condemns mismatches made out of greed but at the same time recommends prudence in choosing a marital partner equal in social background and wealth. Satire persists as the predominant mode for the attack on marriage-as-trade, but the harsh, sweeping indictments of the early era become one extreme in a spectrum of attack whose other extreme tends toward gothic sentimentalism. At the center of the spectrum is lighter, more fashionable, satiric-comic poetry. This type of satire is prevalent in mid-century, but later in the period satire increasingly begins to alternate with a more empathetic, feminized celebratory mode. Poems with such alternations can make us cognizant of the contradictory, even hypocritical, stances of marriage poets who romanticize free choice in love but warn against imprudent matches.

Especially with poems such as these, one must give credence to revisionist critics who argue that the flaw is in companionate ideology itself. It perpetuates patriarchal control under the illusion of freedom of choice. Such contradictions must eventually collapse, and, by the end of the century, satire finally gives way to full-blown romanticization of the ideal. The majority of male and female poets opt for feminized celebration over masculine satire as the vehicle for promulgating a thoroughly secular companionate ideology, an ideology driven in large part by class, property, and money.

The Early Era

As satire evolves throughout this era, it attempts increasingly, but sometimes unsuccessfully, to move beyond attacks on the negative reality of marriage for money in the present and the idealization of marriage in a mythical golden age. Early efforts to affirm the companionate ideal in the present or future often fail because poets are paradoxical or ironic, because they are unable to make the shift from satire to celebration, or because they employ cumbersome means to do so. The earliest direct attacks on marriages for money in the Restoration tend to be qualified by witty irony and paradox, while the attacks made in the last twenty years or so of the seventeenth century seem more to be sweeping broadside shots at the social abuse.[2] Attacks become increasingly forthright and generalized toward the end of the era as the opposition to marriage-as-trade gains force and focus.

While sweeping attacks on debased and hellish marriages continue into the eighteenth century, poets (mostly male) also often employ more particularized ways of dramatizing egregious mismatches. Sweeping satiric condemnations persist and even increase in number, but poets also improve on the seventeenth-century satiric-comic tradition of attacking a specific mismatch, especially a marriage in which a young, attractive woman is bound to an old, wealthy man. Early eighteenth-century poets not only give us stereotypical portraits of impotent, unattractive husbands in their dotage as earlier poets had done but also convey their satire in dramatic monologues that create a pointed narrative interest. Speakers introduce biographical detail to involve the reader more personally in the satiric attack. As we will see in the case of Sarah Fyge Egerton, the evocation of pathos through particularized autobiographical narrative can prove more effective than more generalized portraits of stereotypical mismatches. Because of their focus on individual cases, the later poets frequently can take the option of recommending or celebrating marriage between partners matched in age and interests. While poets of the early era search for the most effective means to dramatize their attack on marriage for money, all poets—male and female—represent the marriage of convenience in one way or another as a hellish evil.

A product of the early Restoration that bases its satire on a pattern of contradictory wit is Samuel Butler's perverse little "Satyr upon Marriage." This poem relies heavily on ironic paradox to tease the reader into thought. Butler's speaker ironically commends marriages made in pagan times by "civil Contract" between "two Partners, that set up a Trade," as superior to modern marriages. Marriages at present, says the speaker, are only used as a staging area for gallantry and "modish Lust." What's more, if a marriage that is not more than a business arrangement is set at naught,

> There was no Conscience,
> Nor faith invaded, in the Strictest Sense;
> No Canon of the Church, nor Vow was broke.
> (*Satires* 56; lines 5–9)

It would be a plausible reading of Butler's satire that he seriously advocates marriages by "civil Contract." However, anyone familiar with the intensity of Butler's attack on marriages for money in the marriage debate in *Hudibras* III.i would recognize Butler's irony in "Satyr upon Marriage." We live in a Christian age, not in pagan times, Butler seems actually to be saying. Consequently, those who marry must do so according to the canons of the church and must not violate either conscience or their vows. Through his perverse irony and indirection, Butler can lead us to believe he is a radical, but his underlying position in "Satyr upon Marriage" is no doubt socially traditional and theologically orthodox—hostile to the Calvinist idea of marriage as a "civil Contract" and supportive of the high Anglican conception of it as a sacred "vow" unifying man and woman as "one flesh to signify Christ and the Church" (Bailey 187).

Looking again at the marriage debate in *Hudibras* III.i (1678), we see that Butler employs a pattern of contradictory wit here as well, yet he is more forthright than in "Satyr upon Marriage" in attacking the debasement of marriage to the level of a business deal. In fact, so that people make no mistake about the coarseness of such a mercenary marriage, he has the hard-mouthed widow characterize it as a grotesque beast engaging in some hellish form of sexual congress with its double. It is not the union of partners who give themselves to one another in love but the greedy self-doubling of a kind of hermaphrodite.

> *Marriage is but a Beast*, some say,
> *That carries double in foul way,*
> And therefore 'tis not to be admir'd,

>It should so suddenly be try'd:
>A bargain, at a venture made,
>Between two Part'ners in a *Trade*,
>(For what's infer'd but T'have and t'hold,
>But something past away, and sold?)
>That as it makes but one, of two,
>Reduces all things else, as low:
>And at the best is but a *Mart*
>Between the one, and the other part,
>   (III.i.569–80)

As the widow continues her harangue against the degradation of marriage, she attacks the complicated and entangling entailment of estates. Under these, a husband might be compelled by law to pass on his property to a child born to his wife but not conceived by him. (The wife, on the other hand, was not obligated to own his bastard children.) In addition to entailment, the widow's satiric catalog of abuses includes the lack of any provision for divorce in civil law, the tendency of the wealthy partner to be exploited financially, the prevalence of fashionable affairs in place of marriage (which people are increasingly unwilling to risk), the corrosive force of jealousy ("a kind/Of *Clap*, and *Grincam* of the mind" [701–2]), and the physically corrosive force of venereal disease.

To a large extent, Butler seems to share the widow's negative assessment of marriage as a corrupt institution—a "bargain, at a venture made,/Between two Part'ners in a *Trade*." Throughout the marriage debate she is, for all intents and purposes, Butler's spokesperson. Nevertheless, as Hudibras characterizes her in III.i.757–60, she talks in the cynical voice of a coffeehouse wit or a fashionable libertine railer at marriage. Her hyperbolic narrative is thus slightly suspect, or rather it is not all that Butler wants to say about marriage.

An added dimension of Butler's satire on marriage-as-trade comes from an unexpected source: the mouth of the hypocritical Presbyterian Knight, Hudibras. Throughout *Hudibras*, its hero is repeatedly made ridiculous by the actions and arguments of the sharp-witted widow. Yet in the marriage debate, as one of the commentators in Grey's edition of Hudibras pointed out, there is a curious lapse in the widow's pattern of victories: "The Knight seems to have too much Courage and good Sense to be baffled by the artful Widow; for he defends Matrimony with more Wit, and a greater Justness, than she had discovered in ridiculing it"

(Grey 2: 170; line 757n). When we do read Hudibras's defense of marriage, we are surprised that our hero offers arguments that appear to rescue marriage from its debasement in the widow's marriage-as-trade harangue. Marriage, says Hudibras, and the division of mankind into two sexes were carefully arranged by nature. Marriage has never been out of fashion,

> Unless among the *Amazons*,
> Or *Vestal Fryers*, and *Cloyster'd Nuns*
> Or *Stoicks*, who to bar the *Freaks*,
> And loose Excesses of the *Sex*;
> Preposterously would have all Women,
> Turn'd up, to all the World, in common:
> (III.i.819–24)

Marriage determines inheritances, rights to lands and titles, even the succession to thrones. Peace or war can be established by marriage. Marriage is the foundation of honor; without it

> All women would be of one piece,
> The virtuous *Matron*, and the *Miss*.
> The Nymphs of *chast Diana's Train*,
> The same with those in *Lewkners-lane*;
> (III.i.863–66)

Most important, marriage has the

> Pow'r to settle
> Th'interests of Love, perpetual,
> An *Act* and *Deed*, that makes one Heart
> Become another's counter part,
> And *passes Fines* on Faith and Love
> Inrol'd, and Registred above,
> To seal the slippery knot of Vows,
> Which nothing else but Death can lose:
> (III.i.923–30)

Hudibras's reasons sound convincing. Because they come so close to the standard family order–civil order arguments advanced in the middle and late seventeenth century by Protestant defenders of marriage, it is difficult to dismiss them as the courtly sophistries of a would-be romance hero.

This much and more can be said in support of Hudibras's apology for marriage. On the other side of the question, at least one telling point can be summoned up in defense of the widow's portrayal of marriage as a debased institution. From the moment Hudibras first sights the widow when he is locked in the stocks, his mercenary motives in courtship are blatant. Butler thus adds another dimension to his satire on marriage-as-trade: the dramatic irony of Hudibras's desperate effort to get his hands on the widow's jointure by marrying her.

The point of the satire then may be *not* that Hudibras's elaborate defense of marriage is wrong but that Hudibras exploits sound arguments for debased motives. Or perhaps in a further irony, Butler may be pointing up the hypocrisy of Protestant apologists for marriage who defend marriage for its legal, commercial, and political advantages, not for its proper religious role of uniting two loving souls together in the eyes of heaven. In either case, Hudibras's hypocritical debasement of marriage is clearly evident in the language of business deals and legal jargon that he uses in marriage's defense: "settle/Th'interests," "An *Act* and *Deed*," "*passes Fines* on Faith and Love/Inrol'd, and Registred above." Even when Hudibras proposes marriage to the widow, his crass language sullies the phrases he borrows from the marriage service. Hudibras asks for the widow's

> plighted Faith . . . and Word
> You past in Heaven, on Record.
> Where all Contracts, to have, and t'hold
> Are everlastingly inrol'd,
> (III.i.539–42).

In this we have another symptom of how Hudibras's debased idea of marriage falls short of the spiritual union it should be. As the widow says:

> there are no *Bargains driv'n*
> Nor *Marriages* clap'd up in *Heaven*,
> And that's the reason as some guess,
> There is no Heav'n in Marriages:
> (III.i.545–48)

Butler's attack on marriage-as-trade, no doubt the most ironically complex attack in Restoration verse, goes beyond earlier satires in his ingenious use of the debate format to dramatize contradictory visions: the debased, even hellish state of marriage in Restoration society and the "Heav'n" that should be "in Marriage."

In the late Restoration, satiric attacks on marriage-as-trade offer a vision of marriage for money as negative as Butler's, but without his richly ironic manipulation of contradictory points of view. Poets give us harangues against the corruption of marriage and at the same time try to suggest what marriage should be. The task however of representing the negative and positive in the same poem is not always handled adeptly, and poets sometimes find it difficult to make transitions from their treatments of the hell and heaven of marriage and to integrate the satiric and celebratory modes. This problem of poetic logistics has to do with the hyperbole toward which the myth of marriage as a hell and heaven seems to drive poets and also ultimately with the contradictory attitudes toward marriage and sexuality rooted in Protestant theology.

In *The Malecontent; A Satyr: Being the Sequel of the Progress of Honesty, or a View of Court and City* (1684), Thomas D'Urfey suggests the heaven of marriage by looking back to a mythical golden age:

> Parents of old Conscientiously did prove,
> In th' days of unsophisticated love,
> That Marriage was design'd, and hearts were pair'd above.
>
> (27)

D'Urfey's "hearts were pair'd above" may lament a past when the marital bond was sacramental. The hell of marriage is embodied in a thinly disguised present easily identifiable as the Commonwealth and Restoration; this the "Satirist," the main character and speaker in the poem, attacks broadly. Surveying the general corruptions of the age from a high cliff, the "Satirist" offers an overview of "the general face of Nature," a face which is "Impure/With an Infection spotted beyond Cure." At the center of this infection is the contemporary marriage mart.

> Pride the vain Idol of the Court is made,
> And Love our darling Joy is grown a Trade:
> Beauty is sold as Merchandizing ware,
>   At who gives most like horses in a Fair;
> Settlements, Joyntures, Bargains are your task,
> Your merit is the last dull thing they ask.
>
> (27)

D'Urfey's "Satirist" calls directly for young women to resist marriages arranged by greedy and proud parents since

> Destruction lies in matches where the heart,
>   Instead of being in all, is not part:
>
> (28)

More so than Butler, D'Urfey's speaker emphasizes the importance of hearts and souls being paired; he does so two or three times.

> Their onely question is, whether you know
> The Fool is rich, if he be so
> No matter whether hearts are pair'd or no:
> (27)

A popular writer of songs, tales, satires, melodramas, and farces who was a friend of Charles II and James II, D'Urfey associates marital happiness with a "moderate state" and links unhappiness in marriage with "large heaps of wealth." Whereas Butler treats the connection of money and marriage only negatively, D'Urfey attempts to make the distinction that later marriage satirists and didactic poets will underscore between sufficient wealth and excessive wealth. With this distinction, we see in early form the myth of bourgeois marital happiness, the love-matched couple who live in the rose-covered cottage with just enough (but not too much) income to support their wants.

In contrast, a Restoration woman satirist in the aristocratic courtly tradition, Aphra Behn in "Song" (written before 1689), avoids the problem of treating the positive and negative in the same poem because she dwells almost entirely on the latter. She "deplores"

> Those matches . . . ,
> Whose bartering friends in council meet
> To huddle in a wedding sheet
> Some miserable pair that never met before.
> (Fullard 98)

"True bliss" is possible not for the married couple but only for the lover who, while the marriage brokers negotiate, "digs the richer mine."

A slightly later woman poet, Mary, Lady Chudleigh in "A Dialogue between Alexis and Astrea" (1703), maintains that compatibility of temperament is strongly to be desired, but choice is denied, especially for women, by the economics of matchmaking.

> *Astrea.* When Humors are alike, and Souls agree,
> How sweet! how pleasant must that Union be!
> But oh! that Bliss is but by few possest,
> But few are with the Joys of Friendship blest.
> Marriage is but a fatal Lott'ry made,
> Where some are Gainers, but the most betray'd:

>   The mild and froward, cruel and kind,
>   Are in unequal Chains by Fate confin'd:
>   (Poems 38)

Lady Chudleigh demonstrates a strong satiric awareness of the powerless position of women who have been reduced to trading commodities on the marriage market. In this "fatal Lott'ry," a few are lucky enough to marry their choice, but most end up in disastrous mismatches. Though Lady Chudleigh's satire is mainly negative in thrust, she, unlike Aphra Behn, admits for the few who find a compatible partner the blissful possibility of marriage as a heaven.

Sir Charles Sedley—wit, dramatist, and an associate of Lord Rochester, Lord Buckhurst, Sir Thomas Ogle, and other aristocratic libertines—contrasts the heaven of the ideal marriage with the hell of marriage-as-trade in "The Happy Pair: Or, A Poem on Matrimony" (published 1702 but written earlier). Taking broad satiric swipes at the corruption caused by marriage for money, Sedley's piece also contains idealized portraits of the love-matched couple. In the manner of Juvenal in his sixth satire and of D'Urfey, Sedley portrays a mythical golden age in which marriages were happy. Unlike the polygamous times "e'er Priest-craft did begin," described in the opening of *Absalom and Achitophel* (1681), Sedley's golden age is not a libertine's paradise, but a time when marriages were not debased by avarice and materialism. Sedley's portrayal of such a golden age is typical of conservative or Tory marriage satire that represents the happy couple as an ideal society has fallen away from rather than as a future aspiration.

Somewhat untraditional, however, is the heightened, even ecstatic language with which Sedley describes the quality of love between this couple. This sort of language we would never encounter in *Hudibras*, for example, or in Juvenal's sixth satire.

>   One Clasp, one Hug, one eager Glance was more
>   Than Worlds of Pearl, or Heaps of golden Ore.
>   He prais'd his priz'd Affection next his God,
>   And though[t] his wife the second chiefest Good,
>   Th' Heaven-born Dame brought to his longing Arms
>   Her Soul, her Beauty, and resistless Charms.
>   (16)

The fall from the golden age of love (and the loss of paradise) may have been caused by Adam's betrayal of it in innocence, or love may have been made into a "Malefactor" by Adam's "Lapse." A third possibility is that man's "acquir'd Excesses" have been so "daring" that love has been deemed a sin; here is a new explanation of "Man's First Disobedience."

Whatever the cause for the fall, the consequence, as Sedley portrays it, has been the corruption of the souls of partners who marry for money:

> Man, like the sordid Earth, from which he sprung
> Corrupts his Soul by a base heap of Dung,
> Forgetting the Celestial form he bore,
> He values not the Woman, but her Store:
> . . . .
>   The Woman too no less debas'd than he,
> Gives not her self, but for *Gratuity:*
> Sooths like a Merchant, with inveigling Art,
> Demands her *Joynture*, and keeps back her Heart.
> . . . .
>   Both Sexes now deprave their Noble Kind,
> While sordid Avarice corrupts the Mind.
>
> (17)

Sedley satirically emphasizes mankind's loss of happiness and peace of mind as he focuses with disgusting detail on the laughable and hideous mismatches produced by marrying for money. Using grotesque imagery of the sort that Butler would have been happy to own, Sedley paints vivid portraits of marital freaks and monsters to stand in contrast to his initial portrayal of Godlike man in paradise (18). Harsh satire intensifies as Sedley carries his attack on mismatches to its climax to represent the animallike "mutual Frenzy" of "A clam'rous Husband, and a brawling Wife."

> Hell and confusion seize the Place around,
> Nothing but mutual Frenzy's to be found.
>
> (19)

From this low point, the poet rises to consider the possibility of matches based in mutual love and respect for the other's abilities, but even these are condemned to the hell of failure because of the cynicism inspired by the corruption and greed of our world.

> The Woman loves the Golden Man she Weds.
> We'll think she brings with her Estate a Mind,
> Pure as her Sterling, from its Dross refin'd.

> Yet this is so unlikely to succeed,
> It Murders what it first design'd to Feed.
> He strait concludes her Passion a Pretence,
> Condemns her Soul, and lays the Crime on Sence.
> Argues, she only chose to be his Bride,
> To serve and gratifie her costly Pride:
>
> (21)

The poet presents a marriage "in which equal Passion both does draw," but this also fails since the husband is so preoccupied with business that he neglects to express his love.

The conservative satirist in Sedley continues to resist the celebrator of marriage until the conclusion when Sedley does finally admit the possibility of a couple who find their full happiness in one another:

> Each to the other proves a solid Bliss,
> Rich in themselves, no want of Happiness.
>
> (23)

Unlike Butler and D'Urfey, Sedley actually sets up a good couple to counterpoint his mismatched couples. Sedley's happy "Rustick Couple" possesses a mythic status and inhabits a world that has less reality to it than that the hellish, earth-bound couples inhabit (23). His portrayal of this couple leaves no doubt that the companionate ideal is established in marriage poetry as early as the 1690s. "The Happy Pair" is one of the earliest poems to fuse traditional satiric attacks on debased marriages with the myth of the happy marriage. Right from the start, we see the cost of establishing the ideal that poets will pay throughout the eighteenth century: the particularity and vivid realism of satire is often sacrificed to a nebulous, quasi-mythical celebratory mode.

In the early eighteenth century, as warnings against marriage for money evolve artistically, they increasingly exhibit a secular, romanticized companionate ideology. Satirists persist in making sweeping satiric attacks on the social abuse of arranging marriages for financial advantage, marriages in which money has been substituted for love and sexuality as the binding force. More frequently, however, poets dramatize the evils of the marriage of convenience by focusing on individual couples who are comically, disgustingly, or pathetically mismatched.

This convention of treating individual mismatches goes well back into the seventeenth century when poets such as Waller, Cleveland, and Davenant serve up witty satiric treatments of youth tied to age. These poets usually work in a tradition of wit or high verbal ingenuity. For example, satire in Cavalier poet Edmund Waller's epigram "To One Married to an Old Man" (1645) results from a clever quibble on the idea that marrying an old man is like being buried alive.

> Since thou woulds't needs (bewitch'd with some ill charms!)
> Be bury'd in those monumental arms:
> All we can wish, is—May that earth lie light
> Upon thy tender limbs! And so good night!
> (Chalmers 8: 81)

The quibble succeeds because of the potential of "earth" to carry both literal and figurative meanings. Little is said in general about the evils of marrying for money; the witty portrait speaks for itself.

The wit of Royalist satirist John Cleveland depends more on hyperbolic tropes and ingeniously recondite conceits. In Cleveland's "On an Alderman Who Married a Very Young Wife" (1651), he uses such wit to create comic disgust at the mismatch:

> His brinish Spittle from his Jawes
>   Hangs dingle dangle to his Coate
> Like *Hocus* Pocus when he draws
>   Some yards of riband through his throat.
> (Cleveland 77)

Again, there is little generalized moralizing against the social abuse that led to the particular mismatch.

In the late Restoration and early eighteenth century, poets continue the pattern of grotesque satiric portraits of a mismatched couple exemplified by Waller and Cleveland; at the same time, they move beyond such strained wit to explore affective tonal stances, using the dramatic monologue or autobiographical confession to convey them.[3] Looking at four contrasting poems by Sarah Fyge Egerton and by Joseph Mitchell, we can observe advances in tonal effectiveness in the way Egerton and Mitchell handle the basic convention of ridiculing a mismatched couple.

Sarah Fyge Egerton's "To Orabella, Marry'd to an Old Man" (1703) relies on heavy sarcasm and ingenious, almost Clevelandesque conceits to create disgust in Orabella and the audience:

> The monster Twin whose Brother grew from's Side,
> With all the stench he suffer'd when he dy'd,
> Is a just Emblem of so yok'd a Bride.

> But Ptisick, Gout and Palsie have their Charms,
> And did intice you to his trembling Arms:
> Kind amorous Glances from his hollow Eyes,
> Did your gay Breast with rapturous Joys surprize
> Ah! who can blame to see a yielding Maid,
> By all those blooming Charms to Love betray'd.
>
> (37)

Egerton's mismatched couple is a freakish Siamese twin, joined to the carcass of his putrefied brother. Moving beyond her bizarre metaphysical conceit, Egerton adopts a sisterly tone in chastising Orabella directly for her greed in accepting such a mate.

> What strong Persuasions made you thus to wed,
> With such a Carcass scandalize your Bed?
> Sure 'twas no earthly Gain that charm'd you to't,
> Nothing but hopes of heaven should make me do't.
>
> (36–37)

With such a partner Arabella's marriage will be a hell on earth. It will partake of heaven only in the afterlife, perhaps when she has achieved martyrdom. Egerton may also be saying that her female self-respect would keep her from such a marriage; she could only be compelled to it by fear of damnation for disobedience to her father.

Joseph Mitchell's "To an Humorist, Who Married a Most Ugly Superannuated Maid" (1729) is similar to Egerton's "To Orabella" in his use of heavy sarcasm. However, Mitchell, a Scots dramatist known as "Sir Robert Walpole's Poet," relies less on grotesque Clevelandesque tropes and more on direct exclamations of gross disgust.

> Who ever saw so wide a *Mouth*,
> Stretch'd, like the *Poles*, from North to South?
> The *Lips* how thin! the *Teeth* how black!
> That Sallow *Skin*! that Bow-bent *Back*!
> These hagged *Eyes*! this tow'ring *Nose*!
> *Breath*, that outvies *Beargarden*, *pos*!
> In *Her*, all Imperfections meet,
> And every one outstinks *Fish-street*!
>
> (1: 300–301)

Mitchell's wit is less subtle and his allusions less recondite than Egerton's, though he is sometimes capable of a vein that combines bawdy insult with clever humor:

> But *Thou*, great Hero, durst encounter
> Deformity itself, and mount her,
> Like brave Saint *George*, thou lay'st thy Leg on
> The Top of this prodigious *Dragon*;
>
> (1: 301–2)

Mitchell also does more to create a stage persona for his speaker.

> Ods Zookers, honest, gallant Harry,
> What put it in thy Head to *marry?*
> Or, if thou could'st not help thy Fate,
> Why did'st thou chuse a *monstrous Mate?*
>
> (1: 229–300)

Mitchell's speaker blusters in amazement, rails in contempt, and salts his colloquial speech with fashionable oaths. He is clearly a dramatic character, though a stereotyped one, while Egerton's narrator seems to speak more from the heart. This may have an autobiographical basis since Sarah had an acrimonious relationship with her second husband, Thomas Egerton, a clergyman and wealthy widower twenty years older than she (see Lonsdale 26–27).

Mitchell achieves more tonal dimension and authenticity in another poem treating a mismatch, "To a Young Lady, on Her Marriage with an Old Gentleman" (1729). Though he relies on comically exaggerated tropes to mock Aurora's choice of husband, his figures of speech are not so grotesque as Egerton's nor so gross as his in "To an Humorist."

> Since all thy Fishing but a Frog hath catch'd,
> *Aurora*, now, have I not Cause to rage?
> Shou'd I not grieve, to see thy Morning match'd
> With one, who's in the Evening of his Age?
>
> (240)

More so than the two previous poems, Mitchell gives expression to emotion that is a little more complex than the stock scorn or disgust of the standard mismatch poem. Mitchell's speaker is angry, jealous, and grieved. But above all these, he finally is pitying with more than a tinge of spite.

> More than my own, her Fortune I deplore,
> Who, now condemn'd to monumental Arms,
> Hears the dull Sot upon her Bosom snore,
> Unconscious of his Duty, and her blooming Charms.
>
> (241)

The "Fortune" of Aurora is not the wealth and title (the armorial bearings) of the family she has married into, but the "monumental arms" of her snoring husband, asleep on her breast. Too bad, says the speaker in effect, that Aurora got what she bargained for.

Of the four mismatch poems by Egerton and Mitchell, Egerton's "On My Wedding Day" (1703) is undoubtedly the most untraditional. In fact, the tone of Egerton's poem is not at all satire but an autobiographical lament for the death of her first husband, Edward Field, and, even more, for the failed happiness of her marriage. This marriage, as she tells us, was poisoned by its being forced upon her, presumably by her greedy father. Although she learned near the end to "celebrate" her wedding day, that came too late.

> I learn'd at last to celebrate thee too;
> Tho' it was long e'er I could be content,
> To yield thee more than formal Complement;
> If my first Offering had been Free-Will,
> I then perhaps might have enjoy'd thee still;
> But now thou'rt kept like the first mystick Day,
> When my reluctant Soul did Fate obey,
> And Trembling Tongue with the sad Rites comply'd,
> With timerous Hand th'amazing Knot I ty'd,
> While Vows and Duty check'd the doubting Bride.
>
> (71)

Like the other mismatch poems, this one also warns against arranged marriages. The protest is complicated, however, and made more dramatically authentic by the speaker's mourning, an emotion which finally overcomes her resentment against the way her marriage was made. Because of the speaker's evident honesty in reporting her contradictory personal emotions, the reader is more inclined to take her attack on marriage-as-trade seriously.[4]

A problem faced by satiric narrators in the early era is to find a way to represent the heaven of marriage that will counterpoint their attack on the hell of marriage-as-trade. Poets offering sweeping indictments of the corrupt practice have a more difficult time suggesting the ideal since the celebratory mode tends to clash with the satiric mode and the implied (sacramental) ideal that may underlie it. Sedley's "The Happy Pair" is an illustration of this lack of integration. Poets attacking specific mismatches are perhaps more able to imply a secular companionate ideal by the tone of their attack on the negative reality. In a candid and touching autobiographical piece such as Sarah Egerton's "On My Wedding Day," the reader is given a realistic sense of the happiness that eluded the narrator because of her arranged marriage. Egerton's piece exemplifies the tendency of the most obviously progressive warnings against marriage for money to rely on affective narratorial stances.

THE LATER ERA

In the long eighteenth century among the aristocracy and the upper middle class, the numbers of arranged marriages may well have been on the upswing. There is certainly documentation indicating that the amount paid in marriage portions was increasing significantly.

> The average of the examples collected by Stone for the peerage was £3,800 per daughter in 1600–24, £7,800 in 1650–74, and £9,700 by 1675–1724. Before the end of the seventeenth century the precedent of portions of £25,000 for girls who were not their fathers' heiresses, or even only daughters, had been set by the Russells, Dukes of Bedford, and in the eighteenth century other ducal families felt constrained to follow it. (Clay 27)

Perhaps because large marriage portions were so much a fact of life, especially among the upper and upper middle classes, the ambivalence toward marriage for money may increase in some later era poetry. A number of didactic poets seem to intensify their condemnation of marriage-as-trade. At the same time they may acknowledge the importance of money in keeping the wolf from the door and counsel prudence in choosing a mate who is similar in age, interests, wealth, and social background. This ambivalence can be judged as contradictory. It tends to taint the companionate ideal with the hypocrisies of the moneyed classes that fostered it. We see how these hypocrisies become more blatant as satire weakens, evolves toward and alternates with the sentimental and the comic, and finally yields to romantic celebration.[5]

In spite of, or perhaps because of, the increase in the size of the portions paid, much later era verse persists in straightforward condemnation of marriage-as-trade. Some harsh traditional satire still appears as in *Marriage à la Mode: An Humorous Tale* (1746), and a new romantic-sentimental subgroup is enlisted in the attack. More common than these two extremes is the lighter satiric-comic verse by such fashionable poets as Cambridge, Shenstone, and Cowper. Later in the century, as exemplified in Francis Dobbs's *Modern Matrimony* (1773), the satiric mode increasingly alternates with the celebratory mode, and, by the end of the period, celebration finally pushes satire to the back burner. Though celebration unmistakably establishes the companionate ideal, the softening and eventual displacement of the satiric attack on marriage debased by money amounts finally to a significant loss of ethically based social criticism. Such criticism persists in the prose of writers such as Mary Wollstonecraft and in the novels of Smollett, Burney, Austen, Radcliffe, and others, but it mainly disappears from poetry.

Before mid-century, one of the favorite formats for attacks on marriage-as-trade becomes the realistic verse narrative; a good example of such a protonovel is *Marriage à la Mode: An Humorous Tale* (1746).[6] Even though this piece calls itself a humorous tale, it stands as an indicator that harsh satire, filled with graphic detail, persisted well into the eighteenth century. Six cantos long in iambic tetrameter couplets, *Marriage à la Mode* explicates Hogarth's six prints by the same title; it is a direct commentary on the prints as well as a satiric tale in its own right.[7] As both the tale and the prints are constructed, they are an exaggerated demonstration of the train of ill consequences that can result from a typical eighteenth-century, upper-middle- or upper-class marriage settlement. In its ultrarealism, the narrative sequence takes on a mythic force in dramatizing how rapidly a marriage for money can deteriorate. As the poet says,

> Whatever Parents may foresee,
> Marriage, they say, is Fate's Decree;
> But nicely scan the present Age,
> And you may tell without Presage,
> It is a Bargain wildly driv'n.
> Without the Interpose of Heav'n.
>
> (3)

Though they both operate at the mythic level, the achievement of the tale and the prints is that they offer so much concrete detail that the thesis of the satire becomes credible. Both are vivid delineations of the hell that marriage-as-a-bargain can become.

In contrast to the narrative *Marriage à la Mode* is Stephen Duck's romantic verse narrative *Alrick and Isabel* (1740). Featuring a sensationalized sentimentality, this tale dramatizes the grotesquely tragic consequences of parents' forcing a daughter to marry a man she does not love. Raymond's failed courtship of Isabel and her arranged marriage to the noble Alrick are the fare we have come to expect in such romantic tales; so is

Raymond's joining the army in order to sacrifice himself in some heroic enterprise. A satiric-gothic dimension is added when Isabel unknowingly consumes her slain lover's heart for dinner. Dying on the battlefield, Raymond had requested it be sent to her. Alrick in his jealousy surreptitiously introduces it into her main dish, which she unknowingly commends as "a sav'ry pleasant meat" (14).

Whether or not Duck is purposely being camp, the heart-for-dinner business verges on silliness, especially when Isabella purposely devours the last morsel after Alrick tells her what she has eaten. Duck's tale, however, is notable for an early use of courtly love arguments in a century that usually rigorously avoided treating adultery sympathetically, a century in which, according to de Rougemont, the courtly myth was eclipsed and there was a resurgence of marriage as "the basic institution" (206–9).

We see this sympathy in the conclusion where the power of romantic love is celebrated.

> In vain we for our Children make a Feast,
> If loathing Nature sickens at the Taste.
> Nature is free, and cannot Force approve
> In any kind; and least of all, in Love.
> For Love's a God tenacious of his Right,
> Whom only voluntary Vows delight.
> (16)

Alrick and Isabel does not, of course, approve adultery in any direct sense, though the underlying sentiment inclines toward it. Isabel's consumption of Raymond's heart may have sexual resonances. The reader, however, is permitted to sympathize with Isabel's vicariously adulterous repast only because she should rightfully have been allowed to marry Raymond. The attack on marriage-as-trade is effective in *Marriage à la Mode* because of its ultrarealistic narrative detail; it works in *Alrick and Isabel* because of the bizarre emotionality of the plot. *Alrick and Isabel* is an early manifestation of the romantic gothic strain that becomes so popular in the novel in the late eighteenth century, especially among women writers. Conflicts in this strain very often pit the affective sensibility, even the sexuality of a heroine, against the legal and socioeconomic restrictions of a patriarchal society.

Such conflicts are sometimes dramatized by women writers in verse narratives that anticipate or parallel those in novels.[8] An interesting example is Mary Collier's versification of "Spectator Vol. the Fifth. Numb. 375" (1762). In this tale, which seems an analog of Richardson's *Pamela*

(1740), the eldest daughter of a London middle-class family who have experienced financial reversals is pursued by an aristocrat with base designs (Collier 54–59). The daughter's problem is not that her parents force her to marry a man she despises but that the neighboring lord takes advantage of their economic plight when he proposes to take her on as his mistress. When the daughter refuses his dishonorable proposal, he recognizes her merits and marries her. Coincidentally, the mother unexpectedly receives payment of a long due debt so that we are not asked to believe that the aristocrat weds a completely portionless bride. This Cinderella story is a romantic one, and its sentimental celebration of the love marriage is a manifestation of a popular response to the way money could subvert wedlock.

Satire, as I said, remains the basic mode for condemnation of marriage-as-trade throughout most of the later era, even when it is mixed with comedy as it usually is. Satiric-comic verse can vary from the insulting to the fanciful with several shades of irony filling the middle of the spectrum. What makes such satiric poetry partly comic is that there is some acceptance of the social evil attacked. This never takes the form of approval but of cynical or bemused resignation to marriage for money as a fact of life. Often this resignation is directed toward a marriage that has already occurred or that will occur inevitably. Underlying the outward resignation to the social importance of wealth, there is almost always the sentiment that marriage for money is a debasement and that marriage for companionship is preferable.

Verses Occasioned by the Marriage and the Game Act (1753) by Richard Owen Cambridge, an Oxford-educated country gentleman and imitator of Pope, is on the surface playful and fanciful, a kind of comic pastoral. Miss Jenny goes down to her seat in the country, "quite sick of the town." She reassures a hare that now no poacher will dare to be seen with a gun or snare. This may be, the hare tells her, but her father may shoot the hare. In the same way, the provisions of the Hardwicke Marriage Act of 1753 will protect her from a clandestine marriage with a social interloper, but it will not save her from an ill-advised marriage with one of her own social class that her father might arrange for her.[9]

> By this act you are safe from each amorous spark,
> From the ensign, the curate, the butler, the clerk;
> But the first booby 'squire that shall knock at your gate,
> With a crack'd constitution and a mortgag'd estate

Shall transform (then adieu the poor pastoral life)
The contemplative nymph to a mope of a wife:
With your fortune redeem his confiscated lands,
And your father the foremost to publish the banns.
                                    (Chalmers 18: 291)

Cambridge's piece is a light, clever fantasy, yet the satire is direct enough. We are shown her father's power to ruin her life by marrying her to a "booby 'squire" "With a crack'd constitution and a mortgag'd estate."

Less fanciful and more insulting is William Shenstone's "To the Memory of an Agreeable Lady Bury'd in Marriage to a Person Undeserving Her." Printed in Dodsley's *Miscellany* (1758), this light but stinging piece attacks not so much a marriage of convenience as a marriage of desperation.

Gratia's unfortunate choice is treated only in the last stanza, yet the whole poem builds toward the comic clincher. Initially, the poet sets the stage for the conclusion by telling us with some seriousness of the wisdom of enduring a lesser evil to avoid a greater:

> 'Twas always held, and ever will,
>   By sage mankind, discreeter
> T'anticipate a lesser ill
>   Then undergo a greater.
>   (6: 216)

Shenstone gives us several straightforward applications of this wisdom; the last one concerns marriage:

> With numerous ills in single life
>   The bachelor's attended;
> Such to avoid, he takes a wife——
>   And much the case is mended.
>   (6: 216)

For the final application involving Gratia's marriage, the pattern is the same, but there is an added bite.

> Poor Gratia, in her twentieth year,
>   Foreseeing future woe,
> Chose to attend a *monkey* here,
>   Before an *ape* below.
>   (6: 216)

Proverbially, old maids are threatened with the humiliation of leading apes in hell. For Gratia, who married for financial security, her punishment will not be in her afterlife but in her unfortunate choice of a husband. Perhaps indicative of the increasing participation of young people in choosing a mate is Shenstone's blaming Gratia for her choice, not her parents.

Comic in a higher and more eloquent way is the irony in Cowper's "Happy the Man Whose Amorous Flame Has Found" (written c. 1750–55).[10] Cowper's poem seems to celebrate the happiness of a man who has fallen in love with and married a woman with money. On the surface at least, the poet approves of a social system that can sanction such fortuitous coincidences. Underneath, however, Cowper's attitude is strongly satiric as the progressions in his irony soon suggest.

> Happy the Man whose amorous Flame has found
> The Glorious Sanction of ten thousand pound,
> But happier he whose Eyes securely stray
> Where Thirty thousand mark the glittering way;
>
> (1:50)

The target of the irony is made clear when the poet treats the parents' attitude toward the young man who would marry a woman without a portion:

> Not so the Youth shall fare whose luckless Flame
> Haply shall light on some unmoney'd Dame;
> For him shall throb the trembling Parent's Heart,
> And sage Advice this Constant Truth Impart:
> My Son, let thy Principles correct:
> Love may allure, but Int'rest should direct.
> Venus when naked charms the Fool alone;
> Let but the Goddess put her Armour on,
> Her Golden Arms, that kindle keen Desire,
> The Grave shall worship and the wise admire.
>
> (1:50)

Better than any eighteenth-century poet previous to him, Cowper exposes the hypocrisy of the advice that love should always be controlled by prudence. Prudence is never counseled by parents to young men who have been lucky enough to fall in love with a woman with a large portion. Using the figure of Venus in golden armor (as opposed to naked),

Cowper symbolically reveals the wisdom of parents to be an artificial imposition on natural love, a barrier imposed by greed. Cowper's irony is deftly handled. He employs it not only to satirize the greed and hypocrisy of arranged marriages but also to praise marriage based on natural love. Unlike some poets who celebrate the bliss of marital love, Cowper magnificently avoids jejune enthusiasm.

Handling comically the contradiction between love and prudence, Cowper is an exception among poets of the later era treating marriage for money. In many didactic or celebratory poems, the formula of the couple as equally matched in sharing joys and sorrows may partially conceal more prudential concerns such as temperament, age, social background, and wealth. In other uses of this formula, poets may be more direct in stressing prudential concerns, even while they condemn marriage for money.

The "conduct poem" allegory "The Marriage of the Myrtle and the Yew. A Fable" (1758) is overt in discouraging Delia not to marry "beneath herself." When Delia (the Myrtle) makes an unfortunate marriage with her "Cousin" yew, the poet condemns the union. The yew is never to be placed in the garden or "to be borne by nymphs of taste," even though it is "fair, and large, and good" (Dodsley 3: 265–68). In "Marriage. Vision VII," Dr. Nathaniel Cotton, a general practitioner and the proprietor of a private madhouse, censures those who "barter youth and bloom for gold." Yet after "Poverty, that famish'd fiend," makes the prospective groom turn pale in fear, Hymen has "Love and Riches" join their hands (*Visions in Verse* [2nd ed., 1751]).

George Jeffreys explicitly praises a union based on "well-weigh'd choice." In "The Happy Pair; Occasioned by the Wedding of the Right Hon. the Lord and Lady Carnarvon, on the 22nd of March 1753" (1754), this praise is embedded in an extended and curious treatment of the marriage purified submotif.[11]

> We long had triumph'd in a warlike race,
> Fruit of the gen'rous love and warm embrace,
> Ere *Hymen's* couch, to sordid views resign'd,
> Unnerv'd the body, and debas'd the mind;
> Hands without hearts debauch'd by sloth,
> Too oft have sunk us to a feeble growth;
> And pleasure, tainted at the fountain-head,
> Has with degen'rate streams the land o'erspread:

> But, wise, and happy, in a well-weigh'd choice
> *Carnarvan* shall the growing age rejoice;
> His nuptial torch, advanc'd by noble birth,
> And bright with mutual love and mutual worth,
> Like That of *Egypt's Pharos*, shall extend
> Its lustre far, Love's voyage to befriend;
> Thro' stormy seas the Nymphs and Swains shall guide
> Clear of the rocks and shelves on either side,
> Instructed well the haven to explore,
> And timely lighted to the blissful shore.
>
> (399)

Jeffreys's use of the formula of the equally matched couple puts more emphasis on good matching than equality. His opposition to arranged marriages seems mainly that they foster unions in which at least one of the partners is genetically inferior or diseased. Partners are chosen for their estates and not for their health, intelligence, beauty, heart, or character. The result is not only the degradation of the institution of marriage but the genetic debasement of English bloodlines. The phrase "pleasure, tainted at the fountain-head" suggests both congenital debilitation, for example, inherited madness, and the actual infection of spouses and progeny by a venereal disease such as syphilis. Though much less vivid in its metaphor, Jeffreys's passage can serve as a mid-century analog to Blake's later description in "London" (1794) of the "youthful harlot's curse" which

> Blasts the new-born Infants tear,
> And blights with plagues the Marriage hearse.
>
> (27)

At the same time Jeffreys's proto-Darwinian concerns evoke the twentieth-century specter of racial elitism and eugenics.

For Jeffreys the "well-weigh'd choice" in the pairing of Lord and Lady Carnarvon makes for marriage that is "bright with mutual love and mutual worth." The union is not necessarily a romantic love match, though the couple do have an equally shared love for each other. The idea of "mutual worth" is likewise an important one, even though it leaves some things unsaid. Certainly, "mutual worth" includes the idea of a common social background and money in both families. Jeffreys attacks the debasement of *"Hymen's* couch" by "sordid views," but we know for a fact that Lord Carnarvon did not marry a charming but penniless milkmaid.

James Brydges (1721–89), the oldest son of Henry Brydges (2nd Duke of Chandos), married Margaret, daughter of John Nicoll, who brought with her a marriage settlement of £150,000 (Valentine 112).

Jeffreys's use of the formula of the equally matched couple with its emphasis on "mutual love and mutual worth" might by itself imply that love and personal qualifications were the sole considerations in the match. Yet Jeffreys also tells us that Carnarvon's nuptial torch is "advanc'd by noble birth." The reader is forced to wonder how much of its lustre ("like that of *Egypt's Pharos*") is due to the "mutual love and mutual worth" and how much to Carnarvon's noble title.

In his celebration of Lord and Lady Carnarvon's marriage, Jeffreys politely underplays the importance of rank and wealth, and in doing so he may call attention to it all the more. Clergyman and headmaster James Cawthorn in "The Temple of Hymen. A Tale" (1771) is franker in treating it as a consideration in forming equal matches. Cawthorn thus involves himself in a more obvious contradiction. At the same time he cautions young people prudentially not to marry above or below their rank, Cawthorn offers a forceful and extensive condemnation of arranged marriages and affirms the agency of love in rescuing marriage from its corruptions by the three demons: "Ambition, Vanity, and Riches."

As Cawthorn handles the contradiction within his allegory, it seems less severe than in fact it is. Since love can be so "whimsical and wild," Hymen orders Goody Prudence to follow Cupid and make sure the couple in love reflect on practical considerations such as where their next meal is coming from:

> Instruct those hearts his arrows hit,
> To pause, and have a little wit:
> Bid them reflect, amidst their heat,
> 'Tis necessary Love should eat;
> That in his most ecstatic billing
> He possibly may want a shilling.
> (Chalmers 14: 253)

Cawthorn plays down the importance of love by making Goody Prudence, not Love, responsible for encouraging young couples to form a solid union based on equality in temperament, social background, and age. Hymen instructs Goody to

> Persuade them, ere they first engage,
> To study temper, rank, and age,

> To march beneath my holy banners,
> Congenial in their tastes and manners,
> Completing just as Heav'n design'd,
> An union both of sex and mind.
>
> (14: 253)

That wealth is an important consideration in forming a marriage Cawthorn artfully stresses again in the conclusion of the poem where Goody Prudence performs another job, that of checking the "houses,/Estates, and minds, of both the spouses" (note the order of priorities). When she finds them "exact to form and law,/The settlement without a flaw," she then gives the couple permission to wed.

With his unobtrusive emphasis on the importance of rank and money, Cawthorn does seem to have it both ways. He praises love and freedom of choice as a way of ridding the world of the curse of arranged marriages, yet "Goody Prudence," whoever she is, makes sure that the couple have paid attention to property and wealth in forming their matches. Admittedly, there is a difference between marrying outside one's rank or age solely for mercenary considerations and marrying an equal in rank, wealth, age, temperament, and intelligence to ensure compatibility and happiness. Cawthorn would no doubt insist on such a distinction. However, as long as one makes wealth and rank a consideration, there is a good possibility that it will come into conflict with love's insistence on freedom of choice. Cawthorn may have reconciled the contradiction by plot manipulation within his poem, but for all that, the contradiction still stands.

In the didactic poets who follow Cawthorn, we find an increasing tendency to ignore the contradiction in which they involve themselves as they condemn marriages for money yet at the same time acknowledge its importance in helping a marriage to survive.

In the three books of *The Nuptials* (1761), an eighty-six page didactic poem in Miltonic blank verse, Richard Shepherd focuses centrally on the problem of forming equal matches, and he advises his readers at length on avoiding "Precipitancy in Marriage," on making their own judgments of potential mates, and on the importance of equality in age and attractiveness. He especially emphasizes "The Misery of the Married State under the Pressure of real Poverty" (2). Initially Shepherd's attitude toward the importance of money does not seem hypocritical, but as he develops his position, striking contradictions emerge.

Shepherd cautions against matches made for money and interest without the binding force of mutual love:

> This, of connubial Bliss the Soul, in vain
> We hope to find 'midst Pageantry and State:
> Vain Thought, to bribe the Power of spotless Love
> With Gold, or Gems, or purple's regal Wear.
>   (20)

At the same time, he concedes that gold does have its uses: to keep "the rude Hand of Want" from harrowing the beauty of one's wife or to avoid hearing the "Plaints of Hunger's keen Demand" from one's children, "those dear pledges of your mutual Joys" (24–25). Shepherd articulates these uses in a plaintive, sentimentalized tone so that only a cynic would accuse him of sanctioning greed. Shepherd, however, neglects to say how one gets gold if one lacks it oneself or if one does not marry someone who has it.

He then abruptly jumps from warnings against poverty to praise a marriage with a "strong and equal Aptitude for Love" (25). From such marriages "derives"

> The Body Health, and Strength the active Mind:
> On the hale Birth propitious Nature smiles,
> And all the Graces all their Influence pour.
>   (25)

And where does one find examples of such marriages? Where indeed but among the poor!

> Go to the humble Roof of lowly Swains,
> Where venal Guardian never sold his Charge;
> Where viler Parent never doom'd his Child
> If Duty's rare Excess may merit Blame,
> Too, too obsequious, to a loath'd Embrace:
>   (26)

Shepherd seems unaware of his stunning contradiction as he shifts almost one hundred and eighty degrees from middle-class prudence to a romantic idealization of poverty. While it is not necessarily a contradiction to condemn marriage for money and at the same time to acknowledge that one needs it to survive, it is hypocritical to caution readers against poverty, as Shepherd does, and then in the next breath to idealize it.

In *Modern Matrimony. A Poem* (1773), Francis Dobbs—Irish lawyer, politician, and pamphleteer—may be even harsher than Shepherd in condemning the bartering of the joys of marriage for a "mammon trade." At the same time, his praise of the ideal union formed in love, the marriage of Strephon and Arabella, is more warmly enthusiastic than Shepherd's. At one point, he shows that a match formed between a couple equal in fortune and in years cannot be happy, if there is not mutual love.

> But lo! gay Florio with his spouse appears;
> In fortune equal—equal in their years:
> Their prudent fathers saw the match was fit;
> What could their godly children do?—Submit.
> 'Tis true, strangers to each, the other came;
> But what of that?—Sure princes do the same.
> They might be happy—bliss might yet be won;
> The odds were not, a *million quite—to one*;
> But oh! ill luck awaits the fated pair,
> And Doctor's Commons ends the wedding year!
>   (10)

Dobbs takes a more romantic stance than Shepherd, the most romantic we have seen so far, as he asserts the primacy of love over prudence. Yet in the midst of his sharply drawn contrasts between sordid mismatches and ecstatic love unions, Dobbs also grants that money is important to happiness.

> Yet prudence sometimes must the bands forbear—
> Nor do I think that love can live on air—
> A competence ought to still on marriage wait;
> Else sad and wretched is the marriage state:
> The more their fondness—still the greater woe—
>   (19)

Dobbs qualifies his qualification by saying that, though a couple requires a "competence," they need not live in "gaudy splendour." Yet he allows that the existence of great wealth may not destroy a marriage. Dobbs does not seem especially concerned whether both partners come to the marriage with money. As long as there is a sufficient amount, love can flourish. Where the money comes from, he does not say, but one must assume that at least one of the partners must bring it to the marriage. Dobbs's poem offers an excellent illustration of the tendency of advice poets using the equally matched formula to blur the prudential and the romantic in sentimentalizing the companionate ideal.

In poems of the later era, contradiction is evident not only in the confusion of the prudential and romantic but in abrupt or frequently alternating shifts from satire to celebration. In one sizable passage in *Marriage: A Poetical Essay* (1748), Robert Shiells addresses parents who would forbid matches because they are not financially advantageous. Shiells, a Scots Jacobite who worked on Johnson's *Dictionary*, has his speaker shift from a pleading tone of appeal to satiric denunciation and back again.

> Nor ye, the Parents, with commanding Nod,
> Forbid the Match: O! think, when youthful Blood
> Ran thro' your turgid Veins, how strong ye felt
> The direful Throbbings of retarded Bliss!
> Yourselves have tasted Love, and Age cannot
> Forget the Days of Youth: Sometimes reflect
> On that impatient State, and say, ye Sires,
> Say, can your rigid Awe forbid the Pair
> To taste connubial Bliss? Can cruel Awe
> Dissolve the Ties of Love, or sordid Gain
> Retard the nuptial Bed? O! Custom vile!
> Which traffics Hearts, and stains the sacred Rites
> With grov'lling Views. How oft does Merit stand
> Neglected all! and she, her Sex's Pride,
> The wond'rous Fair of each bewitching Grace
> And ev'ry Charm possess'd! how oft does she
> Drag on a Maiden Life, who might have grac'd
> Young Damon's Arms, and spent her Prime of Days
> In Prolific? . . .
>
> (10–11)

Using the highly wrought diction and syntax of the Miltonic-Thomsonian descriptive tradition, Shiells works on his readers with both sentiment and satire. His speaker first appeals to the memory of his readers' youth to stir their sympathy: "O! think, when youthful Blood/Ran thro' your turgid Veins." He next dips into his satiric arsenal of rhetorical weaponry: ringing *exclamatio*, wilting rhetorical questions, and devastating invective (see lines 9–19 above). Though Shiells's verse may be too highly wrought for modern tastes, we may admire his smooth ambidextrousness as he varies his attack.

In *Modern Matrimony. A Poem,* Dobbs relies even more obviously than Shiells on alternating modes. Contrasts in mode complement and reinforce the thematic oppositions that run throughout his poem: between true love and the betrayal of it in the marriage of convenience, between natural sexual bliss and the forced ecstasy of the young groom for the old withered dame, and between marriage conducted in earlier times according to "Nature's Laws" and marriage of today corrupted by greed and hypocrisy. Most highly featured is the contrast between Strephon and Arabella's companionate marriage and Lucinda's marriage for "pomp of dress and costly show."

Within his central modal contrast between satire and celebration, Dobbs employs a highly diverse range of poetic stances and tones. These vary from mildly erotic picture painting—

> Draw back the veil that hides th'inraptur'd pair;
> Let him behold, where lies the blooming fair;
> Let him be witness of the fond embrace;
> The dear emotion of each speaking face;
> The soft delicious glance be too reveal'd;
> The melting eye, half open, half conceal'd:
>
> (3)

—to idealizing reminiscence:

> In earlier times, our generous youth disdain'd
> To be, by honours, or by wealth restrain'd;
> By Nature led, by Nature's laws inspir'd,
> Where sense, where beauty join'd, they still admir'd;
> Where e'er an Emma bloom'd, an Henry came,
> And Nut-brown maids were not uncommon theme.
>
> (4)

He can also shift from stern moralistic condemnation, forceful and compressed in the manner of Samuel Johnson, to clever, coy satire, suggestive of Pope's Horatian personae (see Dobbs 6, 8; lines 3–6, 1–4). Dobbs usually employs the celebratory mode seriously, but in at least one curious passage he uses sarcasm to blend ecstatic exclamations with grossly repulsive satiric mockery:

> O happy youth! instruct my willing muse,
> To paint those transports, I must still refuse—
> O happy youth! instruct me to display,

> Those joys supreme, that crown'd thy bridal day—
> Instruct me to display that blissful night,
> Which gave to thee, such exquisite delight—
> When in your arms you clasp'd the willing fair,
> Her beauteous head adorn'd with hoary hair;
> Her dim, dim eyes, with scalding rheum red,
> Rolling on thee, and languishingly dead;
> Her charming lips, of crimson once possess'd,
> Now pale, and toothless, to thy lips are press'd;
>
> (5)

Like the opening of Dryden's *MacFlecknoe* (1682, 1684), the satire in this passage is at first not evident, and it is only after we are well into the passage (in the eighth line) that the sarcasm begins to subvert the praise with such words as "hoary," "dim," and "scalding." The ease with which Dobbs can undermine the celebratory mode may be evidence of his poetic skill, but it also attests to how perilously close his celebratory mode can be to the bathetic. Dobbs may purposely overdo the celebration in this passage, but effectively it is not dissimilar to other passages of straightforward praise in *Modern Matrimony* (13). There is finally not that much difference between Dobbs's satiric and straightforward uses of celebration; both verge on bathos.

While satire and celebration alternate throughout most of Dobbs's poem, it is finally celebration that prevails in the concluding two pages. Here Dobbs turns from condemnation of marriage-as-trade to write a paean to the happy life of "rural bliss" he will spend with his Flora. Friends will often grace their "humble dwelling." They will spend winter days in pleasing talk, or Flora will sometimes "touch the trembling string;/And tender sonnets with her music sing—." Picturing the happy times he and Flora will spend together, the poet paints an Edenic image of the hot summer days when they will bask in the luxury of nature.

> When mid-day suns, with scorching heat o'erpower
> We'll seek some lonely shade, or fragrant bow'r;
> There listen to each tuneful songster's note,
> And catch soft sound from ev'ry warbler's throat:
> Our languid limbs repose beneath some shade,
> That Nature's bounty hath for lovers made;
> There, in the sweet sequester'd scene, we'll prove
> Those nameless joys that wait on mutual love.—
>
> (22)

The paradise in which Dobbs's blissful couple repose is sensuous and fecund, yet still romantically stylized.

By the end of the eighteenth century the predominant mode of attack on the hell of marriage corrupted by a materialist society is the counter-myth of the companionate marriage as heaven. The secular paradises poets create often have a mildly erotic appeal. Yet the energy in these domestic heavens may be languid and the emotion underlying them escapist. The male poets celebrating their blisses may have thought they were breaking new ground by treating natural sexual processes decently in a context of heightened emotionality. Yet the mythical unreality of such celebrations makes them inadequate heavens to stand in contrast to the marital hells represented so vividly in earlier satires on marriage-as-trade.

CHAPTER FIVE

Evolving Types

ESPECIALLY IN CHAPTERS 1, 2, AND 3, WE HAVE seen that poets writing on marriage tend less to employ traditional poetic genres than to use formats that have their counterparts in prose pieces treating marriage. Tract and polemical poems, dialogues, advice poems, and conduct books in verse, verse epistles, and verse tales have their distinctive qualities as poetry, but their development is often closely parallel to prose works using the same format. Grub Street poets, those catering to popular tastes, tend to rely most on poetic formats with prose counterparts.

A minority of marriage poetry, especially in the early era, does rely on traditional poetic genres—the epigram, the ballad, the eclogue, the elegy, the ode, and the epithalamium. Nevertheless, the practitioners of these types, even in the Restoration, tend often to adhere rather loosely to formal organizing principles set by classical and by Renaissance models. Poets often treat genres with much freedom, modifying them or mocking them as suits their purposes.

As the eighteenth century progresses, adherence to the prescribed models becomes even looser, and, in some cases, the genre itself loses its continuity, appearing only sporadically if at all. Instead of poetry written in the traditional genres, adhering loosely to the expectations about what could be done in each genre, later era poets tend to work in an undifferentiated lyric mode depending more and more on "popular emotional effects." According to Eric Rothstein, this poetry "calls for the reader to join the speaker in looking and/or feeling, so as to demand a social kinship" (Rothstein 100). Many of these poems have a "reduced range for the sake of intensity, and still others have author-speakers who announce their own involvement with the poetic process, thereby appealing for an improvisatory kinship with the person going through the process of reading." A social factor contributing to the breakdown of the traditional genres may have been an increase in the number of poets who never studied the Latin and Greek poets in the original language. Many women poets fall into this category, and their rise in numbers no doubt contributes to the shift away from traditional genres toward the lyrically effusive mode (see Lonsdale; Anne Williams).

Tracing the evolution of marriage verse from satire to celebration, we have seen, especially in the previous chapter, that it follows the tendency identified by Rothstein. In the later era, poems in traditional genres appear less frequently, and we discover greater quantities of undifferentiated verse in the celebratory mode. This verse emotionally affirms marriage in a voice that is more intense, empathetic, and lyrically effusive than in earlier eras. Celebrating the companionate marriage and domesticity, such poetry gives expression to a more feminized sensibility. Satire survives, sometimes in lowbrow, facetious compilations offering a grab bag of prose and verse.[1] Yet as earlier chapters have demonstrated, especially the preceding one, it is the celebratory mode that increases in importance and finally comes to predominate.

As we consider in this chapter the minority of poets working with distinctly identifiable traditional types, we will be looking at evolutionary patterns that are often attenuated or that stop altogether. Existing patterns are usually not chronologically neat. Over the course of the period, more and more marriage poems claiming to be of a traditional type exhibit a loss of identifying generic features and an increase in the importance of the speaker's emotive, empathetic role vis-à-vis the reader. Poets who persist in working with distinct types tend to be exceptional in one way or another. They may be translators working with classical or Renaissance texts, they may be especially fine poets who still hold to the old models in spite of the popular tendency to drift away from them, or they may be using a type self-consciously to create a special emphasis. Another group purposely experiments with types alien to the period—the sonnet and the hymn, for example—to create more intense emotional effects. In doing so, they begin a practice that the Romantics were to develop in fertile directions.[2]

The most significant evolution of a poetic type occurs with a special form of the ode, the epithalamium, which traditionally has been most directly celebratory of marriage. During the course of the long eighteenth century, the epithalamium not only moves toward a more effusively empathetic narrator but also tends to replace intricate tropes, which indirectly provide cosmic sanction for the wedding, with the narrator's direct social affirmation through tone of voice. As epithalamiasts turn away from evoking spiritual or natural forces to reinforce their celebration, the net effect is the secularization of the idea of bliss.

Though most evident in the epithalamium, we can detect a more empathetic, less harshly moralistic narratorial stance in many of the other poetic types, beginning with the one traditionally conceived as the most coldly satiric, the epigram.

The Epigram

Hugh Holman has observed that "in the eighteenth century the spirit though not the form of the epigram continued." To avoid discussing poems that are epigrams only in "spirit," I confine myself to those that follow the Renaissance pattern of "a short poem consisting of two parts, an introduction stating the occasion or setting the tone, and a conclusion sharply and tersely giv[ing] the main point." Epigrams "sum up what is to be made permanently memorable, as though it were an inscription." Hence they are "characterized by compression, pointedness, clarity, balance, and polish" (Holman 163).

The period under study did not produce the outpouring of epigrams in the classical manner that Ben Jonson, Sir John Harrington, and other early seventeenth-century poets did. Even so, the form was practiced successfully by many poets. Since the epigram by its nature is ironic and incisive, its handling of the topic of marriage is usually by association satiric. Poets writing epigrams—the large majority I have found are male—often give expression to traditional antifeminist, antimatrimonial attitudes in portraying hellish marriages with wit and cynicism. Because of its associations, the form itself does not allow for much liberalization of attitudes, though a few poems late in the period exhibit this to a degree.

In the middle and late seventeenth century, we find a number of clever satiric epigrams by Edmund Waller, Alexander Brome, Charles Cotton, and Sir Charles Sedley that treat mismatches and duplicitous wives with typical hardness. The early eighteenth century is represented by several epigrams by Swift and two by George Woodward that mainly hold to the satiric antimatrimonial stances of the seventeenth century. In the late eighteenth century the form of these epigrams remains generally consistent with that of earlier practitioners; there is not much these poets could do to vary it. A slight alternation in tone is, however, detectable. All four examples are witty and satirical, but the satire loses some of its cynical edge in three of them. The speakers may be shifting slightly toward a more sympathetic, emotionally involved stance of the sort described by Rothstein. Along with this may come a softening of patriarchal attitudes.

The stance of the earliest epigram writers often involves confronting the reader or the subject addressed with an unalterable, negative fact of married life. This fact may be the projected outcome of an immoral or unwise course of behavior, but it is often presented as an evil that the author can do nothing about and for which he will therefore feel no sympathy. He may even turn away from his subject's misfortune. Edmund Waller, as we have already seen, offers a clever quibble on the idea that a woman's marrying an old man is like being buried alive:

> Since thou woulds't needs (bewitch'd with some ill charms!)
> Be bury'd in those monumental arms:
> All we can wish, is—May that earth lie light
> Upon thy tender limbs! And so good night!
> (Chalmers 8: 81; original date 1645)

The seeming solicitude of "May the earth lie light/Upon thy tender limbs!" is turned aside by the poet's cold dismissal of the woman's plight. In his heart, the poet may be against such mismatches, but his outward satiric stance is an unsympathetic one. Once a woman has committed herself to such a union, there is no remedy.

A similar cynical attitude toward a bad marriage appears in Charles Cotton's pithy, fast moving translation (1689) of Martial's epigram 35 from his eighth book:

> Since y'are alike in manners, and in life,
> A wicked husband, and a wicked wife,
> I wonder much you are so full of strife!
> (Chalmers 6: 766)

More than fifty years later (in 1747) Reverend Josiah Relph of Sebergham, Cumberland, translated the same epigram by Martial (Relph 51). The satiric force of both poems comes less from the poet's surprised discovery of the illogic of the couple's behavior than from his cynical recognition of the hellish perfection of their marriage.

In "Bithinicus, Lib. 2. Ep. 12" and in "To Flavia," Sir Charles Sedley relies on a playing off of appearance against reality in his exposure of the evil cunning of unfaithful wives. Each poem offers a cynical, unflinching exposure of hypocrisy. There is no pity even for the illness-feigning wife whose husband, Bithinicus, cruelly wishes her dead.

A number of Swift's epigrams reveal a curious preoccupation with wives who beat their husbands and vice versa. In their exposure of abuse in the concluding couplets, Swift's poems end on the traditional hard note that Restoration epigrams do:

> . . . .
> Three Duels he fought, thrice ventur'd his Life
> Went home, and was cudgell'd again by his Wife.
> . . . .
> A Kinder Wife was never born,
> She combs his Head, and finds him Horn.
> . . . .
> Dye Joan and Will; give Bess to Ned,
> And ev'ry day she combs his Head.
> (Swift 1: 327–28)

Swift's repeated portrayal of wives who "comb" their husbands' heads (and cuckold them) may be an expression of his patriarchal concern as a clergyman that husbands exert their God-given dominion over their wives. However, the epigrams Swift has left us present no such rationale for their focus on marital cruelty. Swift assumes the traditional antimatrimonial cynicism of earlier epigram writers.

George Woodward in two epigrams included in his *Poems on Several Occasions* (1730) likewise adheres to a traditional antimatrimonial stance in urging the reader not to marry. With cold wit, Woodward's speaker concludes:

> I'd sooner twenty broken *Ribs* abide,
> Than e'er have *One* transform'd into a Bride.
> (114)

Turning to three remaining epigrams from the later era, we find ambivalence in each poet's final attitude. Catherine Jemmat's epigram "On the Marriage of a Handsome Couple" (1766) may even have been intended as a compliment:

> If fools (as they say) spring from parents of sense,
>   And ugly half-monsters from two that are fair;

> 'Tis much to be dreaded, a little while hence,
>   We shall have a strangebreed from this new-marry'd pair.
>
>   (191)

If the couple are to produce a "strangebreed," then by the logic of Jemmat's major premise, they must have intelligence and beauty. We are somewhat baffled by this roundabout compliment, since we expect the final revelation of an epigram to be negative and satiric. This is apparently not the case for this woman poet who may be using the epigram for purposes of social affirmation.

William Cowper has also given us two epigrams. (The first I already touched on in chapter 2.) Cowper delights as much in a pun as the earlier poets. Yet, in his first epigram, Cowper's final revelation, like Catherine Jemmat's, does not exactly show us an evil that the poet identifies, but one for which he refuses sympathy.

> If John marries Mary, and Mary alone,
> 'Tis a very good match between Mary and John,
> Should John wed a score, oh! the claws and the scratches!
> It can't be a match:—'tis a bundle of matches.
>
>   (1: 232; see 501–2n)

The final phrase "bundle of matches" is ingeniously chosen, but it does not quite work like those in epigrams from the earlier era. Instead of exposing the evils of a plurality of wives as proposed by Madan in his tract *Thelyphthora* (1780), Cowper creates further interest by his punning metaphor. Perhaps because Cowper is too artful in his choice of phrase, he creates a corrupting curiosity rather than revealing a hard truth. We may wonder what sort of flare-ups John would experience if he were married to a score.

A second epigram by Cowper, on *Thelyphthora*, carries the poet's disapproval of Madan's argument that a husband should take a woman he seduces as a second wife.

> Oh rare Device! the Wife betray'd,
> The Modest, chaste, Domestic Woman,
> To Save a worthless, Wanton Jade,
> From being, what she would be, Common.
>
>   (1: 232)

As it begins in sarcasm, the poem ends with the word "Common" on a heavily patriarchal note of dismissal, roughly similar to the stinging conclusion of earlier epigrams. Even so, the stance of moral outrage Cowper adopts toward the proposal seems alien to the hard, cynical attitude of the earlier epigram. Even more alien is the affirmation of the "modest, chaste" wife's domesticity. In its form, the epigram is a most restricted poetic type, but in the late eighteenth century even it may show a loosening of attitude and a detectable shift from witty, detached denigration to emotive indignation and backhanded affirmation.

THE BALLAD

In ballads treating marriage, the shift in attitude in the later era is more marked. It is also easier to account for by the distinction between broadside ballads and art ballads. Broadside ballads, which were printed in two columns on folio sheets, were the "yellow journals" of their day. Sold on the streets by hawkers, they featured such sensationalized subject matter as natural calamities, "accidents, dying speeches of criminals, miraculous events, religious and political harangues" (Holman 62). Usually offering first-person narrative accounts that were often satirical, broadside ballads were crude productions. Art ballads, in contrast, often use the four-line stanza of traditional ballads, but they present more complicated narrative situations handled with more literary craftsmanship. The stance of the narrator in an art ballad is usually more self-aware and sophisticated.[3]

Broadside ballads handling marriage do not usually occur after the seventeenth century, while art ballads do not appear until after the middle of the eighteenth. Broadside ballads treating marriage feature wives who cuckold or otherwise humiliate possessive, dim-witted husbands. Violence is endemic in this world, and the male reader of that era must have experienced it vicariously, not so much rejoicing in the wife's victory as taking pleasure in the suffering of the husband. His underlying attitude might have been that since all husbands are bound to suffer at the hands of their wives, better the husband in the poem than he.

The broadside ballad treating marriage is well illustrated by *The Married Mans Complaint* from the British Library collection called the Douce Ballads. A second example is the ballad entitled "Golden Garland" (ca. 1680), included in the *Penny Merriments* assembled by Samuel Pepys and recently reprinted by Roger Thompson. In *The Married Mans Complaint* the tone of the speaker alternates between a lament for his situation and a vivid descriptive narrative in which he chronicles his wife's daily behavior: lying in bed till noon, coming home at night drunk as a sot, and beating him. The substance of the poem remains at this basic level:

conflicts over expenses, over freedom of action, and over dominion in general. The speaker seems not at all aware that he is a character in a ballad, and he voices realistic-sounding complaints.

"Golden Garland," a continuous narrative done in four-line stanzas with no refrain, tells the story of a barber who is unfaithful to his wife with a "Girl of the Game" at a local tavern. He is robbed by her of his money and the plate he had ordered up for their love feast. Even more embarrassing,

> he was forced to send for his Wife,
> To bring him some money to pay for the loss,
> And thus the poor Barber he met with a cross
> The barber was noble, both gallant & great,
> But now he hath paid for his Drinking in plate;
> Let other Shavers be warn'd by his fate
> Lest you should be sorry when it is too late.
> (Thompson 287)

As with many broadside ballads, "Golden Garland" concludes with a moral warning, yet after reading a number of such pieces, one suspects that the didactic function of the narrative is quite secondary to its quasi-sensational value as entertainment. Ballad readers, as I said, had an insatiable appetite for seeing husbands cuckolded or humiliated. They, along with the readers of chapbooks and other "penny merriments," were evidently not a progressive nor sensitive lot.[4]

By the time Cowper and Shenstone published ballads treating marriage, we encounter a set of attitudes that is more liberal by comparison, though certainly not by revisionist standards. Cowper's "A New Ballad Intitled The Sorrowfull Husband's Garland or The Grey Mare the Better Horse" (1763) is presented by a verbose, folksy narrator who offers running commentary and asides on the details—or lack of them—in his story. His intrusiveness breaks the verisimilitude that the older ballads usually strictly maintained.

> No great Matter Where, how it happen'd, or When,
> You'll not presently hear such a Frolick again;
> How to kill a good Husband a Jade of a Wife
> Thought proper to Counterfeit death to the Life.
>
> This Wife had a Title—I cannot say Which,
> Whether Brimstone or Baggage or Vixen or each—

> But lest We should wrong her as haply we shall,
> If we give her but one We'll e'en give her them all.
>
> Our Couple agreed then their Lodging to take
> At a Distance, for a peace and good Neighbourhood sake,
> Since for Banging and Bruising they car'd not a Rush,
> And never could part till they'd had t'other Brush.
>
> Yet both were so Manfull and both were so Stout
> That the Nicest of Judges have still been in doubt
> Whose Talons could draw the most Blood at a Scratch,
> So it must be confest 'twas an Excellent Match.
>
> (51)

To get at the husband, the wife has him informed that she is dead. The husband, who has learned somehow that his wife really is not dead, now realizes that since his wife has confessed she is dead, he now may have the legal option to take a "new Wife in her Stead." In this "New Ballad" there is no knockdown physical violence, only the effort of the couple to undo each other by verbal treachery. The permutations of this treachery are much too sophisticated for the traditional ballad, but Cowper no doubt assumed his middle-class readers would take more pleasure in a battle of wits than in a physical battle of the sexes. The poet's goal is, however, traditionally didactic, to make his readers sensitive to the way a comic-seeming battle of wits can turn a marriage into a hell of mutual destructiveness, the sort of marriage featured in earlier broadside ballads.

Shenstone's "A Ballad" (1765) chronicles the unwillingness of a smart young thing from London to marry a squire from Lincolnshire and move to the country.

> To give up the opera, the park, and the ball,
> For to view the stag's horns in an old country-hall;
> To have neither China nor India to see!
> Nor a laceman to plague in the morning—not she!
>
> (Chalmers 13: 303)

Such wonderful overstatement in dramatizing the spoiled young woman's objections to leaving London seem entirely alien to the lower-class, gritty level of conflict of the broadside ballad. But perhaps that is part of Shenstone's joke as the conclusion reveals it. The affected young society woman is unwilling to marry the plain but honest young squire from Lincolnshire, not because she is so attached to the sophisticated pleasures of London life but because she is carrying on an amorous intrigue with a nobleman with whom she elopes to Scotland. Even though she conceals her perfidy, she is shown finally to be of no higher character than the cuckolding wives of the broadside ballads.

Shenstone uses the ballad form didactically as a vehicle to assist the reader in judging the young woman's behavior. In doing so, he, as did Cowper, moves beyond the generic limits of the broadside ballad. Both poets provide examples of the ways in which a traditional poetic type could be expanded to produce amusing and good-humored moralizations on marriage. In these poets the antifeminist crudities of the broadside ballad are softened, though patriarchal attitudes toward female misbehavior are still quite evident. The title of the wife in Cowper's ballad, he drolly tells us, may actually be "Brimstone or Baggage or Vixen or each." The London hothouse flower in Shenstone's ballad talks "like a wit," but the Latin epigraph—"trahit sua quemque voluptas"—implies that she is a whore.

The Eclogue

In the period under study *eclogue* came to have a "restricted meaning of a formal pastoral poem following the techniques derived from the *Idylls* of Theocritus (third century B.C.)" and the pastorals of Virgil (Holman 147). Eclogues in the strict sense of a dialogue or singing match between love-sick swains do not appear in large quantities as such, though the type was frequently employed in the pastorals and mock pastorals of Ambrose Philips, Pope, Gay, and others. The three examples we will look at are, in chronological order, a 1718 translation by William Bewick of a Latin eclogue by the fifteenth-century Italian, Giovanni Battista Spagnoli Mantovano (Mantuan), an English eclogue by John Gay (1720), and an anonymous 1733 adaptation of Virgil's first eclogue. Predictably, the translation of Mantuan's eclogue exhibits more stock antifeminist and antimatrimonial attitudes than the poem by Gay or the adaptation of Virgil. From these examples, we can see that later poets are softer in attitude and more celebratory in tone.

Alphus: or, The Fourth Eclogue of Baptist Mantuan, A Carmelite; Being a Satyr Against Women features a dialogue between two rustics, the goatherds Alphus and Janus. The latter laments the fate of his goatboy smitten with love for a charming maid. Becoming inattentive, the boy nearly loses a goat and his own life. Alphus answers Janus's lament with a satire against women and wives and their sexual power over men. Mantuan is credited with the introduction of satire into the eclogue form, and in the early eighteenth century such traditional antimatrimonialism still evidently attracted readers.

The second eclogue, John Gay's "The Espousal. A Sober Eclogue. Between two of the People called Quakers" (1720), is the most domesticated of the three and the loosest in following the conventions of the genre. Gay may use *eclogue* in his title only in the sense of a dialogue containing little action, though the designation "A Sober Eclogue" suggests a contrast between Caleb and Tabitha's outward reserved demeanor as Quakers and their inner passions as lovers in debate.

In the dialogue itself, their plainness as Quakers conflicts ironically with their worldliness as lovers. Caleb wants to marry Tabitha, but she feels he is not "sober" enough. He wears "ribbands, flounces, furbelows" (242). Caleb admits to some youthful frailties of this sort, but he is hurt by Tabitha's pointing them out to him, especially since she now wears a watch, a "golden toy" that Josiah gave her when he led her "through the garden's walk,/And mingled melting kisses with his talk." Each grows warmer in protesting his or her love, and each concludes by passionately renouncing the worldliness the other objects to and by affirming an espousal. In this "sober Eclogue" the passion of the lovers finally overflows the bounds of their Puritan scruples. As the poet says,

> *True love is nature unrestrain'd by law.*
> This tenet all the holy sect allows.
> So *Tabitha* took earnest of a spouse.
>   (244)

Gay himself pushes against the generic limits of the eclogue to present a delightful picture of love conquering legalism. The poem works well because Gay has taken charming liberties with the eclogue form. At the same time, Gay's use of dramatic irony saves him from the sentimental.

This is not quite the case with the last poem, *The Happy Marriage: An Eclogue* (1733), whose adaptation of the eclogue form is less playful and more openly celebratory. Virgil's first eclogue contains Tityrus's praise of the stability and prosperity the god Rome has brought into his life. In loosely adapting Virgil's poem, *The Happy Marriage* offers Damon's tribute to the content that Hymen has given him. Induced by reason, Damon has forsaken the roving life and the pleasures of the tavern for the more solid happiness of marriage. Damon converts the skeptical bachelor Moeris into a believer in the happiness of marriage and closes the dialogue with an invitation to Moeris to join him for dinner and observe his wife first hand. Adapting the eclogue to untraditional uses, this piece offers an effusive celebration of the companionate marriage.

The Elegy

An elegy may be defined as a "sustained and formal poem setting forth the poet's meditations upon death or another solemn theme" (Holman 151). In marriage poems that are considered elegies or that use the word *elegy* in their titles, it is not always easy to find poets sustaining a formal and serious mood and not veering off into something else: semiautobiographical love laments, sentimentalized pathos, unintentionally bathetic effusions, or purposeful comedy and satire. The elegy was never a tightly defined genre, and it becomes even looser as it is used to express softer and more effusive stances toward marriage and love.

In the early era, the elegy did not at first offer an open flow of emotion unchecked by wit or irony. The little poem "An Elegy on a Lady That Died Before Her Intended Nuptials" (1661) by Royalist poet and satirist Alexander Brome seems to depend less on the steady evocation of a elegiac mood and more on the drawing of tropes that have a metaphysical grotesquerie.

> Excuse me, sir, passion will swell that's pent,
> Thank not my tears, I cannot but lament
> To see a lady, ready for your bed,
> To Death's embraces yield her maidenhead;
> (111–12)

Swift's "An Elegy on Dicky and Dolly" (written 1728) is not a serious elegy at all but a lampoon of a husband whose sorrow for his deceased wife is hypocritical:

> Dick lost in Doll, a Wife Tender and Dear,
> But Dick lost by Doll, twelve hundred a Year,
> A loss that Dick thought, no Mortal cou'd bear.
> (Swift 430)

Swift mocks the elegiac mood to show that Dick's grief is not based on a true appreciation of his wife's tenderness and devotion.

Pope teaches the elegy to flow steadily and openly. Next to Gray's "Elegy Written in a Country Churchyard," Pope's *Eloisa to Abelard* (1717) contains some of the most finely sustained and best-controlled evocations of the elegiac mood in the century. Its concern with marriage, however, is peripheral to its fascination with the "Unfortunate passion" of the two lovers. Marriage, especially the lovers' secret marriage, figures importantly in the actual history of Eloisa and Abelard, yet, in adapting these materials, Pope makes it sound as if the couple has remained unmarried and as if Eloisa's only marriage is to Christ (when she takes the veil). Indeed, in one passionate outburst (lines 73–80), Eloisa espouses what sounds like the standard late seventeenth-century libertine argument.

In *Poetic Strain*, Anne Williams argues that in the course of the century most of the traditional genres—satire, elegy, pastoral, tragedy—open into a mode that she calls lyric. Williams herself treats *Eloisa to Abelard* as a verse epistle that is "appropriated" by the lyric mode. She might well have treated Pope's poem as an elegy that is taken over by the lyric. Pope sustains the elegiac mood finely for long stretches in *Eloisa to Abelard*, yet several passages jump out as passionate lyrical effusions, expressions of the intensity of her love. Indicative perhaps of Pope's attraction to the courtly love tradition, he does not, as later love poets of his era do, use the effusive mode in support of the companionate marriage.

Not just lyrical effusion but sentimental pathos verging on bathos becomes a hallmark for a group of poems in which the speaker laments a spouse who has died or in which the speaker himself is about to die and is writing a farewell letter to a spouse. One hesitates to call all these poems elegies, though I suppose they ultimately derive from that genre. Examples of the group are George Woodward's "A Letter from a Lady to Her Husband in Spain, in Her Last Sickness" (1730), Elizabeth Rowe's "Upon the Death of Her Husband" (1719), and "An Epistle from Alexias, a Noble Roman, to His Wife, Whom He Left on His Wedding-Day, with a Design to Visit the Eastern Churches" (1739), Moses Browne's "Verses on the Death of a Dear and Most Lov'd Wife. Written Just upon Recovery from Illness, Anno 1737" (1739), and Mary Monck's poignant "Verses Written on Her Death-Bed at Bath, to Her Husband in London" (1755).

Another example of this group that does stay more within the bounds of the elegiac mood is Letitia Barbauld's imitation (1773) of one of the elegies from Ovid's *Tristia*. A poet and writer with a large literary acquaintance, Barbauld was known especially for her liberal political opinions and her works for children. However, she was well able to adapt the classical elegy to a celebration of domesticity. She has Ovid write from exile in Tomis on the Black Sea coast and lament that he will live out the remainder of his life among strangers, cut off from the comforts that an old man might expect to have. Throughout most of her imitation, Mrs. Barbauld avoids the sentimental in giving the reader a moving expression of the poet's sorrow in being absent from home. Yet, reflecting the more positive attitude toward marriage of her era, Mrs. Barbauld could not resist one significant domesticating emendation:

> I bend beneath the weight of broken years,
> Averse to change, and chill'd with causeless fears,
> The season now invites me to retire
> To the dear lares of my household fire;
> To homely scenes of calm domestic peace,
> A poet's leisure, and an old man's ease;
> To wear the remnant of uncertain life
> In the fond bosom of a faithful wife;
> In safe repose my last few years to spend,
> Nor fearful nor impatient of their end.
>
> (89)

In the Latin original, the third from last line reads, "inque sinu dominae carisque sodalibus inque." In the Loeb Classical Library edition, A. L. Wheeler renders this as, "peacefully growing old in my lady's embrace, among my dear comrades." More tellingly, L. R. Lind in a 1975 translation gives us, "upon the breast of my mistress and among my dear comrades." Revealing of her high valuation of marital domesticity is Mrs. Barbauld's imitation, which reads: "In the fond bosom of a faithful wife." As she partially indicates in her title "Ovid to His Wife," her intention was to turn Ovid's elegy into a touching tribute to wedded love and fidelity. In creating this tribute, Mrs. Barbauld does, however, use the type with more restraint than most mid-century elegies treating a dying spouse.

No poet, even one from the dying-spouse group, is as effusive as Abraham Portal in *Nuptial Elegies* (3rd ed., 1775). In these four extended pastoral outpourings, Portal attempts to show the maturing of marital love through four stages or seasons: "Fruition" or spring, "The Disappointment of Passion" or summer, "The Triumph of Reason" or fall, and "The Winter of Love." Unfortunately for modern readers, none of the poet's celebrations of wedded bliss features much realism. The first elegy is the most ecstatic with its anticipation of the "rapt'rous Hours" "when by our Side, . . . / The little Pledges of our Love shall play" (6). Elegy 2 with its representation of a wifely tear soon kissed away is only slightly less "rapt'rous," and elegies 3 and 4, which are supposed to celebrate mature love, continue to rely on etherealized language:

> Their mutual Wants to mutual Pleasures tend,
>   To aid each other, O, what pure Delight!
> Exhaustless Source of Joy, blest Hours to Spend
>   In mutual Proofs of Love's sublimest Height!
>   (20)

In the later era, the vicissitudes of marriage are excluded from the elegy as ecstatic voices celebrating the companionate marriage drown out the crabbed antimatrimonialism of earlier satire. Of the traditional genres examined so far—the epithalamium, the epigram, the ballad, the eclogue, and the elegy—we see that the elegy treating marriage retains its original identity most loosely. Instead of lamenting death or loss, the elegy in the late eighteenth century has almost entirely been appropriated by the lyric.

The Ode

An ode may be defined as a "single, unified strain of exalted lyrical verse, directed to a single purpose, and dealing with one theme. In manner, the ode is an elaborate lyric, expressed in language, dignified, sincere, and imaginative and intellectual in tone" (Holman 306). The ode treating marriage goes through the same evolution as the ode in general in the period under study, though not all of the stages of the evolution are exemplified. Broadly speaking, the movement of the ode is from the irregular "Pindarique effusions" of Cowley and Crashaw through the more refined and rationalized (yet still irregular) Pindarique odes of Dryden to the briefer and simpler Horatian odes of the early and mid-eighteenth century. The tendency is toward stanzaic regularity, though "older notions of the ode as *beau desordre* did persist among certain writers, especially the humorists" (Shuster 238). Ultimately, romantic poets—Wordsworth and Shelley, for example—would experiment grandly with more irregular or unconventional patterns.

In odes treating marriage, the movement, in spite of the tendency toward stanzaic regularity, is in the direction of lyrical effusiveness, especially in the impassioned celebration of a particular "happy marriage."

Even as early as Dryden, we find a finely controlled outpouring of lyrical intensity in his "Pindarique" marriage ode "On the Marriage of the Fair and Vertuous Lady, Mrs. Anastasia Stafford, . . ." (written 1686–88?). Though it lacks the sheer virtuosity in meter and language of "A Song for St. Cecilia's Day" or "Alexander's Feast," "On the Marriage of Mrs. Anastasia Stafford" is still a dramatically powerful celebration of marriage.

> See then a bridegroom worthy such a bride!
> Never was happy pair so fitly tied;
> Never were virtues more allied;
> United in a most auspicious hour—
> A martyr's daughter weds a confessor!
> (Dryden 852; lines 70–74)

From Dryden's elevated drama to the scandalmongering pettiness of "Ill News after Marriage. To Miss E———ds. An Ode." is quite a falling off. Yet the regularizing of the ode in the early eighteenth century sometimes produces such fashionable trifles as this in four-line stanzas of alternating tetrameter and trimeter.

> When good Miss *Teddy* first was told
>   That poor L—d *Nan* was married;
> It made her very Blood run cold,
>   Nay, some thought she'd miscarried.
>
> She flung about the House like mad,
>   And made such a strange Pother,
> They swore that she was drunk, or had
>   Just seen her drunken Mother.
> (33; first two stanzas only)

Printed in *Court Whispers: or, A Magazine of Wit. A Satyr for the Country* (1743), "Ill News after Marriage" is a crude personal attack on Miss E———ds whose love for a Lord Nan has been balked by his marriage to another. The last nine stanzas are delivered in the first person by the target of the satire in a kind of mad song which amounts to a rationalization for promiscuity. If readers are not meant to judge her effusions as unbalanced, at least they are meant to judge her moral values as askew. What makes this poem an ode may simply be that the speech of Miss E———ds is in fact a kind of disordered outpouring, a satiric treatment of the feminine sensibility under stress. Later odes treat women's romantic passions with more sympathy.[5]

William Thompson's "To a Friend on His Marriage. An Ode" (1757), an Horatian ode in iambic pentameter quatrains, is considerably more elevated in language than "Ill News after Marriage." It also obviously celebrates a particularly happy marriage, though not simply in a freely flowing, effusive style. With its heavy personification and its use of metaphoric phrases like "the golden tide of time" and adjectives such as "peculiar white" (describing the quality of the morning light), Thompson, a rector at Hampton Poyle with South Weston in Oxfordshire, reminds us of the sometimes precious diction of Collins's odes.

Once Thompson's ode shifts into the voice of the muse addressing the bridegroom, the language does begin to flow more warmly and naturally.

> "I own the radiant magic of her eyes,
> But more the graces of her soul admire;
> Those may lay traps for lover, fops and flies,
> But these the husband and the Muse inspire."
>
> (Chalmers 15: 22)

Though "To a Friend on His Marriage" has a controlled syntactical balance and antithesis suggestive of Denham, Dryden, or Pope (e.g., in stanza 6), a lyrical outpouring of feelings distinguishes much of it. Thompson's ode points backward to Augustan syntactical and metrical patterns and forward to the more lyrical, effusive mode that increasingly characterizes odes in the late eighteenth and early nineteenth centuries.

William Cowper's "Ode. Supposed to be Written on the Marriage of a Friend" (first printing 1825) stands as an illustration of that lyrical tendency, though certainly not as an example of its excesses. Written in six-line stanzas, which were favored even over the quatrain by ode writers in the later era, Cowper's ode is spoken in the voice of Orpheus addressing his lyre. It repeats the pattern of having an impassioned speaker deliver the ode—a pattern we have already seen in "Ill News after Marriage" and in Thompson's ode.

Cowper's emphasis falls on the power of music (or poetry) to arouse joy in the auditor (in this case, Euridice). Analogously, it dwells on the power of beauty (Euridice's in particular) to cheer the poet and guide his heart. The reciprocal nature of the joy is important to the underlying religious nature of the poet's marital union:

> The God propitious join'd our willing hands,
> And Hymen wreathed us in his rosy bands.
>
> (1: 49; lines 23–24)

Giving depth to their union is the idea that it is not superficial physical beauty which provides the purest and the most lasting pleasure:

> Yet not the beaming eye, or placid brow,
>   Or golden tresses, hid the subtle dart;
> To charms superior far than those I bow,
>   And nobler worth enslaves my vanquish'd heart;
> The beauty, elegance, and grace combined,
> Which beam transcendant from that angel mind;
>
> While vulgar passions—meteors of a day,
>   Expire before the chilling blasts of age,
> Our holy flame, with pure and steady ray,
>   Its glooms shall brighten, and its pangs assuage;
> By Virtue (sacred vestal) fed, shall shine,
> And warm our fainting souls with energy divine.
>
> (1: 49–50; lines 25–36)

Cowper's idea might be seen simply as an elaboration of the commonplace that beauty is no more than skin deep. Close reading shows the idea to be less a commonplace than a philosophical insight with transcendental overtones. Rather than attempting to elevate the dignity of his ode simply by elevating the language, Cowper takes the more substantial route of adding a religious dimension to his theme. Unlike the efforts of many contemporaries to make the ode more musical, Cowper's lyricism has a sustaining spiritual resonance. Although Cowper is obviously interested in the idea of music as a medium through which lyrical feeling can be more deeply expressed, he avoids the bathetically effusive mode of some late eighteenth-century ode writers who celebrate the companionate marriage (see Shuster 223). During the course of the century, the ode, a type traditionally given to lyrical effusiveness, evolves into an apt vehicle for expressing a more affective stance toward marriage. Cowper's ode is an illustration of how finely this can be done.

THE EPITHALAMIUM

The only traditional poetic type exclusively identified with the topic of marriage is the epithalamium. It is a type that is rooted in ancient fertility ceremonies and the animistic pastoral tradition that emerges from them. As Virginia Tufte has shown, fragments of the epithalamia can be found as early as the end of the seventh century B.C. in Sappho's poetry, and in Theocritus's "Idyll 18" it becomes formally identified with the pastoral tradition. The best classical epithalamist is Catullus, whose "Carmen 61" provided "almost a catalogue of [nature-centered] scenes, themes, actions, and images" for the English epithalamists of the Renaissance and early seventeenth century (Tufte, *The Poetry of Marriage* 24). In the medieval period the two most important epithalamia are the Canticles or Song of Songs attributed to Solomon and the 44th Psalm of the Vulgate, "Eructavit cor meum" (71). For medieval commentators, these are not secular love songs but celebrations of the mystical union between Christ and his church. Many epithalamia penned in England in the sixteenth, seventeenth, and eighteenth centuries celebrate the wedding of a noble or royal couple. Traditionally, poets use the type to affirm parallels in natural, social, and cosmic hierarchies.

With Spenser's *Epithalamion* of 1594 and his *Prothalamion* (1596), the English epithalamium becomes more specifically indebted to the nature-centered tradition of Catullus and to other major epithalamic traditions, especially the Christian. It also becomes more individualized, since Spenser wrote his poem to celebrate his own wedding. An intricate and richly structured poem, Spenser's *Epithalamion* sets the standard for succeeding epithalamia as it draws on many elaborate conventions to produce a personal lyric in which natural and spiritual forces echo the narrator's praise of his bride and their marriage. One critic suggests that the world of this poem is made up of concentric spheres emanating outward. At the center of the focus is the couple, then their social context, next their natural setting, then the mythological beings that inhabit the cosmos of the poem, and finally, above all, the Christian heaven.[6]

After Spenser, epithalamia become quite popular. Jonson included several in his masques, and Donne composed two in the witty metaphysical style. Tufte notes "graceful works in the genre by Thomas Campion, Michael Drayton, Henry Peacham, Thomas Carew, Thomas Vaughan, Francis Quarles, Andrew Marvell, and others" (*The Poetry of Marriage* 232). Superior to all but Spenser's poem are the five composed by Herrick, the most notable of which is "A Nuptial Song or Epithalamie on Sir Clipsy Crew and His Lady" (1648). In this poem as in Spenser's, the rich, curious, and beautiful phenomenological world of the wedding consistently evokes an encompassing realm.

Except for passing mention of epithalamia by Dryden, Prior, and

Smart, Tufte breaks off her examination with the Restoration.[7] She does observe that in the later period the type tends to be "patriotic and general rather than personal." She also points to its increasing tendency to become formula-ridden, a tendency that reaches its nadir with Elkanah Settle (*The Poetry of Marriage* 252). Samuel Johnson pointed out in *Idler* 12 that Settle "had a standing epithalamium 'of which only the first and last leaves were varied occasionally, and the intermediate pages were, by general terms, left applicable alike to every character'" (325n55). Tufte's writing off the eighteenth century has some justification, for certainly the period produced many occasional epithalamia. Penned on commission for the weddings of aristocrats and the wealthy, these poems are filled with ceremonious flattery and conventionalized ecstasy.[8] Yet the decline of the epithalamium is a gradual one, and among the many formulaic poems are a number that are both artistically and culturally significant. We will look at a few of these as we examine how the type slowly loses its religious resonances and replaces them with social and emotional affirmation. As the idea of marriage becomes more secular, epithalamia celebrate the value of marriage in terms subject to physical and psychological verification. Epithalamia by women poets follow a similar evolutionary pattern, increasingly placing emphasis on the role of the social virtues in creating happiness.

Late seventeenth- and eighteenth-century epithalamia tend to be shorter and less formally structured than those of the Renaissance, especially Spenser's. The various conventions employed by the earlier poets such as the invocation to the Muse, the decking of the bridal path with flowers, and the welcoming of the night are often simplified or eliminated entirely. In the period under study, epithalamia are usually not composed of distinctly structured parts in which each part handles a conventional topic and in which the temporal order of the ceremony evokes a supernatural or cosmic order. Rather the shorter poems of this period can be held together illogically by witty conceit but mainly are unified by the force or sentiment or emotional association between poet and reader.

A few of the most interesting epithalamia are so because they are not occasional, glorifying a particular eighteenth-century couple, but because they write of a wedding occurring in the mythic past or in some rusticated setting. This framing ostensibly gives the poets more freedom to glorify the religious significance of the wedding, though it is doubtful that they do. Instead of evoking a cosmic order that stands behind the temporal ceremony, these rusticated epithalamia may simply give social affirmation to the wedding celebrated.

Examining the particular lines of evolution of the epithalamium, we will see that the main movement is increasingly toward emotional affirmation. A few later poems persist in witty affirmation, and another interesting later subgroup uses the fictive frame of the rusticated epithalamium or returns to a more elaborately structured Spenserian model. All three types—the epithalamium of emotional affirmation, the witty epithalamium, and the Spenserian or rusticated epithalamium—celebrate marriage in a more worldly, less mystical way that increasingly recognizes its social and psychological benefits.

In the main line of development toward emotional affirmation, the earliest Restoration poems tend to rely on a metaphysical or cavalier style wit to evoke the heaven-sent joy of the ceremony. This is the case, as we will see in chapter 6, with Katherine Philips's finely understated "Rosannia's *Private Marriage*" (1664); it is also true of William Davenant's "Upon the Nuptial of Charles Lord Herbert, and the Lady M. Villers" (1673). When Royalist Davenant writes, "The Priest, with words devoutly said,/ Shall ripen her a Wife" (238), we see that the ceremony is entirely in tune with the natural-supernatural order and gives sanction to a fertility that was begun by God, working through time.

Instead of positively evoking a supernatural order, other early epithalamia may do so in the negative in a mock epithalamium. In a poem such as "The Quaker's Wedding" (1673) by Matthew Stevenson, a friend of the Royalist satirist Alexander Brome, the speaker employs his wit to show how the unorthodox Quaker ceremony has violated some principle of heavenly order.[9]

> How Heaven approv'd the juggle you may tell,
> When Thunder, Lightning, and a Tempest fell:
> So dreadful too, though at one clap it stopt,
> Confusion waited on both Men, and Meat;
> Their Marriage and their Feast were both a cheat.
> And wedding and no wedding brought before ye,
> The Devil doubtless was the Directorie,
> Some Hellebor restore 'um to recant,
> This sordid League, and senseless Covenant,
> O that such vileness should affront the Sun!
>
> (80)

Working in a conservative tradition of Restoration anti-Puritan satire suggestive of *Hudibras*, Stevenson shows cosmic and social forces set at sixes and sevens by the Quaker's antiwedding.

Later Restoration and early eighteenth-century epithalamia often continue to imply that the ceremony has some connection with a supernatural principle, but the way the connection is established often becomes formularized or contrived. Poets depend on novelties of wit or, even worse, on stock praise to celebrate the significance of a wedding. For example, in Davenant's "Epithalamium. The Morning after the Marriage of the Earl of Barrymore with Mrs. Martha Laurence" (1673), one of the standard theological rationales for marriage—the production of offspring—is wittily belittled so that the poet can carry off his ingenious flattery. A sense of the cosmic significance of marriage or its place in the natural order seems lost in the roundabout compliment.

For some epithalamists in this era, Spenser still remains the model, but the conventions and the personages are demythologized. John Pomfret's "On the Marriage of the Earl of A——— with the Countess of S———" (2nd ed. 1707) offers a curious opening somewhat similar to the passage in Spenser's *Epithalamion* in which the hours and graces are summoned and ordered to "Helpe addorne my beautifullest bride" (line 105). In Spenser's *Epithalamion* the "houres" are "begot/In Joves sweet paradice, of Day and Night" and the graces are "ye three handmayds of the Cyprian Queene,/The which doe still addorne my beautifullest bride." In Pomfret's poem,

> While Hymen does his sacred rites prepare,
> The busy nymphs attend the trembling fair;
> (Chalmers 8: 323)

The attendants here are only "busy nymphs," not mythological creatures who inhabit some supernatural realm. They are probably no more than the flesh-and-blood friends and kin of the bride who assist her in dressing.

Spenser describes in an enticingly specific catalog the features of the bride's outward beauty and then "the inward beauty of her lively spright" or soul. Pomfret, in contrast, affirms the bride's outward virtues more generally, and when he treats her inward attractions, he focuses on their more naturalistic manifestations of the bride's physiology:

> Whose veins are swell'd with an unusual heat,
> And eager pulses with strange motions beat:
> (Chalmers 8: 323)

Although Pomfret assures us that "the raptures of Cosmelia's love/Are next, if only next, to those above," the poet focuses less on supernatural analogues to the bride's physical state than on the physical intensity of her conflicting passions.

Women epithalamists may also exhibit a similar replacement of the religious with emotional affirmation of the natural charms of youth and beauty. In "Lines Occasion'd by the Marriage of Edward Herbert Esquire, and Mrs. Elizabeth Herbert" (1713), Anne Finch, Countess of Winchilsea, gives us a Cupid who is little more than a stylized figure:

> Cupid one day ask'd his Mother,
>   When she meant that he shou'd Wed?
> You're too Young, my Boy, she said:
>   Nor has Nature made another
>   Fit to match with *Cupid's* Bed.
>
> *Cupid* then her Sight directed
>   To a lately Wedded Pair;
> Where Himself the Match effected;
>   They as Youthful, they as Fair.
>
> Having by Example carry'd
>   This first Point in the Dispute;
> WORSELEY next he said's not Marry'd:
>   Her's with *Cupid's* Charms may suit.
>   (Winchilsea 55–56)

The contrived fiction of Cupid lends little spiritual vitality to the wedding, but the poet's cleverness and light touch tend to divert us from that fact. More important, her kind concern that her friend Worseley marry gives the poem a positive sympathetic force.[10]

In the early eighteenth century, an increasing number of epithalamia appear that depend more on the poet's empathetic affirmation of the social joys of the wedding than on his or her evocation (by wit or otherwise) of a cosmic order that informs the temporal ceremony. Such is the case with "On the Marriage of Alexander Brodie of Brodie, Lord Lyon King of Arms, and Mrs. Mary Sleigh" (1728) by Allan Ramsay, Scots poet and important figure in Edinburgh literary society. In this piece, heaven does join in the process of approving the marriage, but the couple achieves a "*humane* Bliss complete" (italics mine). Significantly, it is the poet who informs the couple of heaven's approval. In his last stanza the poet calls on cosmic principles to sustain the marriage; however, he is the agent primarily responsible for conveying the blessing.

Similarly, in Henry Travers's "An Epistle to a Painter, Occasioned by the Marriage of the Honourable Mrs. XXXX" (1731), the device of the instructions-to-the-painter allows the poet to emphasize his own moral agency in affirming the marriage as he tells the painter to arrange the tutelary graces in proper order. In "To Mr. Daniel Booth, Jun. on His Marriage" (1739) by Moses Browne, Vicar of Olney, Bucks, cosmic forces are invoked to shed a beneficent influence on the marriage:

> O may each Planet of benignant Pow'r
> Mark with white Omens that auspicious Hour!
> Serene as o'er thy blissful *Parents* shed
> Indulgent Rays, and bless'd their genial Bed:
>
> (262)

Nevertheless, it is the poet's affirmation of the groom's social virtues (like those of his parents) that is most important in this piece.

By mid-century, the poet's emotional affirmation often outweighs any sanction that supernatural or natural principles can lend to the wedding. Such is the case in "Epithalamium by Mr. D——" printed in Dodsley's *Miscellany* (1758). The poet shows us by his various tropes that "Nature wills/Such union." This is illustrated especially by the way "*Loddona's* cold and inactive" stream picks up force when "married to jovial *Thames*" (5.103–4).[11]

Yet, in spite of the poet's mention of nature's support, it is his empathetic blessing of the couple's social fitness that prevails.

> Her lyre
> She strung,—a friendly voluntary strain.
> "Hail (she began) distinguish'd pair! how fit
> To join in wedded love, each other's choice!
> Bridegroom, thy taste is elegant indeed,
> And fingers nice, that on some sunny bank
> In beauty's garden cull'd so fair a flow'r,
> To thine transplanted from her native soil."
>
> (5: 103)

The poet uses a Muse figure to convey approval, and in so doing, he calls attention to his own (and society's) agency in affirming the marriage.

Social affirmation of specific weddings need not always occur in the effusive, empathetic strain, although that strain (as we shall see in chapter 6) does continue to develop strongly in the later era. Even well after mid-century, it can occur in the witty, good-humored poems, the second type of epithalamium. James Robertson in "On Mr. D———'s Marriage with Miss E———" (1767) employs a whimsical mythological fiction to sweeten his moralizing about the sanctity of the marriage vow and the social virtues necessary in a wife. The fiction also makes his flattery of the bridal couple less overt. The clever evocation of the Roman mythological deities adds little spiritual dimension to the wedding being celebrated. Robertson simply uses Jove, Cupid, and Hymen as cute puppets to affirm Mr. D———'s choice of a bride with all the proper social virtues.

Robertson is just as capable of using his wit not to charm and flatter. In "To Mr. Y———, on His Marriage with a Most Joyous Lady" (1770), Robertson ingeniously falls into the effusive, empathetic strain so popular in his time, but he employs it with cutting irony to satirize.

> Tho' some talk of your Marriage queerly,
> I wish you Joy, *Tom*, most sincerely;
> And Joy that Husband must possess,
> Whose Wife's the Source of *Joyousness*:
> Whose Wife has Hundreds happy made,
> Quite mistress of the *joyous* Trade;
> What endless Joys to him are known,
> Who all those Joys now calls his own;
> Too much for one poor Man to bear,
> With Friends you'll therefore kindly share.
>
> I hope, dear Tom, you've now for Life
> Got a most *joyous*, active Wife;
> To whom both *Will* and *Pow'r* are given,
> Of making Spousy free of Heaven;
> And who—(*Can* Love be more exprest?)
> Wou'd damn herself to make you blest.
>
> Your Friends all wish you Joy, and hope
> You've now of Joy—a *Cornu-Cope*:—
> One *Cornu-Cope* perhaps won't do;
> Why then, dear Tom, We wish you *Two*.
>
> (176)

Robertson cruelly mocks his friend's unfortunate choice of a wife and her cuckolding of him. In this mock epithalamium Tom's wife embodies the opposite of a positive cosmic or natural force. Instead of being a true cornucopia, heaven blessed in her fertility, she is a prolific social liability, cuckolding her husband with growing promiscuity. Robertson broadly parodies the effusive strain and points up its potential for bathos.

Many epithalamia that we have seen so far are occasional poems honoring an actual historic couple. They hold to the traditional form of the epithalamia only loosely, so loosely that it could be argued that a number of them no longer fit the category. These poems lack not only the form of the longer Renaissance epithalamia; many have also lost almost all sense of a cosmic or natural order standing behind the ceremony celebrated.

A few epithalamia of the third type do, however, appear in the eighteenth century that hark back to the longer, more elaborately structured style of Spenser and the classical epithalamists. In some cases, the model may not be Spenser but the rusticated epithalamia whose prototype is John Suckling's "A Ballad upon a Wedding" (1646).[12] Suckling's speaker emphasizes the strange, almost enchanted beauty of the West Country wedding he beholds. Though he says little directly about its cosmic or supernatural background, this is suggested by the quaintness or charming purity of the wedding praised by the narrator.

Both the Spenserian and the rusticated epithalamia may have been written out of a nostalgia for an era in which the ceremony of a wedding held more spiritual significance, either as a Christian sacrament or as a natural event with cosmic reverberations. Significantly, in adopting older, more elaborate models for their epithalamia, eighteenth-century poets usually affirm the emotional ambience of the older poems, not their religiosity. A delightful piece that might be identified as belonging to the subgenre of the rusticated epithalamium is N. Brown's "The North-Country Wedding," which Matthew Concanen published in *Miscellaneous Poems* in 1724 (1–15). Describing a wedding between Willy and the "matchless Moggy," Brown's poem has many of the hallmarks of the earlier epithalamia of Spenser, Herrick, and Suckling. Even so, it does little to invoke a supernatural order that would lend a religious dimension to the temporal ceremony. Brown's poem recreates the decor of the older epithalamia without their deeper significance. Portraying the country customs and all the characters and merriment of a north-country wedding, Brown's epithalamium mainly aims to present a scene of warm fellowship and communal joy that socially fashionable weddings of his era may have lacked.

The greatest charm of "The North-Country Wedding" is its cast of sentimentalized country characters suggestive of those in Goldsmith's *The Deserted Village* (1770), though handled here with more comic realism. Most vivid of these is a stage Irishman at whom some of Brown's readers took offense, even though the caricature is fairly mild. There is also a "goodly Dame/Of ruddy Aspect, and enormous Size." She mumbles through an embarrassed tribute to the joys of matrimony, interrupting it with personal interjections.

The entire poem is a fiction, a pure celebration of matrimony in that it makes no reference to an actual historical couple. Perhaps the pervasiveness of occasional epithalamia written for hire prompted Brown to celebrate a rusticated, warmly sentimentalized marriage rather than its coldly fashionable urban reality.

Concanen not only prints Brown's rusticated epithalamium but a similar one by James Ward entitled "Epithalamium on the Marriage of Felim and Oonah" (328–36). Painting a picture of another happy country wedding, Ward makes less use than Brown of comic realism and emphasizes the simplicity and happiness of the vaguely Celtic pastoral setting. Like Brown's poem, Ward's is long enough to treat some of the standard activities of the formal epithalamium: the rustic dance for which the "Jolly Piper" plays, the "Bridal Supper," which "unskill'd Cleanliness prepares," and the leading of the bride to bed by the virgins (332). Like Brown's epithalamium, Ward's clearly places itself in opposition to the fashionable society wedding and the poems that celebrate them. Ward's epithalamium achieves its force from the social virtues of Felim and Oonah's wedding: its honest simplicity, not its echoes of the supernatural or enchanted.

Later epithalamia by women work in the tradition of the rusticated subgenre but go further in emphasizing the honest simplicity and the warm emotional ambience of the occasion.[13] Elizabeth Frances Amherst, sister to Lord Jeffrey Amherst, in "The Welford Wedding" (MS ca. 1740–50) celebrates a Northamptonshire wedding in verses with a domesticated Blakean energy punctuated with anapestic rhythms. Male and female wedding guests

> Jump and skip and caper and brawl,
> Frisk in the drawing-room, romp in the hall,
> (Lonsdale 181)

This may be a fashionable wedding where "*Pates de veau* and transmogrified meats" are served. Yet it is filled with a cast of lovable countrified characters such as Parson Strother, Lady Bustle, and dear Warner who plays a harp no one can dance to—"Tinkle cum tinkle, and sweet flat and sharp." In spite of its social panoply, the wedding is affirmed by its joyful and spontaneous energy.

Priscilla Pointon's "Letter to a Sister, Giving an Account of the Author's

Wedding-Day" (written ca. 1788) is not in the strict sense an epithalamium; however, it offers a celebratory report of a rusticated wedding "in a small country church" at Shotwig near Chester. Working in an informal epistolary style, the blind Lichfield-born poetess writes for her sister a chatty recreation of the day's events: to the church in a post-coach and four, making a "great show" in church with "white gloves and ribbons," regaling the Vicar "with plum-cake and wine," dining at Parkgate "On fish, lamb, and ducks, puddings, tarts, whips, my dear," and then more refreshments later in the day. The couple have obviously expended some effort to appear fashionable:

> The nymphs and the swains all in ranks did appear,
> To see us fine folks, for sure, fine we must be,
> When powdered, and dressed a la mode de Paris!
> (Lonsdale 275)

Yet the realism of the narrator allows us to cut through the mythological decor. This down-to-earth epithalamium gives us the drama of a blind, middle-aged woman enjoying her day in the sun.

Epithalamia that broadly imitate the Spenserian model are, like the rusticated epithalamia, more concerned with emotional affirmation than sanctioning the temporal with the supernatural. An epithalamium that seems closer in both manner and substance to the Spenserian model than Brown's and Ward's is Allan Ramsay's "A Pastoral Epithalamium" (date not established). Ramsay's piece has a setting occupied by shepherds, primroses, rocks, rivulets, and "cattarchs." One of the shepherds in the dialogue also invokes the supernatural in the person of the god Pan. Yet, as with most eighteenth-century epithalamia, close reading reveals its underlying concern is social affirmation and moral counsel:

> Strephon
> Well he deserves her, and the gods are just
> To put so fair a jewell in his trust,
> Who knows to manage well what he intends.
> (3: 328–29)

Ramsay's piece is a curious combination of eighteenth-century wine in a Renaissance bottle.

Another example that differs from the shorter, informal epithalamia most common in the eighteenth century is William Thompson's "Epithalamium on the Royal Nuptials, in May, 1736" (1757). Treating the marriage of Frederick, Prince of Wales, to Augusta, daughter of Frederick II, Duke of Saxe-Gotha, this poem celebrates a very fashionable wedding. The heavy use of mythology and personification along with Spenserian diction and stanza give Thompson's piece a fantastic air, highly suggestive of the Renaissance epithalamia. The problem with the Spenserian imitation is that the mythology generally lacks natural vitality, and the gods and goddesses that appear tend mainly to be decorative accessories to the poet's praise of this most auspicious match. The gods are reduced to the status of jewels on the bride's dress, and the Spenserian decor of the poem only slightly masks Thompson's use of the mid-century effusive strain. As with Brown's, Ward's, Amherst's, Pointon's, and Ramsay's epithalamia, the main activity of Thompson's poem turns out to be approval of the wedding as a model social event.

As we have seen in this section, the epithalamium moves beyond its elaborately structured Renaissance pattern of bodying forth a supernatural order through the temporal ceremony. Adopting simpler structures for their mainly occasional epithalamia, poets turn increasingly toward emotional affirmation through a secularized companionate ideology. This pattern, as this chapter shows, occurs to a significant degree in many traditional poetic types.

CHAPTER SIX

Real Bliss

BETWEEN 1650 AND 1800, IT IS NOT JUST IN TRAditional genres that celebration becomes more secular; in all marriage verse, ideas of joy, bliss, or rapture undergo a significant shift away from a theologically defined ideal, whether Roman Catholic, Calvinist, or Anglican. This shift is a manifestation of the general secularization of religious values in this era, an erosion produced by numerous factors that social historians usually mention, including the inroads of enlightenment rationalism, skepticism, and empiricism on traditional belief and church doctrine; the increasing pressures of capitalist enterprise as an arbiter of values in daily life; the consequent growth in the importance of marriage as vehicle for social and economic advancement; and the developing scientific interest in human physiology and psychology, especially attention to the physical and mental processes of sexuality. More generally, the shift is an expression of an ideology that locates happiness in domestic affection rather than the bliss that God confers through marriage. It is predominantly the male poets who celebrate women in their role as wives as the source of bliss, though many poets strongly support the new myth of bliss in domesticity. Probably this is not only because it romanticizes marital love but because it gives women the illusion of equality.

In their zeal to counter the two libertine arguments, didactic poets, especially in the later era, often attempt to make marriage more appealing to male readers by celebrating a wife's role as wholesome companion and pleasure-giver. Sexuality in wedlock is made to seem more enjoyable (and more healthy) than promiscuous sexuality. An unfortunate by-product of this emphasis on marital sexuality is to reinforce the tendency to regard women as commodities on the marriage market, though within the ideology of domesticity, the wife becomes a commodity of a higher order, a leisure class exhibit or plaything (a projection of male possession fantasies) or even an angelic woman of refined sensibilities who civilizes or spiritually uplifts her brutish husband.

Since the shifts under scrutiny in this chapter can manifest themselves as a confusing variety of notions about the locus of bliss and its nature, for purposes of tracing their permutations and particular implications, these notions can be sorted into four categories, descending from the most spiritual to the most secular.

(1) At the zenith, joy in marital love can be viewed as the result of divine grace, which is associated with the spiritual character of the marital union. In Roman Catholic theology, God confers grace on the partners in their sacramental union. For Anglicans, marriage "does not convey any spiritual grace whereby sin is remitted"; nevertheless, "its inward and spiritual grace is the sanctification of coitus and the attainment of everlasting life through the education of children in the true faith" (Bailey 186). Even in Puritan doctrine, grace "necessarily precedes the decision of two Christian persons to marry and is in a certain way the cause of that decision" (J. T. Johnson 47). In either case the bliss deriving from God's "grace" is mystical, sacred, or divine in its nature and thus eternal.

(2) In a less mysterious religious sense, joy may come more simply from the union of two souls in one body for the purposes of procreation and for faithfulness and companionship. In this sense, joy is a gift of heaven that accompanies the act of procreation and encourages it.

(3) In a more secular sense, the joy or bliss of marriage may be an outcome of domestic tranquillity or the happiness of living together in physical or material comfort. Eighteenth-century poems that celebrate the joy of a married couple living in a love nest or in the proverbial rose-covered cottage usually mean *joy* in this sense.

(4) Finally, in the lowest and most naturalistic sense, joy or bliss can be a pleasurable sensation, specifically sexual gratification.

The overall shift of joy or bliss in the period is from the religious and mystical toward the secular and naturalistic. Nevertheless, because of the multiple meanings of these terms, it would be difficult to demonstrate a simple evolutionary progression by a chronological tracing through all the poetry. We will look consequently at four separate chronological movements under each of the four working definitions just offered.

Examining the ideas of bliss in poetry of the early era, we will see initially a fairly even distribution among the four senses. Bliss in the highest spiritual sense tends to disappear quickly, and bliss meaning sexual pleasure is mainly treated satirically. As we progress through the early era, bliss in the less mysterious religious sense and in the higher secular sense, especially the latter, are predominant.

In later era poetry, the secular senses (3 and 4) move into prominence, with sexual bliss beginning to be treated in a naturalistic or even a positive way. Curiously, although the high mystical sense seems to have been totally lost in the later era, some religious poets (at least one of them a woman) begin to celebrate a divine joy or ecstasy inspired by the domestic bliss of marital love. These poets do not celebrate a bliss that comes to man miraculously through the spiritual medium of the holy estate of marriage. Rather they replace sense 1 with a more rationalized spiritual bliss that proceeds from the virtuous conduct or the religious vocation of one or both of the partners. This celebration is in line with the way eighteenth-century poetry demystifies the supernatural and replaces it with an emphasis on the secular bliss of domesticity. The religious poets, however, go a step further in attempting to respiritualize the secular.

Looking at the movement of poetry under each definition, we will discover that the modal shifts in the early era, except in sense 4, are from understated and witty celebration to the more lyrical and ecstatic. In the later era celebration predominates in all four senses, and the overall tendency is toward the profuse and ecstatic, verging on one hand on sentimentality and on the other on the religious sublime. In both directions, bliss comes to be celebrated by both male and female poets within a companionate ideology glorifying a feminized affective sensibility.

The Early Era

Of those early era poets who use the words *joy* or *bliss* (or a closely related concept) in sense 1, very few do so with the full theological implications expressed above. Poets rarely speak directly of marriage as a sacrament. This is not surprising since the post-Reformation Anglican church officially denied this title to marriage.

The church did, however, claim for this "holy estate" or "state of life" all the virtues of a sacrament. For High Church Anglican theologians as for Catholic theologians, one of the key defining qualities of marriage was its mystical or metaphysical status:

> Starting from our Lord's adaptation of the pronouncement in Genesis that when a man and woman are joined together in marriage "they shall be one flesh" and St. Paul's use of the word "mystery" to expound the union, Christianity [i.e., high Anglicans and Catholics] developed a theology of the sacramental nature of marriage [but not a Sacrament as such]. Where God had accomplished union of creatures he could, and did, bestow a special grace for the more perfect fulfillment of the same. As Origen says: "It is God who united the two into one, so that from the time the woman is joined with her husband, they are two no longer. And since God united them, therefore those who have been united by God have received a grace." Man and woman are thus united by marriage in a mystical degree even as Christ is united to his Bride the Church. (Haw 26; bracketed comments are mine)

Poets who *do* treat the joy or bliss of marriage in the high spiritual sense, though they do not identify marriage as a sacrament, usually suggest clearly the metaphysical or mystical status of the union. They may also refer to the heavenly or God-given pattern or symbol of eternal love as a central reality of marriage. In conservative Anglican theology, marriage is seen as an indissoluble union that is above the law of man: "What God hath joined together let no man put asunder." The union is sealed by the bride and groom in a religious vow before the altar of God. The consummation of the marriage is, however, required to give the union the highest degree of firmness (Haw 25). In their oblique and not so oblique reference to marital sexuality, a few of the poets reflect this awareness as well.

Poets differ in the degree to which they recognize the theological significance of marriage. In the fine and understated heroic couplets of "Rosannia's *Private Marriage*" (1664), Katherine Philips seems to dismiss any religious meaning Rosannia's marriage might have when she scorns public religious ceremony.

> It was a wise and kind design of Fate,
> That none should this day's glory celebrate:
> For 'twere in vain to keep a time which is
> Above the reach of all Solemnities,

> The greatest Actions pass without a noise,
> And Tumults but prophane diviner Joyes.
> Silence with things transcendent nearest suits,
> The greatest Emperours are serv'd by Mutes,
> And as in ancient time the Deities
> To their own Priest reveal'd no Mysteries
> Until they were from all the World retir'd,
> And in some Cave made fit to be inspir'd,
> So when *Rosannia* (who hath them out-vied,
> And with more Justice might be Deified;
> Who if she had their Rites and altars, we
> Should hardly think it were Idolatry)
> Had found a breast that did deserve to be
> Receptacle of her Divinity;
> It was not fit the gazing World should know
> When she convey'd her self to him, or how.
>
> (106–7)

A paradox grows out of the lack of formal ceremony in Rosannia's marriage. In conceits reminiscent of Marvell and the late metaphysicals, Katherine Philips does after all acknowledge the mystical nature of the event that has transpired, the "diviner Joyes" and "Mysteries" of the marriage. Indeed, by Rosannia's Puritan-like rejection of ritual, the speaker is able to emphasize the theological significance of the union and make it more "transcendent." That there may actually be elements of conservative Anglican theology in Philips's poem need not surprise us. "Although she had grown up in a Puritan family and married into a Puritan ruling class, Philips's sympathies were Royalist" (Greer 186).

A similar conception of marriage, though with less emphasis on the mystical nature of the bliss, is again presented by Katherine Philips in her understated epithalamium "To My Dear Sister, Mrs. C. P. on Her Nuptial":

> We will not like those men our offerings pay
> Who crown the cup, then think they crown the day.
> We make no garlands, nor an altar build,
> Which help not Joy, but Ostentation yield.
> Where mirth is justly grounded these wild toyes
>
> . . . .
>
> But these shall be my great Solemnities,
> *Orinda's* wishes for *Cassandra's* bliss

> May her Content be as unmix'd and pure
> As my Affection, and like that endure;
> And that strong Happiness may she still find
> Not owning to her Fortune, but her Mind.
>
> (52)

Though Katherine Philips does not mention God, her description of her sister's "Content" as "unmix'd and pure" strongly suggests that her joy will be spiritual in nature. This is also implied by the poet's locating her sister's future happiness in "Mind," rather than in a physical entity such as Fortune. That the union will be held together by a spiritual love (between "Souls") is suggested as well by the last stanza where the poet continues her blessing of the couple:

> May nothing accidental e're appear
> But what shall with new bonds their Souls endear.
>
> (53)

More directly sacramental and mystical, but in a mechanistic way, is Dryden's pindarique ode (written 1696–98, published 1812) "On the Marriage of the Fair and Vertuous Lady, Mrs. Anastasia Stafford, with That Worthy and Pious Gent. George Holman, Esq" (Dryden 850). Dryden celebrates God's conferring bliss through the agency of the bride's martyred father, Viscount Stafford (1614–80), who was "executed for complicity in the Popish Plot" (*The Poems of John Dryden* 4: 2089).

Other poems can be found that emphasize the mystical nature of marriage and at the same time stress, more naturalistically, the God-given joys that accompany the act of procreation or that stem from companionship in marriage. These poems use joy in both the higher and lower spiritual senses and also possibly in a high secular sense. As Grub Street formula poems relying on heavily overstated celebration as their mode, these pieces may represent a clergyman's effort to evoke the newly popular pro-companionate sensibility.

An Answer to the Pleasures of a Single Life (1701) emphasizes the sacred nature of wedlock, that it is not an anthropological coincidence but a gift of God out of love for mankind:

> And so he than by his alwise Direction,
> Both souls united with the like affection;
> So very sweetly and with such delight,
> The swiftest Winged Minutes take their flight,
> And thus Gods love to Mankind did dispence,

> The sacred Wedlock, which did then commence;
> Not founded as some Criticks say, by chance;
> But Heaven it self, did this blest State advance.
> Not subject to the various Revolutions,
> Of fickle fading human Institutions.
> A Married life was first contriv'd above,
> To be an Emblem of Eternal Love;
> And after by Divine Indulgence sent,
> To be the Crown of Man, and Wife's content;
>
> (3)

Happiness in wedlock is unmistakably divine or "sacred" in nature. The poet stresses marriage's indissolubility by saying that it is "not subject to" the changes of "fickle fading human institutions." The use of the phrase "To be an Emblem of Eternal Love" is however somewhat problematic. It retains the sense of marriage as a sacred union, though the word "Emblem" may lessen the sacramental reality of that union: it may be only the symbol or type of eternal love and not itself an emanation of God's love.

An Answer to the Pleasures of a Single Life also celebrates the less mystical joys of marital companionship (sense 2 and perhaps 3). It describes appealingly the sweetness and delight with which the swiftest "Minutes take their flight" when the couple are joined in "like affection." The poet may also refer obliquely to the sexual pleasures of marriage when he praises marriage as "the Crown of Man and Wife's content."

If *An Answer to the Pleasures of a Single Life* emphasizes the sacred nature of the marital union and also praises its more earthly joys, *Wedlock Vindicated* (1702) uses a profusion of similes to focus on the physical joys of marriage as types of divine bliss. This poem works upward from earthly bliss to heavenly bliss rather than, as the former poem does, downward from the agency of God:

> Marry'd Couples joyntly share in Bliss,
> Enjoy true Charms, and seldom do amiss:
> Their very Courting Days are Types Divine,
> Who like two Angels they in Love combine:
> Their love, like Starry Meteors in the Sky,
> Sparkles and blazes in each others Eye:
> In Innocence they imitate the Dove.
> And represent true lasting Joys above:
> Where Marriage first, was by Divine Command,

> To join true Lovers in a Sacred Band,
> In order to prevent all boundless Lust,
> Decreed this Heavenly Order for the Just:
> For seeing that our Lives were but a Span,
> He gave the Female as a Joy to Man:
>
>   (4)

The *Wedlock Vindicated* poet, identified on the title page as "a Lady," is concerned to show how marriage legitimizes sexual pleasure and gives it divine sanction. The poet's similes—like "Angels," "Starry Meteors," and the "Dove"—all glorify the purity of marital love and its heavenly origin. In contrast, the poet represents sexual relations outside marriage as less pleasurable because "Strange stings of Conscience wou'd our Hearts anoy." The reasoning of the poet is a curious mixture of spirituality and pragmatism. In the same breath she urges marriage because it "represents true lasting Joys above" and because its joys are more solid. Her tone is often quite secular, at times frankly acknowledging her pleasure in sex.

> One word unto the *Men* before I go,
> For they'r the Creatures I desire to know:
> Let them but move the matter, we'll comply
> All Women love the sport as well as I,
> They'l Marry, go to Bed and multiply.
>
>   (6)

Another Grub Street formula poem that shows a blend of bliss in the higher and lower spiritual senses (more sense 2 than 1) is *The Batchelor's Choice, or, The Happy Wish. A Poem* (1707). This piece is mainly a celebration of the power of love in civilizing men's brutish passions and bringing about good marriages. It does, however, grant, though only briefly and indirectly, the force of heaven in designing the marital union and giving us "bliss" through it. Of the three Grub Street examples treating the idea of joy in marriage in senses 1 and 2, *The Batchelor's Choice* offers the most secular rationales.

Celebrating the power of beauty to civilize men, the *Batchelor's Choice* poet provides several sexually charged anecdotes, most notably that of the Roman youth Stultus who is wrested out of the brutish stupidity his name denotes by the sight of a beauteous lady asleep. These stories, says the poet,

> with glimm'ring Light do prove,
> There's Destiny in Marriage, and in Love;
> A Sympathy in their Souls, which inspires,
> With Reciprocal Passions and Desires;
>
> *As If when Heaven first their Frame designed,*
> *Created them two Bodies, but one Mind.*
>
> (10)

What the poet extols seems an eighteenth-century religious version of simpatico. The poet may simply be praising the power of sexual attraction between man and woman, but the mention of "destiny" and the emphasis on God's design in the matter suggests the Calvinist idea of a grace or special providence that brings together a couple who are specially created for each other (see Johnson 47). In such union a spiritual force is clearly at work, though God is present at one remove since he acts as a creator of the providence, not as the source of grace acting through the sacrament.

Such ways of explaining God's role in creating the happiness of marriage may involve a degree of rationalization of God's powers, an effort to identify them with already existing natural forces. Broadly speaking, *The Batchelor's Choice* usually tries to give both heaven and earth their due when it locates the source of bliss in marriage.

> It is the only Bliss that can be given
> To us on Earth, or receiv'd by us from Heaven,
> No Change or Crosses should our Love Impair,
> But in ev'ry State alike it should appear.
>
> (13)

According to popular myth and the traditional moralists, earthly pleasure is notoriously changeable and evanescent. Since the poet has extolled so highly the power of bliss to hold a marriage together, he has also to glorify, as he does in his concluding couplet, the eternality and immutability of that bliss.

Under sense 2, we find poems that celebrate the earthly joys of marriage given to us by God. These poems, however, lay almost no stress on the mystical or sacramental. Two of the chief joys of marriage under this sense are the pleasures of procreation and the pleasures of companionship. In the two examples—both from the 1690s—the celebratory mode is strong, though not hyperbolic. In Dryden's piece (the second), the blisses of marriage are more finely and aptly praised than in Hugh Newman's Grub Street piece. Though he uses *bliss* elsewhere with a meaning close to sense 1, Newman's usage in *A Poem in Praise of Marrying for Love* (1698) is unmistakably in the lower spiritual sense; it is contained in a passage glorifying God's wisdom in setting up marriage.

> This to th'Allwise Creator known,
> He pitti'd MAN shou'd be alone;
> And that his Blisses might not be
> Bound up in Incommunity;
> He rais'd for Help and Propagation,
> That After-Work of the Creation,
> That Polish'd, Curious Fabrick, WOMAN,
> To share the World's vast Stock in Common.
>
> (3)

Man's "blisses" are a direct function of woman's role as a helpmeet and a bearer of children. Interestingly, Newman later in the poem says that in Woman's "stupendious Features shine/ Mixtures of Humane and Divine." Yet in the passage just cited and the one previous to it, he repeatedly refers to woman in material terms, especially those that suggest her role in propagating the species. She is "That After-Work of Creation," "That Polish'd, Curious Fabrick," and, most revealingly, "the Treasure-House of Nature" (3). Probably middle-class and Protestant in background, Newman has a penchant for praising spiritual attributes in materialistic terms, and in his opening he does just that with marriage in general:

> What greater blessing can be given
> From the Immensest Stores of Heaven?
> Heav'n, from whose boundless Treasures flow
> All good we can possess below,
>
> (1)

The blessing of marriage glorified clearly descends from God, but in Newman's metaphor it is presented not as a spiritual grace but as "boundless Treasures," a delight that would have a palpable physical appeal.

In *Eleonora: A Panegyrical Poem* (1692), John Dryden praises the intensity of love between Eleonora and her husband. Having just praised Eleonora for her loving subordination, Dryden turns to emphasize the equality of their passion:

> In equal Fires the blissful couple burn'd:
> One Joy possess'd 'em both, and in one Grief they mourn'd.
> His Passion still improv'd: he lov'd so fast
> As if he fear'd each day wou'd be her last.
>
> (Dryden 474; lines 184–86)

The couple are unified by their passion in the sense that they are placed on an equal basis by the joys and griefs they share. They also may be unified in that their sexual attraction is mutual. There is no definite indication that their love should be understood as unifying them in the mystical sense, unless "blissful" is taken to suggest beatitude. But then such bliss is not beset by fears that it will be used up, as this couple's is. "Blissful" more likely refers to the joy of the couple in emotional closeness or to their shared sexual ecstasy. Both Dryden and Newman imply that bliss may be perishable, but in Newman's poem this is because he talks about it almost crassly in material terms. In Dryden's poem, more rightfully, bliss is transitory because of human mortality.

Turning to sense 3, we find poems which use joy or bliss in a more secular context. God's role in producing this happiness is either not mentioned or is implied only obliquely. Happiness often involves the enjoyment of peace or domestic tranquillity, or it may be linked with married life in a secular paradise, a pleasant country retreat or a rose-covered cottage. Secular paradises in Grub Street formula poems of the turn of the century are often the flip sides of the marital hells that many of the Grub Street satirists describe. The myth simply has been inverted. It is curious that in the description of these paradises we find some of the earliest occurrences of bliss in sense 3.

In drawing these paradises, poets are indebted to the account of Eden in Genesis, but more so to the fourth book of *Paradise Lost*. Milton gives us a delightful description of Adam and Eve in "thir blissful Bower" on the evening of their nuptial:

> In shadier Bower
> More sacred and sequester'd, though but feign'd,
> *Pan* or *Silvanus* never slept, nor Nymph,
> Nor *Faunus* haunted. Here in close recess
> With Flowers, Garlands, and sweet-smelling Herbs
> Espoused *Eve* deckt first her nuptial Bed,
> And heav'nly Quires the Hymenaean sung,
>
> (4.704–11)

In his famous apostrophe to "wedded love," Milton praises marriage as a "Perpetual Fountain of Domestic sweets." Milton's lush, mythologized descriptions and his richly sensuous language undoubtedly inspired formula poets in their glorification of the secular domestic bliss of marriage, though as time went on, Grub Street poets may have drawn upon one another's hyperbole rather than from *Paradise Lost* directly.

In *Wedlock a Paradice* (1701), the paradise celebrated is a domesticated prelapsarian garden enjoyed with a wife who lacks any of Eve's faults. Indeed, the wife praised in this poem seems a virtual angel.

> Tho' I had Failing she was Errour free,
> And shun'd 'em by observing 'em in me;
> Her Goodness never wanted some Device,
> To always make my Home a *Paradice*.
> Bless'd Woman, were it not for thee alone,
> My Life no true felicity had known:
> O happy Wife, thou only faithful Friend,
> That Husband never can enough Commend,
> On thee in time of need we truly may depend.
> 'Twas from thy Charms that I with pleasure see,
> My self reviv'd in my own Progenie,
> And by thy Consolations do I find,
> The Cares of Life made easy to my Mind;
>
> (7)

At least in this passage, God's role in creating woman or in designing her as childbearer or companion is not mentioned. Rather the divinity of woman in these various roles almost seems to supplant God's. Woman herself is made to seem the source of goodness and felicity. Similarly, she, rather than God, becomes the one man turns to for succor and consolation. No mention, incidentally, is made concerning whom woman turns to for consolation.

A second example of a Grub Street poem paradise occurs in *The Ladies Choice* (1702). In this piece, the secularization is even more evident as the poet replaces God with the pagan deities Hymen and Cupid:

> And yet but half our Thanks we owe the Boy,
> He gives us Love, 'tis *Hymen* gives us Joy;
> Well might the Poets feign those Gods a-kin,
> For we are only Happy where they join.
> As when *Aurora* does the Bridal Morn

> With an uncommon Gayety Adorn
> From its Illustrious Pride with ease we may
> Foretel the Brightness of the coming Day:
> So when true Love the Sacred Tye precedes,
> Secure of Happiness that Couple weds;
> No Threat'ning Storms do e'er Molest their Joy,
> Nor Anxious Quarrels do their Peace destroy;
> Their days slide on in securest ease,
> And Circle in Eternal Rounds of Bliss.
>
> (13)

The always peaceful, always happy marriage union in this poem approaches the marriage of romance or fairy tale in which the couple "lives happily ever after." In such a relationship, the days "Circle in Eternal Rounds of Bliss." There is an eternity in this joy, but it is not the spiritual eternity of God's love or blessing. Rather there is the impossible and even frightening notion that earthly bliss is unceasing or can be everlastingly repeated. (Perhaps it is recycled.) Whether the poet is saying that the day-to-day life of the couple will be eternally happy or whether he is suggesting their sex lives will be eternally ecstatic, the idea of bliss becomes fantastic. Marriage poets increasingly draw such etherealized secular paradises, and it becomes the basis for the romantic myth of love in a cottage, a myth that still has popular currency in the twentieth century.[1]

Sense 4 uses of *bliss* or *joy* carry the most naturalistic sense. Bliss here may mean pleasurable sensation or, more specifically, sexual gratification. Sense 4 uses can be found throughout the early era, though they are almost entirely in satiric or witty pieces. This is not surprising for, as Lawrence Stone points out, the overwhelming majority of eighteenth-century moralists did not consider sexual attraction by itself as a sound basis for marriage (Stone 281–82). It is understandable that poets would mock those who seek only sensual pleasure in marriage or would satirize marriages in which bliss has been reduced to routine or feigned sensation.

The latter is the case in "Prologue from *An Evening's Love*" (1671) in which Dryden offers the audience an elaborate comic simile comparing a playwright to a husband. The energetic new playwright is like an overactive bridegroom on his wedding night. In his vigor he misses the mark.

> When first our Poet sets himself to write,
> Like a Bridegroom on his Wedding night
> He layd about him, and did so bestir him,
> His Muse could never lye in quiet for him:
>
> (Dryden 122; lines 1–4)

The veteran playwright, in contrast, is more like the older husband for whom lovemaking has become a tiresome routine:

> But now his Honey-moon is gone and past,
> Yet the ungrateful drudgery must last:
> And he is bound, as civil Husbands do,
> To strain himself, in compliance to you:
> To write in pain, and counterfeit a bliss,
> Like the faint smackings of an after kiss.
>
> (122; lines 5–10)

Bliss in this poem means sensual gratification. In fact, when Dryden describes the civil husband who must "counterfeit a bliss," he is talking about feigning an orgasm or making it seem more intense. In either case, bliss in marriage has been reduced to the lowest and most physical level, a level characterized by polite pretense and faint sensation ("Like the faint smackings of an after kiss"). While physical sensations were held by the materialist philosophers to be the only reality that could be authenticated, the physical pleasure in the obligatory lovemaking Dryden shows us proves an elusive entity.

Dryden as moralist may not have condoned the reduction of marital bliss to the level of physical sensation; however, in this prologue he does not articulate this judgment. He only points wittily to the world's way of dealing with such failures of bliss: patronizing a new poet as a wife would take on a fresh lover.

> But you, like Wives ill pleas'd, supply his want;
> Each writing Monsieur is a fresh Gallant:
> And though, perhaps, 'twas done as well before,
> Yet there's something in a new amour.
> Your several Poets work with several tools,
> One gets you wits, another gets you fools:
> This pleases you with some by-stroke of wit,
> This finds some cranny, that was never hit.
>
> (122; lines 11–18)

The notion of poets' different tools giving different pleasures may tickle us, yet the pleasure ironically celebrated is not suggestive of marital fidelity or of marital bliss in a higher sense. Both Dryden and the poet-gallant he treats could be characterized as playing around.

Another sense 4 use of "bliss" in a comic context is found in a early eighteenth-century poem attributed to W. Plaxton, *Advice to New-Married Husbands, in Hudibrastick Verse* (1712). Plaxton paints essentially the same picture of the husband straining himself in marital lovemaking and attempting to force pleasure. Plaxton's tone however is less cynically libertine than Dryden's and more coarsely good-humored and roughly sympathetic.

> Tom, when the heat of Battle's over,
> Man grows a tame and quiet Lover;
> When Honey Moon is in the wain,
> It's Joys cannot return again;
> Then Kisses Cold and sapless grow,
> And tir'd we are with what we do;
> We toil and sweat with endless Pain,
> Imaginary Bliss to gain:
> Lock'd to the Oar, like Galley Slaves
> In Chains we tug 'gainst Wind and Waves;
> And when we've Row'd the best we can do,
> We're recompenc'd with Tongue Strappado.
>
> (5–6)

Both Dryden and Plaxton describe the same marital dilemma and the same effort by a husband to "counterfeit" a bliss. Both are disparaging in their portrayal of the joy of lovemaking. Yet not only is the tone of each passage different, but so is the message. Given the natural fact that the pleasure of marital lovemaking often palls, Dryden's speaker goes on to describe in his witty trope the recourse of unsatisfied wives who take a "fresh Gallant." The speaker's attitude toward such infidelity seems on the surface objective, but close below this attitude may be a worldly cynicism that winks at the practice or smiles at a wife's search for sexual variety. The message may be that the husband who has lost his sexual vitality deserves to be cuckolded.

Plaxton's speaker, on the other hand, offers comic consolation to the overtaxed husband whose wife treats his Herculean drudgery so thanklessly. Plaxton encourages husbands (and possibly wives as well) to laugh at the loss of physical pleasure in lovemaking and to take it in stride.

As a substitute, Plaxton recommends not taking a mistress (or a "fresh Gallant") but the joys of claret and tobacco.

> Render the Marriage Halter easy,
> And with ten thousand Joys can please thee:
> . . . .
> Divine *Tobacco*, which gives ease,
> To all our Pain and Miseries;
> Composes Thoughts, makes Minds sedate,
> Adds Gravity to *Church* and *State*;
>
> (7)

Regardless of the low opinion we may have of the long-term benefits of wine and tobacco to one's health, many would grant that they are better pleasure substitutes for a tired marriage than infidelity. Of course, once the joy of marriage has been reduced to sensual gratification, then one begins to make such odious substitutions. Perhaps at the deepest level, both Dryden and Plaxton would agree that bliss in marriage should be founded on something higher and less evanescent than sexual pleasure. That argument is tacitly implicit in the comic and satiric stances of most poets treating bliss in sense 4 in the early era.

The Later Era

After 1725, ideas of joy, bliss, or rapture are based primarily in the secular or material senses. Bliss is often seen to be a function of domestic tranquillity, the compatibility of the couples matched, or their living together in physical or material comfort (sense 3). Also celebrated with some frequency is bliss in the most naturalistic sense: pleasurable sensation, specifically sexual gratification (sense 4). Still appearing, though with less frequency, is the religious sense of bliss (2) as deriving from the union of two souls in marriage for purposes of procreation and for faithfulness and companionship. As in the early era, occurrences of joy in sense 2 are usually mixed with occurrences in the more secular senses. I have not discovered uses of bliss in the sacramental sense (1) in any poem of the later era. No poet talks about joy in marital love as a result of divine grace that precedes from the mystical character of the marital union.

Several religious poets do, however, use a poem on marriage as an occasion to celebrate a divine joy or ecstasy that is fed by the pursuit of virtue. This joy does not usually derive directly from the sacramental character of marriage itself but is coincidental with it or even external to it. In an age in which the secular and physical senses of bliss are prevalent, it is curious how the religious poets link a high spiritual sense to a lower meaning. It is almost as if such poets attempt to compensate for the loss of the high mystical sense in *bliss* by forcibly grafting a religious meaning to obviously secular meanings. As the idea of joy and bliss in marriage shifts toward the secular, these poets romantically seem to be trying to reverse the stream. Domesticity becomes the source of goodness in middle-class life, and some poets take the further step of finding God in marriage and the family. Over the course of the century, the incorporation of secular, even physical bliss into the poetic idea of marriage is a major force in undermining the libertine arguments.[2]

Choice of modes in middle and late eighteenth-century poetic treatments of bliss is roughly a function of the senses being handled. Treatments of bliss in sense 3 or higher tend mainly to be celebrations, and the celebrations generally become more intense and ecstatic as the century progresses. In those poems where a religious meaning is grafted onto a lower meaning, celebration often pushes the ecstatic into the realm of the religious sublime or bathetically into the sentimental, even the mawkish. Treatments of bliss in senses 3 and 4 may also be in the didactic mode as poets advise young couples how to achieve bliss in marriage. In their most pragmatic form, these advice poems may operate at the level of the modern sex manual.

In order to see the shift toward the secular illustrated in detail, let us first examine poems using bliss in senses 2, 3, and 4. We can then turn to consider a few religious poets who graft higher senses onto lower.

Some secular celebrations of bliss in marriage do retain, sometimes only in a small way, some sense of the spiritual joy of marriage. We can find this, for example, in the two rustic epithalamia published in 1724 by Matthew Concanen in *Miscellaneous Poems*. In the first of these, N. Brown's "The North-Country Wedding," we discover a fairly overt celebration of bliss in senses 3 and 4.

> Now through the Welkin wide rose Morn
> Display'd her Charms, and with her Ray dispenc'd
> Joy to the World; but greater Joy to none,
> Then dawning glow'd in *Willy's* amorous Breast;
> (*Miscellaneous Poems* 1)

The groom's feelings of "greater Joy" are an obvious function of his anticipation of a happy social occasion filled with comradery and customary festivities (a possible sense-3 meaning). They are also no doubt based on his sexual expectations. Though the wedding night is not envisaged in explicit detail, the final lines do show us the couple "encircled in each other's Arms,/To reap the Harvest of a plenteous Bliss." The reference to the procreative function of marriage could be taken as entirely naturalistic, a celebration of sexual fertility, yet "Bliss" may well also carry the sense of a blessing (a sense-2 meaning).

What may be implied in Brown's epithalamium is stated directly in James Ward's "Epithalamium on the Marriage of Felim and Oonah" (1724). Intent on celebrating the innocent happiness of the occasion by direct poetic incantation, each stanza in this poem gives us the same refrain:

> Happy Virgin! happy Youth!
>   Happy *Oonah, Felim* loves thee!
>   Happy *Felim, Oonah* loves thee!
> Beauty's the Reward of Truth.
>   (*Miscellaneous Poems* 329)

The assertion that beauty is not simply a physical phenomenon but derives from truth may involve the notion that the joy of marriage proceeds from the purity of the couple being joined. There may be a suggestion that God's agency is responsible for making the couple sexually attractive to each other (another possible sense-2 meaning).

As the couple observe the joyous frolics of the youths and lasses in their wedding games, their "Wishes greater Joys pursue" (334). In the final scene in which the couple are bedded, they are told by the poet to "Seize the long'd for, honest Joys" (sense 4). At the same time, there is direct mention of the procreative function of marriage, which will "crown" their "joy."

> So may Love and Marriage shed
> All their Blessings on your Bed,
> And a young *Felim*, lovely Boy,
> In nine Months come to crown your Joy.
> So may each Day be full of Bliss,
> And ev'ry Night be sweet as This.
>   (336)

Portraying the birth of a boy as one of the "Blessings" "shed" by marriage, Ward's epithalamium suggests that the couple's joy will be made complete by the marriage-sanctified gift of childbirth. This bliss conferred by marriage is derived partly from one of the standard religious rationales for marriage: procreation.

Though bliss sometimes retains a theological sense, it most usually occurs in the later era in a secular sense. Joy or bliss referring to the happiness of a well-matched couple living together in domestic tranquillity (sense 3) becomes a prevalent idea, though it occurs less frequently alone than in combination with bliss meaning sexual pleasure. Poets seem quite willing to recognize the importance of a vital sexuality as an adjunct of marital companionship. We can look at two examples of sense 3 by itself before we turn to several examples in combination with sense 4.

Using "Joys" almost wholly in the higher secular sense is Joseph Mitchell's "Verses to the Right Honourable the Lady Sommerville, On Her Marriage" (1729). The poet apostrophizes wedded love, which he praises as based in Reason:

> Reign, *wedded Love*, on Reason founded strong!
> Thou Source of *Kindred*, and thou Soul of *Song*!
> In *Thee*, the Lover meets no treacherous Smile;
> No faithless Snares his manag'd Heart beguile.
> What tho' to *One* thou do'st Desire confine?
> Thy Bounds are *Eden*, a Restraint divine!
> Sweetly associate, *He* sustains no Care,
> That she disarms not by her Right to share.
> Her Joys are heighten'd by the Part he bears,
> And all her Words are Musick to his Ears.
>   (1: 368)

For Mitchell, marriage is a social arrangement that legislates monogamy and provides for the procreation of children. He sees the restraints of monogamy as ensuring happiness by forbidding promiscuity and guaranteeing a mutually sustaining companionship. That Mitchell calls marriage a "restraint divine" may be his acknowledgment that marriage vows are made in the sight of God. However, it is more likely he means the couple will find the restrictiveness of monogamy a social good. In this rather unusual imitation of Milton's "Hail! Wedded Love" paean (*Paradise Lost* 4.750–75), Mitchell offers an almost purely secular view of marriage. At the same time, he suggests very little about its physical joys.

Similar to Mitchell's poem, Catherine Jemmat's "The Reply" (1755) uses the word bliss almost wholly in its high secular sense, though there may be a slight suggestion of its theological source (sense 2). "The Reply," we may recall, is a recently married young man's answer to a query offered in "Verses, Written to a Friend on His Marriage" (1755). In the query poem, the speaker asks the "wild" and "roving" young man who has so long resisted marriage how he came at last to submit "to the chain." The former "weather-cock" replies that he is "No more with empty pleasures fir'd" and is "now to real bliss retir'd, . . ."

> Exchanging care and transient toys,
> For wish'd content and lasting joys;
> (82)

The convert, it seems, has not acquired a young lady who has just outward charms that will fade with time. His love, he assures us, has all the inner qualities that make her a compatible mate: a "bright" Mind, "a gaiety with innocence," "Bewitching manners void of art," and "A chearful, firm, yet feeling heart." We must admit that his is not necessarily a marriage of soulmates; however, the speaker has at least gotten beyond his wife's face and shape in enumerating her virtues. He aspires to the ideal of companionship in marriage, but essentially on a secular basis. The speaker has found a delightful and charming young woman whose personal and social virtues promise a harmonious marriage. He does not dwell on her sexual attractiveness because that might suggest he has not risen above his previous libertinism. Like Mitchell's narrator, Jemmat's speaker celebrates a bliss that is secular but not sensual. Both poets are supporters of the new pro-marriage ideology, but have not embraced an affective stance sufficiently to affirm sexuality.

Occurrences of joy or bliss in sense 3 are most often joined with bliss in the lowest sense of physical or sexual pleasure. This is clearly the most frequent combination in the later era, and its prevalence is a prime indicator of the naturalistic emphasis that was being partially admitted to secular celebrations of bliss. Most poets are hesitant to praise the sexual pleasure of marriage by itself, but many poets, even those who are religious in theme, are willing to treat sex as a concomitant of marital companionship, of a couple's living together in tranquillity and comfort. Especially when the lower secular sense is mixed with the higher secular sense, sexual pleasure need not be handled in the comically derogatory contexts in which it usually appears in the early era.

Many examples can be found of celebratory poems that affirm both companionship and sexuality. In the ode "To a Friend, on His Marriage

(1748), Thomas Warton the Elder, Professor of Poetry at Oxford, uses mythological deities and allegorical personifications to celebrate the concomitants of a happy marriage. Among the personages in attendance are

> *Hymen*, an ever-blazing Torch who bears,
> And *Love* great God of Raptures—not the Boy
> Who blindly wont to favour guilty Joy,
> But who presiding o'er chaste Marriage-Hours,
> All the soft Luxury of Fondness pours,
> While no harsh Jars the mutual Bliss controul,
> But Wish meets Wish, and Soul cements to Soul.
> (120–21)

In spite of Warton's stipulation that the "Marriage-Hours" are "chaste" and in spite of his telling us that "Soul cements Soul," his choice of language suggests physical passion, even sensation—"great God of Raptures," "soft Luxury of Fondness," "mutual Bliss" "cements." We know that the poet is not just praising sexual ecstasy. He, in fact, is celebrating a virtuous union between an emotionally compatible couple, yet the concluding flippant couplet implies that much of the vitality in the marriage will be sexual:

> Go, trifling Wits, insipidly deride
> The constant Husband, and the tender Bride;
> Rail at the real Bliss ye never knew,
> Grow impotent and rotten in a Stew.
> (121)

Warton attacks pointedly the libertine satirists who mock fidelity and warmth of affection by mocking marriage. More broadly, he dismisses the cynicism and the emotional bankruptcy of any who are unable to appreciate the couples' warmly affectionate sexuality. Warton's use of *bliss* in sense 3 clearly has a sense-4 dimension to it.

Even the religious poet and nonjuror John Byrom can use *bliss* in a secular sense that probably includes the idea of sexual joys. In "On the Marriage of Edward Greaves, Esq." (1749), a lighter occasional piece addressed to a newly married friend, Byrom calls on Greaves and his bride to return to Manchester from the south and share their happiness with their friends at home.

> Return, I say, ye wand'ring Couple, home!
> Settle, and House, and cease, henceforth, to roam!

> If ye would keep your Promises for Life,
> Of Loving Husband and obedient Wife:
> Here, amongst us, let all your moments flow,
> With all the bliss that Marriage can bestow!
>
> (3:41)

The "humorous insistence" on Greaves's return, which "almost reads like a parody of 'Ducite ab urbe domum, mea carmina, ducite Daphnim'" (40), is intended to call the couple back from the sophisticated pleasures of London social life to the simpler joys of life among their friends. The force of the invocation is essentially comic with the suggestion that "*all* the bliss that Marriage can bestow" [italics mine] will "flow" more readily if the couple are at home. The poet may even be implying that marital sex will be more blissful back home in Manchester.

There is the additional suggestion, possibly comic as well, that the couple will keep their marital vows more readily in Manchester. The poet may be saying that living among familiar friends and simpler pleasures the couple will be at ease to enjoy themselves in less artificial ways. He may be hinting that there will be fewer temptations at home to be unfaithful because he and others will be keeping an eye on them. Or perhaps he simply wants to share as a friend in the joyful, spiritual energies the newly married couple will be experiencing. In either case, bliss in sense 4 seems to occur as a kind of resonant frequency to many of the sense-3 meanings that are primary in Byrom's poem. Despite the mention of the couples' marriage vows, this piece by an avowedly religious poet celebrates bliss in predominantly secular or worldly senses; these include the pleasures of sex.

Didactic poets of the later era tend, like the mainly celebratory poets, to focus heavily on the bliss that comes from marital companionship. Most didactic poets increasingly link bliss in sense 3 with bliss in sense 4. For these poets the pleasures of a couple living together in domestic harmony become romantically fused with the joys of sex.

In *The Nuptials* (1761), a "Didactick Poem" in three books done in Miltonic blank verse, Richard Shepherd celebrates a secular bliss that derives in large part from the companionship of a congenial match. Shepherd instructs his (male) readers to rise above their sexual passions to a love that takes pleasure in a constant social relationship with the opposite sex. He acknowledges the power of instinct, but he urges his readers to subordinate it to a higher and more refined kind of love. For Shepherd,

Adam's problem in paradise was not that he lacked a mate but that he needed companionship:

> Why need I tell, that our primoeval Sire
> In Paradise sought Bliss in vain: For where,
> Or what is Bliss, of social Love devoid?
>
> (6)

Shepherd sees man as designed by Nature to live in a connubial relationship. He musters somewhat questionable arguments to convince his readers that the joys of companionship are higher than, even separate from, the instinctive pleasures of sexuality as it is experienced by animals.[3]

In directly urging youth to fix on higher and more lasting pleasures than physical gratification, Shepherd treads the same ground as almost all eighteenth-century moralists:

> I charge thee Youth, I charge thee on the Risk
> Of many a tedious Day, to fix thy Bliss
> On surer Basis than a vermeil Lip:
> For Beauty's fairest Fabrick envious Time
> Shall moulder; and then where are all thy Joys?
>
> (15)

Marital joy for Richard Shepherd is essentially a natural phenomenon. However, it is not simply physical sensation or instinct. It is established by the power that rules in nature in order to bind a couple together in a joyful tie. This is made evident in the epithalamium sung by the character Colin-Clout in the conclusion.

> Hail to the Power, that rules the hallowed Rites
>   And spotless Honour of the Nuptial Bed;
> That the prompt Hands, as Love the Hearts, unites,
>   O *Hymen,* here thy genial Influence shed.
>
> (81)

If marital bliss for Richard Shepherd is a social outgrowth of the natural order, this is essentially also the case for another didactic poet, Francis Dobbs. In *Modern Matrimony. A Poem* (1773), Dobbs concludes by celebrating the "mutual love" that is nurtured in a closely bonded marital union over time:

> If ever grief, or sickness, should appear;
> My Flora shall experience all my care—

Her pleasure still shall be my greatest joy;
The bliss of pleasing sure can never cloy—
Each day, each year, fresh happiness shall give;
Affection ever in each breast shall live—
Through ev'ry scene of life, we'll fondly prove,
Those matchless joys that wait on mutual love.
                                        (22–23)

As with Shepherd's poem, the joy that Dobbs's couple experiences in comforting one another in suffering is essentially secular bliss, even though it involves the idea of self-sacrifice. Dobbs, however, does not distinguish this sort of joy from the pleasures of sex as sharply as Shepherd does. For Dobbs, the physical bliss of marriage is an integral part of marital happiness, although for the sake of propriety he refuses to dwell poetically on its raptures.

Thus far my muse hath dar'd to try her wing—
My muse, tho' daring, dares not further sing:—
Such bliss as their's, what language can convey!
No words can paint it—nor no lines display.—
O happy pair! in ecstasy repose;
                                        (13)

Dobbs's exclamations on the raptures of marital sexuality may have inflamed the imagination of the eighteenth-century reader more than explicit description would. Because he is vague, he creates disproportionate expectations. He does not give us marriage manual pictures à la *The Joy of Sex*, but his idea of domestic bliss certainly includes sexual pleasure.

Although the sexuality in Ann Holmes's *An Epic Poem on Adam and Eve* (1800) is more covert, this late pastoral celebration, like Dobbs's didactic poem, involves an inextricable mixing of the idea of joy in companionship (sense 3) and joy in physical love (sense 4). Consider, for example, when Adam and Eve first pledge their love to each other:

He claspt her to his breast, unto his lips
Prest her white hand and said, thou fair possessor
Of my heart, dearer to me thou art than
Worlds on Worlds; my partner thou in joy or grief
My solace and my comfort through this life
Must be. . . .
                                        (11)

As Adam's action of clasping Eve and his promise to care for her "in joy and grief" are inseparable, so essentially, within the romantic aura of Holmes's poem, are the bliss of mutual solace and the physical pleasure of Adam's protective embrace.

While the increasing tendency for most didactic and celebratory poems in the late eighteenth century is to treat bliss in sense 3 and sense 4 as interconnected, perhaps in a kind of romantic unity, a few poems, especially didactic ones working in the Miltonic descriptive tradition, sometimes celebrate sexual bliss apart from the joys of a well-matched couples' living together in companionship, in domestic tranquillity, and in material comfort. This separation sometimes does not persist throughout an entire poem, but it does occur particularly in sections of "marriage manual" poems that give advice on and at the same time celebrate (marital) lovemaking. These direct celebrations of the bliss of sexual pleasure tend to be exceptional, though they do foreshadow the increasingly physiological idea of bliss as pleasurable sensation, a conception that becomes predominant in the late nineteenth and twentieth centuries.

In *The Oeconomy of Love. A Poetical Essay* (1736), which went through numerous eighteenth-century editions, Dr. John Armstrong, Scots physician and poet, offers a quasi-scientific tour through human sexuality. Beginning with puberty, he describes and gives medical information concerning such physiological phenomena as pubic hair, wet dreams, and menstruation. He also offers moral and practical advice on masturbation, prostitution, heterosexual intercourse, and homosexuality. In an initial note to the reader, Armstrong claims that his "little juvenile Performance" was "intended as a parody of some of the Didactick Poets." However, his intent is more serious than he suggests, more scientifically didactic than parodic.

In his opening Armstrong invokes "Love" and tells the reader he sings:

> Thy bounties, Love, in thy soft raptures when
> Timeliest the melting pairs indulge, and how
> Best to improve the genial joy, how shun
> The snakes that under flow'ry pleasure lurk,
>
> (1)

In spite of the Miltonic elevation and periphrasis, phrases such as "soft raptures," "the genial joy," and "flow'ry pleasure" point unmistakably to sexual gratification.[4] Armstrong's entire poem could be read as a sex manual rather than as a marriage manual. This is so even though the context for Armstrong's treatment of coitus is marriage and even though in his opening he not only apostrophizes "Love" but also "Hymen." ("*Hymen, raise/Aloft thy sacred torch. Your gifts I sing*" [2]).

In the large majority of instances, bliss and joy in *The Oeconomy of Love* refer narrowly to sexual gratification. Advising young men to wait until twenty to marry, Armstrong tells them to

> shun the soft embrace
> Emasculent, till twice ten years and more
> Have steel'd thy nerves, and let the holy rite
> Licence the bliss. . . .
>
> (8)

Cautioning young men against masturbation, he says histrionically,

> Banish from thy shades
> Th' ungenerous, selfish, solitary joy.
> Hold, Saticide, thy hand! . . .
>
> (9)

Having warned new husbands not to be violent or "precipitant" in the act of defloration, he instructs them, on the other hand, that they should not slack on the job: "Nor droop because the door/Of bliss seems shut and barricado'd strong" (15). When he advises young men not to indulge excessively in marital sex, he tells them to "let discretion guard the hour of bliss,/Virtuous in pleasure" (20). Armstrong counsels his readers that

> Other joys,
> Other pursuits, their equal share demand
> Of cultivation . . .
>
> (32)

But even "joys" in this passage glances back at sexual bliss—"the sovereign joy," the "unexhausted source of universal joy," which he has just apostrophized (30).

A second "marriage manual" poem, Robert Shiells's *Marriage: A Poetical Essay* (1748), is somewhat more balanced than Armstrong's in treating marital bliss. Shiells's focus is more centrally marriage, and his concern goes beyond sexuality in the narrow sense to include childbirth, nursing, and education of children. Shiells also uses bliss in more varied senses— in the high secular sense and in several instances in a spiritual sense.

Toward the end of his poem Shiells builds on the lower senses to urge his readers to rise to higher pleasures that provide "ceaseless bliss."

Even so, in the largest number of instances, bliss does mean sexual gratification (sense 4). "Cloister'd Maids,"

> deny'd the Sweets
> Of *happy Wedlock*, pine their Days away
> Strangers to Bliss . . .
>
> (8)

Parents who would deny a young couple permission to marry are reminded of how strongly they "felt/The direful Throbbings of retarded Bliss!" They should not forbid the "Pair/To taste connubial Bliss" (10). The young woman who is forced to marry an old man, "jejun'd and dry," is "lost to Bliss" (13). When the married couple approach orgasm, "It comes! high Consummation, smiling, comes/With all it's [*sic*] Train of Bliss! . . ." Experiencing orgasm, the couple, "With trembl'ing Limbs, and Face of rosy glow,/Sinks in the blended Bliss" (20).

A seeming exception to the increasing tendency to secularize the idea of bliss is the linking by religious poets of a high spiritual meaning of *bliss* with a lower secular meaning. What is significant about the spiritual joy celebrated in this group of poems is that it does not flow directly from the sacrament of marriage in a mystical sense. Rather it proceeds from the virtuous conduct or the religious vocation of one or both of the partners, and the happiness may be a reward they achieve in heaven. In these poems, marriage is used as a vehicle for the glorification of religious ecstasy. Although the yoking of physical bliss with such high ecstasy seems an original one, it is probably not since the connection had been frequently celebrated in Renaissance and early seventeenth-century epithalamia. The eighteenth-century religious poets, however, must work hard to reestablish the link. It is almost as if the religious poets are attempting to reimpose, even force a spiritual meaning on *bliss* in the face of its increasing secularization. Thus, instead of celebrating the bliss of the individual's private spiritual relationship with God, the religious poets of the later era increasingly dramatize affective relationships within the family that provide surrogates for religious emotionality.

George Woodward's "A Letter from a Lady to Her Husband in Spain, in Her Last Sickness" (1730) is an early attempt to link the pleasures of companionship with the idea of religious bliss in the afterlife (63).[5] The poem's promise that "Pious Souls will reign in endless Bliss" serves as the "Lady's" consolation as she is dying separated from her husband and from the pleasures of their wedded life together.

> But that I spend my latest Hours, intent
> On those dear Pleasures of a Life well-spent,
> On those dear Pleasures, which with Thee I've found,
> Pleasures, which few can taste in Wedlock bound;
> And ever and anon Reflect with Pain,
> That all soon must end, and ne'er return again.
>
> (62)

The pleasures of companionship with her husband that the "Lady" commends are clearly secular in nature (sense 3), even though few "in Wedlock bound" can taste them. But the "endless Bliss" with which "Pious Souls" will "reign" is distinctly religious in its sense. What is curious is the way the two ideas of *bliss* are juxtaposed and fused.

More striking in its glorification of religious bliss is Mrs. Elizabeth Rowe's "An Epistle from Alexias, a Noble Roman, to His Wife, Whom He Left on His Wedding Day, with a Design to Visit the Eastern Churches" (1739). This piece may draw its emotion from the death of her husband, the young scholar Thomas Rowe, an event she mourned in "Upon the Death of Her Husband" (see Lonsdale 49–51). Rowe, who died of consumption after five years of marriage and whom she names Alexis in the latter poem, is no doubt the model for Alexias. This dying speaker, an early Christian missionary, has spent no time living with his wife. His references to pleasures are overtly an expectation of what the afterlife will be and less directly a reflection on the pleasures of companionship and sexuality that he never enjoyed in his marriage.

> A Nobler view my virtue now excites,
> And pleasure's charming name my soul invites;
> The boundless joys, the crown, the vast reward,
> In heav'n, for steadfast piety prepar'd.
> My tow'ring thoughts in raptur'd sallies rove,
> Thro' all the wide resplendent worlds above;
> I view the inmost glories of the skies,
> And paradise lies open to my eyes;
>
> (1: 153)

What is significant about Alexias's language describing heaven is that he uses many words that secular poets (Armstrong for example) employ to praise companionship and the physical bliss of marriage. We find, for example, "excites," "pleasures," "joys," "raptur'd," "paradise," and "blissful." Mrs. Rowe is forthright in using language suggesting physical rapture to describe religious ecstasy:

> Whole floods of joy come pouring on my soul,
> And high the flowing tides of pleasure roll.
>
> (1: 153)

Even some of the more naturalistic poets such as Dobbs do not describe sexual sensations with as much sensual power as Mrs. Rowe does religious ecstasy.

One should not conclude that Mrs. Rowe was unaware of the sort of language she was using. In the final four lines of Alexias's letter, she makes explicit the equation between sexual and religious "transport."

> With transport there, with transport all divine,
> My lov'd *Emilia*, shall my soul meet thine:
> To endless years our raptures we'll improve,
> And spend a whole eternity in love.
>
> (1: 153)

What was submerged metaphor now becomes an overt equation; physical rapture is elevated to the status of spiritual ecstasy. This is no complicated witty inversion of the physical and spiritual such as Donne and the metaphysicals often dramatized. Rather in Mrs. Rowe's poem spiritual ecstasy *is* physical rapture.

A finer incorporation of the physical joys of marriage into a celebration of its spiritual joys is William Cowper in "Ode. Supposed to be Written on the Marriage of a Friend" (written between 1748 and 1763). Unlike Woodward's and Rowe's, Cowper's equation does not seem hyperbolically forced but "divinely" inspired. Cowper carefully builds the metaphoric link between secular bliss and heavenly bliss so that it becomes integral to the poem. He works gradually up the ladder to the culminating idea of a spiritual love that "warms our fainting souls with energy divine." The speaker, who is supposedly a lover just recently married, invokes the magic of Orpheus's lyre and encourages him to rise above the charming of rocks and trees to "paint a lover's bliss—a lover's pain—" (8). The role of Orpheus's lyre will be to bring pleasure to Eurydice:

> From her sweet brow to chase the gloom of care,
> To check that tear that dims the beaming eye,

> To bid her heart the rising sigh forbear,
>   And flush her orient cheek with brighter joy,
> In that dear breast soft sympathy to move,
> And touch the springs of rapture and of love.
>   (1: 49; lines 13–18)

The role of the lyre corresponds metaphorically to the shamanic role of the poet in bringing pleasure to the reader and conveying the extent of his (the poet's) love for his bride. The poet approaches this task with an extended light metaphor that allows him to transcend earthly notions of joy and happiness. The most important light trope is that of the "radiant star of love." This may stand for the physical beauty of his bride, particularly her beaming eye. Beyond his pleasure in this, the joy he receives from his love transcends her physical beauty as her virtues "beam" from her "angel mind."

> Yet not the beaming eye, or placid brow,
>   Or golden tresses, hid the subtle dart;
> To charms superior far than those I bow,
>   And nobler worth enslaves my vanquish'd heart;
> The beauty, elegance, and grace combined,
> Which beam transcendant from that angel mind
>
> While vulgar passions—meteors of day,
>   Expire before the chilling blasts of age,
> Our holy flame, with pure and steady ray,
>   Its glooms shall brighten, and its pangs assuage;
> By Virtue (sacred vestal) fed, shall shine,
> And warm our fainting souls with energy divine.
>   (lines 25–36)

Continuing the light metaphor, Cowper contrasts the cold, temporary light of meteors—suggestive of "vulgar passions"—to "our holy flame" whose "pure and steady ray" warms "our fainting souls with energy divine." Physical passions like meteors "expire" with the coldness of old age, but the spiritual love he has for his bride will warm them with its Godlike qualities. By introducing a superphysical element into the conclusion, the poet, like Orpheus, has performed a species of magic with his song and converted earthly pleasure into a kind of heavenly joy.

   Compared to the other religious poets, Cowper is exceptional in his more skillful manner of celebrating the religious sublimity of physical ecstasy. Even so, all the religious poets—Woodward, Rowe, and Cowper—run counter to the predominant shift toward the secular that poets of the period exhibit. Two of the major progressive results of this secularization are the weakening of the patriarchal authority of the Anglican Church, especially as it prohibited divorce and remarriage, and the establishment of the ideals of companionship and domesticity. A negative result, which we have just considered, is the loss of an explicitly theological ideology of marriage that gave it a sacramental or sacred status. Without this status, people may have been more inclined to dissolve marriage for trivial or selfish reasons (see Stone, *Letters*). For this loss, religious poets attempted to compensate by endowing affective marital relationships with spiritualized emotionality. Most, as we have seen, were not successful in doing so. Negative results of secularization, which revisionist critics stress and which we will consider next, include the masking of inequality and subordination by companionate ideology and the limitation of women's selfhood and spheres of activity by domesticity.

CHAPTER SEVEN

Dominion o'er the Breeches

❦

Dominion is a pervasive topic in marriage verse in the long eighteenth century, and, for modern critics, its insistence on women's subordination is one of its most controversial issues. As I showed in my introductory chapter, progressive historians mostly attempt to treat male dominion objectively. It is seen as an historically explainable, though no doubt lamentable, feature of the companionate model. Revisionist feminism views the ideology of male superiority as skewing the promised blissful equality of the companionate household because the entire edifice of domesticity is constructed on a foundation of patriarchy. As revisionists might see the paradise of late eighteenth-century domesticity, it is not Adam's and Eve's disobeying God that causes them to fall from bliss. Rather it is the husband's assuming that he is Godlike and that his wife should obey him. It is appropriate then that we consider the dominion question in this late chapter. We are brought finally to ask whether the evolution of a secularized companionate ideology is positive in any respect.

The dominion question is rooted in the Biblical myth of Eve's disobedience and in the patriarchal injunctions of the marriage liturgy. In the *Book of Common Prayer*, for example, husbands are enjoined to "love your wives even as Christ also loved the Church and gave himself to it." Wives are instructed to "submit yourselves unto your husbands, as unto the Lord. For the husband is the head of the wife, even as Christ is head of the Church; and he is the Saviour of the body." In addition, husbands must promise to "love her, comfort her, honour, and keep her in sickness and in health," while wives vow to "obey him, serve him, love, honour, and keep him in sickness and in health" (1760 ed.). The theological insistence on the wife's obedience in Roman Catholic, Lutheran, Calvinist, and Anglican theology is a fact of cultural history; the interesting question is how poets—male and female—reacted to the obvious inequality in the injunctions and the vows.

More so than with all the other topics treated, progressive views on the dominion question are slow to evolve. The reasons for this are not simply that patriarchy is so firmly entrenched in the religious, socioeconomic, legal, and cultural structures of England. In poetry, the reasons are, more immediately, that the myth of women's disobedience and of her wish to dominate men is so strong, pervasive, and enduring. Thus, although modern readers might assume that one satirical attack on a domineering wife is like another, it is worth looking at them closely to see the sociopolitical bases of the myth at the beginning of the Restoration and how by the end of the Restoration the myth grows vulnerable by becoming archetypal and hyperbolic. In the early eighteenth century, as we will also see, the myth is softened and secularized as satire is cut with comedy. Having followed this evolution, we can turn with more understanding to criticisms of the myth and to attacks on tyrannical male dominion, especially those from women's pens.

In spite of the call for equality in a limited number of pieces, the dominion question is not resolved in the eighteenth century, only displaced. In a similar way, the theological justifications for male dominion are ignored, though the social principle continues to be affirmed. Poets, especially didactic and celebratory poets, eschew polemics as they advise husbands to be "kinder and gentler" in exercising their authority or as they celebrate the marriage in which mutual love supplants the struggle for sovereignty. Didactic poets—mostly male—also attempt to placate wives by enforcing the myth of the woman who stoops to conquer. Even women poets, a number of whom in the early era are outspoken in attacking woman's subjugation in marriage, tend in the later era to accede to the pervasive secular myth of the woman who prevails by her domestic virtues, beauty, good humor, and compliance. Revisionist critics would see later era women poets as deluded or co-opted by the prevalent male-fostered ideology because this idea perpetuates women's powerlessness. We can, however, appreciate the stance of such women poets if we acknowledge that power can be exercised in various spheres, not just in the public world of business, politics, and law. Although later era women poets celebrated power in domesticity, it still in effect was power. The very fact that women were paying attention to the issue of power raised a protofeminist consciousness and, in the long run, advanced the struggle for equality in the public arena.

The Early Era

Examining the attitudes toward dominion in marriage that we pick out of the stewpot of social controversy, formula, convention, and myth in the early era, we will look first at the popular verse, especially the satire, that reinforces the idea of male sovereignty. This will be viewed in four categories. The first category includes harsh Restoration satire in which the myth is weakened by overstatement and generalization; in a second category, early eighteenth-century satire is softened by comedy. In a third category, we find the significant minority of verse, a portion of it by outspoken women poets, which criticizes male sovereignty as tyrannical or hypocritical. If this poetry, mainly in the didactic and celebratory modes, does not exemplify a weakening of the idea of patriarchal authority, it at least challenges it seriously.[1] Finally, we will examine a fourth category of poems, also mainly in these modes, that glorifies a marriage in which mutual (romantic) love displaces the struggle over dominion. This stance becomes prevalent in the later era.

Satire reinforcing the myth of the shrewish, aggressive wife undergoes significant modifications in the late seventeenth century. Previous to the Interregnum, attacks on women for wearing the breeches can be found, though they are not especially frequent. During the Civil Wars and Commonwealth, they increase significantly in number, and satirists mention specifically the involvement of women in the political and religious causes of the 1640s and 1650s.[2] After the Restoration, attacks remain at a fairly high frequency. Early Restoration satires on women usurping men's dominion maintain an element of topicality, while in the late Restoration they become more universalized.

The broad pattern of evolution in the Restoration is from the topical to the general, a movement that is increasingly toward the mythical. Instead of mocking historical women who usurp dominion by their involvement in Interregnum politics and religion, later poets portray domineering wives who are archetypally hellish. Conversely, satirists increasingly lament the loss of a paradisal golden age in which wives were subservient. Some poets establish a vague connection between this age and a pre–Civil War era, but later its status becomes more fabulous. Based on these patterns, it would seem that, at least initially, the misogynist animus of Restoration satire is in large part a reaction to women's increased visibility during the Interregnum as political activists and as members of religious sects, even as preachers. When Restoration satire attacks the excesses of the era through which it has just passed, it turns against women's untraditional sociopolitical behavior as a symbol of that era. Attacks on assertive women persist in the Restoration perhaps as a carry-over from Interregnum satire or perhaps because women continue to be visible in new roles.[3] No doubt, the misogyny of the Restoration satire is reinforced by traditional ideologies including clerical hostility toward marriage, middle-class prudential concerns that young men take the responsibilities of married life seriously, and the "intensity and volatility of homosocial relationships" in the sixteenth and seventeenth centuries (see chapter 1, stage one). However, it is to the Interregnum that satirists turn repeatedly for their negative paradigms.

It is instructive to see how satirists of the Interregnum formulate their attack on assertive women and how that attack is rooted solidly in the politics of the time. The Royalist satirist John Taylor, for example, in the prose *Diseases of the Times or the Distempers of the Commonwealth* (1643) scores "the dangerous disease of Feminine Divinity": "These would reforme the Church, and under that pretence deforme it, but that will be a rare World when women shall weare the breeches & men peticotes, this greatly tingleth in the eares of the world." Taylor's main concern is with women's meddling in church affairs in their effort to reform religious practice. His satiric representation of women wearing the breeches is used both to trivialize the impact women reformers will have and to show how out of place their involvement in religious affairs is.

Henry Neville's *Newes from the New Exchange, or the Commonwealth of Ladies, Drawn to Life, in Their Severall Characters and Concernments* (1650) is also pointedly topical, but the burden of his prose attack is more broadly the freer life-style that women of the time were leading. Neville employs wonderfully vivid realism to contrast the former peaceful, domestic activities of English women and the present unconventional, rebellious political involvements of the "Ladies-*Rampant*." Many satirists treating the dominion question, even Juvenal in the opening of his sixth satire, describe a mythical past or golden age when women were obedient to their husbands. Neville, in contrast, seems to give us an actual view of women's life-styles in the eras before and during the Civil Wars. He offers pointed and obscene lampoons, mostly of actual Roundhead women, as he names the historical personages who will attend his parliament. He then informs us in gossipy, unseemly detail what they have done to deserve to be there.

A significant link between Royalist topical satire and more archetypal Restoration satire occurs in one of the greatest conduits of Interregnum popular verse to the Restoration reader, Butler's *Hudibras*.[4] Butler's general attack on the domineering wife in the skimmington scene in part 2, canto 2 frames a concentrated passage of topical satire on women for their involvement in the Good Old Cause. Butler expects us to see this particular attack as an instance of a universal satiric pattern.

The skimmington is one of those rough village ceremonies or violent recreational activities upon which Hudibras and Ralpho always seem to stumble in their peregrinations. As with the bearbaiting in part 1, Hudibras's abusive verbal harangue against the villagers' raucous mockery of the domineering wife and the henpecked husband precipitates more violence: the villagers throw rotten eggs and manure at the Presbyterian knight and his Anabaptist squire. The satire in this whole situation carries a universalized, archetypal force as "hard words" repeatedly produce more civil disorder and violence.

In inveighing against the skimmington, Hudibras condemns the village ceremony as "an Antichristian Opera"; Butler ironically plays up Hudibras's distorted assessment of what he sees by describing the ceremony as a Roman procession honoring a military triumph. Adding an air of mythical universality to the satire, Butler honors the domineering wife as the victorious hero:

> Next after, on a Raw-bon'd Steed,
> The Conqueror's *Standard-bearer* rid,
> And bore aloft before the *Champion*
> A *Petticoat* displaid, and Rampant;
> Near whome the *Amazon* triumphant
> Bestrid her beast, . . .
>   (II.ii.637–42)

The henpecked husband is treated as the humiliated warrior, overcome by the champion:

> and on the *Rump* on't
> Sate *Face* to *Tayl*, and *Bum* to *Bum*,

> Arm'd with a *Spindle* and a *Distaff*,
> Which as he rod, she made him twist off;
> > (II.ii.642–46)

Butler's satire continues in an archetypal vein as he extends the epic fiction jocularly.

Butler's accusations up to this point are timeless, and the mock-heroic elements do little to limit the intended universality of his satire. However, as Hudibras continues his speech explaining the significance of the skimmington to Ralpho, Butler introduces topical, anti-Puritan satire in a concentrated passage of about forty lines. Hudibras pays tribute to the wives of the "Saints" for their contributions to the "Good Old Cause" and alludes specifically to various demonstrations and quasi-military activities carried out by women as members of the London mob in the 1640s.

> *Women*, that left no stone unturn'd,
> In which the *Cause* might be concern'd:
> Brought in their childrens *spoons*, and *whistles*,
> To purchase *Swords, Carbines*, and *Pistols*:
> > (II.ii.777–80)

Hudibras introduces this passage of topical satire as a response to the treatment of the woman in the skimmington. When he describes the procession as "an Antichristian Opera," he says it is designed

> To scandalize that *Sex*, for scoulding,
> To whom the *Saints* are so beholding,
> > (II.ii.773–74)

The archetypal thrust of this dramatic irony may well be that Hudibras defends a woman mocked for wearing the breeches in a household by referring to a "mob" of women who have moved beyond their traditional sphere of activity into the larger world of politics. Butler uses the topical satire on the "London mob" to provide a specific context for his archetypal mockery of the topsy-turvy world of domineering wives and henpecked husbands.

After *Hudibras*, satires attacking wives who would gain dominion tend to lose most of their topical force. Though a few make brief reference to the behavior of women in the Restoration, more tend to compare an unspecific present with the behavior of women in a mythical past. Later in the Restoration (after the publication of *Paradise Lost* in 1667), poets become progressively more explicit in drawing on the Garden of Eden story to fill out this myth. As one might expect, the portrayal of wives' behavior in these unsophisticated popular satires tends to run to stereotyped extremes, the mythical hell and heaven dramatized by so many popular marriage poets. As the domineering wife becomes more obviously mythical, the way is prepared for a challenge to the myth by the increasing celebration of her counterpart, the good wife.

This is the case in a pair of broadside ballads from the 1670s entitled *The Married Mans Complaint* and *The Married Mans Best Portion*. In *The Married Mans Complaint*, as the subtitle informs us, the husband "took a Shrow [sic] instead of a Saint" to wife. The strife in this ballad is timeless. The first page features a woodcut of a man and wife threatening each other with spades or hoes held in the left hand, while each pulls with the right on the opposite sides of a pair of breeches. With this universal icon in front of him, the reader is not surprised to discover repeated instances of the wife's self-indulgence and bullying. Indeed, such behavior occurs every day in a regular pattern:

> If she lyes abed till twelve a clock
>   yet I must say nothing to it,
> To make a caudle or warm her smock
>   I dare not say much but do it,
> Or else with a bed staffe my noodle she'l greet
> In such a rude manner you'd laugh for to see't
> Although I desire they never should meet.
>
> [2]

The poem concludes with the husband in another timeless pose, always threatening to get the better of his wife "tomorrow":

> If I get the better as I hope I shall
>   For I mean to by tomorrow,
> I'le knock her bold face against the wall
>   and make her for to know sorrow,
> But if that the hen should beat the Cock
> Amongst all my Neighbors they will me mock
> Because I went down of my knees to the smock
> I wish I had never been married been married,
> I wish I had never been married.
>
> [2]

Whether he really intends to beat his wife or whether he is simply making threats to salve his ego, this husband is plagued *not* with a wife whose freer behavior is a manifestation of the political turmoil of the times but with a timeless phenomenon, a wife from hell. In antithetical contrast, in *The Married Mans Best Portion*, which is celebratory, we get a conventional idealization of a good, obedient wife. Her virtue is timeless and inexhaustible as she is sent from heaven.

Other popular satires that treat the domineering wife tend to do so similarly in archetypal terms or offer only tenuous links with the Restoration. Printed under the title *Female Excellence: or, Woman Display'd in Several Satyrick Poems* (1679), "A Satyr upon Woman's Usurpation" simply offers a broad contrast between an unspecified past and present.

> *Woman* was made Man's Sovereignty to own;
> *Man*, as the Monarch, was to rule alone.
> She created was a Slave, and made to dread
> The angry frowns of Man, her Lord and Head.
> Heaven did to him his Power delegate;
> O're all the Universe he made him great:
> . . . .
> Once she was happy, but her towring pride
> Could not Superior, God or Man abide:
> *Man's* now enslav'd, imperious *Woman* reigns
> And governs Monarchs with her golden chains:
> She is so prone by nature to comptroul,
> That she must govern, or destroy man's Soul.
> (4–5)

A second satire from 1679, "A Satyr against Woman," makes quite a similar accusation and is only slightly more specific about time context:

> By their Base Condescention Females sway
> Who were by Nature Destin'd to Obey;
> For Woman in this Foppish Age and Nation
> Like Adam, Lords it o're the whole creation;
> Nay she does more, than *Adam* e're cou'd doe,
> She names the Beasts, and sometimes makes them too.
> Yet Man this Thing first Weds, then bears it'n Van
> The Turkish Ensign, th'o' a Christian.
> How shamefully dos Man on Woman dote?
> The Breeches warp unto the Petticoate?
> (*A Ternary of Satires* 21)

Though this piece may be referring to the Restoration when it points its finger at "this Foppish Age and Nation," it is actually no more topical than "A Satyr upon Woman's Usurpation." Both satires are really interested in the discrepancy between the Biblical myth of woman's subservience and the social reality of woman's behavior. Though "by Nature" or by heavenly design a wife was supposed to be inferior to her husband, she might well be superior to him physically or intellectually. Perhaps it was the tension in Restoration culture between antifeminist ideology and actuality that helped inspire so many Restoration satires on domineering women.

That archetypal Restoration satires on domineering wives are in part a self-conscious response to the Biblical myth of woman's subservience appears more obviously in a verse satire of 1686 by M.S. entitled *The Great Birth of Man* (2nd ed.), a reworking of *Paradise Lost*. Whereas Milton's portrayal of Adam and Eve as helpmeets tends to put the dominion struggle in a positive context, the author of *The Great Birth of Man* takes every opportunity to present Eve's actions in an antifeminist light. Eve responds to Satan's invitation to eat the apple not just with the hope that she may obtain Godlike knowledge (as in *Paradise Lost*). In this satire she has the additional fantasy that she may become Adam's superior.

> Alas! Poor *Adam*, now I shall be more
> Your Soverain, than you was mine before.
> Your narrow Soul, like mine, durst not Aspire,
> Nor is't compos'd of such a Fire.
>
> (9)

Eve's seduction of Adam is likewise a much more treacherous act in the second poem than in Milton's. The Eve of *The Great Birth of Man* actively persuades Adam to eat the apple.

The Great Birth of Man is overtly antifeminist in another way. On expelling Adam and Eve from the Garden, God is explicit in repeating the Biblical curse that Eve will experience "the Pangs of Death" in giving birth and that she will be ruled by her husband:

> Know 'tis our Pleasure, Ratif'd in Heav'n,
> Strictest Obedience you shall pay to Men.
> All your desires, in his just Pow'r shall rest,
> To suffer, as his Judgment thinks it best.
> 'Tis our Command, who Grasp the Worlds great Ball,
> That Man shall be the Sov'rain Lord of all.
>
> (22)

In *Paradise Lost*, it should be remembered, Milton does not have God, Michael, or Adam raise the issue of Eve's subordination. Rather as Adam and Eve are leaving Paradise, Eve herself says:

> But now lead on;
> In me is no delay; with thee to go
> Is to stay here; without thee here to stay
> Is to go hence unwilling; thou to me
> Art all things under Heaven, all places thou,
> Who for my willful crime art banished hence.
> (12.614–19)

Eve's last words in Milton's poem emphasize her equality in companionship rather than her subordination. This is so in spite of Adam's earlier despairing remarks (in 10.889–908) about the impossibility of finding a fit mate or of forming a relationship in "strait conjunction with this sex."

Though M.S., the author of *The Great Birth of Man*, follows *Paradise Lost* with a rough fidelity, why does he make Eve more treacherous and why does he emphasize the final curse of her subordination to man? The likely explanation is that the author is caught up in the myth. Writing in the satiric mode, the author feels obligated to give us a disobedient Eve in a hellish marriage fraught with conflict over dominion rather than a marriage which at least aspires to a heavenlike harmony. For the author of *The Great Birth of Man*, the mythical archetype is stronger than Milton's more sympathetic portrayal of Eve's character and prevails over it. The poet, however, is aware that he is manipulating myth to appeal to his readers, and in that awareness lies the myth's eventual demise.

In the satire of the first two decades of the eighteenth century, domineering wife accusations persist as does reinforcement of male sovereignty. Some early eighteenth-century poets continue to produce harsh, even hostile indictments of women who do not obey their husbands. Another perhaps larger group mellow their satire with comedy. A subtle distinction can be made in these decades between the harsher satires that attack women for asserting dominion or aspiring to a Godlike superiority and the more comic satires that chastise men for being vulnerable to women's wiles. Satires of the latter sort, which become more prevalent as the eighteenth century advances, seem somewhat more progressive in their recognition that men often allow or want women to have dominion over them. They also employ less Biblical allusion and manifest less concern with the theological implications of women's disobedience. By modern standards, however, none of these satires could conceivably be called hostile to woman's subjection in marriage.

Those early eighteenth-century satires that do make harsh attacks on wives for their assertive behavior are most similar to Restoration satires of domineering wives. *Female Apostacy: Or, the True-born English-woman: A Satyr* (1705) uses the Eden motif in much the same way as *The Great Birth of Man*. Satan completes his seduction of woman by promising her that she will "be like God, Supreme and Great;/(And what wou'd not a Woman do for that?)"(1). *The Fifteen Comforts of a Wanton Wife* (1706/7), one of the fifteen-format poems, attacks domineering wives strongly and directly:

> When thus she'as made her silly Husband bend,
> She'll never let him have the upper hand.
> She manages Affairs, while he (poor Soul)
> Consents, because he's fearful to controul;
>
> (2)

The more comic satires, in contrast, place more emphasis on man's vulnerability to control. Tom Brown of Grub Street fame, in "A Satire on Marriage" (1707–8), uses a bawdy sailing metaphor and double and triple rhymes to contrast the husband's titular power with the wife's natural power.

> The husband's the pilot, the wife is the ocean,
> He always in danger, she always in motion,
> And he that in wedlock twice hazards his carcass,
> Twice ventures a drowning, and faith that's a hard case;
> Ev'n at our own weapons the females defeat us,
> And death, only death, can sign our *Quietus*.
>
> (*Works* 1: 58)

For Brown, a woman is less a human individual than a force of nature. The reference to women defeating men with their own weapons may be Brown's comic acknowledgment of biological fact; men are incapable of making love as many times in succession as women are. The emphasis falls on men's limitations and vulnerability.

Another example of a satire cut with comedy is in William Plaxton's *Advice to New-Married Husbands, in Hudibrastick Verse* (1712). In this coarsely humorous poem with its bump-along tetrameters and Hudibrastic double and triple rhymes, Plaxton's concern is with a husband's vulnerability. Writing in a comic-satiric didactic mode, Plaxton gives serious and not so serious advice to young men who have just become husbands. Plaxton asserts man's dominion in marriage and encourages young husbands to uphold it:

> Thy Birth-right, Breeches, Lad maintain,
> The proper Garniture of Man. (11)
> . . . .
> Man rules, and shou'd the Sceptre sway,
> Whilst the Help-meet ought to obey.
> (12)

If a wife does not obey or if she is unfaithful, the solution is near at hand. He may

> Send her to Bristol, to Ned . . . er,
> For *Best Virginia*, he'll exchange her;
> Two Hogsheads for a lusty Jade,
> (12–13)

Instances of wife sale have been noted in England even as late as the nineteenth century.[5] Nevertheless, I believe that Plaxton's advice, as cruel as it sounds, is crudely facetious.

Plaxton's plain-speaking advisor has great faith in tobacco, and he concludes by recommending it as a universal remedy for all ills, marital or otherwise. He also counsels good humor, though not necessarily tenderness, as the proper response to wifely anger:

> Keep up thy courage, cheer thy Soul,
> Love *Mall*, but let her not controul;
> What if she pet, shed Tears, and frown,
> Laugh at her Folly;—she'll ha' done;
> Never dry up her Tears with Kisses,
> The more she cryes, the less she pisses.
> (16)

Whether such jocular humor constitutes a mellowing of the tone in which poets counsel husbands to control their wives, the reader can best judge. However, Plaxton's advice to combine love with firmness certainly seems a slight improvement over the speaker's vindictive desire to knock his wife's "bold face against the wall" in *The Married Mans Complaint*.

An unmistakable indication of the softening of the convention of attacking domineering wives is the comic use of it by a woman poet. In "Reformation" (1713), Anne Finch, Countess of Winchilsea, gives us a short tale in heroic couplets dramatizing a gentleman's inability to control his "wrangling and reproving wife" (Lonsdale 21). In an effort to endue his wife with a "calmer habit" of mind, the husband sends her to the country where her "wisely froward" ways will not trouble him or the servants. On her return, he discovers that while in her pastoral retreat she could not refrain from railing at the local shepherds and maids, even though she had no share in their concerns. The husband resigns himself to her dominance and passively awaits the ruin she will bring "like reformers who in states abound." Anne Finch's use of the domineering wife convention places her in the male satiric tradition. However, her manner of portraying a husband at a loss to control his wife may be an acknowledgment of the biological fact that women are in some ways stronger than men or that some women are more assertive than some men.

In a final example, "A Quiet Life, and A Good Name" (1719), Swift, like Plaxton, slightly modifies the conventions of harsh Restoration-style satire by introducing a humorous, didactic narrative spiced by knockabout comedy. Husband Dick is not in control of his wife. Nell abuses Dick both with her tongue and Dick's staff, but Dick will not correct her out of fear of scandal. His friend Will (and the poet) berate him for his false patience and mistaken pride. The Punch-and-Judy violence in Swift's poem is obviously derived from the popular ballad tradition that we saw exemplified by *The Married Mans Complaint*. Yet Swift is also close in comic spirit to a poet like Plaxton. In fact, in both poems the husband is advised to deal with an aggressive wife by exchanging her for a quantity of tobacco. In Swift's poem, friend Will recommends wife sale with callous comedy:

> If she were Mine, and had such Tricks,
> I'd teach her how to handle Sticks:
> Z—ds I would ship her for Jamaica
> And truck the Carrion for Tobacco,
>   (Swift 1: 220; lines 29–31)

Swift's satire is didactic, more strongly so than Plaxton's, and Swift's concern as a paternalistic moralist that a husband control his wife may well be seriously based in Christian marriage doctrine. This doctrine stressed the husband's obligation to control his wife even perhaps more than a wife's duty to be obedient to her husband. Yet, to make this serious point, Swift chooses a farcical vehicle, one that parodies the popular format for satire of domineering wives. Such tactics serve to soften the myth and finally to discredit it.

So far we have looked at poems—all of them predominantly in the satiric mode—that attack domineering wives and reinforce male sovereignty. What of the poems that criticize male sovereignty as tyrannical or hypocritical, or of the poems that glorify a marriage in which mutual love displaces the struggle over dominion (and creates an equal partnership)? These poems, clearly in the minority in the Restoration and somewhat less so in the early eighteenth century, are not primarily in the satiric mode. The majority operate in the didactic mode, the celebratory mode, or both, and each of these creates different expectations. We would not look for a poet acting as a moral advisor to savage a domineering wife, nor would we expect a poet to celebrate a marriage riven by strife over dominion.

Let us consider first the poems that criticize male sovereignty. In almost all cases, these do not challenge the principle of male sovereignty but point to individuals or types of men who abuse their dominion, usually by being tyrannical or hypocritical. Even if male sovereignty itself is criticized, no poem suggests that it be replaced by female sovereignty or by marital equality defined in legal terms.

"The Union of Friendship" (1675) by Richard Leigh, an actor in the Duke of York's company, attacks male sovereignty by describing subordination within a household as tyrannical:

> If it be lawful to compare
> A lesser, with a *greater Sphere*,
> Each *House*, a Kingdom is in short
> And govern'd, like the *Turkish Court*.
> The *Wife*, no *Office* seems to have
> But of the *Husbands* prime she-*Slave*.
> For she apart no *Rights* can claim,
> Nor has no title to her *Name*.
>
> (49)

In spite of Leigh's comparison of dominion in a household to Turkish absolutism, he is not advocating reform of the laws defining a woman's rights in marriage. Rather he is contrasting the principle of subordination in marriage to the principle of equality that governs in friendship. Friendship, the poet tells us in metaphysical-style conceits, is superior to marriage because the parties meet in freedom and equality.

> *Two Sexes, Marriage* does unite,
> And makes both, one *Hermaphrodite*.
> But *Friendship*, has the pow'r alone,
> To make two, of the *same Sex, one*.
>
> (49)

Paradoxically, the union of friendship has a purity of motive and a naturalness marriage lacks.

Leigh shows a fine sensitivity to the way dominion can poison a relationship and deprive the subordinate partner of selfhood. He is also one of the few poets to treat questions of primogeniture and subordination as they affect the eldest and the younger son. As a younger son himself, Leigh was no doubt sensitive to the issue. Even so, Leigh's poem is hardly reformist in intent. It might be more accurately described as a pleasures-of-the-single-life poem that treats male sovereignty critically.

A criticism of dominion is found in *Sylvia's Revenge, or, A Satyr against Man* (1688), attributed to Richard Ames. His attack is not so much on male tyranny as hypocrisy. In this poem, the speaker, who is supposedly the offending Sylvia of Robert Gould's *Love Giv'n O're* (1682), offers, in return for the attack on her, devastating sketches of various types of fops or single men about town. She then does the same for types of husbands. After hitting the type in each case with satiric accuracy and comic charm, Sylvia comes to the main target in her catalog: hypocrisy. Echoing the ranting mode of Gould, she uses her revelation of husbandly character flaws as a basis for questioning men's right to rule over women.

> Are these ye *Gods*, the Sov'reigns we must own?
> Must we before these golden Calves bow down?
> Forgive us Heaven if we renounce the Elves,
> We'll make a Common-Wealth among ourselves:
> Where, by the Laws that we shall then Ordain,
> We'll make it Capital to mention *Man*.
>
> (18)

If a woman who joins the "Common-Wealth" does "maintain a League with that detested Creature *Man*," she will first be counseled, then threatened, and finally left to suffer without pity the curse of a husband.

Proposing a commonwealth of women from which men would be banished, Sylvia would seem to be advocating a form of female sovereignty. The proposal of a one-sex kingdom or community is, however, not a new one in literature, nor is it one that need be taken at face value. The idea goes back as far as the myth of the Amazons, and it was as current as the play *The Women's Conquest* (1671) by Edward Howard, brother of the dramatist Sir Robert Howard. Howard's tragicomedy is an excellent indicator of the lack of seriousness with which the idea of a woman's commonwealth could be treated. As a single-sex commonwealth becomes a vehicle to reassert the principle of male dominion, so Sylvia's commonwealth is a stick with which to beat men and draw their attention to women at the same time. Sylvia's proposal has the same force as the oaths sworn by the members of the lady club in Congreve's *The Way of the World* (1700) who vow to shun all men forever (2.1). Like Mrs. Marwood, we expect to hear Sylvia proposing next "to carry her aversion to man one step further by marrying one."

Anyone with some familiarity with Richard Ames's poetry would not expect sincere advocacy of women's rights in marriage from him. As Felicity Nussbaum rightly points out: "*Sylvia's Revenge* does not argue for women's superiority or even for women's equality. It focuses on a simple reversal of men's fears that women are inconstant by detailing the inconstancy of every fop in town and warning the female sex against marriage. It argues against men but it does not argue for women" (*The Brink* 36). Like other satires by Ames, Gould, and other Grub Street versifiers, *Sylvia's Revenge* illustrates a turnabout poem, a formula poem that counterattacks the attacker, praises what had been satirized, or satirizes what had been praised. Such about-faces were motivated by the demands of the Grub Street market. To sell another poem, Ames would argue a position or write in a mode antithetically opposite to the one that had just appeared.

Though this seesawing alternation between satire and celebration is prompted by the marketplace, the significance of the alternation rises above it. Between 1680 and 1705, Ames and other Grub Street poets stand alternately on either side of this archetypal modal alternation. As poets could praise wives just as facilely as they could satirize them, so the way is opened for celebration increasingly to become a predominant mode in marriage verse.

The rising celebratory mode is well exemplified by another Grub Street poem that also criticizes the idea of male dominion. *Wedlock a Paradise:*

or, A Defence of Woman's Liberty Against Man's Tyranny (1701) comes as close as any we have seen so far to serious feminist advocacy. The position of its male speaker on the dominion question sounds, even perhaps by revisionist standards, supportive of women's rights in marriage.

> Since more than all these Comforts we enjoy
> In the fair Sex, whom we too oft decoy,
> And then misuse, as if kind Heaven gave
> Woman, not as a Partner but a Slave,
> Vain empty Thought that Man has all the sway,
> And Woman, tho' more perfect, must Obey
> A harsh Decree, and but of late made good,
> Since we have basely Chill'd the Female Blood,
> Who were long since to Arms and Arts apply'd,
> And in heroick Actions lay their Pride,
>
> (7–8)

The suggestion that women's blood has been "basely chill'd" in recent times may contain a sharp sociological insight into the impact of the myth of the "fair sex" on the freedom of action of women. In *The Rise of the Novel* Ian Watt suggests that, as families gained bourgeois status, wives effectively lost equality as they became "leisure exhibits engaging in no heavier economic tasks than the more delicate and supervisory operations of housewifery" (161). In poor households women traditionally had worked beside men in the fields as well as carrying out household tasks and caring for children. In the eighteenth century "a conspicuously weak constitution was both an assertion of delicacy and a presumptive claim to a similar future." Watt's explanation supports a revisionist analysis of the roles of women.

It is more credible, however, that in remarking on the "base chilling of Female Blood," the *Wedlock a Paradice* poet is simply offering a broad contrast between the unheroic character of modern women and the achievement in "Arms and Arts" of female "worthies" of ancient history and legend, a topic for celebration by Grub Street writers in the seventeenth century.[6] As the poet develops this contrast, he soon tips his hand by overstatement. In proving his point that male dominion is a recent innovation, the speaker offers sketches of the lives of such questionable female worthies as Semyramis of Assyria and Valasque of Bohemia. He argues not just for women's equality but for the superiority of women. Because his argument is so hyperbolic, one suspects that the poet's idealizations are more a function of the laudatory mode he uses than a seriously felt position. As with Ames, the poet who penned *Wedlock a Paradice* has done an about-face. In reply to *The Pleasures of a Single Life* (1701), which attacks a disobedient wife and demeans women, *Wedlock a Paradice* undertakes to free women from the accusation of disobedience and to praise them for their virtues. Obviously, neither the heavenly wife nor the hellish wife is an accurate portrait of the historical diversity of wives in eighteenth-century England. Whoever these women were in actuality, we do not see them in the satiric or celebratory mode of these Grub Street poems.

If *Wedlock a Paradice* is not a sincere critique of male dominion, a number of poems by women are, though even these have formulaic elements in their stance.[7] The most significant of these is Lady Chudleigh's *The Ladies Defence: or, The Bride-Woman's Counsellor Answer'd: A Poem in a Dialogue between Sir John Brute, Sir William Loveall, Melissa, and a Parson* (1701). As already discussed, the character of the Parson is intended to represent the Rev. John Sprint who published in 1699 *The Bride Woman's Counsellor. Being a Sermon Preach'd at a Wedding, May the 11th, 1699, at Sherbourn, in Dorsetshire*. In his sermon, Sprint took it upon himself to chastise women for their ungovernable tempers and their unreasonable behavior. He baldly lectured women on their duty to obey their husbands: "God and Nature hath given the Husband Authority to Command, and the wife is bound to obey, however unnecessary she may think it to be" (13–14).[8]

Lady Chudleigh found Sprint's insistence on blind obedience more than a little ridiculous, but even more, I believe, she was offended by Sprint's tone: "Had he treated us with a little more Respect, and instead of the surly Sourness of a Cynick, express'd himself with the good Humour of an English Man, and the soft and indearing Mildness of a Christian, I should have thought my self oblig'd to have return'd him Thanks for his Instructions" ("Preface to the Reader" [vii]). The poem she wrote in reply to Sprint adheres to the conventions of the Grub Street tract poem; it is polemical and uses hyperbole and verbal irony heavily. Even so, Lady Chudleigh's poem has more literary richness than the typical tract piece and deserves closer attention, especially as its literary qualities are pertinent to the question of how far-reaching its critique of male sovereignty is.

What is most difficult to reconcile in *The Ladies Defence* is the apparent contradiction between Lady Chudleigh's professed support for male sovereignty in "The Epistle Dedicatory," in "The Preface to the Reader," and in sections of the text and her outspoken mockery of the idea of "Arbitrary Sway" by men she offers through the character of Melissa, a character who seems to be her mouthpiece. The reader is not sure which to take seriously and must decide between at least two explanations: (1) The assent to the idea of male dominion is lip service; perhaps this is Lady Chudleigh's ruse to avoid being accused of heretical or subversive views. (2) Melissa's attacks on male dominion are more or less dramatic overstatements designed to point up the hypocrisy in Sprint's authoritarian stance. In this sense, it is not so much male sovereignty under attack as Sprint's overbearing tone.[9]

Though readers may differ, I incline more to the second explanation without dismissing the first. In fact, it sometimes appears that Lady Chudleigh may have it both ways: she sometimes seems to counsel obedience grudgingly or ironically, yet in other instances, she seems to do so quite straightforwardly. For example, in "The Epistle Dedicatory" she recommends obedience to women married to "Men of brutish unsociable Tempers, to Monsters in Humane Shape, to Persons who are at open defiance with their Reason, and fond of nothing but their Folly, and under no other Government but that of their irregular Passions." Wives of such men, advises the author with apparent complaisance, should "pay 'em as much Respect, and . . . obey their Commands with as much readiness, as if they were the best and most indearing Husbands in the World." One may suspect irony here, though the author justifies her advice by saying it will silence critics and give women the self-satisfaction of being virtuous. This tone is not quite straightforward; the self-righteousness of the martyr colors it.

In contrast, in "The Preface to the Reader," the author advises men that once they have secured their wives' affections by their "reciprocal Esteem," they "need not doubt of their Obedience." Unlike the advice in "The Epistle Dedicatory," this seems quite direct and sincere.

The poem itself has much of the effectiveness and some of the humor of a problem comedy. Our response to its literary qualities must inevitably affect how far-reaching we take its attack on male dominion. The characters are clearly types whose positions on issues are of necessity somewhat overstated.[10] The Parson is both zealous and self-satisfied in having taught wives

> their Husbands to Obey and Please,
> And to their Humours sacrifice their Ease:
> Give up their Reason, and their Wills resign,
> And every Look, and every Thought confine.
> (2–3)

Given the apparent extremism of the Parson's position, Melissa's attack on male sovereignty can sometimes seem calmly reasonable. Challenging men's title to such dominion over women, Melissa often appeals to logic:

> Must Men command, and we alone obey,
> As if design'd for Arbitrary Sway:
> Born petty Monarchs, and, like Homer's Gods,
> See all subjected to their haughty Nods?
>
> (3)

At the same time a significant share of anger invades Melissa's character as her initial stridency turns to controlled mockery and sarcasm. Is the rage a dramatic stance in which Lady Chudleigh has no emotional stake, or is Lady Chudleigh so involved in Melissa's character that the latter often articulates Lady Chudleigh's rage in undisguised form?

A good portion of Melissa's anger does seem to be motivated by Lady Chudleigh's Parson-baiting rather than by her attack on male sovereignty in principle. What incenses Lady Chudleigh–Melissa is the double standard of a figure like Sprint who demands the primitive virtues of absolute passive obedience from women but who has been willing evidently to apply relaxed standards in judging men.

Through the righteously provoked Melissa, Lady Chudleigh brings Sprint to account for a corollary hypocrisy. Though Christian men are required to show love to their wives, Sprint insists that the wives must show obedience *before* husbands can be more loving. Says the Parson:

> Our Love on their Obedience does depend,
> We will be kind, when they do no more offend.
>
> (8)

Melissa–Lady Chudleigh is especially angered by the Parson's portrayal of women as men's intellectual inferiors who must as puppets win favors from men by humoring them or wheedling. The Parson's insistence on the unthinking obedience of wives is made so upsetting to Melissa because Lady Chudleigh believes that women are not inferior to men by nature but by education.

In the debate over woman's intellectual capacity, the Parson bears the brunt of Melissa–Lady Chudleigh's attack rather than the tyrannical, antiintellectual husband, Sir John Brute, or the rather frivolous Don Juan, Sir William Loveall. Admittedly, the views of the latter two men on educating women are barbaric. Sir William, who earlier expressed his reverence for women, shows his true colors when he opposes educating women because then they will laugh at frivolous suitors and only men of sense will have a chance with them. Sir John, a thoroughgoing knuckle-dragger, opposes books on more primitive though equally pragmatic grounds.

> By Heav'n I wish 'twere by the Laws decreed
> They never more should be allow'd to Read.
> Books are the Bane of States, and the Plagues of Life.
> But both conjoyn'd, when studied by a Wife:
> They nourish Factions, and increase Debate,
> Teach needless things, and causeless Fears create.
>
> (16)

In contrast, the Parson respects books and learning and has, it seems, taken a hint or two from a play in writing his sermons. In his pride, however, the Parson would not have women learn from books directly but only through preceptors like him. In Lady Chudleigh's thinking, this makes him more reprehensible than the other two because as a clergyman and man of letters, he should have respect for women's intellectual capabilities.

The Parson's denial of books to women determines the curious final stance Lady Chudleigh has Melissa take. Women, Melissa vows in noble disdain, will respond to male hypocrisy by leading humble, virtuous, obedient lives dedicated to intellectual and moral self-improvement. Men will never have to upbraid them with want of duty and women will be kind to themselves by ensuring both their education and salvation. In the conclusion of the poem, Melissa espouses a kind of Christian feminism (which Lady Chudleigh also strongly recommends to women in "The Epistle Dedicatory"). Women who are condemned to hellish subordination will ensure their attainment of heaven hereafter by their piety and intellectual pursuits.

All in all, *The Ladies Defence* is a powerful poem. Although Lady Chudleigh's stance may finally be too polemical, especially since she does not distance herself sufficiently from Melissa, the poem's dramatic realism allows it to move some distance beyond the simple heaven-hell polarizations of the Grub Street formula poem. *The Ladies Defence* is far from being simplistic or one-dimensional. It has an expanding field of meaning that stems from its rich use of irony and dramatic characterization.[11]

It is not especially easy to sum up in one sentence Lady Chudleigh's attitude toward the idea of male dominion, nor perhaps should one try. It can be said she was sharply critical of the idea itself, though she was evidently more upset by the manner and tone with which women were advised to obey their husbands. As she says in "The Preface to the Reader," men who respect women's capacity to be educated, who treat them with civility, who choose wives for their virtues and intelligence, who treat them as friends, who do not interfere in women's jurisdictions in the household, "would not only win their Love, but preserve it, and engage 'em in reciprocal Esteem; and when once they have secur'd their Affection, they need not doubt of their Obedience" (ii).

Lady Chudleigh's poem, though published anonymously, attracted the attention of other women poets and encouraged at least one to write a tribute to her espousal of the cause of women. Elizabeth Thomas in "To the Lady Chudleigh, The Anonymous Author of the Lady's Defence" (1722) tells us of her reaction to Sprint's sermon. From the "*pompous* Title Page" she expected "*sage Advice*," giving women "good rules" to guide them in their conduct, but when she discovered its "*Malignant* Humour" and its lack of "*Charity* and *Sense*," her patience snapped. Dramatizing this, she offers an exasperated critique of male dominion that is like Lady Chudleigh's in striking more at male brutality in enforcing dominion than at the enslavement of sovereignty itself.

> *Poor Sex*, cried I, with *Malice* still opprest,
> By Knaves, and Fools, on e'ry Side *distrest*!
> Long have we drag'd a servile heavy Chain,
> Yet were our Souls *too noble* to complain:
> For *Quiet Sake*, we own'd the barb'rous Sway,
> And tamely did their rigid Laws obey.
> Such mild Submission, *gen'rous Minds* would own,
> But *savage Men* are not with Mildness won;
> Our *Duty* cannot calm their brutal Rage,
> Nor silent *Virtue*, Thirst of Rule asswage.
>
> (146)

Thomas's anger and her desire for someone to champion the female cause are more than satisfied when she reads Chudleigh's poem, recommended to her by a male friend.

The strongest and most scathing attack on unjust and hypocritical male dominion occurs in Lady Mary Wortley Montagu's "Epistle from Mrs. Yonge to Her Husband" (written 1724 but not published until 1972). Recently reprinted and discussed briefly in the fifth edition of *The Norton*

Anthology of English Literature (1: 1974–76), this heroic epistle, ascribed to the hand of Mrs. Yonge, is based on a 1724 Parliamentary divorce case in which the "notorious libertine" William Yonge publicly exposed his wife Mary's indiscretions with a Colonel Norton and was granted a divorce along with his wife's dowry and a major portion of her estate. The use of pathetic complaint for satiric purposes is a conventional feature of the Grub Street tradition, especially in the various pseudofeminist replies to Gould's *Love Giv'n O're*.

Lady Mary's poem, however, does not rely on falsified pathos. The anger and deeply felt intensity with which her speaker denounces her husband's hypocrisy in particular and the tyranny of the legal system and of custom in general make this one of the most authentic-sounding indictments of male dominion in the eighteenth century. The Norton editor, Lawrence Lipking, does not surprise us when he implies that the poem was not published during the eighteenth century because its attack was too outspoken. Although the poem is an unusual one, it evidently expressed a hostility toward the double standard that many women (and men) had come to feel.

> From whence is this unjust distinction grown?
> Are we not formed with passions like your own?
> Nature with equal fire our souls endued,
> Our minds as haughty, and as warm our blood;
> (lines 24–28)

We should, however, understand that "Epistle from Mrs. Yonge" is intended less to effect reform of the legal structure supporting male dominion than to create sympathy for the pathetic situation of the speaker and wives in general. As Lady Chudleigh's spokeswoman Melissa does, Lady Mary Montagu's Mary Yonge looks to heaven (not the legal system) for justice.

> Just heaven! (for sure in heaven does justice reign,
> Though tricks below that sacred name profane)
> To you appealing I submit my cause,
> Nor fear a judgment from impartial laws.
> (lines 15–18)

By their appeal to a heavenly or a natural justice, both Lady Chudleigh and Lady Mary Montagu reinforce their call on society to respect the dignity and humanity of women.

Of the critiques of male dominion by women poets, Lady Chudleigh's and Lady Mary Montagu's are the most developed and the most telling. As Michael Suarez has shown, the attack is mounted forcefully by a number of other women poets of the early and middle eighteenth century including Sarah Fyge Egerton, Mary Leapor, and Elizabeth Tollet. All three employ the trope of woman as slave in her various social roles, most disturbingly that of wife. As women poets repeat the trope, it retains its ideological impact even as it becomes formularized (see also Lonsdale 136).

In "The Emulation" (1703), Egerton elaborates on the complaint against male tyranny initiated by Lady Chudleigh in *The Ladies Defence* and "To the Ladies" (1703):

> Say tyrant Custom, why must we obey
> The impositions of thy haughty sway;
> From the first dawn of Life unto the Grave,
> Poor Womankind's in every State a Slave,
> The Nurse, the Mistress, Parent and the Swain,
> For Love she must, there's none escape that pain;
> Then comes the last, the *fatal* Slavery:
> The Husband with insulting Tyranny
> Can have ill Manners justify'd by Law;
> For Men all join to keep the Wife in awe.
>
> (108)

The trope of the "wife in bondage" is continued in "An Essay on Woman" of 1746 by Mary Leapor, self-educated daughter of a gardener (see Lonsdale 207–8). It is given a Popean dramatic brilliance in Elizabeth Tollet's "Hypatia" (1724).[12]

> What cruel laws depress the female kind
> To humble cares and servile tasks confined!
> In gilded toys their florid bloom to spend,
> And empty glories that in age must end:
> For amorous youth to spread the artful snares,
> And by their triumphs to enlarge their cares.
> For, once engaged in the domestic chain,
> Compare the sorrows, and compute the gain;
> What happiness can servitude afford?
> A will resigned to an imperious lord,

> Or slave to avarice, to beauty bind,
> Or soured with spleen, or ranging unconfined.
> That haughty man, unrivalled and alone,
> May boast the world of science all his own:
> As barb'rous tyrants, to secure their sway,
> Conclude that ignorance will best obey.
> (Lonsdale 99–100)

In women poets' diatribes on male tyranny, we discover a strongly articulated protofeminist awareness, an expression of women's anger at the oppressive roles in which they are cast by society, roles that stultify their intellectual and artistic potential. Undoubtedly, the attacks by women poets on women's servitude are authentic responses to blatant social inequalities. At the same time, as women poets repeat the trope, it becomes a formula in much the same way that the libertine attack on the imprisonment of marriage does. In fact, the attack on male tyranny by women poets borrows many of its tropes from the first and second male libertine arguments.

To say that this attack often becomes conventionalized is perhaps to say why it eventually loses its social impact. An additional and more important reason may be the rise to fashionable ascendancy of the companionate model. While the ideology that supported the male libertine arguments was being discredited in the early and middle eighteenth century, the myth of the fair sex that served as an ideological platform for the attack on the libertine arguments was gaining considerable sympathy. It is probably the rise of this male-fostered myth that bolsters domesticity which causes women's polemical condemnations of wifely servitude to abate in the last half of the century.

We have looked at poems—satirical, didactic, and celebratory—that are critical of male sovereignty, especially as men abuse their dominion by being tyrannical or hypocritical. These poems generally do not carry a political intent in the narrow sense, and even the outspoken poems by women seem more concerned with altering social attitudes than with proposing legislation that would significantly improve women's status in marriage. Even less seriously reformist are the early era poems by men that displace the struggle over dominion either by suggesting cavalierly that women are the power behind the throne or romantically that mutual love can form an equal partnership. These mainly didactic and celebratory poems, though progressive in stance, do not challenge male dominion directly. It is poems taking this tack that we will see flourishing most vigorously in the later era.

Not unexpectedly, it is to Richard Ames that we turn for an early example of a poem that pushes the dominion question aside to praise equality in love. His use of the laudatory mode in *The Pleasures of Love and Marriage, A Poem in Praise of the Fair Sex* (1691) is another illustration of a turnabout. *The Pleasures of Love and Marriage* is written as a reply to Ames's vitriolic satire *The Folly of Love* (1691), which savages women. Knowing Ames's penchant for Jekyll and Hyde about-faces does not encourage our faith in his sincerity, and Ames worsens his credibility by opening in a laudatory mode that plunges over the verge into fulsomeness.

> *Divinest Sex*, compos'd of purer *Mold*!
> (We only are the Ore, but you the Gold.)
> How shall I justly *Treat* so vast a *Theme*,
> Where *meanly to Commend* were to *Blaspheme*?
> (1)

After five pages or so of this excess, Ames settles down to more pedestrian hyperbole as he offers an overstated defense of women against the overstated accusations of his earlier poem.

On the dominion question, Ames first takes the tack of praising women as the power behind the throne. He thus displaces the standard legal and theological rationales for male dominion. Ames argues that men may boast of raising empires and building cities. However, while men pretend to rule the world, women keep it "in its constant state" and encourage "*Man* in all his *sweat* and *toils*."

> 'Tis *Woman* makes the ravish'd *Poet* Write,
> 'Tis Lovely *Woman* makes the *Soldier* Fight;
> (6)

Not only does woman rule man by inspiring him and rewarding him, but woman has a second function. In Ames's male-centered but romantic interpretation of woman's roles, she is a civilizing force whose influence is necessary to keep men from degenerating into animals:

> Should that *soft Sex* refuse the World to Bless,
> Twou'd soon be *Chaos* all, or *Wilderness*;
> A *Herd*, without *Civility* or *Rules*,

> A *Drove* of Drinking, Cheating, Fighting *Fools*;
> All *Mad* to kick each other off the *Stage*,
> Their very *Race* destroy'd in one short *Age*.
> 'Twas Beauty first made Laws, did Monsters bind,
> Reform'd the *World* and civiliz'd *Mankind*;
>
> (7)

In passages such as this, we already have a full articulation of the myth of the fair sex, a myth which, as Richard Clancey, Ian Watt, and Ellen Pollak show, comes to the fore as the eighteenth century progresses. Ames credits women with teaching mankind "first to turn the Fruitful Soyl," while men who were the warriors considered themselves superior. "But which is the best Title, *Bold* or *Wise*?" Ames asks. Siding with women in this anthropological contrast, Ames answers, "Wise."

As with all myths, there are elements of truth in this one, and it is tempting to point to the kernel of accuracy that may be contained in Ames's fiction. Anthropology has shown us that in many primitive societies men are the hunters, and women are the farmers, doing most of the manual labor in the village. We also know that civilization began to develop beyond the nomadic state when men (or rather women) began to cultivate the land. It was at this point that cities were first built. By praising the civilizing virtues of women as cultivators of the soil and denigrating the warrior attributes of men, Ames may in fact be proposing to his reader new models for masculine behavior. As Susan Staves suggests, "As the culture became more a bourgeois culture of men who rejected the personal use of violence, where better to look for examples of how people manage without violence than among women?" (186).

After first displacing the dominion question by presenting woman as the power behind the throne and as a civilizing force, Ames next displaces it by proposing a romantic (or possibly a Christian) model in which the couple are so in love that neither strives for mastery:

> Thrice Happy they in those soft *Fetters* ty'd,
> The Fatal Sisters only can divide;
> Who for no other Mastry ever strove,
> But whether of the two should better Love,
>
> (20)

The pattern of love displacing or muting the struggle over dominion is not only advanced by Ames but by a number of male poets—both Grub

Street and polite—between approximately 1690 and 1720. As we might anticipate, many of these poems are celebratory, perhaps after the precedent set by Ames. In *A Poem in Praise of Marrying for Love* (1698), the author, Hugh Newman, commends the "Seraphick Charms" of woman given to her by heaven so that man's "desires" would be "confin'd alone/ To her, whom Fate has made his own." She

> with Pious Conduct, still
> Squares the Just Limits of his Will;
> And studies, with delight and ease,
> Not how to Rule, but how to please.
> (3–4)

The praise of Newman, who may be a clergyman, is really no more than Protestant doctrine on marriage dressed up in romantic trappings. His sensitivity to the injustice of women's subordination is minimal, even less than Ames's, but at least he is not offensive in the manner of Sprint.

Newman advances in only one minor respect beyond the orthodox position that the wife must serve and obey her husband. The wife in Newman's poem "pleases," rather than simply submitting. The distinction is a subtle one, but a somewhat more active role for the wife is clearly implied, especially when we keep in mind that pleasing a husband was for Newman a way of ruling him.

In *Eleonora: A Panegyrical Poem Dedicated to the Memory of the Late Countess of Abingdon* (1692), even Dryden gives us a version of displacement, one that may be more progressive than Newman's. Eleonora stands in this laudatory piece as the "Pattern" of the "best Wife, the best Mother, and the best of Friends."

> Love and Obedience to her Lord she bore,
> She much obey'd, him but she lov'd him more.
> Not aw'd to Duty by superior sway;
> But taught by his Indulgence to obey.
> Thus we love God as Author of our good;
> So Subjects love just Kings, or so they shou'd.
> Nor was it with Ingratitude return'd;
> In equal Fires the blissful Couple burn'd:
> One Joy possess'd 'em both, and in one Grief they mourn'd.
> (Dryden 473–74; lines 176–84)

Eleonora offers both love and obedience, but the love is clearly a stronger force than the obedience. Given the final couplet especially, the displacement may seem only a romantic one, a secularization of Christian doctrine. Yet when Dryden emphasizes the husband's maintaining his wife's obedience not by "asserting his authority" but by bestowing "love and favor," he adopts at least one major emphasis of Protestant marriage theology. As William and Malleville Haller point out in "The Puritan Art of Love," the husband's obligation "to love the woman God gave him is stressed by many seventeenth-century preachers and conduct book writers on marriage." This is true especially but certainly not exclusively of those the Hallers label Puritan. In this tradition, "The more he loves her the more she will obey him. 'A good husband will make a good wife; a good John a good Joane'"(265).

In the long eighteenth century, we have seen that theological conceptions of conjugal love are secularized and softened by popular romantic ideals. As the Hallers put it, "From magnifying the religious significance of marriage Puritan thought easily proceeded to magnify the emotional, romantic and idealistic aspects of the marriage relation" (265). A mixture of the religious and the romantic conceptions of love are behind Dryden's final couplet:

> In equal Fires the blissful Couple burn'd:
> One Joy possess'd 'em both, and in one Grief they mourn'd.
> (Dryden 474: lines 183–84)

"Blissful" (in 183) may suggest beatitude, but it is more likely it refers to the joy of the couple's emotional closeness and to their shared sexual ecstasy.

A much more simplistic and blatant secularization is behind the displacement of the dominion question in a Grub Street poem, *The Ladies Choice* (1702). In this dialogue, mainly in the didactic mode, Belinda advises the fifteen-year-old Melissa on the choice of a husband. Belinda takes an interesting stance in granting that marriage involves subordination or, at least, serious restrictions on a wife's freedom. Having said this, Melissa flies right over the problem (with the help of Cupid):

> So to my Lover I'd my Heart resign,
> The Conquest his, the Glory should be mine.
> With mutual Love my Nuptials shou'd be Blest,
> Then to my Arms I'd call the Welcome Guest,
> And Celebrate with Joy great *Hymen's* Feast.
>
> Marriage is Bondage; but where *Cupid* Reigns
> The Yoke is easie; Glorious are the Chains:

> His Fetters please, nor wish we to be Free,
> But Glory in the Loss of Liberty:
>
> (12–13)

In this romanticized piece, "*Cupid* reigns," so the question whether the husband or wife has the sovereignty does not really seem at issue. Of course, if "the Nuptials" no longer were to be blessed by "mutual Love" or if Cupid should happen to fly off someday, the wife might find herself quite resentful of her "Chains."

If *The Ladies Choice* tries to make dominion palatable to young women by appealing to their romantic imagination, Samuel Jackson in *The Duty of a Wife* (1707) takes a more prudential stance. Jackson not only shows love displacing the husband's concern about his dominion. He suggests slyly that once a wife gains her husband's love by obedience, then she can rule him and get what she wants (as long as it is not evil):

> First, therefore see your Husbands you Obey,
> Strive to please them, and then perhaps you may,
> In time rule them, for if ever they find,
> You love them, and are subject to their Mind;
> They'll love you, and let you do what you will,
> (Provided you do nothing that is Ill)
> But first if you'l observe the lines below,
> How you must win their love I'll plain show.
>
> [1]

Jackson offers what may have been for his women readers an attractive rationale for their being obedient. Even so, the woman who reads on in the poem would have found that there are numerous tasks and obligations required to "please" one's husband. These include not scolding or brawling when he comes home from the tavern after "a Cup too much," starting a fire in his room and laying out dry clothes when he comes home wet, not despising him if she should happen to be richer than he, avoiding scolding in general to get her way, being chaste in order to avoid jealous spies who might report her wayward behavior to him, and not slighting her husband if he should fall into affliction or become old. Before a wife could "rule" her husband, a good amount of work had obviously to be put into winning his love.

Jackson anticipates the objections of wives who protest such obedience.

> Perhaps you'l say, 'tis hard we must Obey,
> When we to Rule, are full as fit as they;

> What have we done, what have we committed,
> That we to Rule should not be admitted?
>
> (8)

Jackson responds to his rhetorical question with two arguments. In the first, he makes the predictable reference to the story of Eve's disobedience in Gen. 3:16. His second argument is that women by nature are not as fit to rule as men.

> Nature made them not as fit to bear the Pain,
> And the Fatigue that's undergone by Men:
> For they cannot withstand invading Foes,
> Neither can they indure the Wounds and Blows,
> That are given in Fight, and therefore 'tis fit
> To those that defend them they should submit;
>
> (8)

Ames denigrates the warrior attributes of men to praise women as a civilizing force and thus displaces the dominion question. Jackson praises the warrior attributes of men to justify men's dominion. In either case men end up in control. The only difference is how bluntly or tactfully dominion is affirmed.

As we move further into the eighteenth century, we encounter more didactic poems in which a less heavy handed, more reasonable and tactful husband is featured. A softening of the style by which husbands affirm their dominion is evident in these pieces. For example, in dialogue VI of Ned Ward's *Nuptial Dialogues and Debates* (1723), we are offered a revealing debate "Between a pert Lady and her Spouse, concerning Superiority in Wedlock." The husband's defense of his sovereignty, though condescending, *sounds* reasonable and tolerant:

> Husbands, like Princes, tho' they bear command,
> Scorn to chastise with too severe a Hand:
> Yet, if a King does too indulgent prove,
> And makes his subjects happy in his Love,
> Th'ingrateful People will be apt, like you,
> To deem his Royal Clemencies their due;
>
> (1: 50)

In contrast, the wife's assertion of her equality may be meant to be undercut since Ward makes her rely so obviously on protofeminist polemics.

> Wives, by Experience, know their Husbands would
> Be Monarchs, nay, be Tyrants, if they could:
> But Women that are wise, their Frowns withstand,
> And scorn to truckle to each proud Command.
> . . . .
> But Man has no Dominion o'er his Bride,
> More than what's founded on his churlish Pride
> The Wife's his Partner, and has Right to share
> His greatest Fortunes, well as meanest Fare.
>
> (1: 49–50)

The husband finally does affirm his dominion, and his tone still sounds reasonable. He does not rant angrily as he makes it clear that subordination is not slavery but a "lawful Duty" that involves an "easy Servitude."

> Slav'ry's a modern, canting Term, in Vogue
> With stubborn Wives, and each rebellious R—gue,
> Who hating to submit, would bear the sway
> O're those just Pow'rs they should by Law obey.
> The Apprentice bound for seven Years to serve,
> That the dull Fool may neither hang or starve;
> The Woman ty'd in Marriage-Bonds for Life,
> To be a faithful and obedient Wife;
> The Subject fetter'd to his Prince's Cause
> By sacred Oaths, Religion, and the Laws;
> All hate the Yoke, desiring to be free,
> And stile their lawful Duty, Slavery;
> Forgetting still the Safety and the Good
> Th'enjoy in such an easy Servitude.
>
> (1: 54)

Offering a secular justification of male dominion, the husband points out that subordination is the common lot in civilization, and all resent it, even those whose yoke is easy.

If Ward's husband affirms his authority in a paternalistic tone made to seem reasonable, "The True Woman's Man" (1729) by Henry Carey—writer of farces, comic operas, and burlesques—seems to be defining a new model for husbandly behavior; he rejects extremes to establish an idealized norm, which he suggests will be popular with the ladies. In celebrating this norm, Carey is at the same time paying tribute to his friend

George Rivers, Esquire. Carey's first step in his definition is to reject out of hand the "women's men":

> In the opinion of the vulgar crowd
> No merit is to women's men allow'd,
> But tattling, dandling, loit'ring all the day,
> And trifling life's most precious hours away.
> Let such as these, when caught in wedlock's share,
> Be the coquette or stern virago's share;
>
> (199)

"Women's men" were evidently those who shared with women in social activities usually pursued exclusively by them; Carey scorns such men. In contrast is the "true woman's man" whom he praises with slightly tempered machismo:

> But to a girl of honour, worth, and sense
> Let no such coxcomb dare to make pretence.
> Be hers the gay, the generous, the brave,
> No surly tyrant, nor yet henpeck'd slave;
> But one who will instruct, approve, defend,
> A constant lover and a faithful friend,
> Who, by his conduct, shall acquire such fame,
> She shall with pride and pleasure wear his name.
>
> (199)

The true woman's man, the one women would have for a beau or a husband rather than a pet, manifests his dominion by positive personal traits and by the roles he plays. He will "instruct" (as a teacher), "approve" (as a moralist or judge), and "defend" (as a soldier). Most important, he is brave (but no surly tyrant) and constant and faithful (but not a "henpeck'd slave"). Such a man is embodied in his friend Rivers, and such a man, Carey asserts, represents a more humanized model for husbandly dominion than the authoritarian patriarch or the feminized "woman's man."

Neither Ward nor Carey actually weaken the principle of male sovereignty, though both insist on it in a way meant to be more appealing than that taken by earlier moralists. In the course of the eighteenth century, as we will see next, the style by which dominion is affirmed in male satiric and didactic poetry does continue to soften and secularize. This softening—along with the amplification of the myth of the "fair sex" and the continued displacement of the dominion question by praise of the companionate marriage—is no doubt an additional factor in making women poets of the later era less sharply polemical in their criticism of dominion.

THE LATER ERA

Although the patriarchal idea that husbands should hold sovereignty over their wives remains in place, the number of harsh satiric attacks on domineering wives declines significantly in the later era. Appearing with more frequency are lighter satires that emphasize, sometimes ironically, the power of women to get men to do their bidding by their emotional influence or sexual attractiveness. Didactic poems counsel women to obedience but advise them to gain influence over men by humoring them. Conversely, didactic poems advise husbands to assert their control over wives, not by force but by capitulating to them in small matters.

Marriage verse of this era focuses less on conflicts produced by assertive or hellish wives and more on ways to avoid such conflicts. Disputes over sovereignty are to be displaced by love or tactful submission. Women are advised to stoop to conquer, and men at least outwardly are to be more chivalrous. By this time, a new style for the husband to affirm his sovereignty is clearly evolving. Unfortunately, the new chivalrousness is a feature of a new myth, and there is often condescension in the new, more liberal male stance toward the angelic "fair sex."

Though some harsh satires on domineering wives do occur in this era, especially in popular verse, attacks on women's challenge to men's sovereignty are usually lighter and more entertainingly indirect, especially in polite verse.[13] This is the case in Thomas Parnell's narrative satire "Hesiod: or, The Rise of Woman" (1726), based on the myth of Pandora's box as related by Hesiod. In Parnell's poem, when Pandora comes to man bearing her "golden coffer," his marriage to her results in his loss of dominion. When Pandora opens her box, she brings forth not just evil in general but the specific tribulations of men attributable to women. Chief of these is man's sexual attraction to woman and all that controlled insanity inspired by it:

> The days of whining, and of wild intrigues,
> Commenc'd, or finish'd, with the breach of leagues;
> The mean designs of well-dissembled love;
> The sordid matches never join'd above;
> Abroad the labour, and, at home the noise,

>   (Man's double suff'rings for domestic joys)
>   The curse of jealousy, expence, and strife;
>   Divorce, the publick brand of shameful life;
>   The rival's sword; the qualm that takes the Fair;
>   Disdain for passion, passion in despair—
>   These, and a thousand, yet unnam'd we find;
>   Ah fear the thousand, yet unnam'd behind!
>   (13–14)

Loss of dominion in Parnell's poem means not so much that the male is verbally or physically abused by the female but that she has the power of sexual attractiveness that stimulates irrational, reprehensible behavior both in him and in other men. Of course, women must be held responsible as well for irrational behavior. However, in Parnell's somewhat chivalrous poem the onus falls on male difficulties in fending off female charms. All the gods and goddesses—Vulcan, Venus, Juno, Minerva, Hermes, Apollo, the Graces, and Fair Flora—contribute to making Pandora irresistibly charming. It is no wonder that man would put his dominion in jeopardy by marrying her. Pandora's power—and that of women in general—is presented as formidable indeed. Even poets such as Hesiod who insult women in their songs are vulnerable. (Hesiod himself was mistakenly stabbed by the jealous kindred of a woman who had eloped with her lover.) Cupid, says the poet, will not suffer his empire to be mocked with impunity.

Unlike traditional satire on domineering women, Parnell's Pandora narrative shows women exerting power over men not by physical or verbal force but by the power of their sexual attractiveness. Richard Jago's "Female Empire. A True History" (1784), an even lighter poem than Parnell's, bases its comedic satire on this very distinction. Jago, a clergyman of Cornish descent, contrasts two wives' differing manners of getting their way with their husbands. "Female Empire" first gives us Chloe who gets her husband's attention by "streaming eyes" or "hysterics"; Chloe resorts to a time-honored form of woman's rhetoric. Celia, on the other hand, chooses a more forceful (and traditional) means of persuasion: she belabors her husband about the head with a poker. Celia, of course, is the hellish wife of earlier satire, mocked for abusing her husband. Jago, however, does not satirize her directly. Rather he scorns Celia's violence, archly acknowledging the forcefulness of Chloe's means of persuasion:

>   Victorious sex! alike your art,
>   And puissance we dread;

> For if you cannot break our heart,
>   'Tis plain you'll break our head.
>
> Place me, ye gods, beneath the throne
>   Which gentle smiles environ,
> And I'll submission gladly own,
>   Without a rod of iron.
>   (Chalmers 17: 312)

From the poet's point of view, the issue is not how women can gain dominion over men. For that the poker might be more effective. The question is rather how women can manipulate men to win concessions from them. For this, the poet sees the tearful plea or the complaisant smile as more effective. Most males would agree with the poet since they would rather surrender to charm than brute force, and female charm does have its idyllic, even Edenic resonances in the male imagination. Even so, the speaker's preference for charm over force is demeaning since it neglects to suggest that women are capable of rational argument or that women in many instances might have justice or the natural superiority of intellect on their side. Though chivalrous, the final attitude of the speaker in Jago's poem is condescending.

More or less condescending for similar reasons are several advice poems that attempt to recognize women's power and to instruct them to use it properly to gain influence over their husbands. Though the modern reader might be put off by the patronizing tone of these pieces, by the standards of the time they are clearly an advance in courtliness over the earlier conduct books in verse that recommend obedience more bluntly.

This is certainly the case with Pope's "Epistle to Miss Blount, with the Works of Voiture" (1712). Though written in 1712, the "Epistle to Miss Blount" is much closer in tone to other mid-century didactic works than to those of the earlier era. Like these mid-century works as well, Pope's epistle, for all its sensitivity, ends up perpetuating the traditional ideal of the wife who suffers all in good humor.

Pope sees women as unnecessarily oppressing themselves and other women by their adherence to social forms and custom, an unnatural adherence that is due to pride.

> Too much *your Sex* is by their Forms confin'd,
> Severe to all, but most to Womankind;
> Custom, grown blind with Age, must be your Guide
> Your Pleasure is a Vice, but not your Pride;

> By Nature yielding, stubborn but for Fame;
> Made Slaves by Honour, and made Fools by Shame.
>
> (169–70; lines 31–36)

If women's subjection to the tyranny of social forms is to a large extent self-imposed, their domination by a husband is not:

> Marriage may all those petty Tyrants chace,
> But sets up One, a greater, in their Place;
> Well might you wish for change, by those accurst,
> But the last Tyrant ever proves the worst.
> Still in Constraint your suff'ring Sex remains,
> Or bound in formal, or in real Chains;
> Whole Years neglected for some months ador'd,
> The fawning Servant turns a haughty Lord;
>
> (170; lines 37–44)

Pope is critical both of women's self-imposed subordination to social forms and their real subordination in marriage. He opposes the latter by recommending the only sure course of action an eighteenth-century English woman could take to avoid a despotic husband: stay single.

> Ah quit not the free Innocence of Life!
> For the dull Glory of a virtuous Wife!
> Nor let the false Shows, or empty Titles please:
> Aim not at Joy, but rest content with Ease.
>
> (lines 45–48)

To be sure, not all women married out of desire for "Shows" and "Titles." In many cases, a woman's independent status was difficult to maintain without being humiliatingly dependent on friends or relatives; marriage was not just an indulgence but a social and economic necessity. Pope may recognize this when he comes to the point of the poem and the reason for his extended reference to Voiture:

> But, Madam, if the Fates withstand, and you
> Are destin'd *Hymen's* willing Victim too,
> Trust not too much your now resistless Charms,
> Those, Age, or Sickness, soon or late, disarms;
> *Good Humour* only teaches Charms to last
> Still makes new Conquests, and maintains the past:
>
> (lines 57–62)

By "Good Humour" Pope probably means the "Humour, Wit, ... native Ease and Grace" that characterized Voiture's life and works and that Pope hopes will distinguish his life and Patty Blount's.

> His Heart, his Mistress and his Friend did Share;
> His Time, the Muse, the Witty, and the Fair.
> Thus wisely careless, innocently gay,
> Chearful, he play'd the Trifle, Life, away,
> (169; lines 9–12)

Pope fears that Patty Blount's marriage may cut her off from him. He uses the extended allusion to Voiture not just to offer moral advice about the spirit in which she should conduct her life; he also employs Voiture's life as a literal model that will sanction the continuation of his relationship with Patty Blount:

> Thus *Voiture's* early Care still shone the same,
> And *Monthausier was only chang'd in Name*:
> By this, ev'n now they live, ev'n now they charm,
> Their Wit still sparkling and their Flames still warm.
> (170–71; lines 69–72)

In his "wisely careless" and "innocently gay" life-style, Voiture was able to continue his correspondence, even after she married, with Julie Lucine d'Angennes, duchesse de Monthausier and eldest daughter of the Marquise de Rambouillet (170; note 70). Pope wants to do the same with Patty Blount:

> Now crown'd with Myrtle, on th' *Elysian* Coast,
> Amid those Lovers, joys his gentle Ghost,
> Pleas'd while with Smiles his happy Lines you view,
> And finds a fairer Rambouillet in you.
> The brightest Eyes of *France* inspir'd his Muse,
> The brightest Eyes of *Britain* now peruse,
> And dead as living, 'tis our Author's Pride,
> Still to charm those who charm the World beside.
> (171; lines 73–80)

In a fashion we have come to expect from Pope, he tops off his elaborate advice and charming compliments with the piquant sauce of witty egotism. Pope's recommendation of "Good Humor" is thus in part self-serving.

Though Pope shows sensitivity to the way women can be enslaved in marriage, his counsel at base amounts to a repetition of the patriarchal conduct book advice given to women for coping with a tyrannical or ill-humored husband: namely, the wife should not contradict him but accede to his wishes in good humor. By doing so, she may shame him into treating her more kindly. Pope says to Patty Blount that she should trust her "Good Humour," and not her beauty, to maintain her power. This advice is not patronizing on the face of it; however, the underlying force of it may be since "Good Humour" belittles the pain a woman can experience in subordinating herself to male dominion, especially if it is tyrannical or abusive. In advising Patty Blount, Pope in effect says that if she marries she must accede to her subservience gracefully.

One must dig a bit to uncover the patronizing attitude underneath Pope's chivalrous tone. In several advice poems of the mid-century, it is easier to detect. Samuel Wesley the Younger's *The Battle of the Sexes: A Poem* (1723), a Popean mock epic (in modified Spenserian stanza), treats the respective powers of the sexes in courtship. The speaker for Samuel Wesley, who was a headmaster and the elder brother of John and Charles, offers direct advice to the ladies on the importance of not being arrogant in courtship:

> Tho' Man does awful Rule o'er Woman bear,
> Not sprung from greater Worth, but right Divine;
> Yet she shall in her Turn Dominion share,
> E'er to his Will her Empire she resign;
> But while she reigns her Mildness let her Show,
> And well employ the quickly-fleeting Time;
> Not unrewarded shall her Mercy go,
> And strictest Justice shall o'er take her Arms.
> Gently shall those be rul'd, who gently sway'd;
> Abject shall those obey, who haughty were obey'd.
>
> (36)

For Wesley there is no question about the dominion of men in marriage; it is a God-given right. What is interesting is his chivalrous aspersion of dominion to women in courtship and the psychology and logic of his appeal to them not to be tyrannical in their temporary role as masters.

One is hard put to know how to take this appeal. Is it meant as token flattery or is it a veiled threat? If the poet is flattering women by magnifying the importance of their dominion in courtship, then he is guilty of a kind of reverse condescension. If, on the other hand, the poet is warning women not to be too arrogant or standoffish or they will be treated harshly in turn, then he can be called to account both for the heavy handedness of his counsel and its illogic. Husbands may be tyrannical to a wife in marriage whether or not she is haughty in courtship.

In the way he pays attention to women's power in courtship, Wesley's stance is chivalrous. In poems that are more strictly conduct books in verse, we find such gallantry recommended to the husband as the style with which he should enforce his sovereignty. In order to affirm their sovereignty in large matters, husbands are advised to accede to their wives in small ones. The converse of this is the myth of the wife who stoops to conquer. Advice poems of the later era frequently tell wives that they will gain sway over their husbands by the complaisance and charm with which they obey them.

In Francis Blyth's *Advice to a Friend on His Marriage, A Poem* (1735), the poet counsels the new husband directly on how best to maintain his dominion in marriage. The wife is to be treated chivalrously, even kindly, in order to forestall "Matrimonial strife." The husband should occasionally allow her the victory, so that in the long run he will prevail.

> What would you lose, tho' you at Times submit?
> Complacence ne'er was Forfeiture of Wit.
> Reclaim'd in Sense, tho' suffer'd to subdue,
> Grateful in turn, She'll next submit to You.
> Th'Idea, which She's fond of, never thwart;
> But nobly lose your Point, and gain her Heart.
>
> (17)

Granted, some husbands would not operate under any higher motivation, yet there is an appeal to the husband's self-interest in Blyth's advice that makes it seem calculating and manipulative.[14]

If Blyth's poem gives the husband advice on how to maintain his control by chivalrous behavior, Thomas Mariott's *Female Conduct* (1759) instructs the wife on the advantageous use of her subordinate position. Mariott's tone is mildly paternalistic and preachy, though he frequently tries to lighten his prescriptiveness with witty play and rhetorical flourish. On the question of the wife's duty to obey her husband, he is quite direct in stating that the husband has dominion. Mariott then employs the "stoops-to-conquer" myth in a well-developed form:

> Hence ev'ry Wife her Husband must obey,
> She, by Compliance, can her Ruler sway;
> Strong, without Strength, she triumphs o'er the Heart,
> What Nature gives not, she acquires by Art;
> Preeminence, herself debasing, gains,
> By yielding conquers, and by serving reigns;
> Her soft Endearments, her fierce Master tame,
> As *Greece*, with Arts, *Rome's* conquering Arms o'ercame;
>
> (18)

Mariott softens the force of the husband's dominion by emphasizing the wife's ability to "sway" "by Compliance." He reinforces this with several embellishing oxymorons ("strong, without strength," "yielding conquers" and "serving reigns").

In a passage reminiscent of the description of the power of Belinda's beauty in canto 2.19–28 of *The Rape of the Lock*, Mariott elaborates at some length on the "proper tools" of women's power over men: beauty and flattery. For the unmarried women especially, beauty is a potent weapon. The poet presents the woman who would use it as a soldier armed with weaponry: "Well disciplin'd to use her Arms;/To know the Force of her Artillery." Mariott cautions woman, in using her beauty, that she does not ensnare herself in her own trap and fall victim to a young man's wiles. It is safer and wiser for a woman to depend on flattery to get her way. Speaking as a man of "Learning," Mariott lets her in on the secret of how powerful an ("unlearn'd") woman may be when practicing this "art" on (educated) men.

> Sages, who moral Precepts finest Spin,
> Such Flattery, in Maids, can deem no Sin,
> By Nature weak, the Woman stronger grows,
> By this smooth Art, and can our Strength oppose;
> Whether the Art to please, or Flatt'ry call'd,
> By this, each human Heart may be inthrall'd;
> Hence, she unlearn'd, our Learning can outdo,
> Thro's Wedlock's Maze, this is her guiding Clue.
>
> (27–28)

Mariott unashamedly fosters the myth of the fair sex who is physically weak (and uneducated), but powerful in subterfuge. In his chivalrous condescension he encourages women to practice flattery, an "art" that poets usually regard with contempt when practiced by men. So confident is the poet in his masculine superiority that he can reveal how vulnerable men are to women's power.

By the time of Mariott's *Female Conduct* in 1759, the myth of the angelically submissive but victorious wife had been well established in didactic poetry. It is thus fair game for those who would celebrate it or romanticize it further. This occurs in numerous poems, including those by women. Letitia Barbauld's "The Rights of Woman" (written ca. 1795) does not as such propagate the myth of the woman who stoops to conquer; she does, however, use verbal irony as a stick to beat down women who are too militant in asserting feminine claims on men's respect and sympathy.

> Try all that wit and art suggest to bend
> Of thy imperial foe the stubborn knee;
> Make treacherous Man thy subject, not thy friend;
> Thou mayst command, but never canst be free.
>
> (Lonsdale 306)

Though her poem may have been specifically intended as a critique of Mary Wollstonecraft's *Vindication of the Rights of Woman* (1792), Mrs. Barbauld's more general point seems to be that the (mutual) inclination toward connubial tenderness and affection is stronger and more natural than the assertion of gender superiority.[15] The woman who attains victory over men by the justice of her powers as a woman will finally

> abandon each ambitious thought;
> Conquest or rule thy heart shall feebly move,
> In Nature's school, . . .
>
> (Lonsdale 306)

For Mrs. Barbauld, the myth of equality in marital companionship and affection displaces the struggle for equal rights for women as a social group.

Similarly, in "[The Power of Women]" (written 1798) by Matilda Betham, a single woman who strove for independence as an artist, the speaker disdains women's participation in the "mechanic arts," warfare, or "the search for sordid gain" (502). She upholds the myth of women as the power behind the throne. Women control the world by controlling men, who do not realize they are enchained:

> So that the captive wanders unconfined,
> And has no sovereign but o'er his mind!
>
> (Lonsdale 503)

Neither poet encourages women to build a career or to seek economic self-sufficiency.

An even more romantic handling of the myth occurs in a late work by Ann Holmes entitled *An Epic Poem on Adam and Eve* (1800). More a mild erotic fantasy in the pastoral mode than a serious reworking of Miltonic themes, this piece begins with the creation of Eve and ends, interestingly enough, before her temptation by the serpent. Ann Holmes celebrates the marital bliss of our first parents in the garden and lavishes attention on the innocent sensuousness of Adam and Eve's equally innocent pleasures among the flora and fauna. In this mythical setting the question of dominion is used to enhance the romantic appeal of Adam and Eve's relationship. Eve's vow of submission to Adam is charming in its surrender to his mastery:

> O Adam she reply'd, what place
> Hast thou for me assign'd, that with the name
> Of partner thou dost honour me a hight,
> To which I never must aspire, lest I
> Presumptuous should be deem'd, me, who
> Much inferior am, that when with thee
> Compar'd, and with thy nobleness of mind,
> Thy solid judgment and thy sense secure,
> A mirror they do prove, wherein I all
> My imperfections see; therefore, be thou
> My teacher and my guide; o'er my weak senses
> Arbitrary reign: shield and protect I pray
> This feeble frame, lest any should the same
> Oppose; and in return, thou shalt me all
> Obedience find:
>
> (11; lines 248–62)

In Eve's speech it is the sentiment of surrender and the sexual frissons that surround it that are more important than the issue of dominion and any argument that might arise concerning it. Whereas Restoration adaptations of *Paradise Lost* focused pointedly on the power struggle between our first parents and on Eve's desire for superiority over Adam, this piece almost completely displaces that struggle to emphasize the happiness of the couple as they wander au naturel through the snakeless garden. By the end of the era the argument over dominion, in a few poems at least, has entered the realm of romantic myth, and idealizations of woman's power to conquer by her charming surrender to her husband become more and more overtly Edenic.

In the later era, then, satire lightens, and didactic and celebratory poems come to the fore. As it is throughout the eighteenth century, the husband's sovereignty is still supported, but poems advise or celebrate a more chivalrous manner for him to maintain his dominion. Wives, conversely, are still to be obedient, but the myth of the fair sex, which emphasizes women's power to sway men by beauty or feminine wiles, gains strong currency. Conduct poems especially affirm a fashionable complaisance for female readers aspiring to politeness.

We have already considered a number of early and mid-century attacks by women poets on male tyranny in marriage. A concern with paternal and husbandly injustice is dramatized in at least one later era poem by a woman. Lady Dorothea DuBois in "A True Tale" (1764) tells the thinly veiled autobiographical story of the husband and father, Anglesus, who deserts his wife, Anna, and his eldest daughter, Dorinda, to take up with a tenant's daughter who gains influence over his "fickle Mind." The mother nurtures the daughter and, by a pension given her by the king, supports Dorinda in her marriage to a foreigner. When Anglesus, worn out by his dissolute life, is on his deathbed, Dorinda in filial "Gratitude and Love" decides to visit him. Attempting to do so, she is mistreated by a "numerous Throng" of his "Ruffians" who threaten and abuse her and take her prisoner. When she is freed after great distress, her husband can only rebuke her for her decision to visit. The mother, after Anglesus dies, must go to law to claim her rights as wife (1–27). Such a narrative indirectly questions what women gain by playing the traditional dutiful roles a patriarchal society expects of them.

Also by a woman is a later era poem that finds the ideology of domesticity restrictive. In Jane West's "To a Friend on Her Marriage, 1784," the speaker laments women's confinement to household duties and encourages her newly married friend to undertake an active social life of charitable activities while still maintaining an orderly household (Lonsdale 280–82; see also chapter 6 of this book). West's advisor does not, however, encourage women to develop independent careers, nor does she criticize male dominion. She finds the ideology of domesticity limiting, but does not finally reject it. Even so, her advice to eighteenth-century women to take on outside responsibilities while keeping the home fires burning may foreshadow the dilemmas faced by many women of the late twentieth century. This includes those who choose to maintain a career and a home or those who are compelled to do so because they are single parents, have unassisting spouses, or need the income.

After the middle of the century, the large majority of poets—male and female—idealize the power of a woman who uses her beauty, good humor, and complaisance to please a husband or father and thus to get her way. A very few poets suggest, as Jane West does, that domesticity may be restrictive or, as Lady Dorothea DuBois does, that, by relying on their power to please, women may degrade themselves and ultimately become vulnerable to male abuse or neglect. This is unlike the first half of the century when, as we recall, a vocal minority of women poets such as Lady Chudleigh, Lady Mary Montagu, and Hetty Wright sharply denounce husbandly tyranny. Not only do the women of this era question the justice of male dominion, but a few pre-1750 poets offered the very critiques of domesticity that revisionist feminism finds wanting in women's poetry of the later era.

It is worth looking back at two of these pre-1750 pieces to remind ourselves briefly of the dramatic stances and ideology women poets turn away from after mid-century. These two pieces are also significant since they avoid the conventional tropes that pre-1750 women poets frequently use in attacking male tyranny.

Mary Barber's "The Conclusion of a Letter to the Rev. Mr. C——." (1734) (Fullard 300–302) contains a completely charming attack on the narrow-minded type of male who insists on a wife's obedience and would confine her to housewifely duties designed to serve only him. With a mischievousness suggestive of Swift, who served as her mentor, Barber offers an ironic re-creation of such a would-be husband's voice.

> If ever I marry, I'll choose me a spouse
> That shall *serve* and *obey*, as she's bound by her vows;
> That shall, when I'm dressing, attend like a valet;
> Then go to the kitchen and study my palate.
> She has wisdom enough that keeps out of the dirt,
> And can make a good *pudding*, and cut out a *shirt*.
> What good's a dame that will pore on a book?
> No!—give me the wife that shall save me a cook.
>
> (Fullard 301)

Barber not only mocks the selfishness underlying the speaker's ideology of domesticity. She concludes her poem by having her autobiographical persona provide her son Constantine with more liberal expectations in a wife, should he marry. The persona urges him to respect his wife's intellect and to treat her as a friend and companion, not a servant. Contrary to the male ideology, which sees an educated woman as likely to neglect her domestic duties, Barber advises her son that a woman "By learning made humble, not thence taking airs," is less likely "To despise, or neglect, her domestic affairs." More important, an educated woman makes a better mother (Fullard 302). Barber does not disdain domesticity, but she does not view it as woman's exclusive path to fulfillment.

Anne Irwin in "An Epistle to Mr. Pope Occasioned by his Characters of Women" (1736) defends women against Pope's characterizations in "To a Lady." She stresses lack of education as the chief cause of female folly. Writing as a satirist in the tradition of Pope, she does not deny that women can be trifling, idle, slothful, or vain, but she assigns the cause to nurture, not to nature.

> Can female youth, left to weak woman's care,
> Misled by custom (folly's fruitful heir;)
> Told that their charms a monarch might enslave,
> That beauty like the god can kill or save;
> . . . .
> Can they resist, when soothing pleasure woos;
> Preserve their virtue, when their fame they lose?
> Can they on other themes converse or write,
> Than what they hear all day, and dream all night?
>   (Fullard 304–5)

Women attempt to rule men by their sexual attractiveness because they are not trained to respect virtue and truth. Women have "heads" that are "toyshops" because they have not been taught to aspire to anything more worthwhile. Irwin directly attacks the submissive and manipulative roles women play because such roles demonstrate the "savage waste" of their minds.

Unlike Barber and Irwin, women poets of the late eighteenth century usually avoid direct attacks on the confinement of women to uneducated domesticity. Women's voices protesting wifely subjection can be heard in post-1750 prose tracts such as Wollstonecraft's *A Vindication of the Rights of Woman* (1792) and outspokenly in novels by women. Yet, with a few exceptions, such voices are silent in poetry. As the shift from satire to celebration is a loss to the vitality of poetry in the later era, so the gradual falling away from the polemical indignation and the dramatic pathos and ingenuity of a Mary Chudleigh, a Mary Montagu, a Hetty Wright, or a Mary Barber finally weakens the protofeminist critique of male dominion. With this critique muted, most women poets embrace companionate ideology and domesticity unquestioningly and argue that housewifely virtue, a charming complaisance, and beauty are tools to power. For late eighteenth-century women poets such as Letitia Barbauld, Matilda Betham, and Ann Holmes, the struggle for equality is displaced by the celebration of affective companionship and women's emotional and sexual power over men. Revisionists find poets who celebrate such powers delude women into complacency, into a failure to pursue power in public life.

This is largely true. Yet we should not automatically assume that all influence women exercise through companionship and domesticity is delusory. Holding such influence in contempt or seeing it as counterprogressive does not deny that wives and mothers did and still do trade on the sentimentalization of their roles as domestic angels, guardians of the home front, kitchen bosses, and bedroom despots and still use them to get their way with men and to exert moral, social, and even political suasion. Women traditionally have also had considerable behind-the-scenes influence in the economic arena, if only as consumers and marriageable commodities. The problem with such influence is obviously that women who employed it usually had to accede to male dominion in the legal, business and professional, and political spheres. One does not have to be a revisionist feminist to judge this subordination as tantamount to servitude. If ever women achieve full equality in public life, perhaps they will be freer to enjoy the positive influences they can effect through companionship and domesticity.

CHAPTER EIGHT

A Union Both of Sex and Mind

I F LATE EIGHTEENTH-CENTURY MARRIAGE POETS did not resolve the issue of dominion in marriage but rather displaced it, how finally should the ideology of companionship be assessed? Are there any poets who move beyond sentimental and hazily romantic formulae to offer substantially realistic representations of what companionship entails? The answer is that some poems transcend the formulae, though their existence is overshadowed by the preponderance of those who do not.

The Husband and Wife as Friends

One of the defining expectations of the companionate ideal is that the couple should be friends, that is, companions sharing common interests and activities, both at work and at play. The idea of the husband and wife as friends is slow to develop in marriage poetry perhaps because there is a traditional theological resistance to the idea. Aquinas, for example, rejects the notion of woman as a helpmate to man, "since man can be more efficiently helped by another man in other works." Aquinas takes God's statement in Gen. 2:18 ("let us make him a helper like to himself") to mean that woman will be a helper in the work of generation (*Summa Theologica* 2: 489; 1.92.1).

Since man indulges his greatest passion with his wife in the act of procreation, he has traditionally had difficulty exerting self-control to work calmly beside her. Wives also complain about husbands who spend too much time in the wives' workplaces as a distraction or annoyance. In *Paradise Lost*, Eve offers the latter reason when she persuades Adam that they should work separately in the garden (9.205–25).

Similarly, the idea of a married couple pursuing leisure activities together may have been fraught with cultural reservations. When husband and wife share all their activities—sex, work, recreation—the unbroken closeness may put a strain on the most compatible of couples. Further, the sharing of leisure activities specifically may have been an intrusion on traditional male or female same-sex associations which, as I pointed out in chapter 1, flourished in England, especially early in the period under study. Concerning the "intensity and volatility of homosocial relationships" in the sixteenth and seventeenth centuries, Gillis says: "Friendship was often as consuming as a love affair, and therefore a major psychological reason why both men and women approached marriage so late and so ambivalently, knowing full well that this meant an end to so many well-developed and emotionally sustaining associations of very long years of bachelor and spinsterhood" (24). In Richardson's *Pamela*, we see the force of "homosocial relationships" when, shortly before their marriage, Mr. B must deal with three brother rakes who ride noisily into his courtyard with the intention of compelling him to join them in a "merry tour" from house to house in the neighboring countryside. Mr. B is well aware that his beloved Pamela's society is more desirable than that of his comrades, and he rids himself of their company by a ruse (266–68).

Perhaps because of such sociocultural forces militating against the idea of a married couple as friends, poets resort to romantic or sentimental formulae. Of the treatments of friendship I have found, three present the author's relationship with his wife in affected, almost mawkish terms. A fourth, by John Scott of Amwell, manages to be less sentimental.

Moses Browne's "Verses on the Death of a Dear and Most Lov'd Wife. Written Just upon Recovery from Illness, Anno 1727" has a kind of poignancy that can readily be viewed as melodramatic, even though the poem has the ring of truth to it. The speaker in this dramatic monologue has just recovered from a near fatal illness only to discover to his horror that his wife has died in childbirth. The speaker's exclamations of loss and sorrow contain an emotion-filled tribute to his wife as friend and companion:

> Am I restor'd, kind Heaven! from dreaded Woes
> To Health, to vig'rous Strength, to fresh Repose?

> O what Returns are just, his grateful Dues,
> Who from the Tomb my wasted Form renews!
> But where is *She*?—ah where! the lov'd the kind!
> Long to my Heart by closest Ties conjoin'd,
> Who us'd my Cares to sooth, my Joys to raise,
> Soft, sweet Companion of my pleasing Days?
> Who but so late, with fondest Fears possest,
> My sick'ning Side with watchful Tendance press'd,
> Kiss'd my pale Lips, my Hand desponding wrung,
> And o'er my Clay-cold Breast impassion'd hung.
> Alas! how soon in *Childbed's* tort'rous Throws
> My *Suffering Dear* has left her Life and Woes!
>
> (451–52)

With its focus on his wife as the "soft, sweet Companion of my pleasing Days," this poem is clearly an expression of the companionate ideal, but the speaker's wife is more than a friend with whom he shared leisure time activities. She is a loving comforter, almost a mother-figure to whom the speaker can no longer turn for support. Bathed in self-pity for his pathetic state, the author on beginning to regain his strength is forced to transfer his self-pity to his wife. And because she is not there, his pity is again thrown back on himself. Browne's poem does have some emotional depth, but the author achieves it mainly by submerging us in the speaker's pool of tears.

A little less melodramatic than Browne's verses is an ecstatic tribute to friendship in marriage in Nathaniel Cotton's *Marriage. Vision VII* (1751).

> In wedlock when the sexes meet,
> Friendship is only then complete.
> "Blest state! where souls each other draw,
> Where love is liberty and law!"
> The choicest blessing found below,
> That man can wish, or Heaven bestow!
> Trust me, these raptures are divine,
> For lovely Chloe once was mine!
> Nor fear the varnish of my style,
> Tho' poet, I'm estranged to guile.
> Ah me! my faithful lips impart
> The genuine language of my heart!
>
> (Chalmers 8: 40)

Reaching for a special sincerity, Cotton cuts through the polished allegorical format of his *Vision* ("the varnish of his style") to confess, in an autobiographical aside, his love for Chloe, evidently a wife that he has lost. Cotton's exclamations concerning the "divine raptures" of the married state seem out of place with the idea of friendship and may lead the reader to think more of a sexual union than companionship. Yet later era poets do often elevate friendship to romantic heights and praise it ecstatically.

John Langhorne's *Precepts of Conjugal Happiness* (1767) uses Miltonic allegory in a serious effort to advise his sister Maria on the ills as well as the pleasures of the married state. He refers to the "darker hour" she must "bear" when she must "drag the chains of Care" (427) or be "opprest" by some "transient grief." He counsels tellingly against "the wrong conduct of our hopes and fears" and says that Hope and Fancy must be controlled by Truth. He warns her especially against the "green-eyed monster" (Chalmers 16: 427).

> Of one dark foe, one dangerous foe beware!
> Like Hecla's mountain, while his heart's in flame,
> His aspect's cold,—and Jealousy's his name.
>   (16: 427)

He even advises her not to be disenchanted

> When love's warm breast, from rapture's trembling height,
> Falls to the temperate measures of delight;
> When calm delight to easy friendship turns,
> Grieve not that Hymen's torch more gently burns.
>   (16: 427)

Yet in spite of this solid sense for the evils of marriage, Langhorne concludes on a strongly idealizing note. He celebrates the "charm connubial" that "like a stream . . . glides/Through life's fair vale, with no unequal tides, . . ." (428). His penultimate verse stanza, an ecstatic paean to this "charm," overpowers his earlier didactic warnings:

> O bliss beyond what lonely life can know,
> The soul-felt sympathy of joy and woe!
> That magic charm which makes e'en sorrow dear,
> And turns to pleasure the partaken tear!
>   (16: 428)

Langhorne's earlier sensible, semirealistic cautions about the evils of marriage are finally drowned out by his swelling hymn to the heavenly bliss of companionship.

The latest praise of friendship is curiously the least bathetic. In a sonnet-length tribute entitled "The Author to His Wife" (1782), the Quaker poet John Scott of Amwell mixes more restrained, heartfelt compliments with the sort of hyperbole we have just seen in Cotton's and Browne's verses.

> Friend of my heart, by fav'ring Heav'n bestow'd,
> My lov'd companion on life's various road!
> Now six swift years have wing'd their flight away
> Since yon bright Sun have adorn'd our nuptial day—
> For thy sweet smiles, that all my cares remove,
> Sooth all my griefs, and all my joys improve;
>
> (Chalmers 17: 492)

Like Browne's wife, Scott's is a comforter whose "smiles . . . sooth all my griefs." Like Cotton's Chloe, Scott's wife is a blessing bestowed by heaven. At the same time, she is a companion in a more ordinary sense ("My lov'd companion on life's various road"). He praises her not so much for the raptures he experiences with her as for her "sweet converse," "prudence lively," and relaxed sensibleness. There is a slightly more substantial sense of what his friendship with his wife must have been, though that sense is limited and marred by the conventional heightening of Scott's praise. We do not, for example, see them fly-fishing together. Though Scott of Amwell comes closest to a concretely delineated description of what friendship in marriage means, none of the four employing the formula of the couple as friends manages to rise above a conventionality of phrasing that vitiates sincerity. None avoids the sticky trap of sentimentality. All four illustrate the tendency of later era verse to represent the companionate ideal hazily.

Idealizing Companionship

In the last thirty years of the century, praises of the companionate marriage can become quite effusively romantic, idealizing a happy union and not mentioning such concerns as friendship or equality in temperament, age, rank, or wealth. The pastoral genres that these pieces employ may predispose them to such etherealized effusions.

Thomas Chatterton's "The Happy Pair" is essentially a pastoral song in dialogue that was printed with *The Revenge, a Burletta,* acted in Marybone Gardens in 1770. In alternating stanzas, Lucy and Strephon celebrate the bliss of their married life together. Not one somber note is struck in the entire song, and the closest it comes to treating hardship is Strephon's description of how his love of Lucy sustains him in his labor in an open field.

> Blest with thee, the sultry day
> Flies on wings of down away,
> Labr'ing o'er the yellow plain,
> Open to the sun and rain,
> All my painful labours fly.
> When I think my Lucy's nigh.
> (Chalmers 15: 488)

Though there may be some echoes of the formula of equality in sharing joy and sorrow, Chatterton seems more intent on apotheosizing the domestic bliss of marital love.

> Godlike Hymen, ever reign
> Ruler of the happy train,
> Lift thy flaming torch above
> All the flights of wanton love,
> Peaceful, solid, blest, serene,
> Triumph in the married scene.
> (15: 488)

Chatterton gives the secular bliss of marriage—even "the flights of wanton love"—a divine status. The nature of this divinity seems, however, to be pagan rather than Christian.

Similar to Chatterton's song in rapturous celebration of marital happiness are Abraham Portal's *Nuptial Elegies,* a series of four pastoral effusions published in 1775 (3rd ed.). Miltonic in a bad sense, these pieces sometimes echo the formula of the couple made one by love. The romantic aura is so pervasive that we get a very limited sense of the reality of marital love. For example, in describing the way their love will unify them, Corin says,

> Our Hopes, our Fears, our Joys, our Hearts, our Hands,
> Are all in everlasting Union tied.
> (5)

Praising the way their love will make even the drudgery of labor pleasurable, Corin sings:

> How sweet henceforth, shall be my daily Toil,
>   When *Silvia's* Happiness that Toil requites;
> For *her*, I tend the Flock and till the Soil,
>   That Thought shall change my Labours to Delights.
>
> (7)

Emphasis falls mainly on the couple's common experience of joy; a balanced sense of the difficulties of marital love is lacking. In poems such as these, we see the negative culmination of the growing tendency to romanticize marriage, a tendency that becomes progressively more evident in the various formulae used predominantly by male celebrators of the companionate marriage.

Only in a limited number of poems in the later era do we find a countertendency, an effort to cut through the myths and formulae and to delineate concretely what companionship may entail. Significantly, a number of these are by women poets.[1] In "Consolatory Verses to Her Husband" (1748), Laetitia Pilkington offers a wife's encouragement in adversity.

> No more, lov'd partner of my soul,
>   At disappointments grieve,
> Can flowing tears our fate controul,
>   Or fights our woes relieve?
>
> Adversity is virtue's school
>   To those who right discern;
> Let us observe each painful rule,
>   And each hard lesson learn.
>
> (*Poems by Eminent Ladies* 2: 212)

Her speaker's message is implicitly that the disappointments and tensions of marriage may severely test the companionate ideal. It is refreshing to hear a woman poet making this point, even if it is rather ironically appropriate coming from Laetitia Pilkington, whose marriage with her clergyman husband gained a notoriety for profligate conduct, on his part at least (see Lonsdale 136).

In "On the Author's Husband Desiring Her to Write Some Verses" (written ca. 1780), Mary Whatley offers up, on her husband's request, the standard idealization of the equality in companionship, an idealization many women endorsed, especially as affective sharing between husband and wife made for a loving climate in which children could be nurtured. Whatley, however, playfully challenges this idealization, although she does not undercut it.

> The mutual interest all reserve disclaiming,
> The scheme of pleasure each for other framing,
> The kindling transports of parental love,
> Which the sweet smiles of innocence can move,
> Are thine alone, O Hymen! to bestow,
> Which hearts that do not feel them cannot know:—
> —But hark!—my darling infant cries,
> And each poetic fancy flies.
> (Lonsdale 262)

With the comic interruption of her ecstatic flight by her baby's crying, Whatley makes us aware that the companionate ideal is after all a poetic creation. Reality does not destroy the myth, but women from time to time may have cause to smile at it.

In her "Letter to Miss E. B. on Marriage" (1777), Mary Savage almost entirely avoids the standard idealizations of companionship. Savage describes herself as a busy housewife who had "the care of a large family" (Lonsdale 345). Her experience evidently provided her with sharp insights into psychological causes of marital discord. Her speaker dwells particularly on the male ego's need for power and on male rationalizations of the double standard. She also stresses to her correspondent the importance of "a strong desire to please" (Lonsdale 349). She is quite evenhanded in observing how both sexes "take great pains to come together,/Then squabble for a straw or feather." Her message is a down-to-earth, humanized one reminiscent of the Augustan satirists, but without their paternalistic bias:

> That neither sex must think to find
> Perfection in the human kind;
> Each has a fool's cap—and a bell—
> And, what is worse, can't always tell
> (While they have got it on their head)
> How far astray they may be lead.
> (Lonsdale 349)

A poem by a male carrying a similar message is William Cowper's "Mutual Forbearance Necessary to the Happiness of the Married State" (1782). Though this piece concludes with a celebration of marital love that unifies the couple through sickness and old age, the conceptualization of that love is not facile or superficially sanguine. Cowper prefaces his concluding affirmation of mutual love with a mildly satirical vignette in which he dramatizes a failure of communication between husband and wife. The husband's deafness leads him to gross misunderstandings of his wife. Exasperated by his handicap, she scorns him bitterly under her breath. Cowper's moral is a solid one, based on a realistic perception of what living together in marriage involves:

> The kindest and the happiest pair
> Will find occasion to forbear;
> And something ev'ry day they live,
> To pity and perhaps forgive.
> But if infirmities, that fall
> In common to the lot of all,
> A blemish or a sense impair'd,
> Are crimes so little to be spar'd,
> Then farewell all, that must create
> The comfort of the wedded state;
> Instead of harmony, 'tis jar,
> And tumult and intestine war.
>   (Chalmers 8: 657)

Cowper's didactic poem is grounded in a satiric vision of how lack of forbearance can cause a marriage to degenerate into domestic warfare, the hell on earth of the early era satirists. Because his moral counsel is built on such a substantial foundation, it can support the celebratory passage with which his poem concludes:

> The Love, that cheers life's latest stage,
> Proof against sickness and old age,
> Preserv'd by virtue from declension,
> Becomes not weary of attention;
> But lives, when that exterior grace,
> Which first inspir'd the flame, decays.
> 'Tis gentle, delicate, and kind,
> To faults compassionate or blind,

> And will with sympathy endure
> Those evils, it would gladly cure:
> (8: 657)

In contrast to the etherealizations of marital love that often appear in the late eighteenth century, Cowper's poem is not vitiated by an undue tendency to idealize or sentimentalize. In exceptional poems such as Pilkington's, Whatley's, or Cowper's we do get a flesh-and-blood portrayal of the sacrifices and self-restraint that true companionship entails.

Clearly, the idea of companionship is an increasingly popular one in poetry of the middle and late eighteenth century, but in many of the verses that celebrate it, it is expressed in romanticized formulae of little substance. Even in more down-to-earth didactic poems, prudent advice to marry an equal in temperament, age, wealth, and social background may be contradicted or masked by romantic idealizations. Marital companionship is celebrated more and more as a secularized heaven, perhaps as a substitute for the religiosity that this rational age was losing. As many late eighteenth-century poets present it, this heaven is insubstantial. It underplays or ignores such negative emotions as dissatisfaction, boredom, conflict, jealousy, anger, and hurt—emotions that are just as much a part of marriage as the heavenly joy of companionship.[2] Such a romanticizing of marriage blinds women and men to its social and legal inequities and to the way popular myths can stereotype marital roles and restrict selfhood.

In making a heaven of hell, marriage poetry's greatest loss may have been satire. Certainly, male poets of the later era had to move beyond the antifeminist, antimatrimonial biases of earlier satirists and didactic poets. The unsympathetic patriarchal stances of the majority of those writers would not do in a more refined age in which civilized men prided themselves in their outward respect for women's aspirations and sensibilities. In making the transition, however, many poets lost a sense of the negatives in marriage, a view necessary to ballast their idealization of it.

Though numbers of marriage satires can still be found in the later era, especially in jocular Grub Street compilations, the absence of the contribution of the great and not so great Restoration and Augustan satirists is an egregious one. The later era has its comprehensive satirists—Charles Churchill and other poets who attack the general taste of the times. It also has its well-bred "social and occasional satire" by such "well-to-do amateurs" as William Shenstone, Richard Graves, Richard Owen Cambridge, and Christopher Anstey (Rothstein 122). Many of these satirists, however, do not write on marriage, and those that do tend toward fashionable comic verse with more affective narratorial stances. In the later era, poetry generally shows less of the slashing wit and intellectual vitality of the earlier poets. It also is missing the polemical, which adds so much gusto to the verse of the earlier era. I am speaking not only of the work of Butler, Dryden, Rochester, Swift and Pope but also of the large number of talented lesser poets—both male and female—who thrived on marriage controversy and added their moral arguments to the pungent stewpot, poets such as Charles Sedley and Richard Ames, Mary Chudleigh and Elizabeth Thomas. The pro-companionate ideology required celebratory poetry to establish it, but it needed satire to counterpoint it, to give it substance and flavor. An indication of the perspective satire might have supplied in larger quantities is offered by a few late works critical of the new ideology.

The first of these, the anonymous *The Divorce* (1779), ironically celebrates the most controversial by-product of the companionate ideal: civil divorce. As society placed more emphasis on equality in temperament and character and stressed the importance of happiness in a match, it became more willing to tolerate divorce in cases of incompatibility, though legally the incompatibility had to be confirmed by infidelity. Parliamentary divorces following civil suits of criminal conversation became much more common in the later era. Such divorces could be procured only by men, and women had to have recourse to consistory courts to procure judicial separations from unfaithful or abusive husbands. In the late eighteenth century, not only was there an increase in civil divorce but also a sharp rise in separations from bed and board granted by consistory courts. In such judicial separations, wives were no longer the principal suitors in this era as female adultery seems to have become significantly more frequent (Stone, letter, 6 December 1989).

In *The Divorce*, the poet hails these new trends with less joy than cynicism as he points backward to the older theological ideal of marriage as an indivisible sacramental union:

> Thus, in the Case before us now,
> Men *were oblig'd* to keep their Vow;
> Nor could evade the Laws of Heaven;
> When once the Priest a Wife had given,
> To have and hold, in Peace and Strife,
> And love, and *cherish*, during Life;

> Whither attach'd by Love—or *Money*,
> A lasting *Tye*—was Matrimony.
>
> (7)

Acknowledging the corruption of marriage for money, the poet nevertheless insists on matrimony as a knot tied by God—one not to be untied by humans. In the present age, the poet says, untying is what men and women are doing.

> —But we, who scorn the musty Rules,
> That stern Religion taught her Fools,
> Have set at length the matter right,
> And prov'd it as a juster Rite,
> To find a flaw—and *kindly* sever
> Whom Fate *unkindly* yok'd together.
> Hail, blest Divorce! each happy Belle
> Thy kind Effect is proud to tell;
> 'Tis thou can'st set the Wanton free,
> And rid the Wretch from Slavery!
> Both Wives and Husbands thee adore;
> —The Name of *Cuckold* is no more;
>
> (7)

The focus in the subsequent anecdote of Flavia is mainly on women's recourse to divorce, an attack which may be sexist since women could not themselves procure a Parliamentary divorce, nor could they defend themselves against accusations in criminal conversation suits that were often collusive. The poet may, however, be referring to the increase in judicial separations in which women were either the plaintiff or the defendant (see note 1.12). In either case, the satirist does not just point to the exploitation by women; he indicts "Both Wives and Husbands" for the debasement of marriage. His wonderfully ironic parody of Milton's "Hail, Wedded Love" hymn tells us that people undermine religion and honor when they exploit legal mechanisms for selfish ends.

A juster and more delightful parody of Milton's hymn is offered by the character Obtuse Angle in Blake's *An Island in the Moon* (1784 or later).

> Hail Matrimony made of Love
> To thy wide gates how great a drove
> On purpose to be yok'd do come
> Widows & maids & Youths also

> That lightly trip on beauty's toe
> Or sit on beauty's bum
>
> (450–51)

Blake's stance is antifeminist to the extent that he focuses especially on women's uncritical enthusiasm for matrimony and on their central place in the new myth of marriage as a heaven of maternal domesticity.

> Hail fingerfooted lovely Creatures
> The females of our human Natures
> Formed to suckle all Mankind
> 'Tis you that come in time of need
> Without you we should never Breed
> Or any Comfort find.
>
> (450)

Blake captures perfectly the elements of a feminized companionate ideal as they developed from the fourth book of *Paradise Lost* and holds them up for delicious ridicule. But more than this, he questions from a radical perspective the value of matrimony as an institution and the unthinking willingness of women to give up their freedom to it.[3]

> The universal Poultice this
> To cure whatever is amiss
> In damsel or in Widow gay
> It makes them smile it makes them skip
> Like Birds just cured of the pip
> They chirp & hop away
>
> Then come ye Maidens come ye Swains
> Come & be eased of all your pains
> In Matrimony's Golden cage—
>
> (451)

Blake employs what sounds like an early era male libertine argument for sexual freedom, but he is actually directing a revolutionary argument to women. He is asking them to consider whether the fashionable pro-companionate ideology, strongly embraced by many women, is truly in their best interests.

In the satire Blake offers, we find one poet's challenge to the myth of marriage as heaven that so many male poets of the period worked enthusiastically to affirm. His final trope—"Matrimony's Golden cage"—shows women that, in spite of its attractiveness, marriage is still the creation of a cultural system that promises women solace but actually imprisons them. The companionate ideal prevents women from seeing marriage as an institution debased by the material interests of a class-conscious society, a society in which women are treated as prized birds to be displayed but not allowed their freedom. In this society, women are nurturers and domestic and sexual servants, and their assumed natural role is to "suckle all Mankind." Though there is a grandiose cast to this characterization of women's role, its underlying sarcasm, though not its satiric intent, is probably no more progressive than Iago's "To suckle fools and chronicle small beer." Blake, however, is suggesting that our conception of women's role should not be restricted to nurture or domesticity. His revolutionary critique of companionate ideology points finally to a more vital, realistic, and humanized model for marriage. It places men and women in roles that encompass both opposition and friendship, conflict and harmony, hell and heaven.

CHAPTER NINE

What Comes After?

IT IS WORTH ASKING FINALLY WHAT MARRIAGE POetry gains and loses after the eighteenth century by its celebration of marriage as heaven. Certainly, as the progressive historians demonstrate, the emergence of the companionate model amounts to a revolutionary humanization of the institution of marriage. If, in fact, couples previous to the eighteenth century were matched mainly to serve their parents' social or financial advantage and if indeed couples in the late eighteenth century begin to marry with some concern for personal compatibility, common background, and feelings of affection, that indeed is a change to set the world on end. Though the companionate model may have gained wide acceptance only among the upper and the upper middle classes in the late eighteenth century, it still must be hailed as a major step in the liberalization of English society. Especially for women who suffered most as financial pawns in the marriage of convenience, the shift in a broad sense should be seen as part of a protofeminist impetus that calls women's attention to their common interest as women and that emphasizes their status as rational beings demanding the same respect as men. The impetus gains a political force in the very late eighteenth century and nineteenth century from such strong advocates for women's rights as Mary Wollstonecraft and John Stuart Mill. In the mid-nineteenth century, the impetus manifests itself in reforms in the marriage laws, most importantly the Matrimonial Causes Act of

1857, which allows divorce for selected causes in a secular court with the permission to remarry. It leads ultimately to the twentieth-century campaign for women's suffrage and full equality under the law.[1]

While the emergence of the companionate model can be hailed as social progress, the Protestant ideologies that nourished it and the ideology of domesticity to which it gives rise possess seriously problematic features. Chief of these is the myth of male dominion and female submissiveness that the companionate ideal perpetuates under romantic disguises. For a corollary reason, the rise of the celebratory mode in marriage verse must be taken as a problematic literary direction. By the end of the eighteenth century, the insistence of the celebratory mode on idealizing marriage often makes for romantic etherealizations. As satire was declining, the way was opened for the sentimentalization of marriage and women's role in it. This becomes a primary tendency in much nineteenth-century poetry, especially in Victorian popular verse but also in the poets of the high culture as well. In Coventry Patmore's *The Angel in the House* (1858), marital love is quintessentially a heaven on earth, a heaven that, in the husband's imagination, may even be superior to the love he will encounter in heaven itself.

> Vaughan, when his kind Wife's eyes were dry,
>   Said, "This thought crosses me, my Dove;
> "If Heaven should proffer, when we die,
>   "Some unconceiv'd, superior love,
> "How take the exchange without despair,
>   "Without worse folly how refuse?"
>   (152)

In this reductio ad absurdum of the marriage-as-heaven metaphor, marriage can be an earthly heaven that is better than the heaven of traditional theology.

To be sure, some marriage poetry in the nineteenth century does not sentimentalize the domestic blisses of marriage. Yet, throughout the nineteenth century, a split between the idealization of marriage and the realistic portrayal of it persists in all but a very few poets. One might say that the separation between the celebratory and the satiric mode that runs throughout Restoration and eighteenth-century poetry is perpetuated in the nineteenth century in the tendency of poets either to idealize marriage or to treat it with dark realism. Indeed, in nineteenth-century poetry the opposition between the heaven and hell of marriage seems to become even more pronounced and complicated than it was in the long eighteenth century.

Looking briefly at what happens to the satiric and celebratory traditions in later poetry, we can see on a broad canvas how this develops.

Satire on marriage does not flourish in nineteenth-century poetry. When poets of this century do employ satire, its morality is often different from the unsympathetic, judgmental morality of a Swift or Pope. Rather than indicting the folly of individual behavior, marriage satirists often point to society's hypocrisies or cruelties. Byron, for example, in canto 1 of *Don Juan* (1819) mocks the shallowness of Donna Julia's social conscience. When she is confronted by the reality of her passion for Don Juan, her honor and virtue go by the board, and Byron grins to see Nature assert itself. Thackeray, in the strongly ironic "Damages, Two Hundred Pounds" (*The Oxford Book of Satirical Verse* 227–29), lays bare in concrete detail a husband's psychological and physical abuse of his wife as it is revealed in the testimony at a divorce trial. In partial contrast to Byron's recognition of the woman of natural urges who tries to hide behind the mask of social respectability, Thackeray inclines toward a sentimentalization of the wife's plight. He shows us the wronged woman who stands behind the jury's narrowly conventional and legalistic judgment against her. In satire, nineteenth-century poets often tend to sustain one side or other of the dichotomized attitude toward woman as an angel or a loose woman. In this sense, they perpetuate the myths of the eighteenth century.[2]

In the eighteenth century, the emergence of the sentimental or gothic verse tale treating "star-crossed lovers," barred by circumstance or birth from marrying, owes a small debt to satire, particularly satire on marriage for money. However, as Stephen Duck's *Alrick and Isabel* (1740) shows, such verse tales mainly traffic in melodramatic sentiments. In the early nineteenth century, as Wordsworth's *Vaudracour and Julia* (1820) illustrates, gothic tales of this sort are the refined verse counterparts of the romantic gothic novel that focuses more sensationally on lovers kept apart by hypocritical social institutions or by corrupt individuals within those institutions. Even in the Victorian period, though the subject matter of verse tales might contain elements of social realism, their plots often remain melodramatic. A good example is Elizabeth Barrett Browning's novel-in-verse *Aurora Leigh* (1856) which treats "a range of interrelated social questions: the place of an independent woman in Victorian society and the problems of poverty and prostitution, of social equality and individual fulfillment, especially fulfillment in women's lives." The plot, however, remains "fantastic" (W. Johnson 55).

To find realistic verse narratives in nineteenth-century literature that do not sentimentalize marriage, we must turn to a poet such as George Crabbe. Though Crabbe published most of his poetry in the very early nineteenth century, he remains in many respects an eighteenth-century satirist. Though not squarely in the tradition of Swift and Pope, he does offer clear-sighted moral judgments on a gallery of couples, many of whom have entered marriage under some romantic delusion. In part 2 of *The Parish Register* and in a number of Crabbe's later tales such as "The Equal Marriage," "The Wife and Widow," and "Belinda Waters," Crabbe dramatizes the negative consequences that usually result from such delusions.

In the later tales (all published after *The Parish Register*), Crabbe somewhat curtails his role as a moralizing narrator and presents narratives that are more like short stories in opening and concluding simply with a thematic generalization. Crabbe still intrudes from time to time as an omniscient narrator offering moral observations. However, the direction of Crabbe's development is toward the more naturalistic. In Crabbe's tendency to avoid the sentimentalized judgment and in his faithful attention to realistic detail, Crabbe embodies the best of the old satiric verse narrative tradition and looks forward to the more darkly realistic psychological poems of the middle and late nineteenth century.[3]

Mid-nineteenth-century poems such as George Meredith's sonnet series *Modern Love* (1862) and many of Browning's dramatic monologues treating marriage may well be descended from the older satiric tradition. Both poets' realistic concern with the force of marital delusion and of disillusionment places them in this tradition. Even so, the two mid-Victorian poets rely to a large degree on first-person narration of marital partners who are involved in conventional, stale, or failed marriages. With this sort of narration, objective moral or satiric commentary becomes difficult if not impossible to manage. This, of course, is the essence of Meredith's and Browning's poetic strategy as they involve the reader in complex epistemological and psychological questions concerning what point of view is the truthful one. Such poetry is no longer satire, at least not satire of the Restoration and eighteenth-century sort in which the narrator finally takes an identifiable and consistent moral position.

If the satiric tradition dissipates in the nineteenth century, the celebratory tradition flourishes in several different and significant directions. In the major poetry of the high Romantics, especially in Blake, Wordsworth, and Coleridge, the topic of marriage is not generally treated directly.[4] However, as Meyer Abrams (*Natural Supernaturalism*) and other critics have pointed out, Blake, Wordsworth, and Coleridge employ in several important poems a marriage metaphor to symbolize the essential union that they recognize as existing between the individual mind (of the poet) and the universe that it perceives (Abrams 27–28 and 27–46). Reacting against the epistemological divorce between the mind and the objective world brought about by Lockean and Humean empiricism, the Romantic poets, as Michael Daly points out, are "convinced of the mind's power to transform or half-create the world of its perception, to effect its own perceptual apocalypse by recognizing its active and creative role as perceiver in the universe which is organically and dynamically harmonious" (*DA* 2254-A).

The high Romantics' significant use of the marriage metaphor, as Michael Daly also explains, is based upon the practice of the Biblical prophets; however, it depends heavily as well on the "tradition of the epithalamium or marriage hymn in English literature." Although the major Romantics did not write much about marriage directly, they did find the spirit of the epithalamium especially appealing as they did that of other "sublime genre[s]," such as the ode and the epic. According to Daly, the "sensuous or 'pagan' quality deriving from the Song of Songs and long a part of the epithalamium tradition could serve them in their expression of revolt against the oppression of the orthodox restrictions which had characterized the eighteenth century" (*The Marriage Metaphor* 5).[5] Thus, in Wordsworth's preface to the 1814 edition of *The Excursion*,

> the discerning intellect of Man,
> When wedded to this goodly universe
> In love and holy passion . . .

shall find paradisal beauty in the "simple produce of the common day." The poem that Wordsworth plans to write will be the epithalamium or "the spousal verse/Of this great consummation" (5: 5; lines 52–58).

For Blake in *The Marriage of Heaven and Hell* there is no "progression" "without contraries," yet the mind of the poet encompasses both heaven and hell and can shift imaginatively from one to the other at will. Blake, however, does not wish to reconcile these two contrary states but to maintain each in its full vitality. Thus, the word "marriage" in the title is in a sense parodied, though Blake may ultimately see the warring of opposites as a marriage in the highest sense. Blake's use of "Heaven" and "Hell" in his title may represent his parody of the heaven-hell dichotomy of eighteenth-century marriage poetry and his attempt to put the celebratory and satiric mode into a new relationship.

Coleridge in *The Rime of the Ancient Mariner* (1797–98) uses the Mariner's communion with the wedding guest to symbolize the Mariner's regaining his faith in the power of the imagination to respiritualize the dead world of the materialist and empirical philosophers. Once the Mariner can perceive spiritual value in the external world, he can love all living things, especially his fellow man. The Mariner's joyous experience of spiritual communality with the perceived world is well symbolized by his attending the wedding feast.

> O sweeter than the marriage-feast,
> 'Tis sweeter far to me,
> To walk together to the kirk
> With a goodly company!—
> (208; lines 596–604)

For Blake, Wordsworth, and Coleridge, the marriage metaphor is an important symbol for the mind's ability to join heaven with earth through the force of love and the imagination. As important as their celebration is, it is not, however, in the literal line of development of nineteenth-century marriage verse.

A Romantic poet who is more directly in the literal line of development, at least in a few of his poems, is Shelley. In a poem such as *Epipsychidion* (1821), the high-flying, Neoplatonic allegory may mask Shelley's revival of the libertine argument for sexual freedom. The poet is direct in articulating his disdain for marriage and for those who abide by its strictures.

> I never was attached to the great sect,
> Whose doctrine is, that each one should select
> Out of the crowd a mistress or a friend,
> And all the rest, though fair and wise, commend
> To cold oblivion, though it is in the code
> Of modern morals, and the beaten road
> Which those poor slaves with weary footsteps tread,
> Who travel to their home among the dead

> By the broad highway of the world, and so
> With one chained friend, perhaps a jealous foe,
> The dreariest and the longest journey go.
>
> (191; lines 147-59)

It is ironic that the first libertine argument, which became progressively more stereotyped and debased in the long eighteenth century, should reappear in the beginning of the nineteenth century in one of the most ethereal of Romantic poems. Throughout nineteenth-century poetry we frequently encounter the feeling that a stale or conventional marriage, especially one made for status or wealth, is not a marriage in fact. In some poets, this feeling is linked with the usually hidden fascination with adultery and the courtly love tradition. This fascination becomes a central ingredient in the Victorian double standard for male and female conduct in marriage. Just as often, however, as in Browning, the Victorian modification of the libertine argument is used to romanticize the noble beautiful lady who is imprisoned in a marriage made for money or status.

Romantic poets such as Shelley who adapt the libertine argument to their purposes are less directly in the main line of development of celebratory marriage verse than are a number of the major Victorian poets. These poets sometimes attempt a fusion of their idealization of marriage with a grimmer, more realistic view of marriage. Yet, in almost every case, the fusion fails, and the idealization and sentimentalization of marriage stand separate from efforts to examine marriage matter-of-factly.

Perhaps the most extreme idealizations are those of Gerard Manley Hopkins and Coventry Patmore, especially the latter. For these Victorians, marriage admittedly has its earthy, sexual dimension. Yet the joys of marriage are unmistakably divine in character. We can see this most obviously in Patmore's *The Angel in the House*. Wendell Stacy Johnson calls Patmore's view of marriage sacramental.[6] However, the beauty which Felix Vaughn enshrines in his wife Honoria is not exactly the bliss of marriage as a holy and mysterious sacrament celebrated by Renaissance and early seventeenth-century poets. Rather it is almost an idolatrous bliss that grows out of the sentimentalization of woman's role in marriage in late eighteenth-century poetry. The "rare and virtuous" spirit that Patmore praises may finally have religious significance, but it is a religious significance romantically imposed rather than a mystical attribute of the sacrament itself. As with the Oxford Movement's revival of emphasis on the ceremonies and rituals of Christianity, Patmore's glorification of the spiritual in marriage is in essence a romantic phenomenon.

The greatest Victorian poets, Tennyson and Browning, especially the former, seem to strive in some of their verse for a fusion of the celebratory and the realistic. Yet almost always the fusion fails as both poets in their increasing pessimism concerning marriage slide across middle ground in their descent from idealization. The center does not hold.

Tennyson begins his poetic career idealizing the isolated maiden who in her loneliness and attraction toward death epitomizes an alienation from love, marriage, and the social world in general. In the poetry of his middle years, Tennyson treats marriage more literally, and in works such as *Two Voices* (1842), *In Memoriam* (1850), and *The Princess* (1847), Tennyson offers an idea of marriage in which the flesh and the spirit are unified and in which the opposing temperaments of the sexes are both joined and modified (W. Johnson chap. 2). Such an idea has decidedly progressive resonances. However, even though the poetry of his middle period offers Tennyson's "most hopeful conception of marriage as an alternative to isolation, to despair, and death," marriage is still presented abstractly and metaphorically; it is still a sweet ideal to be realized in some enlightened, hazy future (W. Johnson 142).

The lack of solidity of this idea perhaps accounts for Tennyson's turning away from it in his later poetry. In *Maud* (1855) and *Idylls of the King* (1859), Tennyson offers his darkest and most realistic portrayal of marriage. The ideal seems to have been disposed of, as Tennyson presents marriage in the context of frustrated love, madness, violence, and warfare (W. Johnson 146–50). In *Idylls* the failures and corruptions of Arthur's world stem directly from the infidelity of Guinevere and the collapse of his marriage. As an inheritor of the eighteenth-century polarization of marriage as a heaven and hell, Tennyson's marriage poetry runs to extremes, never really resting solidly on any middle ground.

Even in Browning, who is implicitly more realistic than Tennyson, there is an overall failure to fuse the ideal and the grimness of the actual. In some of his earlier poetry, Browning's idealizations of noble women trapped in a marriage of convenience may be an expression of romantic "woman worship," which, as Johnson suggests, is often disdainful of marriage. Perhaps influenced by Shelley, Browning even entertains at times a softened version of the libertine argument, that a marriage which is only one in the legal or physical sense, in the true sense may be no marriage at all.

In the poetry published during and directly after his marriage in collections such as *Men and Women* (1855) and *Dramatis Personae* (1864), Browning often deals more realistically with the successes and failures of marriage, with the possibilities of achieving companionship or oneness, if only momentarily, and with the forces that almost inevitably separate couples from each other. Especially in the later collection—and this increasingly becomes the tendency in Browning's late poetry—the emphasis falls on the failure of domestic happiness, on unequal matches, and on unfaithfulness. For Browning, generally, the actuality of marriage and the ideal of "mystical oneness of equals" are in the large majority of cases strongly opposed entities (W. Johnson 251).

It is Arthur Hugh Clough, who in a piece such as *The Bothie of Tober-Na-Vuolich* (1848), comes closer than other poets of his age to joining the "sacramental sense of marriage" with its "earthly, animal reality" (W. Johnson 79). In the "Rachel-and-Leah" allegory, Hobbes writes advice to his friend Philip the poet who is to wed Elspie the highland lass; in this advice, Clough makes an effort, even if gently ironic, to unify the "duality, compound and complex" that is marriage: the "One part heavenly-ideal, the other vulgar and earthy" (*The Bothie* 92). Yet, in later works such as *Amours de Voyage* (1858) and *Dipsychus* (1865), even Clough dramatizes the failure of lovers to achieve intellectual companionship in marriage and to harmonize the constant opposition between the sexual urge and the striving for ideality. Clough's irony allows him to approach a reconciliation of the heaven and hell of marriage more nearly than other Victorian poets, but the gulf is too wide to be bridged. The distance between the ideality and actuality of marriage that broadened in late eighteenth-century verse becomes for many Victorian poets a huge chasm.

With the advent of the modern era, both in Britain and America, poetry on marriage focuses increasingly on the negative reality of marriage, on failed marriages, on the despair of divorce, on the alienation of individuals who have not achieved happiness in a domestic union. Poets often dramatize marriage's failure in a particular depressing instance, an instance that frequently seems drawn from the poet's personal experience. Such is the case in confessional pieces like Stanley Kunitz's "River Road" or Robert Lowell's "The Old Flame" where the speaker turns away from the past failure toward a new but lonely life. Other modern poets treat a specific sterile or unhappy marriage then generalize about the ennui or angst many experience in wedlock. Examples are Dannie Abse's "Portrait of a Marriage," Denise Levertov's "The Ache of Marriage," and Mark Strand's "The Marriage." Poets also dwell on the suffering or imprisonment of an abused wife (or husband), the loss of a widow (or widower), or the bitter inheritance of the child of a broken home.[7] Modern poetry mainly resides on the negative side of the gulf.

The ideal, when it is celebrated, is often treated with cynicism or irony, as an impossible dream, or as a flickering flame in a very dark world. Relatively few modern poems celebrate marriage. We do, of course, have popular greeting card verse that inclines toward the unendurably sentimental. In addition, a few poets in the high tradition such as Ezra Pound, Edith Sitwell, Ivor Winters, Dylan Thomas, and May Sarton have revived the classical and Renaissance epithalamium in pieces that celebrate the universal physical and spiritual harmonies between marriage and the cosmos. More frequently, however, modern epithalamia are written to celebrate the occasion of a friend, relative, or important personage's wedding, and the tribute is particularized or qualified by the situational irony that the couple's happiness must endure in a world indifferent or hostile to it. Among the limited number of modern poets writing epithalamia, a number use it to satirize marriage, while others subvert the epithalamia in order to lay bare their disillusionment or negative experiences in the conjugal union.[8] It is difficult to find much serious verse that is directly supportive of the social institution of marriage in its more ordinary manifestations. We do have advice columns in magazines and newspapers, and many popular experts have written articles and volumes on how to save a marriage or revivify marital lovemaking. Very few of these advisors (with the exception of Ogden Nash) work in verse.

For modern poets the distance between the ideal and the actual is usually so wide that they usually do not try to cross it. Dwelling in a world of despair and alienation for the most part, they cannot see to the other side of the gulf. Even those poets who do treat both the heaven and hell of marriage frequently find the distance unbridgeable between the dream of the ideal marriage and its debased reality. This is well exemplified in "Marriage" (1960) by the American beat poet Gregory Corso. Corso's use of the heaven-hell dichotomy is in some ways suggestive of the early eighteenth-century poets:

> Yet if I should get married and it's Connecticut and snow
> and she gives birth to a child and I am sleepless, worn,
> up for nights, head bowed against a quiet window, the past
>   behind me,

> finding myself in the most common of situations a trembling man
> knowledged with responsibility not twig-smear nor Roman coin
>   soup—
> O what would that be like!
> Surely I'd give it for a nipple a rubber Tacitus
> For a rattle a bag of broken Bach records
> Tack Della Francesca all over its crib
> Sew the Greek alphabet on its bib
> And build for its playpen a roofless Parthenon
>
> No, I doubt I'd be that kind of father
> not rural not snow no quiet window
> but hot smelly tight New York City
> seven flights up, roaches and rats in the walls
> a fat Reichian wife screeching over potatoes Get a job!
> And five nose running brats in love with Batman
> And the neighbors all toothless and dry haired
> like those hag masses of the 18th century
> all wanting to come in and watch TV
> The landlord wants his rent
> Grocery store Blue Cross Gas & Electric Knights of Columbus
> Impossible to lie back and dream Telephone snow, ghost
>   parking—
> No! I should not get married I should never get married!
>
> <div align="right">(<i>A Casebook on the Beat</i> 82)</div>

In his tender portrayal of the responsibilities of fatherhood, Corso draws the heaven of "Connecticut and snow" in human proportions. Yet this dream is easily punctured by the much more graphic hell of "hot smelly tight New York City seven flights up." Between these two extremes, again, the center cannot hold.

In the poetry of Restoration and early eighteenth century, similar dichotomies between the hell and heaven of marriage are repeatedly dramatized. But in at least one important respect, the distance between dream and reality is not so great as it is for the major Victorians or for a modern poet such as Corso. For the majority of poets in the period we have studied, the heaven and hell of marriage are not simply extreme mental possibilities or fantasy renderings of experience, as they are with Corso. They are also representations of proscribed or recommended human behavior. Working more directly with the social reality of marriage, the early era poets repeatedly offer negative examples as well as positive models for conduct.

To the modern sensibility, much Restoration and eighteenth-century marriage satire may appear quite negative, suggestive to some of the cynicism and despair of the bleak marriage verse of the twentieth century. Conversely, celebratory verse, especially in the later era, is increasingly sentimental and idealized, lacking in imagery and tropes that tie the secular joys of marriage to a sacramental ideal or to the fertility of the natural world and the bliss of the cosmos. Though such assessments have truth to them, we must remember that the emphasis of both the satirical and celebratory verse is insistently didactic.

Whereas much modern marriage verse simply confesses or dramatizes the failure of marriage or (much less frequently) romanticizes an idealized union of the secular and the spiritual, most poetry of the long eighteenth century either implicitly or explicitly advises its readers on their marital conduct. Unlike a large number of the modern poets who treat marriage, the earlier poets write under the assumption that the behavior of couples toward each other in marriage is capable of improvement. Even more significant, in their many satires of arranged marriages and their many idealizations of the companionate marriage, the earlier poets give witness to their belief that the institution and society can be bettered, if only through a multiplication of individual instances in which conduct is improved. Though not treated specifically in this study, poems such as Swift's "Baucis and Philemon" (1708) and Prior's "An Epitaph" (1718) are satiric in the broadest and best sense in that they portray individual marriages in which the couple's pursuit of material comforts has subverted all other social and religious values.

As sophisticated or cynical moderns who disdain to read the "Can This Marriage Be Saved?" column in *Ladies Home Journal*, the idea that someone's marriage might actually be improved may strike us as naively optimistic. Even worse, many have grown suspicious of social movements or religious campaigns that offer to rejuvenate the institution of marriage by legal mechanism or moral plan. Many bristle at the programmatic, the doctrinaire, or the evangelistic, especially where it is accompanied by a paternalistic stance. It is certainly true the poetry we have examined is predominantly by males and that the discourse, even in some poems by women, is imbued with patriarchal ideology. However, we are far enough away from this verse that we can often enjoy its prescriptive, witty, and empathetic didacticism. Poems badly distorted by antifeminism can serve as negative examples of it, and even the Grub Street poets can show us the extremes to avoid in our search for the via media between the hell and heaven of marriage. The best male and female poets, especially the satirists, can do even more than this. They can draw us into the hells and heavens they portray. They can make us see how our fears and dreams affect our marital behavior and how husbands and wives can do violence to one another. They can give us a sense for the real frustrations and vicissitudes of marriage, and they can make us wary of the romantic delusion of believing married life will automatically be a heaven on earth, a heaven untinged by unhappiness, dissatisfaction, or the need for religious values, kindness, good judgment, and mutual self-sacrifice. They can also point us toward the heaven of companionate equality, not a marriage in which every moment is domestic bliss but one in which each partner helps to realize the other's fullest and best potential.

NOTES

Preface

1 For feminist criticism that pays careful attention to the role of literary form in creating meaning, see, for example, the articles under the subheading "Gender and Genre" in *Fetter'd or Free?* 8–58.
2 See, for example, Brown, *Alexander Pope*; Nussbaum, *The Brink of All We Hate*. Pollak in *The Poetics of Sexual Myth* argues that Pope reifies sexist myth, while Swift tends to challenge it. For a fictive extrapolation of Swift and Pope's sexist attitudes, see Erica Jong's *Fanny: Being the True History and Adventures of Fanny Hackabout-Jones: A Novel* (1980).

Introduction: The Companionate Ideal and Its Problems

1 A nuclear family is a basic social unit in which the parents and their children live in one household. According to Trumbach "the ideal of domesticity" is that "woman's role in life [is] to love her husband, bear his children, and remain at home to care for them" (166).
2 "Companionate" ideology emphasizes marriage between partners who are compatible in age, interests, and background. It idealizes a union based on friendship and deeply felt affection, though not always romantic love. I use "ideology" to refer to a system of values, not always explicit, held by a culture or class. These values govern "not just political and economic relations but social relations and psychological stresses" (Poovey xiv). In this study, "myths" or "mythology" refers to the tales or legends of a culture or group that embody its ideologies.
3 One current school of historians studying marriage does not address the relationship between ideology and historical fact. Historians following the methodology of the

Cambridge Group for the History of Population and Social Structure are concerned with demographics, and their methodology is essentially statistical analysis. Working with household listings and parish registers in relatively small geographical loci in England and projecting their findings backward into earlier centuries, the Cambridge group, whose chief representative is probably Peter Laslett, have given us factually based explanations for the "sudden spurt in population from roughly the middle of the eighteenth century, after a hundred years of minimal growth" (Macfarlane 20). This increase, they have shown, is not due to an increase in fertility in England. Rather the "age at marriage fell and with it the proportion of men and women who never married, and yet at the same time illegitimate fertility rose sharply and the proportion of pregnant brides also increased" (Macfarlane 26).

The question of what caused this change is an intriguing one. According to E. A. Wrigley, the shift is most likely not due to changes in courtship patterns, in the decision-making process of those who would marry, or in the idea of marriage. Rather more people were marrying at an earlier age because "the inducements to marry grew steadily greater and the disincentives less with the rising real incomes over a period which lasted more than a century" (148). As an historian, Macfarlane goes on to posit tentatively from this that "between the sixteenth and the nineteenth centuries, and possibly earlier, we are looking at a framework of decision making, a set of rules and customs, which remain broadly the same" (Macfarlane 30). Such a view of eighteenth-century marriage essentially discounts the connection between social ideologies and demographic statistics. It sees increases in the popularity of marriage as entirely a function of economic factors. The progressive historians' thesis concerning the emergence of affective individualism and the rise of the companionate marriage holds little force here. It seems implicitly to be denied.

4 Trumbach makes a distinction between patrilinear ties that worked, as inheritance did, through the father and kinship ties that placed each individual at the "center of a unique circle of kinsmen connected to him through both mother and father and through his spouse" (1). For Trumbach, the survival of kinship patterns among the English aristocracy had much to do with the rise of the egalitarian family in the eighteenth century.

5 Porter understates the exclusion of women from the libertine ethos and the important role of women, more than half of polite society, in supporting the attack on the double standard.

6 I use the term "Protestant" to refer not just to Puritans but also to members of the Church of England who were broadly influenced by Calvinist or Lutheran doctrine. I do not refer to the Anglican Church itself as "Protestant." The term "middle class" roughly encompasses the social groups named in the text, but before 1688, the term carries the additional implication of a Whiggish social stratum, which was hostile to the Frenchified culture and the Catholicism of the Stuart Court, as well as the aristocrats (the nobles and gentry) who were supportive of it. I realize, of course, that the Stuart monarchy had support from groups that were technically middle class by income level.

7 See my discussion of bliss in chapter 6 for poetic celebrations of the physical blisses of marriage. Most poets are hazily romantic and oblique in treating the sexual pleasures experienced by wives, and marriage manual poems are usually addressed to male

readers. An exception is Robert Shiells's *Marriage: A Poetical Essay* (1748); it does treat sexual bliss as mutual and characterizes a young woman forced to marry an old man as "lost to Bliss." Venette's *Conjugal Love; Or, the Pleasures of the Marriage Bed Considered in Several Lectures on Human Generation*, a prose work translated from the French and published first in London in 1750, devotes an entire chapter to the sexuality of women and concludes that "women feel less pleasure than men; but their's [sic] is of a longer duration" (121; rpt. in the series Marriage, Sex, and the Family in England 1660–1800). As Patricia Meyer Spacks shows, "well-bred" women were not expected to feel "lust," yet women's novels, letters, and journals repeatedly dramatized their struggles to repress their sexual fantasies and passions.

8   Samuel Johnson articulates a prevalent eighteenth-century justification for the double standard based on the idea that a wife's adultery can disrupt patrilinear inheritance (and thus the social order). The husband's adultery, on the other hand, is in effect a venial trespass: "'Confusion of progeny constitutes the essence of the crime; and therefore a woman who breaks her marriage vow is much more criminal than a man who does it. A man, to be sure, is criminal in the sight of God: but he does not do his wife a very material injury, if he does not insult her; if, for instance, from mere wantonness of appetite, he steals privately to her chambermaid. Sir, a wife ought not greatly to resent this'" (*Boswell's Life* 393–94).

9   See, however, Katherine M. Rogers 185–88 for her discussion of the softening of patriarchal stance in male satires and didactic works.

10 See the second edition of *A Vindication*, edited by Carol Poston, for various supportive and hostile contemporary reactions to Wollstonecraft's essay. These include a derisive verse satire by Richard Polwhele and a personal tribute by Blake. The "Wollstonecraft Debate," as Poston terms it, is one of the best indicators of the intensity of the era's ideological disagreement over where woman's power lies. See also Rendall 55–72.

11 *Norton Anthology of English Literature* 2: 110. For a broadly focused survey of materials treating the social history of eighteenth-century woman in England, see Schnorrenberg; see also Browne, chap. 6 ("Women in Society").

12 Stone's recent work on divorce shows the precipitous increase in the late eighteenth century in Parliamentary divorces. A large number of the criminal conversation suits that prepared the way for a Parliamentary divorce were evidently collusive. "The damages were never paid and returned in these cases. Only husbands could sue for Parliamentary divorce, so that wives were excluded, however unfaithful the husband. Moreover, wives were unable to appear in court to defend their reputation. On the other hand, a majority of cases of separation from bed and board were initiated by wives, either for the husband's adultery or cruelty, or both" (Stone, letter to the author, 20 November 1989). In a subsequent letter (6 December 1989), Stone points to "shaky evidence" for an increase in private separations and "hard evidence" from the records of the Consistory Court of London that show a "sharp rise" in judicial separations. According to Stone, this was "also the belief of contemporaries." The late eighteenth century was exceptional in that the principal suitors before the consistory courts were husbands.

One: Polemic Poems

1 See Pat Rogers 145–74 for a complete discussion of the Fleet and its satiric associations. Many of the popular poems I treat were published in the general vicinity of the Fleet: Warwick-Lane, Blackfriars, Ludgate Street, and Whitefriars. This can be accounted for simply by the fact that the Fleet district, with Stationers Hall off Ludgate Hill, was an established printing and book sales center. Here book shops and street vendors offered the popular and tract poems that sold for as little as a penny and as much as a shilling.

It is tempting to speculate that the Fleet district produced so much marriage poetry because for one hundred and sixty years it was notorious for clandestine marriages performed originally in the chapel of Fleet Prison without the proclamation of banns, license, or taxation. "After 1710 (when chapel marriages without banns became illegal), Fleet marriages spread to taverns throughout the neighborhood" (Baker and Jackson 212). Why some marriage poetry was published in the neighborhood of St. Pauls is easier to account for, especially since most polemical and hortatory poems are moralistic in their concerns. I suspect many of the polemic poets are clerics.

2 In applying Rothstein's perceptive scheme to marriage verse, I use the shift from a theme of power, to an operating principle of interaction, to a posture of sympathy as a way of conceptualizing the evolution in poets' handling of the marriage debate and companionate ideology. This tends to oversimplify the point Rothstein makes that "the same theme or principle could change its force [and the genres it employs] without immediately losing its predominance" (see Rothstein 120).

3 See Powell 88–89 on the popular tradition of controversy concerning all aspects of marriage that erupted in the seventeenth century, especially during the Interregnum. Adding fuel to the fire of controversy over marriage during this era are the four prose tracts of John Milton (1642–45). In these he takes the radical position, perhaps with his personal situation in mind, that divorce *a vinculo* should be allowed in cases of incompatibility (see Halkett). The tradition of prose polemics on marriage continues strongly throughout the long eighteenth century. Though I treat a few of these in some detail, I neglect the large majority.

Though there are numerous prose arguments in the medieval period and the earlier Renaissance that urge marriage or oppose it, most are not so stridently polemical. Of the earlier works, one of the best constructed is Erasmus's sample letter persuading a young man to marry from *De Conscribendis Epistolis* (1522) LB I 414D–24A (25: 129–45). Erasmus evokes numerous justifications for marriage by divine sanction and in human and natural law, and he also goes on to anticipate objections, including the arguments in praise of celibacy and virginity. He is undoubtedly serious in his argument, yet his presentation of it as an example of a letter of persuasion does lend it the quality of a rhetorical exercise. As such, it asks for a contrary argument. In this respect perhaps, it looks forward to the more polemical arguments of the seventeenth century.

4 There is, however, a poem in the *Love Giv'n O'er* series that is protofeminist in the sense that it gives expression to a woman's arguments, not a male poet's stereotyped representation of them. *The Female Advocate, or an Answer to a Late Satyr against the*

Pride, Lust, and Inconstancy of Women, Really Written by a Lady in Vindication of Her Sex (1686) was written by Sarah Fyge Egerton when she was only fourteen. She contends tellingly that vitriolic male satiric attacks on women as hellish monsters have their origin in distortions of the male imagination caused by sexual guilt and fear (see *The Female Advocate* 3; Nussbaum, *The Brink* 20–24). For a biography of Gould, see Sloane.

5 These in turn are based on a late fifteenth-century French poem, *Les Quinze Joyes de Mariage* (1480–90), attributed to Antoine de La Salle. Printed in England in 1509 by Wynken De Worde under the title of *The Fyfteene Joyes of Maryage*, it was reissued in an Elizabethan prose translation called *The Batchelars Banquet* (1602); this version omitted a number of the grosser passages. These were restored in a prose version of 1682 that took the title *The XV Comforts of Rash and Inconsiderate Marriage, or Select Animadversions upon the Miscarriage of a Wedded Life. Done Out of the French*. This piece was answered by another prose piece, *The Woman's Advocate or Fifteen Real Comforts of Matrimony in Requital of the Late Fifteen Sham Comforts . . .* (1682).

These prose pieces continue the debate on marriage and perpetuate the polemical opposition between anti- and pro-marriage ideologies. A. Marsh is identified as the author of *The Ten Pleasures of Marriage Relating All the Delights and Contentment That Are Mask'd under the Bands of Matrimony* (1682). The success of this lengthy prose piece, which reduces the fifteen format to ten, evidently encouraged Marsh to follow it in 1682 with *The Confessions of the New Married Couple, Being the Second Part of the Ten Pleasures of Marriage*. The prose in Marsh's two pieces may often sound sarcastic, but in fact both pieces are essentially serious praise of the pleasures of marriage. They in effect advance a pro-marriage ideology by their realistic, detailed narrative accounts of the problems a couple will encounter and the ways they finally surmount them.

6 One of the final manifestations of the format is the titillatingly ironic *The Fifteen Pleasures of a MaidenHead. Written by Madam B———le* (1707). In this debased, quasi-erotic piece a virgin complains of the sexual frustrations of remaining chaste and not enjoying the pleasures that married women do.

7 See, for example, Egerton, *The Female Advocate* 3–4; *An Answer to the Pleasures of a Single Life* (1701; treated in chap. 2); and "The Shepherd and Truth. By a Young Lady" (1763; Fullard 128–89).

8 See Utley 52–90 for a thorough listing and discussion of the French works that participated in the original "Querelle des femmes," a fifteenth- and sixteenth-century controversy over the merits of celibacy. Among the English and Scots works which perpetuated this debate, Utley lists a number of poems that specifically debate the merits of marriage.

One of the most brilliantly comic prose marriage debates of all time is in book three of Rabelais's *Gargantua and Pantagruel* (1522–24). In Rabelais's contribution to the original French "Querelle des femmes," he does not so much take sides as make the entire debate look silly. Rabelais's clerical hostility to marriage is at a standoff with his humanistic affirmation of the appetites of the flesh. He offers little positive pro-marriage ideology (see discussion of *Hudibras* in note 9).

Another important prose debate is the oratorical contest between Hercules Tasso, a learned philosopher, who speaks against marriage, and Torquato Tasso, the famous epic poet and orator, who defends marriage and has the last word in this battle of learned references. Originally published as *Dello Ammogliarsi* (1595), this pro-marriage work appeared in England as *Of Mariage and Wiving. A Excellent, Pleasant, and Philosophical Controversie between the Two Tassi.* Tr. R. T[ofte] (1599).

In the Restoration and eighteenth century, prose debates published in England include William Walsh's lengthy *Dialogue Concerning Women* (1691). In this witty piece, Mysogynes opens, disparaging the whole idea of the companionate marriage and offering a mean opinion of women's intelligence and moral nature. Philogynes follows, opposing Mysogynes point by point and effectively exploding his every position. After the initial satire, we are finally provided with a gallant defense as Walsh satisfies the desire of his male readers to see women both debased and idealized.

If Walsh's dialogue approaches Rothstein's second stage, a more clear-cut example is found in Bernard Mandeville's two hundred and fourteen page collection of ten prose dialogues entitled *The Virgin Unmask'd; or, Female Dialogues betwixt an Elderly Maiden Lady, and Her Niece, on Several Diverting Discourses on Love, Marriage, Memoirs, and Morals, &c of the Times* (1709). In the debates between the virgin Antonia and her Aunt Lucinda (who warns against marriage), asserting the pro- or antimarriage position may ultimately be less important than emphasizing the empirical method as an operating principle in matters under dispute. Mandeville's empirical point of view leads the reader to a clear-eyed skepticism about the benefits of marriage for women. His stance may be derived in part from mythical glorifications of the single life, but he also exhibits a surprisingly progressive sensitivity to the social disadvantages marriage imposes on women.

Rothstein's third stage is illustrated quite strikingly by F. Douglas's prose *Reflections on Celibacy and Marriage in Four Letters to a Friend* (1771)—rpt. in the series Marriage, Sex, and the Family in England 1660–1800. The entire goal of the letter writer in Douglas's work is to share his affective approval of marriage with his single friend and convert him (and all male readers) to a pro-marriage ideology by his enthusiastic affirmation of it.

9 See, for example, *An Account of Marriage* (1672) in which at least four of the ten heads of argument correspond loosely to points stated by *Hudibras*: Hudibras's point in III.i.809–12 corresponds with argument 2 in *An Account of Marriage*, Hudibras III.i.822–54 with argument 4, and III.i.855–68 with argument 5.

10 A somewhat similar pattern is illustrated in a marriage debate by Swift that inclines toward Rothstein's third stage: "The Grand Question Debated Whether Hamilton's Bawn Should Be Turned into a Barrack or a Malthouse" (1722). When, at the end of this poem, Lady Acheson reveals that she agrees at heart with Hannah's preference for a soldier over a clergyman, she in effect loses the marriage debate by discrediting the woman's position. Women, Swift suggests with sly humor, judge men by outward appearance and social manner. Of course, since Swift wrote the poem in the first place, he has every right to arouse the reader's sympathy for poor deans who are unfairly mocked. It is not so much men who win the debate with women, but the author who triumphs over everyone by his witty appeal for sympathy for clergymen and scholars. At the same time he gives credence to the woman's position if only by his comic attention.

Two: The Rake in Fetters and the Pleasures of a Single Life

1   Recent scholarship on the evolution of the rake's role has focused mostly on drama. The work of Robert Hume, Maximillian E. Novak, John Traugott, Harold Weber, and others sets the standard for scholarship by avoiding monolithic generalizations and insisting on distinctions among types and subtypes.

2   This idea survives in slightly altered form even in the eighteenth century. It crops up in such an unexpected source as Defoe's *Conjugal Lewdness* (1727). In this work husband and wife are counseled to adhere to "matrimonial chastity" and are warned against "irregular Desires" and *"all immoderate use of permitted Beds"* (49).

3   See Turner, chap. 1, for a discussion of the crux of prelapsarian sexuality. One traditional theological view on this question is that Adam and Eve did not have sexual intercourse before the fall. Cf. Marvell's "The Garden" (1681).

4   For varying views of Dryden, see Mark Auburn's introduction to the University of Nebraska Press's edition of *Marriage à la Mode*: "Contemporaries were split: on one hand Dryden could be cited in a pamphlet of 1674 as one who celebrated marriage and married love; on the other his play could be assailed in a comedy of 1672 as one of the antimatrimonial mode" (xxviii); see also Auburn 24n.

5   See Root 64–70 for a discussion of the shift in cultural values that took place after the Glorious Revolution of 1688. Root is mainly concerned with comedy, but he does suggest broadly that the "replacement of the Catholic James II with the Protestant William III and Mary" was viewed by many as a moral renaissance in England, "a rejection of the Stuart lifestyle of extravagance and libertinism." William himself called openly for a "reformation of manners" and publicly set the new moral tone, even though his private conduct drew forth satiric accusations of homosexuality (see O'Neill 17).

6   See, for example, his "Prologue to a New Play, Call'd, *The Disappointment*" (Dryden 321).

7   See especially Behn's "To Mrs. W. on Her Excellent Verses (Writ in Praise of Some I Had Made on the Earl of Rochester) Written in a Fit of Sickness" (4: 171–72), "The Disappointment" (which reworks Rochester's "The Imperfect Enjoyment" from a female point of view), and many of her amorous songs.

8   The *DNB* finds it necessary to defend her reputation from this aspersion: "But we are sure that a woman so witty, so active, and so versatile was not degraded though she might be lamentably unconventional." In Sarah Egerton's monologue "The Repulse to Alcander" (1703), she dramatizes a similar problem with reputation at a personal level. Because the woman speaker did "not damn all [a young man's] little gallantries for vice," the young man took the abusive freedom of assuming her a loose woman and attempting to seduce her; see Lonsdale 27–28.

9   Unlike Wycherley's speaker, William Walsh's witty man of the world in "To His Mistress. Against Marriage" (1692) is not making a plea to seduce; he is refusing to marry a mistress whom he has already enjoyed. But the tone is light, clever, and complimentary enough that we can perhaps overlook that he is dumping her. Walsh's speaker employs the standard first argument, but his light tone and facile logic keep ironic shading at a minimum and admit little skepticism about the libertine ethos he espouses. Walsh has captured the stance and manner of the great poets without their depth.

10   Cf. Elizabeth Thomas's "The Monkey Dance. To a Jealous Wife" (1722), which uses the chained monkey figure to satirize the woman who allows herself to be made jealous by the inevitable insincerity of man. Flatman's companion song, "The Second Part," manages to rise a degree or two above the formulaic by its ironic ending, which accuses Christianity of imposing the bonds of marriage on humanity and thus condemning them to hell (see 121).

11   Attributed to John Pomfret in the Folger Shakespeare Library card catalog. The Philadelphia edition of 1762 fathers the poem on Sir John Dillon. Poems in the series initiated by *The Pleasures of a Single Life* include in chronological order: *An Answer to the Pleasures of a Single Life: or The Comforts of Marriage Confirm'd and Vindicated: With the Misery of Lying Alone, Provd and Asserted* (1701); *Wedlock a Paradice: or, A Defence of Woman's Liberty against Man's Tyranny. In Opposition to a Poem, Entitul'd, The Pleasures of a Single Life, &c* (1701); *Good Advice to the Ladies: Shewing, That as the World Goes and Is Like to Go, the Best Way for Them is to Keep Unmarried* (1702); *Wedlock Vindicated: or, The Ladies Answer to the (Pretended) Good Advice to Them, Proving a Married Life is the Best Way to Support the Reputation of Both Sexes and a Single Life Scandalous, Dangerous and Obnoxious Both to Men and Women. With Seasonable Cautions to Avoid It* (1702); and *Good Advice to Beaus and Batchelours, in Answer to Good Advice to the Ladies* (1705).

12   Recent scholars working with the English antifeminist tradition in the sixteenth, seventeenth, and eighteenth centuries may also treat the antimatrimonial tradition in passing. They sometimes fail to acknowledge that antimatrimonialism and the argument for celibacy are historically one of the chief sources of antifeminist satire. For support of this point and for a reprinting of pertinent classical and medieval texts, see *Chaucer: Sources and Backgrounds*, chap. 8. For examples of critics who evidently overlook the connection, see Wright 500–501, Huebner 22–27, and Nussbaum, *The Brink* 12, 54, 77, 80, 84–85, 96, 100, 101, 106, and 119.

13   Cf. Francis Bacon's essay "Of Marriage and Single Life" (1625).

14   In a letter to the author, David Foxon posits an affinity between *The Pleasures of a Single Life* and its replies and the Gould/Ames formula poems of the 1680s and 1690s. As I have already briefly noted, Robert Gould was, during the first part of his life, a serving man. He was encouraged by John Oldham, who became his mentor. Gould and Richard Ames, the Grub Street hack who imitated him, both echo Oldham's intense Nonconformist hostility against religious, political, and sexual corruption in high places (see Sloane).

15   See, for example, "Antigamus" in *The Oxford Packet* (1714). In this parody of Milton's "L'Allegro," the libido of the speaker asserts itself unashamedly, but the assertion is so bald we suspect irony. For the text, see *Marriage Poems and Satires*.

16   See also the more naturalistically explicit rake's confession that Greene prints under the title "The Debauchee" and fathers on Rochester (72–74). Vieth (227–28) denies the attribution and suggests that the piece is probably by Charles Sackville, Earl of Dorset.

17   The emergence of a protofeminist or feminist consciousness in the culture of Restoration and eighteenth-century England is receiving increasing critical attention. In addition to works already mentioned, see, for example, Rogers; Perry, *The Celebrated Mary Astell* and *Women, Letters, and the Novel*; and Wittreich. Older studies of note include Clancey's unpublished diss. and Reynolds.

THREE: ADVICE POEMS

1. For a charming example from the 1790s of a woman poet using a simple satiric gallery, see Susanna Blamire's "O Jenny Dear, The Word is Gane" (written 1794) (Fullard 135–36). As with Blamire's other Scots dialect poems featuring a female speaker, Blamire's persona seems less concerned with expressing an antimatrimonial, prudential ideology (as earlier poems do) than with showing the reader how each male suitor has a serious character flaw. Blamire's failure to provide a positive portrait may reinforce the poem's satiric, protofeminist insight: contrary to men's inflated view of their worth, women perceive men's shortcomings with a sharp eye, though they are not always in a position to give voice to them as candidly as the speaker does.

2. I am indebted to Nussbaum for her reading of *To a Lady* in light of earlier satires on women and of "Restoration and eighteenth-century conduct books, moral essays, sermons, biographies, and poems directed at a predominantly female audience" ("Pope's 'To a Lady'" 445). As she suggests, Pope's negative characters of women as well as his positive character of Martha Blount should be understood in a context provided by these satiric and didactic works. I agree strongly with Nussbaum that "Martha Blount's lengthy portrait establishes her as an ideal for her sex, a norm against which we measure the highly entertaining but woefully deficient women" (451). I am however less convinced by Nussbaum's argument that the character of Martha Blount is "tinged with irony," that it is difficult to take Pope's idealization entirely seriously when he makes such blanket condemnations of women. As Brown does, Nussbaum finds the portrait of Martha Blount lacking in reality. Similarly, Pollak sees the character of Blount as empty: she has meaning only as "a part and counterpart of man whom she at the same time mirrors and completes" (*The Poetics of Sexual Myth* 109).

    The question here is what does Pope intend to accomplish in his character of a good woman? How purposefully does he set out to undermine the conventional virtues he recommends and celebrates? The irony Nussbaum perceives may be due in large measure to the difficulties inherent in writing in the celebratory mode when it is juxtaposed with the satiric, a problem that becomes more and more severe for later era poets. With his humanized tone and enumeration of Blount's specific virtues, Pope succeeds better than the others in giving his portrait of the good woman a positive substantiality.

3. Prose conduct books have been treated in some detail by twentieth-century criticism. See especially Powell, chap. 4, for a discussion of the domestic conduct book in the sixteenth and early seventeenth centuries. For a checklist of courtesy and conduct books, see Noyes. J. T. Johnson finds an emphasis on mutual society and domestic companionship evolving in Puritan conduct books of the early and middle seventeenth century. Davies is unwilling to identify this emphasis as distinctively Puritan. For a case study of Defoe's conduct manuals, see Curtis, and for manuals of the second half of the eighteenth century, see Hemlow.

4. In *The Rake Reform'd* (1718), for example, it is the death of his fellow rake from debauchery that prompts the rake-narrator to take up a pure life in the country. "A Consolatory Epistle to a Friend Made Unhappy by Marriage" treats a friend's experience in matrimony, while *The Pleasures of a Single Life* (1701) describes the narrator's own hellish marriage.

5. See also lines 20–34 of "Friday: The Toilette. Lydia" by Lady Mary Wortley Montagu (Fullard 293).

6   *Good Advice to Beaus and Bachelours* to a large extent plagiarizes *A Satyr against Love*. *The Fifteen Comforts of a Wanton Wife* (1706/7) purports to offer fifteen separate "comforts," but the whole piece presents an entertainingly coherent narrative devolution. The latter poem lifts a section wholesale from *False Apostacy* (1705) or vice versa. Cf. "the Second Comfort" from the former poem with the last paragraph on p. 2 and with the first two paragraphs on p. 4 of "The Character of a True-Born English-Woman."
7   According to Harold Williams, the object of attack in "Corinna," as first indicated by Hawkesworth in 1755, is Mrs. Delarivier Manley (1662–1724). An author of "some success," she led, according to Williams, "a life of more than questionable morality" (Swift 1: 149). "Corinna" could also be Elizabeth Thomas who is attacked in *The Dunciad* as "Curll's Corinna" (see Lonsdale 33).
8   Cf. Swift's description of the wife's daily activities to Gould's "A Consolatory Epistle to a Friend Made Unhappy by Marriage" (*Poems* 241–44). More than other Augustan satirists, Swift in his poetry treating women and marriage draws on and modifies the formulae of Grub Street poetry. See Nussbaum, "Juvenal, Swift, and *The Folly of Love*" 546–51. Hermann Real, editor of *The Battle of the Books*, points to Swift's acknowledgment of familiarity with at least one major Grub Street poet: "'I have read Mr. *Thomas Brown's* works entire, and had the Honour to be his intimate Friend,' Swift writes in the preface to *A Compleat Collection of Genteel and Ingenious Conversation*" (Swift, *The Battle of the Books*, appendix C, 122; translated from Real's German).
9   See Nussbaum, *The Brink* 26–42 for insights into the conventions of the Rochester, Oldham, Gould, and Ames tradition of vitriolic antifeminist satire. In addition to Swift's poems, the only other marriage poem I have found that uses *progress* in the title is *The Progress of Matrimony* (1733). This is a retitled reissue of an earlier poem *The Rape of the Bride; or Marriage and Hanging go by Destiny . . . A Poem Hudibrastick, in 4 canto's* (2nd ed., 1723). A rather cleverly done comic imitation of *Hudibras*, this piece concerns the alleged rape of a newly married, rich, elderly widow by a young husband. The reissue of 1722 was evidently not retitled to pick up on the popularity of Swift's "The Progress of Marriage" since that poem was not actually printed until 1765.
10 See Hagstrum 195–99 for a discussion of sensibility in *Clarissa*. Perry, *Woman, Letters, and the Novel* discusses eighteenth-century novels that examine the consciousness of women characters as well as their romantic and sexual fantasies. For an extreme case of a heroine's revolt against male authority, which is treated more or less sympathetically, see Ann Masterman Skinn's novel *The Old Maid; or; The History of Miss Ravensworth* (1771). See also Staves's discussion of it in "Matrimonial Discord in Fiction and in Court: The Case of Ann Masterman" (*Fetter'd or Free?* 169–85).

Four: A Bargain Between Two Partners in a Trade

1   As I suggested in chapter 1 and as Winnett (60–118) demonstrates in detail, seventeenth-century Anglican doctrine was ridden with controversy about the indissolubility of marriage and how much and in what ways it preserved the status of a sacrament, if at all. In this chapter and in chapter 6, I do not treat High Church Anglican doctrine as such but rather as a mythical idealization of it in a few conservative satires and celebratory verses respectively.

2 No poet of the early era seriously or wholeheartedly approved of marriage for money. Yet some cynically and ironically accede to or even praise the practice. A good example of such early Restoration irony is "The Wife." This piece is attributed to Alexander Brome, the Royalist poet, by Harold Love in the *Penguin Book of Restoration Verse* 171–72; however, I have been unable to locate it in Brome's *Songs and Poems* (1661). Brome's speaker wittily recommends a marriage of convenience since it is the best his readers can hope for in an imperfect world. It may be that the speaker wishes his advice to marry a "short liv'd and rich" woman to be taken seriously, and the recommendation may seem crass only to modern romantic sensibilities. Nevertheless, we see finally that the poet's advice is not so much to marry for money as not to marry at all. This unbalances his witty paradox and turns his advice to marry a rich and sickly woman into a broader satiric attack on marriage corrupted by greed and cynicism.

3 By 1673 in "To Mistress E. S. Married to an Old Usurer," William Davenant relies not just on cleverly stated tropes but also on a tone made more appealing by the use of a partially developed dramatic monologue. Though he praises the lady's beauty in conceits a little less extreme than Cleveland's, his satiric attack on marriage emerges mainly from his cavalier tone, from his presenting himself as a soldier disinterested in all but conquest.

> Why should a Souldier thus his praises spend,
> On what he loves and cannot comprehend?
> Our work is to attain, not to commend.
> (Davenant 322)

Though a trace of didacticism intrudes into Davenant's poem, he still essentially allows the dramatic situation to speak for itself.

This is somewhat less the case with a talky dramatic monologue by the Grub Street poet Tom Brown. In "A Satire on Marriage. Supposed to be Spoken by One Who Was Threaten'd to be Disinherited, on Condition He Refus'd the Match That Was Offer'd by His Friends" (written ca. 1700), Brown dramatizes the speaker's blatant rebellion against authority: the law, the church, and his "Friends," i.e., his parents.

> For me I'm too much to myself a friend.
> To chuse those evils which this state attend.
> I hate a bargain, when we go to woo,
> Why can't we all things as completely do,
> Without the curate and the lawyer too?
> (*Works*, 8th ed., 1: 248)

Although Brown's satire on marriage-as-trade has a generalized force, it is mainly interesting in the way it gives the stock libertine harangue a personal voice, and, like Davenant's poem, exemplifies the movement toward the exploration of affective stances.

4 Elizabeth Boyd's poem "To Mr. B——k on His Leaving His Mistress for Want of Five-Hundred Pound" (1733) is like Mitchell's and Egerton's pieces in addressing a specific mismatch (Fullard 112). Though Boyd wrote a novel, she does not do as much as the other poets to develop the character of her persona; she relies more on a stock tone of angry contempt liberally spiced with invective and name calling.

5 I have found no poem from the later era that appears to offer forthright praise of

marrying for money, except perhaps for Allan Ramsay's rollicking "Lass with a Lump of Land" (1728) (20: 282).

6   For a verse narrative using a classical setting, see John Moncreiff's *Themistocles, A Satire* (2nd ed., 1759). Themistocles is an Athenian politician who refuses to marry his daughter to a noble fool because marriage is a heaven-sent "blessing."

7   See Paulson 1: 479–85 for the plates and a discussion of them.

8   A late example of a woman poet using a well-characterized female speaker to expose the force of money on male suitors is Susanna Blamire's "I've Gotten a Rock, I've Gotten a Reel" (written before 1794) (Fullard 134). Blamire's dialect-using persona seems a combination social critic and wizened seer, a type who appears in the gothic novel as, for example, a wise old nurse or a comic but visionary servant.

9   The act was mainly designed to regulate clandestine marriages. Its main provisions were to accept as valid only those marriages "which had been solemnized in the parish church of the persons concerned, the banns having been published in the parish church or churches of both upon three Sundays preceding the solemnization. No license for marriage was to be granted in any other church than that of the parish within which one of the persons dwelt." See Haw 150, for additional provisions.

10 Note Cowper's echoing of Pope's "Ode on Solitude" (Pope 265).

11 Jeffreys's "mother Anna seems to have been the sister of James Bridges, Lord Chandos, whose son was first duke of Chandos" (*DNB*). Another use of this formula, less developed than Jeffrey's, is found in Moses Browne's "To Mr. Daniel Booth, Jun. on His Marriage" (1739):

>If thy fair Pattern might our Youth engage,
>No longer Vice shou'd taint th'enormous Age.
>Chaste Love alone shou'd warm each manly Breast,
>And *Marriage* be no more an impious Jest.
>
>(263)

Five: Evolving Types

1   See for example John Single's *Cupid and Hymen: or A Voyage to the Isles of Love and Matrimony. Containing a Most Diverting Account of the Inhabitants of Those Two . . . Countries. Tr. from French. To Which Is Added the Batchelors Estimate or Expenses Attending a Married Life* (1746) and *Gretna Green, or, Cupid's Introductions to the Temple of Hymen; Describing Many Curious Scenes, Love Anecdotes, and Characters, Prose and Verse. Calculated for the Entertainment of Both Sexes* (1798—listed in the checklist under "The Batchelor's Soliloquy").

2   See Curran's excellent discussion of the poetic types cultivated by the Romantics.

3   Somewhere between the broadside ballad and the art ballad, we might place a piece such as Swift's "An Excellent New Ballad: or, The True En———sh D———n to Be Hang'd for a R—pe" (1730). Swift self-consciously uses the sensationalism of the broadside ballad to reinforce his harsh satiric condemnation of the Dean's criminally libertine behavior.

4   See Thompson, *Samuel Pepys' Penny Merriments* 247–96 for additional late seventeenth-century chapbook prose and verse treating marriage. Many of these nonballad pieces

are prose dialogues in which the coarse humor revolves around a husband being cuckolded or humiliated in some way, often by wives who are out of control. In *Unfit for Modest Ears* 96–116, Thompson offers an informative discussion of this and other chapbook materials treating marriage. English writers, he points out, feel the need to justify their humiliation of the husband since in the seventeenth century "Infidelity is no longer an ingenious jape; it is a joke at someone's expense." Thus, "in the numberless cuckolding situations, we have numberless and exhausting explanations" (96). For a discussion of chapbook verse's handling of courtship, see Spufford 168–70.

5 Cf. "Verses by Mrs. M. E———ds, Occasion'd by a Lampoon on L———d A———H———'s Marriage," *Court Whispers* 35–36. Though not identified as an ode, this lampoon of Mrs. E———ds is more obviously an effusive and disordered outpouring. It is however less a mad song than drunken musings.

6 See Greene for a thorough discussion of Spenser's use and modification of classical, medieval, and Renaissance epithalamic conventions. Especially pertinent to my sense of Spenser's poem is Green's discussion of its amplitude: the way the world of the poem is made up of concentric areas emanating outward. At the center of the poem's focus is the couple, then their social context, next their natural setting, then the mythological beings that inhabit the poem, and finally, above all, the Christian heaven.

7 See Tufte 224n54. In the spirit and charm with which he employs mythology and the forms of the classical epithalamia, Prior is something of an exception to the evolutionary pattern illustrated in this section. Such pieces as "To the E of D. upon His Marriage" (written 1685), "A Hymn to Venus, upon a Marriage" (written 1690), and "The Wedding Night" (written 1702) offer social affirmation of the couples' virtues and charms, yet untypically they celebrate, with both wonder and irony, the cosmic forces that give life to a marriage. In contrast, Prior's "To Mr. Charles Montagu, on His Marriage with the Right Honorable the Countess of Manchester" (written 1687) is a witty and heartfelt tribute to a friend that offers mainly social affirmation (2–6, 106–7, 212, 61–62).

8 The one sizable group of poems that I have partially omitted from this study are occasional epithalamia offered in compliment to a specific couple. Since so many of these are formulaic, it would have been repetitive to treat more than a few.

9 See Tufte chap. 2 for a discussion of the antiepithalamium in classical poetry.

10 After Anne Finch, epithalamia by women, like those by men, increasingly affirm the happiness of the couple by praising their physical beauty and social virtues. For the most part, later women epithalamists do not adopt a personal, authentic voice but employ the conventional celebratory rhetoric of their male counterparts. See, for example, Mrs. Barber's "On the Earl of Oxford and Mortimer's Giving His Daughter in Marriage in Oxford Chapel" (1735); Mary Collier's "On the Marriage of George III. Wrote in the Seventy-Second Year of Her Age" (1762); Lady Dorothea DuBois's "Ode on the Marriage and Coronation of Their Most Sacred Majesty King George III and Queen Charlotte" (1764); and Anna Williams's "Essays Occasioned by the Marriage of Miss ——— and Mr ———" (1766). An exception is Mary Jones's witty, offhand "Ode on the Rt. Hon. Lady Henry Beauclerk on Her Marriage" (1757).

11 The author is identified by Eddy 15 as Sneyd Davies. See Tufte 178–88 for the use of the union of rivers as an analogy or metaphor for the union of the couple in

marriage. Christopher Smart in "Epithalamium" (1752) runs somewhat counter to the midcentury trend toward increasing social affirmation. Smart's poem abounds in mythological deities representing natural forces. Though the poet claims to find it "arduous to express" the "eternity" of the bride's happiness, his image of "two coeval pines in Ida's grove" links the social ceremony with the harmonious design of the natural order (198–200).

12 See *Ben Jonson and the Cavalier Poets* 265n7 for an identification of the "rusticated epithalamium."

13 See also Laetitia Pilkington's "The Happy Pair: A Ballad" (1748) (Fullard 116–17) and Catherine Jemmat's "The Rural Lass" (1750) (Fullard 120–22). The latter gives us a young woman rustic as narrator; she not only celebrates the honest simplicity of her wished-for wedding but fully cultivates the mythology of love in a cottage (see chap. 6).

Six: Real Bliss

1 For a more down-to-earth celebration of domestic bliss in marriage, cf. Henry Carey's "The Happy Marriage. *Inscrib'd to Nathaniel Oldham, Esq.*" (1729):

> Thrice blissful wedlock, where a beauteous wife
> Kindly contributes to a social life;
> Where home is made delightful, where each friend
> His option and her conduct must commend.
> Such, Oldham, is thy choice, thy partner such.
> She can't be prais'd, or thou approv'd too much.
>   (200)

Carey's adoption of the ideology of secular domesticity has already turned the wife into a moral exemplar.

2 Joel Porte argues that the evocation of terror in gothic fiction may be "a substitute for discredited religious mystery" (42). It might similarly be said that religious poets of the middle and late eighteenth century celebrate a secular domestic joy as a substitute for bliss in its more mystical religious sense.

3 See Shepherd 9. Shepherd's anthropology may be somewhat faulty for, according to at least one student of human behavior, humans form longer-lasting pair bonds than almost all animals not so much because humans are motivated by *higher* emotions but because the human animal is constituted in such a way that sexuality is more intensely and frequently rewarding (Morris 62–64).

4 See Arthos for a thorough discussion of the poetic use of language for quasi-scientific description. Though it is not poetry, John Cleland's *Memoirs of a Woman of Pleasure* (1748) uses just this sort of elevated and periphrastic Miltonic language to celebrate the mechanisms of human sexuality.

5 Woodward's poem is modeled on a pathetically moving love letter sent by a dying wife to her husband, "a Collonel R———s who is stationed in Spain." This letter was first printed in *The Spectator* 204, Wednesday, 24 October 1711. See the discussion of the elegy in chapter 5 for an identification of a group of lyrically effusive pieces (including Woodward's and Rowe's) in which a husband or wife laments the death of a spouse. The linking of companionate bliss with affective religious emotionality seems a distinctive

feature of eighteenth-century marriage poetry. Treatments of the death of a spouse in earlier marriage verse typically play down the emotionality of companionship in praising the joys of the afterlife. See, for example, "Eliza"'s "To My Husband" (1652) in which she requests that "no blacks be worne for me," but only a "bright Diamond." When this "sparkles" in her husband's eye, he will be reminded by its brightness of her heavenly destination:

> It was my glory I did spring
> From heavens eternall powerful King:
> To his bright Palace heir am I.
> (Greer 144–45)

In her assurance of salvation, "Eliza" purposely understates the pathos of her dying.

SEVEN: DOMINION O'ER THE BREECHES

1 Critics differ on how fully Interregnum challenges to patriarchal authority were carried over into Restoration society. Staves in *Players' Scepters* sees the calling into question of absolute authority within the state, especially by the execution of Charles I, as having lasting repercussions within society. She finds evidence for this in selected statements by protofeminists and progressive theologians, philosophers, and moralists, by precedents set in important divorce cases, and by increasing stress on the feminine in drama, especially in the 1690s. In evident disagreement, Stone asserts that "at the Restoration, the normal authority patterns were more or less restored and that feminist agitation by the urban artisan women of the London 'mob' was a movement without a future" (240). Nussbaum sees in the pamphlet controversy of the Restoration an effort to "reestablish" women's "traditional role" (*The Brink* 12). Pollak (in a comment on Susan Gubar's *The Female Monster* 728) finds in the popular literature of the age "the existence by the 1680s of a pervasive mythology of passive womanhood that upheld a rigorously defined ideal of woman as married, conjugally faithful, modest, good natured, cheerfully tolerant of idleness, and preeminently intent on pleasing her husband."

Critics' assessments of the strength of patriarchal authority in the Restoration depend to a large extent on their primary sources. Nussbaum's and Pollak's observations apply most directly to the popular tract poems and satires I treat in this chapter, Staves's to the protofeminist poems.

2 For a discussion of Interregnum challenges to patriarchal authority, especially by women, see Stone (240), Keith Thomas (54–55), and Higgins (209).

3 In a letter to the author, Rothstein suggests that Restoration misogyny results in part from an increased role for women and an increased political consciousness as the result of the concentration on power relations from the mid-seventeenth century on. In her "Epilogue: How Strong?" (464–70), Fraser concludes that women in the Restoration remained weak in the ideological war of words and in the public arena, but they had gained opportunities for more assertive, masculine roles during the war years. These opportunities did not always persist into peacetime after the Restoration.

4 For Butler's use of Interregnum popular materials, see Horne, "Butler's Use of the Rump in *Hudibras*." For popular imitations of *Hudibras*, see Richards.

5 For a number of eighteenth-century reports of the cruel practice of wife sale, see Hill 118–22.

6   See Noyes's bibliography for a listing of works in this vein. Examples include *The Wonders of the Female World, or A General History of Women* (1682) and Nathaniel Crouch, *Female Excellency, or The Ladies' Glory* (1688).

7   In *A Woman's Case: in an Epistle to Charles Joye, Esq; Deputy Governor of the South-Sea* (1720), an indirect but nevertheless hard-hitting critique of husbandly behavior is offered by Susanna Centlivre, a self-educated playwright of considerable popular success. This slyly ironic verse-letter is an appeal to Joye for a South Sea Company subscription. Centlivre confesses that her dedication of earlier poetry to George, Duke of Wales, got her nothing but her husband's chiding. In fact, she nearly got him dismissed. Now she writes to benefit him (though we can be sure she did not get his thanks after the South Sea bubble burst). For this poem Mrs. Centlivre wins the award for wives whose good intentioned interventions on behalf of husbands only gain their rancor.

Centlivre has left us an unflattering portrait of her financially strapped husband doing the sort of nagging that evidently drove her to write her epistle:

> What did it ever get for me?
> Two years you take a Play to write,
> And I scarce get my Coffee by 't.
> Such swingeing Bills are still to pay
> For Sugar, Chocolate, and Tea,
> I shall be forc'd to run away.
>   (7)

As Centlivre draws her husband, he is finally a cad who promises never to offend "with either male or female friend" if her epistle to Joye succeeds.

8   See Staves, *Players' Scepters* 159–60 for a discussion of the social significance of the debate over male sovereignty in Sprint, Chudleigh, and others. See also *The First English Feminist* 20–26 for Bridget Hill's informative discussion of the stimulus Sprint's sermon provided for other protofeminist or feminist works. Most significantly, Mary Astell's *Some Reflections upon Marriage* (1700) handles many of the same issues with the same emphases as Lady Chudleigh.

9   A third possibility, one not to be discounted, is that the printer tampered with the preface (see Lonsdale 1).

10 See, for example, the first page of the preface where Lady Chudleigh explains Sir John's irreverent reflections on the clergy as not her own thoughts, "but what one might rationally assume a man of his character will say on such occasions."

11 For a less shaded, more unrelenting bashing of husbandly dominion, see Chudleigh's "To the Ladies" (1703) (Lonsdale 3). This piece depends heavily on stereotyping to make its attack forceful: once a wife has promised to obey her husband, "Fierce as an eastern prince he grows,/And all his innate rigour shows." In *The Ladies Defence*, Chudleigh's use of the name Sir John Brute from Vanbrugh's play *The Provok'd Wife* (1697) is a curious allusion. In appropriating this name, did she mean to suggest that both the husband and wife in her poem have their faults, as Sir John and Lady Brute do in *The Provok'd Wife*? In a letter to the author Arthur Scouten suggests that "anyone in London who read poetry surely knew about Vanbrugh's new play" and that "Sir John Brute quickly became the symbol for boorish male mentality." Though Vanbrugh does

make Lady Brute's behavior seem questionable too, I doubt Lady Chudleigh intended her readers to make the association with Vanbrugh's character in the case of Melissa as they would have with Sir John. This is so, especially since Lady Chudleigh does not identify her as Lady Brute.

12 See also "The Condition of Womankind" (1733) whose opening quatrain may have been modeled on Tollet's first four lines (Fullard 289).

13 In the later era, there are a limited number of harsh satiric attacks on domineering women that are just as direct and insulting as those in the Restoration. See, for example, *Women Unmask'd and Dissected; A Satire* (1740), which portrays women forcing their way to power and dominion over men in every role women take on.

14 Even the poet's encouragement to the husband to share pleasant activities with his bride has an appeal to male self-interest. The husband's joys will be greater if he shares them with his marital companion (see 18). "Cynthia," the wife in the poem, is turned into a mechanism that should be employed properly "for greatest user benefit."

15 In his study of Mary Wollstonecraft, Ralph Wardle uses a poem by Mrs. Barbauld as a flagrant illustration of the argument that women rule by pleasing men. Wardle observes that the "majority of women in the eighteenth century accepted their inferior status without complaint" and that women were probably "more eager to retain their own position than to extend it to other women—at the risk of stirring up dissension, which might rob them of their privileges" (139–40).

Eight: A Union Both of Sex and Mind

1 In Mary R. Stockdale's "Song: Conquest" (1798), the wife who speaks recognizes that marriage may often involve adversity, especially as a couple age. However, her plan to address such suffering draws on banal love-in-a-cottage formulae:

> A smile shall ornament my cot,
> To welcome my lov'd swain,
> To gaily cheer life's chequer'd lot,
> And ease his every pain;
>
> (Fullard 143)

2 In the prose debate on marriage between Rasselas and Princess Nekayah in *Rasselas* (1759), Johnson affirms the happiness of marriage over the single life. At the same time he shows how this happiness can be marred in early marriages by folly and immaturity, particularly the rivalry between parents and children. Happiness in late marriages can be prevented by pride, obstinacy, and ingrained habits. Johnson avoids the idealization of many later era poets. At the same time, he disguises the patriarchal tone of his moral warnings by having the princess offer them rather than the prince or Imlac (564–68; chap. 29).

3 A more problematic revolutionary position is taken by Robert Burns in some of his satiric and celebratory verse. Burns's open celebration of free-spirited and spontaneous sexuality is exhilarating, yet it sometimes seems to evoke the traditional male libertine argument as it does in the epigrammatical "On Marriage" (undated). Burns's antimatrimonialist praise of sexual freedom challenges society's mores as hypocritical and unnatural, but he may be criticized for exploitation of the women who were

his sexual partners. In "A Poet's Welcome to His Love-Begotten Daughter; the First Instance That Entitled Him to the Venerable Appelation of Father—" (written 1784–85), Burns mocks the dogma of pro-marriage ideology that true love and affection can only be found within the heaven of matrimonial domesticity. At the same time, his celebration of his fatherhood raises serious questions about his irresponsibility toward his many illegitimate children and their mothers. For a Scots woman poet's celebration of natural sexuality, see "O'er the Muir Amang the Heather" (1792) by Jean Glover, an itinerant street entertainer whose song Burns recorded (Fullard 136–37).

NINE: WHAT COMES AFTER?

1 For a discussion of the feminism of Mary Wollstonecraft, see Rogers chap. 6. Wendell Stacy Johnson 28–33 provides an overview of the nineteenth-century movement for women's rights and offers references to more extended discussions of it. For a treatment of the theological implications of the various significant reforms in marriage legislation in the nineteenth century, see Haw chap. 2.
2 The opposition between woman as goddess and as whore, what Wendell Stacy Johnson calls the "madonna-harlot syndrome," is a staple of nineteenth-century poetry. Some of the most vivid dramatizations of this dichotomy occur in the poetry of Dante Gabriel Rossetti (see W. S. Johnson 86–90).
3 Crabbe's achievement as a marriage poet should not be underrated. See, for example, Shearon.
4 This is not, however, to say that the major Romantics do not treat marriage at all. Take Wordsworth, for example. A quick check of the contents of the five-volume Clarendon Press edition reveals, in addition to *Vaudracour and Julia* (2: 59), a number of minor poems that treat marriage in one way or another. These include "Composed on the Eve of the Marriage of a Friend in the Vale of Grasmere, 1812" (3: 14), "The Matron of Jedborough and Her Husband" (3: 85), and an ecclesiastical sonnet called "The Marriage Ceremony" (3: 397).
5 In a fashion typical of traditional critics of Romantic poetry, Daly treats the indebtedness of Blake, Wordsworth, Coleridge, and the others to the medieval and Renaissance tradition of the epithalamia. Also typically, he pays no direct attention, either positive or negative, to the evolution of this sensibility in the epithalamia of the Restoration and eighteenth century. Tufte also essentially neglects Restoration and eighteenth-century epithalamia (see 251–53).
6 Wendell Stacy Johnson treats the marriage poetry of the major Victorians in significant depth. Since my argument dovetails well with his, my discussion of the major Victorians relies heavily on his study.
7 For example, see respectively Alan Dugan's "Love Song: I and Thou" (1027), Patrick Kavanagh's "Tinker's Wife" (674–75), and James Merrill's "The Broken Home" (1104) in *The Norton Anthology of Modern Poetry*.
8 For an anthology that offers a fine sampling of twentieth-century English and American epithalamia, see *High Wedlock* 252–88. Tufte prints occasional epithalamia by Gertrude Stein (252–55), John Masefield (255–56), Edith Sitwell (266–67), Robert Graves (269–70), and W. H. Auden (275–78). A good example of a satiric epithala-

mium is e e cummings's "this little bride & groom are" (268); in this piece, cummings mocks the reduction of marriage to toy figures on a wedding cake, decked with artificial confections. Tufte also includes C. S. Lewis's "Prelude to Space: An Epithalamium." In this "dark or anti-nuptial poem," Lewis ironically celebrates the impregnation of space by a rocket, which ejaculates the seeds of earthly cruelty and disease into it. Confessional poems that subvert the epithalamium by revealing the disillusionment or the unnatural restrictiveness of marriage include those by Ann Stanford (284–85) and James Merrill (285–86).

An unusual contemporary epithalamium by Wendell Berry, "To Tanya" (1982), celebrates a union based in domesticity but manages to avoid banal and sentimental formulae. In this twenty-fifth anniversary poem to his wife, Berry avoids turning her into his property as he evokes a spirituality within the natural world of their marriage (52).

WORKS CITED

(PRE-1900)

This list includes only collections or works that contain short pieces, usually poems, treated in this study. For references to pre-1900 works published under their own titles, consult the index. Unless indicated otherwise, the place of publication is London.

Ames, Richard. *The Folly of Love.* 1691. See *Satires on Women* in Works Consulted.
Barbauld, Mrs. Letitia. *Poems.* 1772.
Barber, Mary. *Poems on Several Occasions.* 1726.
The Book of Common Prayer. 1549, 1662, 1760.
Brome, Alexander. *Songs and Other Poems.* 1661.
Brown, Thomas. *The Works of Mr. Thomas Brown, Serious and Comical, in Prose and Verse.* 8th ed. 4 vols. Dublin, 1778–79.
———. *The Works of Mr. Thomas Brown, Serious and Comical, in Prose and Verse.* 2 vols. 1707–8.
Browne, Moses. *Poems on Various Subjects. Many Never before Printed.* 1729.
Butler, Samuel. *Hudibras in Three Parts . . . with Large Annotations and a Preface.* Ed. Zachary Grey. 2 vols. 1744.
Chalmers, Alexander, ed. *The Works of the English Poets from Chaucer to Cowper.* 21 vols. 1810.
Chudleigh, Lady Mary. *Poems on Several Occasions by Lady Mary Chudleigh.* 1702.
A Collection of Poems in Six Volumes. By Several Hands. 1758—referred to throughout as Dodsley's *Miscellany.*
Collier, Mary. *Poems on Several Occasions.* 1762.
Court Whispers: or, A Magazine of Wit. A Satyr for the Country. 1743.
Davenant, William. *The Works of Sr. William Davenant Kt . . . Now Published Out of the Authors Originall Copies.* 1672.
[Dixon, Sarah]. *Poems on Several Occasions.* Canterbury, 1740.
Dodsley's *Miscellany.* See *A Collection of Poems in Six Volumes.*
[Drake, Judith]. *An Essay in Defence of the Female Sex.* 1696.

[DuBois, Lady Dorothea]. *Poems on Several Occasions by a Lady of Quality*. Dublin, 1764.
[Egerton,] S[arah] F[yge]. *Poems on Several Occasions, Together with a Pastoral. By Mrs. S. F.* [1703].
[Egerton, Sarah Fyge]. *The Female Advocate*. 1686. See *Satires on Women* in Works Consulted.
Female Excellence: or, Woman Display'd in Several Satyrick Poems. 1679.
Gould, Robert. *Love Giv'n O're*. 1682. See *Satires on Women* in Works Consulted.
———. *Poems Chiefly Consisting of Satyrs and Satyrical Epistles*. 1688/9.
Jeffreys, George. *Miscellanies in Verse and Prose. By George Jeffreys, Esq.* 1754.
Jemmat, Catherine. *Miscellanies in Prose and Verse. By Mrs. Catherine Jemmat. Daughter of the late Admiral Yeo of Plymouth, and Author of Her Own Memoirs*. 1766.
Lennox, Charlotte Ramsay. *Poems on Several Occasions*. 1747.
Miscellaneous Poems, Original and Translated. By Several Hands. Published by Mr. Concanen. 1724.
Miscellaneous Works, Written by his Grace, George, Late Duke of Buckingham. 1704.
Mitchell, Joseph. *Poems on Several Occasions*. 2 vols. 1729.
Moore, Edward, and Henry Brooke. *Fables for the Female Sex*. 2nd ed. 1746.
The Oxford Packet. 1714.
Parnell, Thomas. *Poems on Several Occasions by Dr. Thomas Parnell*. 1726.
Patmore, Coventry Kersey Dighton. *Poems*. 2nd collected ed. 1886.
Philips, Katherine. *Poems. By the Incomparable Mrs. K. P*. 1664.
Poems by Eminent Ladies. 2 vols. Dublin, 1757.
Pomfret, John. *Miscellany Poems on Several Occasions*. 2nd ed. 1707.
Portal, Abraham. *Nuptial Elegies*. 3rd ed. 1775.
Relph, Reverend Josiah, of Sebergham, Cumberland. *A Miscellany of Poems*. Glasgow, 1747.
[Robertson, James]. *Poems, Consisting of Tales, Fables, Epigrams, &c. &c. By Nobody*. 1770.
Robinson, Mary (Darby). *The Poetical Works of the late Mrs. Mary Robinson*. 2 vols. 1806.
Rowe, Elizabeth. *The Miscellaneous Works in Prose and Verse of Mrs. Elizabeth Rowe*. 2 vols. 1729.
Sedley, Sir Charles. *The Works of the Honourable Sir Charles Sedley, Bart*. 2 vols. 1722.
Seymar, William. See *Conjugium Conjurgium* in Works Consulted.
Stevenson, Matthew. *Poems: or, A Miscellany of Sonnets, Satyrs, Drollery, Panegyrics, Elegies, &c*. 1672.
A Ternary of Satires. 1679.
Thomas, Elizabeth. *Miscellany Poems upon Several Subjects*. 1722.
Tollet, Elizabeth. *Poems on Several Occasions*. 2nd ed. [ca. 1760].
Travers, Henry. *Miscellaneous Poems and Translations*. 1721.
Waller, Edmund. *Poems, &c. Written by Mr. Ed. Waller of Beckonsfield, Esquire*. 1645.
Walsh, William. *Letters and Poems, Amorous and Gallant*. 1692.
Ward, Edward. *Nuptial Dialogues and Debates; or, An Useful Prospect, of the Felicities and Discomforts of a Marry'd Life, Incident to all Degrees, from the Throne to the Cottage*. 2 vols. 1723.
Warton, Thomas. *Poems on Several Occasions. By the Reverend Mr. Thomas Warton*. 1748.
Williams, Anna. *Miscellanies in Prose and Verse*. 1766.
Woodward, George. *Poems on Several Occasions*. 1720.

WORKS CONSULTED
(1900 AND AFTER)

This list includes both works cited and consulted. Pre-1900 works appearing in modern reprint editions are listed here.

Abrams, Meyer Howard. *Natural Supernaturalism: Tradition and Revolution in Romantic Literature.* New York: Norton, 1971.

Altick, Richard D. *The Shows of London.* Cambridge, Mass.: Belknap P, 1978.

Aquinas, Saint Thomas. *The Summa Theologica.* Great Books of the Western World 19. Chicago: Encyclopaedia Britannica, 1952.

Armstrong, Nancy. *Desire and Domestic Fiction: A Political History of the Novel.* New York: Oxford UP, 1987.

Arthos, John. *The Language of Natural Description in Eighteenth-Century Poetry.* Ann Arbor: U of Michigan P, 1949.

Atlas, James. "The Battle of the Books." *New York Times Magazine* 5 June 1988: 24–27, 72–73, 75, 85, 94.

Bailey, Derrick Sherwin. *Sexual Relation in Christian Thought.* New York: Harper, 1959.

Baker, Felix, and Peter Jackson. *London: 2000 Years of a City and Its People.* New York: Macmillan, 1974.

Bannet, Eve Tabor. "Rewriting Family Relations: The Role of Lady Novelists in the 18th Century." Third Annual DeBartolo Conference on Eighteenth-Century Studies. Tampa, 11 March 1989.

Barnard, John. "Did Congreve Write *A Satyr against Love?*" *Bulletin of the New York Public Library* 68 (May 1964): 308–22.

Behn, Aphra. *The Works of Aphra Behn.* Ed. Montague Summers. 1915. Vol. 4. New York: Phaeton P, 1967. 4 vols.

Ben Jonson and the Cavalier Poets. Ed. Hugh Maclean. A Norton Critical Edition. New York: Norton, 1974.

Berry, Wendell. "To Tanya." *CoEvolution Quarterly* 36 (Winter 1982): 52.

Blake, William. *The Poetry and Prose of William Blake.* Ed. David V. Erdman. Garden City, N.Y.: Doubleday, 1965.

Bonfield, Lloyd. "Marriage Settlements and the 'Rise of Great Estates': the Demographic Aspect." *Economic History Review* 22 (1979): 482–92.

Boswell's Life of Johnson. Rev. ed. London: Oxford UP, 1953.

Brown, Laura. *Alexander Pope.* Oxford: Blackwell, 1985.

Browne, Alice. *The Eighteenth Century Feminist Mind.* Detroit: Wayne State UP, 1987.

Burns, Robert. *Poems and Songs.* Ed. James Kinsley. London: Oxford UP, 1969.

Butler, Samuel. *Hudibras.* Ed. John Wilders. Oxford: Clarendon P, 1967. Cited throughout as *Hudibras* by part, canto, and line number.

———. *Prose Observations.* Ed. Hugh De Quehen. Oxford: Clarendon P, 1979.

———. *Satires and Miscellaneous Poetry and Prose.* Ed. René Lamar. Cambridge: Cambridge UP, 1928.

Byrom, John. *The Poems of John Byrom.* Ed. Adolphus William Ward. Vol. 2. London: Chetham Society. 2 vols. 1895–1912.

Carey, Henry. *The Poems of Henry Carey.* Ed. Fredrick T. Wood. London: Scholartis P, 1920.

A Casebook on the Beat. Ed. Thomas Parkinson. New York: Crowell, 1961.

Chaucer: Sources and Backgrounds. Ed. Robert P. Miller. New York: Oxford UP, 1977.

Clancey, Richard. "The Augustan Fair-Sex Debate and the Novels of Samuel Richardson." Diss. U of Maryland, 1966.

Clay, Christopher. "Property Settlements, Financial Provision for the Family, and Sale of Land by the Greater Landowners, 1660–1790." *Journal of British Studies* 21 (1981): 18–28.

Cleveland, John. *The Poems of John Cleveland.* Ed. Brian Morris and Eleanor Withington. Oxford: Clarendon P, 1967.

Clough, Arthur Hugh. *The Poems of Arthur Hugh Clough.* Ed. F. L. Mulhouser. 2nd ed. Oxford: Clarendon P, 1974.

Coleridge, Samuel Taylor. *The Poems of Coleridge.* Ed. Ernest Hartley Coleridge. London: Oxford UP, 1912.

Conjugium Conjurgium, or Some Serious Considerations on Marriage. By William Seymar (1673); *Marriage Asserted: In Answer to a Book Entituled Conjugium Conjurgium* (1674). Rpt. in Drydeniana 4: The Life and Times of Seven Major British Writers. New York: Garland, 1976.

Cotton, Charles. *Poems of Charles Cotton, 1620–1687.* Ed. John Beresford. New York: Boni, n.d.

Cowper, William. *The Poems of William Cowper.* Ed. John D. Baird and Charles Ryskamp. Vol. 1. Oxford: Clarendon P, 1980. 2 vols.

Curran, Stuart. *Poetic Form and British Romanticism.* New York: Oxford UP, 1986.

Curtis, Laura A. "A Case Study of Defoe's Domestic Conduct Manuals Suggested by *The Family, Sex, and Marriage in England, 1500–1800.*" *Studies in Eighteenth-Century Culture* 10 (1981): 409–28.

Daly, Michael Joseph. "The Marriage Metaphor and the Prophecy: A Study of the Use of the Epithalamium in the Poetry of Blake, Wordsworth, and Coleridge." *DA* 29 (1969): 2254A. U of Southern California.

———. "The Marriage Metaphor and the Prophecy: A Study of the Use of the Epithalamium in the Poetry of Blake, Wordsworth, and Coleridge." Diss. U of Southern California, 1968.

Davies, Kathleen M. "Continuity and Change in Literary Advice on Marriage." *Marriage and Society: Studies in the Social History of Marriage*. Ed. R. B. Outhwaite. London: Europa, 1981. 58–80.

Defoe, Daniel. *Conjugal Lewdness; or, Matrimonial Whoredom. A Treatise concerning the Use and Abuse of the Marriage Bed*. 1727. Gainesville, Fla.: Scholars' Facsimiles & Reprints, 1967.

DeLauretis, Teresa. "Eccentric Subjects: Feminist Theory and Historical Consciousness." *Feminist Studies* 16 (Spring 1990): 115–50.

———. "Feminist Studies/Critical Studies: Issues, Terms, and Contexts." *Feminist Studies: Critical Studies*. Ed. Teresa DeLauretis. Bloomington: Indiana UP, 1986, 1–19.

de Rougemont, Denis. *Love in the Western World*. Rev. ed. New York: Harper & Row, 1956.

Dictionary of National Biography (DNB). 1917.

Doody, Margaret Anne. *The Daring Muse: Augustan Poetry Reconsidered*. Cambridge: Cambridge UP, 1985.

Dryden, John. *Marriage à la Mode*. Ed. Mark S. Auburn. Lincoln: U of Nebraska P, 1981.

———. *The Poems and Fables of John Dryden*. Ed. James Kinsley. London: Oxford UP, 1970. Cited throughout as Dryden.

———. *The Poems of John Dryden*. Ed. James Kinsley. 4 vols. London: Oxford UP, 1958.

———. *Poems 1693–96*. Berkeley: U of California P, 1974. Vol. 4 of *The Works of John Dryden*. 19 vols. to date.

Eddy, Donald. "Dodsley's Collection of Poems by Several Hands. 6 vols. 1758. Index of Authors." *The Papers of the Bibliographical Society of America* 60 (1966): 9–20.

Erasmus. *Collected Works of Erasmus*. Vol. 25. Toronto: U of Toronto P, 1985. 42 vols to date.

The Female Poets of Great Britain. Ed. Frederic Rowton. 1852. Intro. Marilyn L. Williamson. Detroit: Wayne State UP, 1981.

Fetter'd or Free? British Women Novelists, 1670–1815. Ed. Mary Anne Schofield and Cecilia Macheski. Athens: Ohio UP, 1986.

Finch, Anne. Countess of Winchilsea. See Winchilsea.

The First English Feminist. Reflections Upon Marriage and Other Writings by Mary Astell. Ed. Bridget Hill. New York: St. Martin's P, 1986.

Foxon, David. Letter to the author. 22 June 1986.

Fraser, Antonia. *The Weaker Vessel*. New York: Knopf, 1984.

Fullard, Joyce, ed. *British Women Poets 1660–1800: An Anthology*. Troy, N.Y.: Whitston, 1990.

Gay, John. *Poetry and Prose*. Ed. Vinton A. Dearing and Charles E. Beckwith. Vol. 1. Oxford: Clarendon P, 1974. 2 vols.

George, Charles H., and Katherine. *The Protestant Mind of the English Reformation 1570–1640*. Princeton: Princeton UP, 1961.

Gillis, John R. *For Better, For Worse: British Marriages, 1600 to the Present*. New York: Oxford UP, 1985.

Goreau, Angeline. *Reconstructing Aphra: A Social Biography of Aphra Behn*. New York: Dial P, 1980.

Greene, Graham. *Lord Rochester's Monkey*. New York: Viking, 1974.

Greene, Thomas M. "Spenser and the Epithalamic Convention." *Comparative Literature* 9 (1957): 215–28.

Greer, Germaine, et al., eds. *Kissing the Rod: An Anthology of Seventeenth-Century Women's Verse*. New York: Farrar, Straus, 1989.

Griffith, Reginald Harvey. "Progress Pieces of the Eighteenth Century." *Texas Review* 5 (1920): 218–22.

Hagstrum, Jean. *Sex and Sensibility: Ideal and Erotic Love from Milton to Mozart*. Chicago: U of Chicago P, 1980.

Halkett, John. *Milton and the Idea of Matrimony: A Study of the Divorce Tracts and Paradise Lost*. Yale Studies in English 173. New Haven: Yale UP, 1970.

Haller, William, and Malleville. "The Puritan Art of Love." *HLQ* 5 (1942): 225–72.

Haraway, Donna. "Animal Sociology and a Natural Economy of the Body Politic, Part I: A Political Physiology of Dominance." *Signs* 4 (1978): 21–36.

Harbage, Alfred. *Shakespeare and the Rival Traditions*. New York: Barnes & Noble, 1952.

Harding, Sandra. "Why Has the Sex/Gender System Become Visible Only Now?" *Discovering Reality: Feminist Perspectives on Epistemology, Metaphysics, Methodology, and Philosophy of Science*. Ed. Sandra Harding and Merrill B. Hintikka. Dordrecht, Holland: Reidel, 1983.

Hartsock, Nancy C. M. "The Feminist Standpoint: Developing the Ground for Specifically Feminist Historical Materialism." *Discovering Reality: Feminist Perspectives on Epistemology, Metaphysics, Methodology, and Philosophy of Science*. Ed. Sandra Harding and Merrill B. Hintikka. Dordrecht, Holland: Reidel, 1983.

Haw, Reginald. *The State of Matrimony: An Investigation of the Relationship between Ecclesiastical and Civil Marriage in England after the Reformation, with Consideration of the Laws relating Thereto*. London: Society for Promoting Christian Knowledge (S.P.C.K.), 1952.

Hemlow, Joyce. "Fanny Burney and the Courtesy Books." *PMLA* 65 (1950): 722–61.

Higgins, Patricia. "The Reactions of Women, with Special Reference to Women Petitioners." *Politics, Religion, and the English Civil War*. Ed. Brian Manning. New York: St. Martin's P, 1972. 177–222.

High Wedlock Then Be Honoured: Wedding Poems from Nineteen Countries and Twenty-Five Centuries. Ed. Virginia Tufte. New York: Viking, 1970.

Hill, Bridget, ed. *Eighteenth-Century Women: An Anthology*. London: Allen, 1984.

Holman, C. Hugh. *A Handbook to Literature*. Indianapolis: Bobbs, 1980.

Horne, William C. "Butler's Use of the *Rump* in *Hudibras*." *The Library Chronicle* 27 (Spring 1971): 126–25.

———. "Violence in *Hudibras*: Wit, 'Hard Words,' and the *Rump*." Diss. U of Pennsylvania, 1971.

Huebner, Wayne Vincent. "Convention and Innovation in the Satirical Treatment of Women by Major Satirists of the Early Eighteenth Century." Diss. U of Minnesota, 1964.

Hume, Robert. "The Myth of the Rake in 'Restoration' Comedy." *Studies in Literary Imagination* 10 (1977): 25–55.

Jehlen, Mona. "Archimedes and the Paradox of Feminist Criticism." *Signs* 6 (Summer 1981): 575–601.

Johnson, James Turner. *A Society Ordained by God: English Puritan Marriage Doctrine in the First Half of the Seventeenth Century*. Studies in Christian Ethics Series. Nashville: Abingdon P, 1970.

Johnson, Samuel. *Rasselas, Poems and Selected Prose*. Ed. Bertrand H. Bronson. New York: Holt, 1952.

Johnson, Wendell Stacy. *Sex and Marriage in Victorian Poetry*. Ithaca: Cornell UP, 1975.

Jong, Erica. *Fanny: Being the True History of the Adventures of Fanny Hackabout-Jones*. New York: NAL, 1980.

Lacey, T. A., and R. C. Mortimer. *Marriage in Church and State*. London: Society for Promoting Christian Knowledge (S.P.C.K.), 1947.

Leigh, Richard. *Poems by Richard Leigh*. 1675. Rpt. Hugh McDonald. Oxford: Basil Blackwell, 1947.

Leites, Edmund. *The Puritan Conscience and Modern Sexuality*. New Haven: Yale UP, 1986.

Lewis, C. S. *The Allegory of Love: A Study in Medieval Tradition*. New York: Oxford UP, 1958.

Lonsdale, Roger, ed. *Eighteenth-Century Women Poets*. Oxford: Oxford UP, 1989.

Macfarlane, Alan. *Marriage and Love in England: Modes of Reproduction, 1200–1840*. Oxford: Blackwell, 1986.

Mandeville, Bernard. *The Virgin Unmask'd*. 1709. Ed. Stephen H. Good. Delmar, N.Y.: Scholars' Facsimiles & Reprints, 1975.

Marriage Poems and Satires, 1670–1800. Ed. William C. Horne. Delmar, N.Y.: Scholars' Facsimiles & Reprints, 1986.

Marriage, Sex, and the Family in England 1660–1800. Ed. Randolph Trumbach. New York: Garland, 1986. 44 vols.

Milton, John. *Paradise Lost*. Ed. Merritt Y. Hughes. New York: Odyssey P, 1925.

Moi, Toril. *Sexual/Textual Politics: Feminist Literary Theory*. London: Methuen, 1985.

Morris, Desmond. *The Naked Ape: A Zoologist's Study of the Human Animal*. New York: McGraw, 1967.

The Norton Anthology of English Literature. Ed. Abrams, et al. 5th ed. New York: Norton, 1986. 2 vols.

The Norton Anthology of Modern Poetry. Ed. Richard Ellman and Robert O'Clair. New York: Norton, 1972.

Noyes, Gertrude. *Bibliography of Courtesy and Conduct Books in Seventeenth-Century England*. New Haven: Tuttle, 1927.

Novak, Maximillian E. "Margery Pinchwife's 'London Disease' and the Libertine Offensive of the 1670's." *Studies in the Literary Imagination* 10 (1977): 1–22.

Nussbaum, Felicity. *The Brink of All We Hate: English Satires on Women, 1660–1750*. Lexington, Ky.: U of Kentucky P, 1984.

———. "Juvenal, Swift, and *The Folly of Love*." *ECS* 9 (Summer 1976): 540–52.

———. "Pope's 'To a Lady' and the Eighteenth-Century Woman." *PQ* 54 (1975): 444–56.

Nussbaum, Felicity, and Laura Brown, eds. *The New Eighteenth Century: Theory, Politics, English Literature*. New York: Methuen, 1987.

Oldham, John. *The Work of John Oldham*. 1686. Delmar, N.Y.: Scholars' Facsimiles and Reprints, 1979.

O'Neill, John H. "Sexuality, Deviance, and Moral Character in the Personal Satire of the Restoration." *ECL* 2 (1975): 16–19.

The Oxford Book of Marriage. Ed. Helge Rubinstein. Oxford: Oxford UP, 1990.

The Oxford Book of Satirical Verse. Ed. Geoffrey Grigson. Oxford: Oxford UP, 1980.

Paulson, Ronald. *Hogarth: His Life, Art, and Times*. Vol. 1. New Haven: Yale UP, 1971. 2 vols.

The Penguin Book of Restoration Verse. Ed. Harold Love. Baltimore: Penguin, 1968.

Perry, Ruth. *The Celebrated Mary Astell: An Early English Feminist.* Chicago: U of Chicago P, 1986.

———. *Women, Letters, and the Novel.* New York: AMS, 1980.

Pollak, Ellen. Comment on Susan Gubar's "The Female Monster in Augustan Satire" (*Signs* 2 [Winter 1977]: 280–92). *Signs* 2 (Spring 1978): 728–32.

———. *The Poetics of Sexual Myth: Gender and Ideology in the Verse of Swift and Pope.* Chicago: U of Chicago P, 1985.

Pope, Alexander. *The Poems of Alexander Pope.* Ed. John Butt. London: Methuen, 1962.

Poovey, Mary. "Feminism and Deconstruction." *Feminist Studies* 14 (Spring 1988): 51–65.

———. *The Proper Lady and the Woman Writer: Ideology as Style in the Works of Mary Wollstonecraft, Mary Shelley, and Jane Austen.* Chicago: U of Chicago P, 1984.

Porte, Joel. "In the Hands of an Angry God: Religious Terror in Gothic Fiction." *The Gothic Imagination: Essays in Dark Romanticism.* Ed. G. R. Thompson. Pullman, Wash.: Washington State UP, 1974. 42–64.

Porter, Roy. "Mixed Feelings: The Enlightenment and Sexuality in Eighteenth-Century Britain." *Sexuality in Eighteenth-Century Britain.* Ed. Paul-Gabriel Boucé. Totowa, N. J.: Manchester UP, 1982. 1–27.

Powell, Chilton Latham. *English Domestic Relations 1487–1652: A Study of Matrimony and Family Life in Theory and Practice as Revealed by the Literature, Law, and History of the Period.* New York: Russell, 1917.

Prior, Matthew. *The Literary Works of Matthew Prior.* Ed. H. Bunker Wright and Monroe K. Spears. 2nd ed. Vol. 1. Oxford: Clarendon P, 1971. 2 vols.

Ramsay, Allan. *The Works of Allan Ramsay.* Ed. Burns Martin and John W. Oliver. The Scottish Text Society 2. 1952–61. New York: Johnson Reprint, 1972. 2 vols.

Rendall, Jane. *The Origins of Modern Feminism: Women in Britain, France, and the United States, 1780–1860.* New York: Schocken, 1984.

Reynolds, Myra. *The Learned Lady in England, 1650–1760.* Vassar Semi-Centennial Series. 1920. Gloucester, Mass.: Smith, 1964.

Richards, Edward Ames. *Hudibras in the Burlesque Tradition.* Columbia University Studies in English and Comparative Literature 127. 1927. New York: Octagon, 1972.

Richardson, Samuel. *Pamela or Virtue Rewarded.* New York: Norton, 1958.

Ricks, Christopher. Concluding Remarks. Third Annual DeBartolo Conference on Eighteenth-Century Studies. Tampa, 11 March 1989.

Rochester, John Wilmot, Earl of. *The Complete Poems of Wilmot, Earl of Rochester.* Ed. David M. Vieth. New Haven: Yale UP, 1968.

Rogers, Katherine M. *Feminism in Eighteenth-Century England.* Urbana: U of Illinois P, 1982.

Rogers, Pat. *Hacks and Dunces: Pope, Swift and Grub Street.* London: Methuen, 1980.

Root, Robert L., Jr. "The Problematics of English Comedy 1688–1710." Diss. U of Iowa, 1975.

Rothstein, Eric. *Restoration and Eighteenth-Century Poetry 1660–1780. The Routledge History of English Poetry* 2. Boston: Routledge, 1981.

Satires on Women. Introd. Felicity A. Nussbaum. The Augustan Reprint Society 180. Los Angeles: William Andrews Clark Memorial Library, 1976.

Schnorrenberg, Barbara. "The Eighteenth-Century Englishwoman." *The Women of England from Anglo-Saxon Times to the Present.* Ed. Barbara Kanner. Hamden, Conn.: Archon, 1979. 183–228.

Schucking, Levin L. *The Puritan Family: A Social Study from Literary Sources.* New York: Schocken Books, 1970.

Scouten, Arthur. Letter to the author. 22 August 1988.

Sexual Underworlds of the Enlightenment. Ed. G. S. Rousseau and Roy Porter. Chapel Hill: U of North Carolina P, 1988.

Seymar, William. See *Conjugium Conjurgium.*

Shearon, Forrest B. "The Muse of Hymen: George Crabbe on Marriage." Diss. U of Louisville, 1972.

Shelley, Percy Bysshe. *Selected Poetry and Prose.* Ed. Neill Cameron. New York: Holt, 1951.

Shorter, Edward. *The Making of the Modern Family.* New York: Basic Books, 1975.

Shuster, George N. *The English Ode from Milton to Keats.* Gloucester, Mass.: Smith, 1964.

Sloane, Eugene Hulse. *Robert Gould: Seventeenth Century Satirist.* Diss. U of Pennsylvania, 1940. Philadelphia: U of Pennsylvania P, 1940.

Smart, Christopher. *Miscellaneous Poems English and Latin.* Vol. 4 of *The Poetical Works of Christopher Smart.* Ed. Karina Williamson. Oxford: Clarendon P, 1987. 4 vols. to date.

Spacks, Patricia Meyer. "Ev'ry Woman is at Heart a Rake." *Eighteenth-Century Studies* 8 (1974): 27–46.

Spufford, Margaret. *Small Books and Pleasant Histories: Popular Fiction and Its Readership in Seventeenth Century England.* Athens: U of Georgia P, 1981.

Staves, Susan. *Married Women's Separate Property in England, 1660–1833.* Cambridge, Mass.: Harvard UP, 1990.

———. "Matrimonial Discord in Fiction and in Court: The Case of Ann Masterman." *Fetter'd or Free? British Women Novelists, 1670–1815.* Ed. Mary Anne Schofield and Cecilia Macheski. Athens: Ohio UP, 1986. 169–85.

———. *Players' Scepters: Fictions of Authority in the Restoration.* Lincoln: U of Nebraska P, 1979.

———. "Where is History but in Texts? Reading the History of Marriage." *The Golden & the Brazen World.* Ed. John M. Wallace. Berkeley: U of California P, 1985.

Stone, Lawrence. *The Family, Sex, and Marriage in England, 1500–1800.* New York: Harper, 1977.

———. "Honors, Morals, and Adultery in Eighteenth-Century England: The Action for Criminal Conversation." Third Annual DeBartolo Conference on Eighteenth-Century Studies. Tampa, 10 March 1989.

———. Letters to the author. 20 November 1989 and 6 December 1989.

———. *Road to Divorce: England 1530–1987.* Oxford: Oxford UP, 1990.

Suarez, Michael F., S.J. "'Lawful Plague,' or, The Wife as Slave: Perspectives from Eighteenth-Century Poetry." Third Annual DeBartolo Conference on Eighteenth-Century Studies. Tampa, 10 March 1989.

Swayne, Mattie. "The Progress Piece in the Seventeenth Century." *Texas Studies in English* 16 (1926): 84–92.

Swift, Jonathan. *The Battle of the Books.* Ed. Hermann Josef Real. Berlin: de Gruyter, 1978.

———. *The Poems of Jonathan Swift.* Ed. Harold Williams. 2nd ed. Oxford: Clarendon P, 1958. 2 vols. Cited throughout as Swift.

Thomas, Keith. "Woman and the Civil War Sects." *Past and Present* 12 (1958): 42–62.

Thompson, Roger, ed. *Samuel Pepys' Penny Merriments* . . . . New York: Columbia UP, 1977.

———. *Unfit for Modest Ears: A Study of Pornographic, Obscene, and Bawdy Books Written or*

Published in England in the Second Half of the Seventeenth Century. Totowa, N.J.: Rowman, 1979.

Todd, Janet, ed. *A Dictionary of British and American Woman Writers, 1660–1800.* Totowa, N.J.: Rowman, 1985.

Traugott, John. "The Rake's Progress from Court to Comedy: A Study of Comic Form." *Studies in English Literature* 6 (1966): 281–407.

Troyer, H. W. *Ned Ward of Grub Street.* London: Frank Cass, 1946.

Trumbach, Randolph. *The Rise of the Egalitarian Family: Aristocratic Kinship and Domestic Relations in Eighteenth-Century England.* New York: Academic P, 1978.

Tufte, Virginia J. *The Poetry of Marriage: A Critical History of the Epithalamium.* Los Angeles: Tinnon-Brown, 1968.

Turner, James Grantham. *One Flesh: Paradisal Marriage and Sexual Relations in the Age of Milton.* Oxford: Clarendon P, 1987.

Unauthorized Sexual Behavior during the Enlightenment. Ed. Robert P. Maccubbin. Spec. issue of *Eighteenth-Century Life* 9 (May 1985).

Utley, Francis Lee. *The Crooked Rib: An Analytical Index to the Argument about Women in English and Scots Literature to the End of the Year 1658.* 1944. New York: Octagon, 1970.

Valentine, Alan Chester. *The British Establishment, 1760–1784: An Eighteenth Century Biographical Dictionary.* 1st ed. Norman: U of Oklahoma P, 1970.

Wagner, Peter. *Eros Revived.* London: Secker & Warburg, 1988.

Wardle, Ralph M. *Mary Wollstonecraft.* Lawrence: U of Kansas P, 1951.

Watt, Ian. *The Rise of the Novel: Studies in Defoe, Richardson and Fielding.* Berkeley: U of California P, 1957.

Weber, Harold. *The Restoration Rake-Hero: Transformations in Sexual Understanding in Seventeenth-Century England.* Madison: U of Wisconsin P, 1986.

Williams, Anne. *Prophetic Strain: The Greater Lyric in the Eighteenth Century.* Chicago: U of Chicago P, 1984.

Williamson, Marilyn L. *Raising Their Voices: British Women Writers, 1650–1750.* Detroit: Wayne State UP, 1990.

Winchilsea, Anne Kingsmill Finch, Countess of. *The Poems of Anne Countess of Winchilsea.* Ed. Myra Reynolds. 1902. Rpt. New York: AMS, 1974.

Winnett, Arthur Robert. *Divorce and Remarriage in Anglicanism.* London: Macmillan, 1958.

Wintle, Sarah. "Libertinism and Sexual Politics." *Spirit of Wit: Reconsiderations of Rochester.* Ed. Jeremy Treglown. Hamden, Conn.: Archon, 1982.

Wittreich, Joseph. *Feminist Milton.* Ithaca: Cornell UP, 1987.

Wollstonecraft, Mary. *A Vindication of the Rights of Woman.* Ed. Carol H. Poston. 2nd ed. New York: Norton, 1988.

Wordsworth, William. *The Poetical Works of William Wordsworth.* Ed. E. De Selincourt and Helen Darbishire. 5 vols. Oxford: Clarendon P, 1949.

Wright, Louis B. *Middle-Class Culture in Elizabethan England.* Chapel Hill: U of North Carolina P, 1925.

Wrigley, E. A. "The Growth of Population in Eighteenth-Century England: A Conundrum Resolved." *Past and Present* 98 (Feb. 1983): 121–50.

Wycherley, William. *The Complete Works of William Wycherley.* Ed. Montague Summers. Vol. 4. New York: Russell, 1964. 4 vols.

CHECKLIST OF MARRIAGE POEMS, 1650–1800

The list presented here goes well beyond those titles discussed or referred to in *Making a Heaven of Hell*; the checklist does not, however, attempt to be comprehensive. For each entry, I provide the author's name and dates (where known), the title of the poem, and its initial date of publication; where pertinent, the date of composition follows in parentheses. Titles reprinted in *Marriage Poems and Satires* are designated by an asterisk. Where additional data are pertinent and available, I include it on succeeding lines in the following order:

Contemporary collection(s) in which the work (first) appeared (pagination provided wherever possible).

Modern collection(s) or reprint series. Poems reprinted in Chalmers (see Works Consulted) may also be found in the microcard series *The Library of English Literature* (LEL); LEL numbers have been provided.

ID number in Arthur E. Case, *A Bibliography of English Poetical Miscellanies 1521–1750* (1935; rpt. Folcroft, Pa.: Folcroft, 1970) [abbreviated CASE]; *The Eighteenth-Century Short Title Catalogue* (The Research Libraries Group, Inc.) [ESTC]; David Foxon, *English Verse, 1701–1750*, 2 vols. (Cambridge: Cambridge UP, 1975) [FOX]; or Donald Wing, *Short Title Catalogue of Books Printed in England, Scotland, Ireland, Wales, and British America and of English Books Printed in Other Countries, 1641–1700*, 3 vols. (New York: MLA, 1972) [WNG].

Reel number in microfilm series: *Early English Books, 1641–1700* [EEB] for WNG and *The Eighteenth Century* [EC] for ESTC. In cases in which the microfilm series does not reprint the first edition, the date of the edition reprinted and its ID and/or reel number are supplied in round brackets, viz. { }.

Mode of poem: satiric, celebratory, exemplary, etc.

In cases of uncertainty, data are placed in square brackets. The text for all titles by Rochester is *The Complete Poems of Wilmot, Earl of Rochester*, ed. David M. Vieth; by Swift, *The Poems of Jonathan Swift*, ed. Harold Williams; and by Pope, *The Poems of Alexander Pope*, ed. John Butt (see Works Consulted). For these three important poets as well as for William Blake, Robert Burns, Samuel Butler, John Byrom, John Cleveland, William Cowper, John Dryden, Lady Mary Wortley Montagu, Matthew Prior, and Christopher Smart, I have made no attempt to list the contemporary collection in which the title may have appeared initially. For all these poets, modern editions make such information readily available.

Advice to a widow. 1747.
FOX A76
ESTC T167752
exemplary/satiric

[Ames, Richard] (d. 1693). *Sylvia's revenge, or, a satyr against man: in answer to the satire against woman.* 1688.
WNG A2992D, E, F, or G
EEB reel 1663
satiric

Ames, Richard (d. 1693). *The female fire-ships.* 1691.
WNG A2979
EEB reel 198
satiric

Ames, Richard (d. 1693). *The folly of love; or, an essay upon satyr against woman.* 1691.
Satires on Women, ed. F. Nussbaum. The Augustan Reprint Society 180 (Los Angeles: Clark Library, 1976): 1–27.
WNG A2980
EEB reel 1560: 53
satiric

[Ames, Richard] (d. 1693). *The pleasures of love and marriage, a poem in praise of the fair sex. In requital for the folly of love, and some other late satyrs on women.* 1691.*
WNG A2987
EEB reel 340: 12
satiric

[Ames, Richard] (d. 1693). *Sylvia's complaint or her sexes unhappiness. Being the second part of Sylvia's revenge, or, a satyr against man.* 1692.
WNG A2992a
satiric

[Ames, Richard] (d. 1693). *The rake, or, the libertine's religion, a poem.* 1693.
WNG A2988
EEB reel 832: 20
satiric

Amherst, Elizabeth Frances (later Thomas) (c. 1716–79). The Welford wedding. 1989 (c. 1740–50).
Bodleian MS Eng. poet. e. 109, fos. 47–50.
Lonsdale 181–83
celebratory

An answer to the pleasures of a single life; or, the comforts of marriage confirm'd and vindicated: with the misery of lying alone prov'd and asserted. 1701.*
ESTC N005386
EC reel 2496: 18
anti-satiric

Armstrong, John, M.D. (1709–79). *The oeconomy of love. A poetical essay.* 1736 {1789}.
ESTC T136229 {T074298}
EC reel {1186: 20}
exemplary

Baker, Daniel M. A. (c. 1654–1723), Rector of Fincham. The wife. 1697.
Poems upon Several Occasions (1697) 17–18.
WNG B489A
EEB reel 81: 1
comic

Barbauld, Anna Laetitia (Aiken) (1743–1825). The rights of woman. 1825 (c. 1795).
Works (1825) 1: 185–87.
Lonsdale 305–6
satiric

Barbauld, Anna Letitia (Aiken) (1743–1825). Ovid to his wife: imitated from different parts of his *Tristia*. 1773.
Poems (1773) [1774] 88–94.
ESTC T074946
EC reel 1462: 10
elegiac

Barber, Mary (c. 1690–1757). The conclusion of a letter to the Rev. Mr. C——. 1734.
Poems on Several Occasions (1735) 58–62.
Fullard 300–302
Lonsdale 122–24
ESTC T042623
EC reel 1466: 06
satiric

Barber, Mary (c. 1690–1757). On the Earl of Oxford and Mortimer's giving his daughter in marriage in Oxford chapel. 1735.
Poems on Several Occasions (1735) 269.
ESTC T042623
EC reel 1466: 06
celebratory

Barker, Jane (c. 1652—c.1720). To my friend Exillus, on his persuading me to marry old Damon. 1688.
Poetical Recreations (1688) 14–15.
WNG B770 (for *Poetical Recreations*)
EEB reel 52: 3
anti-marriage advisory

Barker, Jane (c. 1652—c.1720). A virgin life. 1688. Magdalen MS 343, Part III.
Poetical Recreations (1688) 12–13.
A Patch-work Screen for Ladies (1723).
Greer 360–61
WNG B770 (for *Poetical Recreations*)
EEB reel 52: 3
celebratory

The batchelor's choice, or, the happy wish. A poem. 1707.
FOX B3
exemplary

The batchelors and maids answer, to the fifteen comforts of matrimony. Being real encouragement for all single persons, of both sexes to marry as soon as ever they can get wives and husbands, in order to avoid the danger of leading apes in hell; with sutable [sic] directions for that purpose. [1706?]
ESTC N015694
EC reel 2496: 02
anti-satiric

The batchelors soliloquy, in imitation of Hamlet. 1798. *Gretna Green, or, Cupid's Introduction to the Temple of Hymen; Describing Many Curious Scenes, Love Anecdotes, and Characters, in Prose and Verse. Calculated for the Entertainment of Both Sexes.* 1798.
See also Single. *Cupid and Hymen . . .* 1746. 21–22.
satiric

Behn, Aphra (1640–89). The disappointment. 1684.
Poems upon Several Occasions (1684) 70–77.
The Works of Aphra Behn, ed. Montague Summers, 4 vols. (1915; New York: Phaeton, 1967) 4: 178–82.
WNG B1757
EEB reel 525
satiric

Behn, Aphra (1640–89). The golden age. A paraphrase out of French. 1684.
Poems upon Several Occasions (1684) 1–12.
The Works of Aphra Behn, ed. Montague Summers, 4 vols. (1915; New York: Phaeton, 1967) 4: 138–44.
WNG B1757
EEB reel 525
satiric

Behn, Aphra (1640–89). Song. 1755 (before 1689).
Poems by Eminent Ladies, 2 vols. (1755) 1: 163.
Fullard 98
ESTC T042592
satiric

Betham, Matilda (1776–1852). [The power of women]. 1905 (c.1798).
Ernest Betham, A House of Letters (London: Jarrold, 1905) 55–56.
Lonsdale 502
celebratory

Blake, William (1757–1827). Hail matrimony made of love. 1965 (1784).
An Island in the Moon. Ms. fragment.
The Poetry and Prose of William Blake, ed. David V. Erdman (Garden City: Doubleday, 1965) 450–51.
satiric

Blamire, Susanna (1747–94). The Siller Croun. 1790.
The Scots Musical Museum, 4 vols. (Edinburgh, 1853) 3: 249 (song 240).
Fullard 132
satiric/celebratory

Blamire, Susanna (1747–94). I've gotten a rock, I've gotten a reel. 1842 (before 1794).
The Poetical Works of Miss Susanna Blamire (Edinburgh, 1842) 191–92.
Fullard 134
satiric

Blamire, Susanna (1747–94). O Jenny dear, the word is gane. 1842 (1794).
The Poetical Works of Miss Susanna Blamire (Edinburgh, 1842) 238–39.
Fullard 135–36
advisory

[Blyth, Francis] (n.d.). *Advice to a friend on his marriage, a poem.* 1735.
FOX B291
ESTC N001616
exemplary

Boyd, Elizabeth (fl. 1730–40). To Mr. B——k, on his leaving his mistress for want of five-hundred pound. 1733.
The Humorous Miscellany; or Riddles for the Beaux (1733) 15.
Fullard 112
ESTC T070868
EC reel 3843: 19
satiric

Boyd, Elizabeth (fl. 1730–40). Advice to Aurelia. A song. 1733.
The Humorous Miscellany; or Riddles for the Beaux (1733) 31–32.
Fullard 112–13
ESTC T070868
EC reel 3843: 19
satiric

Brome, Alexander (1620–66). An elegy on a lady that died before her intended nuptials. 1661.
Songs and Other Poems (1661) 111–12.
Chalmers 6: 686. LEL 21788
WNG B4852
EEB reel 1399: 12
elegiac

Brome, Alexander (1620–66). Epigram xlv. To a jealous husband. 1661.
Songs and Other Poems (1661) 178.
WNG B4852
EEB reel 1399: 12
witty

Brome, Alexander (1620–66). Epigram xxix. On two wives. 1661.
Songs and Other Poems (1661) 171.
WNG B4852
EEB reel 1399: 12
witty

Brome, Alexander (1620–66). To a gentleman who fell sick of the small pox when he should be married. 1661.
Songs and Other Poems (1661) 106–8.
Chalmers 6: 685–86. LEL 21788
WNG B4852
EEB reel 1399: 12
witty

Brome, Alexander (1620–66). To a widow. 1661.
Songs and Other Poems (1661) 18–19.
WNG B4852
EEB reel 1399: 12
witty

Brome, Alexander (1620–66). To his mistris married to another. 1661.
Songs and Other Poems (1661) 126–27.
WNG B4852

EEB reel 1399: 12
witty

Brome, Alexander (1620–66). The wife. n.d.
Penguin Book of Restoration Verse (Baltimore: Penguin, 1968) 171–72.
witty

Brown, N. (n.d.). The north country wedding. 1724.
Miscellaneous Poems, Original and Translated by Several Hands (1724) 1–15.
ESTC T25249
EC reel 1427: 10
celebratory

Brown, Thomas (1663–1704). A satire on marriage. 1707–8.
The Works of Mr. Thomas Brown, Serious and Comical, in Prose and Verse. 2 vols. (1707–8) 1 (part 2): 86–88.
ESTC T052781
EC reel 2208: 14
satiric

Brown, Thomas (1663–1704). A satire on marriage. Supposed to be spoken by one who was threaten'd to be disinherited, on condition he refus'd the match that was offered him by his friends. 1778–79 (ca.1700).
The Works of Mr. Thomas Brown, Serious and Comical, in Prose and Verse. 8th ed., 4 vols. (Dublin, 1778–79) 1: 247–49.
ESTC N025870
satiric

Brown, Thomas (1663–1704). To a lady, whom he refus'd to marry, because he lov'd her. 1707.
The Works of Mr. Thomas Brown, Serious and Comical, in Prose and Verse. 2 vols. (1707–8) 1 (part 2): 28–29.
ESTC T052781
EC reel 2208: 14
satiric

Browne, Moses, The Rev. (1704–87). To Mr. Daniel Booth, Jun. on his marriage. 1739.
Poems on Various Subjects (1739) 450–52.
ESTC T1083771
elegiac

Browne, Moses, The Rev. (1704–87). Verses on the death of a dear and most lov'd wife. Written just upon recovery from illness, anno 1737. 1739.
Poems on Various Subjects (1739) 450–52.
ESTC T1083771
elegiac

Burns, Robert (1759–96). A poet's welcome to his love-begotten daughter; the first instance that entitled him to venerable appelation of father. (1784–85).
Robert Burns. Poems and Songs, ed. James Kinsley (London: Oxford UP, 1969) 77–78.
satiric

Burns, Robert (1759–96). Epitaph on a henpecked country squire. 1786.
Robert Burns. Poems and Songs, ed. James Kinsley (London: Oxford UP, 1969) 188.
satiric

Burns, Robert (1759–96). My wife's a wanton, wee thing. 1790.
Robert Burns. Poems and Songs, ed. James Kinsley (London: Oxford UP, 1969) 406.
satiric

Burns, Robert (1759–96). Song—sic a wife is willie's wife. 1792.
Robert Burns. Poems and Songs, ed. James Kinsley (London: Oxford UP, 1969) 509.
satiric

Burns, Robert (1759–96). The henpeck'd husband. n.d.
Robert Burns. Poems and Songs, ed. James Kinsley (London: Oxford UP, 1969) 720.
satiric

Burns, Robert (1759–96). On marriage. n.d.

Robert Burns. *Poems and Songs*, ed. James Kinsley (London: Oxford UP, 1969) 718.
satire

Butler, Samuel (1613?–80). *Hudibras* III.i.522–1052. 1678.
Hudibras, ed. John Wilders (Oxford: Oxford UP, 1967) 205–19.
satiric

Butler, Samuel (1613?–80). Satyr upon marriage. 1759 (c. 1670).
Satires and Miscellaneous Poetry and Prose, ed. René Lamar. (Cambridge: Cambridge UP, 1928) 53–59.
satiric

Butler, Samuel (1613?–80). Satyr upon the licentious age of Charles the 2d. 1759 (c. 1670).
Satires and Miscellaneous Poetry and Prose, ed. René Lamar. (Cambridge UP, 1928) 40–45.
satiric

Byrom, John (1692–1763). To his wife. 1739.
The Poems of John Byrom, ed. Adolphus William Ward. 3 vols. in 5 (Manchester: Chetham Society, vol. 34, 1895) 2: 96–99.
laudatory

Byrom, John (1692–1763). On the marriage of Edward Greaves, esq. 1749.
The Poems of John Byrom, ed. Adolphus William Ward. 3 vols. in 5 (Manchester: Chetham Society, vol. 70, 1912) 3: 40–41.
appellant

Cambridge, Richard Owen (1717–1802). *Verses occasioned by the Marriage and the Game Act: both passed the same sessions. Written in the year 1753.* 1753.
Chalmers 18: 291. LEL 21797
witty

Carey, Henry (c. 1687–1743). The contended cuckold. 1737.
The Musical Century. 2 vols. (1737–40) 1: 4.
The Poems of Henry Carey, ed. Frederick T. Wood (London: Scholartis P, 1930) 128.
comic

Carey, Henry (c. 1687–1743). The disparity of youth and age. 1729.
Poems on Several Occasions (1729) 207.
The Poems of Henry Carey, ed. Frederick T. Wood (London: Scholartis P, 1930) 134.
ESTC T042634
EC reel 2744: 12
comic

Carey, Henry (c. 1687–1743). The happy butchers' wives. 1737.
The Musical Century. 2 vols. (1737–40) 1: 30.
The Poems of Henry Carey, ed. Frederick T. Wood (London: Scholartis P, 1930) 127.
comic

Carey, Henry (c. 1687–1743). The happy marriage. *Inscrib'd to Nathaniel Oldham, Esq.* 1729.
Poems on Several Occasions (1729) 107.
The Poems of Henry Carey, ed. Frederick T. Wood (London: Scholartis P, 1930) 200.
ESTC T042634
EC reel 2744: 12
laudatory

Carey, Henry (c. 1687–1743). The happy nuptials. 1733.
The Gentleman's Magazine 3 (November 1733) 599.
The Poems of Henry Carey, ed. Frederick T. Wood (London: Scholartis P, 1930) 74–75.
laudatory

Carey, Henry (c. 1687–1743). The nuptial day. 1734.
Britannia. An Entertainment given at Goodman's Fields Theatre, 11/2/1734.

The Musical Century. 2 vols. (1737–40) 2: 23.
The Poems of Henry Carey, ed. Frederick T. Wood (London: Scholartis P, 1930) 76.
celebratory

Carey, Henry (c. 1687–1743). The true woman's man. Inscrib'd to George Rivers, Esq. 1729.
Poems on Several Occasions (1729) 105–6.
The Poems of Henry Carey, ed. Frederick T. Wood (London: Scholartis P, 1930) 199.
ESTC T042634
EC reel 2744: 12
laudatory

Carey, Henry (c. 1687–1743). The wedding day. Sung by Master Osborne in *The Happy Nuptials.* 1733.
The Happy Nuptials. A Musical Entertainment given at Goodman's Fields Theatre, 12/11/1733.
The Poems of Henry Carey, ed. Frederick T. Wood (London: Scholartis P, 1930) 77.
laudatory

Cawthorn, James (1719–61). The temple of Hymen. A tale. Spoken at the anniversary, 1760. 1771.
Poems. By the Rev. Mr. Cawthorn. Late Master of Tunbridge School (1771) 153–71.
Chalmers 14: 251–54. LEL 21793
ESTC T002143
EC reel 1529: 05
satiric

Celibacy: or, good advice to young fellows to keep single . . . being an answer to matrimony; or, good advice to the ladies, &c. 1739.*
FOX C91
ESTC T131915
satiric

Centlivre or Carroll, Susannah (nee Hughes) (c. 1670–1723). A woman's case: in an epistle to Charles Joye, Esq; Deputy Governor of the South-sea. 1720.
FOX C97

ESTC N024952
appelant

Chatterton, Thomas (1752–70). The happy pair. 1770.
Printed with *The Revenge, a Burletta Acted at Marybone Gardens in 1770* (1795) 45–46.
Chalmers 15: 488. LEL 21794
ESTC T155263
celebratory

Chudleigh, Lady Mary (nee Lee) (1656–1710). The ladies defence: or, the bridewoman's counsellor answer'd: a poem in a dialogue between Sir John Brute, Sir William Loveall, Melissa, and a parson. 1701.*
WNG C3984
EEB reel 1863
satiric

Chudleigh, Lady Mary (nee Lee) (1656–1710). A dialogue between Alexis and Astrea. 1703.
Poems on Several Occasions. By Lady Chudleigh (1703) {1722} 37–39.
ESTC T097275
EC reel {2743: 05}
exemplary/satiric

Chudleigh, Lady Mary (nee Lee) (1656–1710). To the ladies. 1703.
Poems on Several Occasions. By Lady Chudleigh (1703) 40.
Fullard 101–2
ESTC T097275 {T097274}
EC reel {2743: 05}
satiric

Cleveland, John (1613–58). On an alderman who married a very young wife. 1651.
The Poems of John Cleveland, ed. Brian Morris and Eleanor Withington (Oxford: Clarendon P, 1967) 77–78.
satiric

Collier, Mary (1690?–1762). *The woman's labour: an epistle to Mr. Stephen Duck; in answer to his late poem, called The*

Checklist of Marriage Poems

Thresher's Labour. To which are added the three wise sentences taken from the first book of Esdras, ch. iii and iv. 1739.
ESTC T052659
EC reel 1638: 013
exemplary

Collier, Mary (1690?–1762). The happy husband, and the old bachelor. A dialogue. Winchester, 1762.
Poems on Several Occasions (Winchester, 1762) 33–40.
ESTC T125590
celebratory

Collier, Mary (1690?–1762). On the marriage of George III. Wrote in the seventy second year of her age. Winchester, 1762.
Poems on Several Occasions (Winchester, 1762) 60–62.
ESTC T125590
celebratory

Collier, Mary (1690?–1762). Spectator vol. the 5th. numb. 375. Versified. Winchester, 1762.
Poems on Several Occasions (Winchester, 1762) 54–59.
ESTC T125590
celebratory

Concanen (the Elder), Matthew (1701–49). To a jealous husband. 1724.
Miscellaneous Poems, Original and Translated by Several Hands; Published by Mr. Concanen (1724) 60–61.
ESTC T25249
EC reel 1427: 10
satiric

The Condition of Womankind. 1733.
The Gentleman's Magazine 3 (May 1733): 263.
Fullard 289
satiric

[Congreve, William (1670–1729), rev. and corrected] A satyr against love. 1703.
Rpr. by John Barnard, *BNYPL* 68 (May 1964): 308–22.
FOX S43

ESTC N021383
satiric

Cotton, Charles (1630–87). The joys of marriage. 1689.
Poems on Several Occasions (1689) 36–44.
Poems of Charles Cotton, ed. John Beresford (New York: Boni and Livright, n.d.) 318–22.
Chalmers 6: 737. LEL 21788
WNG C6389
EEB reel 274: 14
satiric

Cotton, Charles (1630–87). Martial lib. viii. ep. 35. 1689 (c. 1670).
Poems on Several Occasions (1689) 566.
Chalmers 6: 737. LEL 21788
WNG C6389
EEB reel 274: 14
witty

Cotton, Nathaniel (c. 1707–88). Marriage. Vision vii. 1751.
Visions in Verse for Entertainment and Instruction of Younger Minds (1751) {7th ed. (1767) 91–103}.
Chalmers 18: 39. LEL 21794
ESTC T125423 {T137983}
EC reel {3654: 01}
satiric/exemplary

Cowper, William (1731–1800). Mutual forbearance necessary to the happiness of the married state. 1782.
The Poems of William Cowper, ed. John D. Baird and Charles Ryskamp (Oxford: Clarendon P, 1980) 1: 427–29.
Chalmers 18: 657. LEL 21796
exemplary

Cowper, William (1731–1800). If John marries Mary, and Mary alone. 1824 (1780?).
The Poems of William Cowper, ed. John D. Baird and Charles Ryskamp (Oxford: Clarendon P, 1980) 1: 232.
comic

Cowper, William (1731–1800). Ode. Supposed to be written on the marriage of a friend. 1825 (1748–63).

The Poems of William Cowper, ed. John D. Baird and Charles Ryskamp (Oxford: Clarendon P, 1980) 1: 49–50.
celebratory

Cowper, William (1731–1800). Epigram on Thelyphthora. 1973 (1780).
The Poems of William Cowper, ed. John D. Baird and Charles Ryskamp (Oxford: Clarendon P, 1980) 1: 232.
ironic

Cowper, William (1731–1800). Happy the man whose amorous flame has found. 1973 (1748–63).
The Poems of William Cowper, ed. John D. Baird and Charles Ryskamp (Oxford: Clarendon P, 1980) 1: 50.
comic

Cowper, William (1731–1800). A new ballad intitled the sorrowfull husband's garland or the grey mare the better horse. 1973 (1748–63).
The Poems of William Cowper, ed. John D. Baird and Charles Ryskamp (Oxford: Clarendon P, 1980) 1: 51.
comic

The cuckold's curse, against the state of matrimony. and a satire, on my Lady Tinger a———se. Dublin, 1757.
ESTC T125575
satiric

D———. Epithalamium, by Mr. D———. 1758.
A Collection of Poems in Six Volumes; By Several Hands (1758) 5: 102–4.
ESTC T115890
EC reel 1844: 05
exemplary

Davenant, Sir William (1606–68). Epithalamium. The morning after the marriage of the Earl of Barrymore with Mrs. Martha Laurence. 1673.
The Works of Sr. William Davenant Kt . . . Now Published out of the Authors Original Copies (1673) 310–13.
WNG D320
EEB reel 207: 9
celebratory

Davenant, Sir William (1606–68). To Mistress E. S. married to an old usurer. 1673.
The Works of Sr. William Davenant Kt . . . Now Published out of the Authors Original Copies (1673) 322.
WNG D320
EEB reel 207: 9
satiric

Davenant, Sir William (1606–68). Upon the marriage of the Lady Jane Cavendish with Mr. Cheyney. 1673.
The Works of Sr. William Davenant Kt . . . Now Published out of the Authors Original Copies (1673) 293.
WNG D320
EEB reel 207: 9
celebratory

Davenant, Sir William (1606–68). Upon the nuptials of Charles Lord Herbert, and Lady M. Villers. 1673.
The Works of Sr. William Davenant Kt . . . Now Published out of the Authors Original Copies (1673) 238.
WNG D320
EEB reel 207: 9
celebratory

[Defoe, Daniel (1661?–1731)]. *Good advice to the ladies: shewing, that as the world goes and is like to go, the best way for them is to keep unmarried. By the author of the true-born Englishman.* 1702.
FOX G219
ESTC T068170
anti-satiric

The delights of marriage; being a collecion [sic] of elegant sayings, instructive and diverting, in prose and verse, of the most celebrated authors in praise of that divine institution. 1725?.
ESTC T124802
celebratory

Denham, Sir John (1615–69). Friend-

ship and single life against love and marriage. 1668.
Poems and Translations (1668) 82–88.
Chalmers 7: 246. LEL 21789
WNG D1005
EEB reel 207: 9
witty

Derrick, Samuel (1724–69). A defence of female inconstancy. In an epistle to Robert Tracy, of Coscomb, in Gloucestershire, esq. 1740.
A Collection of Original Poems by Samuel Derrick (1754) {1755} 115–22.
ESTC T135391 {T135392}
EC reel {3913: 03}
satiric

The divorce. 1779.
ESTC N007926
EC reel 1105: 05
satiric

[Dixon, Sarah] (fl. 1716–45). To Mrs. S———. An epigram. Canterbury, 1740.
Poems on Several Occasions (Canterbury, 1740) 46.
ESTC T042620
satiric

Dobbs, Francis (1750–1811). *Modern matrimony. A poem. To which is added, the disappointment. An elegy. By the author of The Irish Chief: or, The Patriot King*. 1773.
ESTC T010080
satiric/celebratory

Dodd, Dr. William (1729–77). To Mr. J———, on the report of Miss ———'s marriage. 1767.
Poems (1767) 117–20.
ESTC T095146
EC reel 2602: 02
elegiac

[Dorman, Joseph] (d. 1754). *The female rake: or, the modern fine lady. An epistle from Libertina to Sylvia. In which is contain'd the à la mode system*. [1735].
FOX D407
ESTC 122375
satiric

Drake, James (1667?–1707?). To the most ingenious Mrs. ——— on her admirable defense of her sex. 1696.
[Drake, Mrs. Judith; STC attributes to Mary Astell]. *An Essay in Defence of the Female Sex* (1696) [xiv–xv].
WNG A4058
EEB reel 9.
laudatory

Dryden, John (1631–1700). Prologue from *An Evening's Love*. 1671.
The Poems and Fables of John Dryden, ed. James Kinsley (London: Oxford UP, 1970) 122–23.
witty

Dryden, John (1631–1700). Epilogue from *Marriage à la Mode*. 1673.
The Poems and Fables of John Dryden, ed. James Kinsley (London: Oxford UP, 1970) 144–45.
witty

Dryden, John (1631–1700). Song from *Marriage à la Mode*. 1673.
The Poems and Fables of John Dryden, ed. James Kinsley (London: Oxford UP, 1970) 145.
witty

Dryden, John (1631–1700). Epilogue from *The Kind Keeper; or, Mr. Limberham: a Comedy*. 1680.
The Poems and Fables of John Dryden, ed. James Kinsley (London: Oxford UP, 1970) 174–75.
satiric

Dryden, John (1631–1700). Prologue spoken at *Mithridates*. 1681.
The Poems and Fables of John Dryden, ed. James Kinsley (London: Oxford UP, 1970) 185–86.
satiric

Dryden, John (1631–1700). Epilogue to *The Princess of Cleves*. 1684.
The Poems and Fables of John Dryden, ed.

James Kinsley (London: Oxford UP, 1970) 316–17.
satiric

Dryden, John (1631–1700). Prologue to a new play, call'd, *The Disappointment: or, The Mother in Fashion*. 1684.
The Poems and Fables of John Dryden, ed. James Kinsley (London: Oxford UP, 1970) 320–21.
satiric

Dryden, John (1631–1700). Eleonora: A panegyrical poem dedicated to the memory of the late Countess of Abingdon. 1692.
The Poems and Fables of John Dryden, ed. James Kinsley (London: Oxford UP, 1970) 475, lines 166–204.
laudatory

Dryden, John (1631–1700). Epilogue to *Henry the Second*. 1693.
The Poems and Fables of John Dryden, ed. James Kinsley (London: Oxford UP, 1970) 482.
didactic

Dryden, John (1631–1700). An epitaph on Lady Whitmore. 1693.
The Poems and Fables of John Dryden, ed. James Kinsley (London: Oxford UP, 1970) 488.
laudatory

Dryden, John (1631–1700). Epilogue from *Love Triumphant*. 1694.
The Poems and Fables of John Dryden, ed. James Kinsley (London: Oxford UP, 1970) 493–94.
satiric

Dryden, John (1631–1700). Baucis and Philemon. Out of the eighth book of Ovid's *Metamorphoses*. 1700.
The Poems and Fables of John Dryden, ed. James Kinsley (London: Oxford UP, 1970) 641–46.
laudatory

Dryden, John (1631–1700). Epilogue from *The Pilgrim*. 1700.
The Poems and Fables of John Dryden, ed. James Kinsley (London: Oxford UP, 1970) 833–35.
satiric

Dryden, John (1631–1700). The monument of a fair maiden lady, who dy'd in Bath, and is there interr'd. 1700.
The Poems and Fables of John Dryden, ed. James Kinsley (London: Oxford UP, 1970) 814–15, esp. lines 19–20.
laudatory

Dryden, John (1631–1700). To my honour'd kinsman, John Driden, of Chesterton in the county of Huntingdon, Esquire. 1700.
The Poems and Fables of John Dryden, ed. James Kinsley (London: Oxford UP, 1970) 605–10, esp. lines 16–30 and 96–116.
laudatory

Dryden, John (1631–1700). On the marriage of the fair and vertuous lady, Mrs. Anastasia Stafford, with that truly worthy and pious gent. George Holman, Esq. A pindarique ode. 1813 (1686–88?).
The Poems and Fables of John Dryden, ed. James Kinsley (London: Oxford UP, 1970) 850–52.
laudatory

Dubois, Lady Dorothea (nee Annesley) (1728–74). A dialogue song. Dublin, 1764.
Poems on Several Occasions by a Lady of Quality (Dublin, 1764) 122.
ESTC T142034
didactic

Dubois, Lady Dorothea (nee Annesley) (1728–74). An emblematic tale. Dublin, 1764.
Poems on Several Occasions by a Lady of Quality (Dublin, 1764) 107–14.
ESTC T142034
didactic

Dubois, Lady Dorothea (nee Annesley)

(1728–74). Ode on the marriage and coronation of their most sacred majesty King George III and Queen Charlotte. Dublin, 1764.
Poems on Several Occasions by a Lady of Quality (Dublin, 1764) 32–37.
ESTC T142034
celebratory

Dubois, Lady Dorothea (nee Annesley) (1728–74). Song. Dublin, 1764.
Poems on Several Occasions by a Lady of Quality (Dublin, 1764) 102.
ESTC T142034
didactic

Dubois, Lady Dorothea (nee Annesley) (1728–74). A true tale. Dublin, 1764.
Poems on Several Occasions by a Lady of Quality (Dublin, 1764) 1–27.
ESTC T142034
didactic

Duck, Stephen (1705–56). *Alrick and Isabel: or, the unhappy marriage. A poem.* 1740.
ESTC T021304
exemplary

[D'Urfey, Thomas] (1653–1723). *The malecontent; a satyr.* 1684.
WNG D2748
EEB reel 490
satiric

The duty of a husband: or, the lady's answer to the duty of a wife. 1707?
FOX D562
ESTC N007513
exemplary

Egerton, Sarah Fyge (1670–1723). The repulse to Alcander. 1703.
Poems on Several Occasions, together with a Pastoral (1703) 25–27.
Lonsdale 27–28
ESTC T125148
EC reel 1406: 26
satiric

Egerton, Sarah Fyge (1670–1723). The emulation. 1703.
Poems on Several Occasions, together with a Pastoral (1703) 108–9.

Lonsdale 31–32
ESTC T125148
EC reel 1406: 26
satiric

Egerton, Sarah Fyge (1670–1723). On my wedding day. 1703.
Poems on Several Occasions, together with a Pastoral (1703) 70–72.
ESTC T125148
EC reel 1406: 26
elegiac

Egerton, Sarah Fyge (1670–1723). To Orabella, marry'd to an old man. 1703.
Poems on Several Occasions, together with a Pastoral (1703) 36–37.
ESTC T125148
EC reel 1406: 26
satiric

Eliza (pen name). To my husband. 1652.
Eliza's Babes: or the Virgins-Offering (1652) 46–47.
Greer 144–45
WNG E526
EEB reel 142: 10
elegiac

Ephelia (Philips, Mrs. Joan) (fl. 1679) To a gentleman that had left a vertuous lady for a miss. 1679.
Female Poems on Several Occasions (1679) 75–77.
WNG P2030
EEB reel 645: 16
satiric

An epithalamium. By a lady. 1731.
The Flower-Piece. A Collection of Miscellany Poems, ed. M. Concanen (1731) 237–39.
Fullard 110–11
ESTC T102877
advisory masked as celebratory

Fawkes, Francis (1720–77) A good wife. 1761.
Original Poems and Translations (1761) 92–94.
Chalmers 16: 247. LEL 21795

ESTC T146589
celebratory

Female apostacy: or, the true-born English-woman: a satyr. 1705.
FOX 86
satiric

Female chastity, truth, and sanctity: satire. 1735.
FOX F88
ESTC T107764
satiric

The female dunces, inscrib'd to Mr. Pope. 1733.
FOX F91
ESTC T035477
satiric

The female monster or, the second part of the world turn'd topsy turvey. A satyr. 1705.
FOX F97
ESTC T000193
satiric

Female qualifications: or, jilts and hypocrites portray'd. A satire, chiefly occasion'd by two pieces, publish'd not long since. The one entitled, woman not inferior to man; and the other woman's superior excellence to man. 1741.
FOX F90
ESTC T166060
satiric

Fenton, Elijah (1683–1730). The widow's wife. A tale. 1717.
Poems on Several Occasions (1717) 128–34.
Chalmers 10: 408. LEL 21791
ESTC T140950
EC reel 1881: 01
witty

Fido, to his bride—written on their wedding day. A sort of epithalamium. 1736.
The Gentleman's Magazine 6 (April 1736): 224.
comic/celebratory

The fifteen comforts of a wanton wife: or, the fool well fitted. Dedicated to the London-cuckolds. 1706/7 i.e. 1707.

ESTC N006484
satiric

The fifteen comforts of matrimony. Or, a looking glass for all those who have enter'd in that holy comfortable state. Wherein are sum'd up all those blessings that attend a married life. Dedicated to batchelors and widdowrs. 1706.
FOX F128
ESTC T183105
satiric

Finch, Anne. See Winchilsea.

Flatman, Thomas (1637–88). The batchelors song. 1674 {1686}.
Poems and Songs, 4th ed. (1686) 120–21.
WNG F1151
EEB reel 379: 40
satiric

Flatman, Thomas (1637–88). The second part, song. 1674 {1686}.
Poems and Songs, 4th ed. (1686) 121.
WNG F1151
EEB reel 379: 40
comic

[Forbes, William, of Disblair] (d. 1714). An essay upon marriage in a letter addressed to a friend. Edinburgh, 1704.
FOX F185
satiric

Gay, John (1685–1732). The espousal. A sober eclogue. Between two of the people called Quakers. 1720.
Poems on Several Occasions, 2 vols. bound as one (1720) 372–368, i.e., 378.
Poetry and Prose, ed. Vinton A. Dearing and Charles E. Beckwith (Oxford: Clarendon P, 1974) 1: 241–44.
T013893
comic

G[lanvil], A[braham], Gent. (n.d.). *The rake reform'd: a poem. In a letter to the rakes of the town.* 1718 [1717].
FOX G171
T138948
exemplary/satiric

Glanvil, John (n.d.). *The happy pair. a new song, sung by Mr. Abell.* [1701?]
ESTC T001567
EC reel 3877: 13
celebratory

Glover, Jean (1758–1801). O'er the muir amang the heather. 1792.
recorded by Robert Burns
Fullard 136–37, 555
celebratory

Golden Garland. n.d.
Samuel Pepys' Penny Merriments, ed. Roger Thompson (New York: Columbia UP, 1977) 286–87.
satiric

Good advice to beaus and batchelours, in answer to good advice to the ladies. By the author of a tale of a tub. 1705.
FOX G218
satiric

A good wife and a bad one. 1709.
The Batchelor's Banquet; or, the Maid's Delight: containing Select Poems on Several Subjects. . . . (1709).
comic

Gould, Robert (d. 1709?). A consolatory epistle to a friend made unhappy by marriage. Or, a scourge for ill wives. 1688/9.*
Poems Chiefly Consisting of Satyrs and Satyrical Epistles (1688/9) 233–49.
WNG G1431
EEB reel 598
satiric

The happy marriage: an eclogue. In imitation of Virgil's Tityrus. With other poems. 1733.
FOX H44
ESTC N001161
exemplary

The happy marriage. Salisbury, [1785?].
ESTC T035987
EC reel 1912: 055
celebratory

Herbert, Nicholas, The Hon. (1706?–1775). Marriage à la mode: or the two sparrows. A fable. 1758. An adaptation of fable 21 from book 4 of Antoine Houdar De La Motte (1672–1731).
A Collection of Poems in Six Volumes; By Several Hands (1758) 3: 205–8.
ESTC T115893
EC reel 1844:05
exemplary

Hill, Aaron (1685–1750). Epitaph on a man and wife, who were buried together and represented quarrelling on their grave. Translated from the Latin. 1726.
Miscellaneous Poems and Translations by Several Hands, Publish'd by Richard Savage (1726) 88.
The Works of the Late Aaron Hill, 4 vols. (1753) 4: 128.
ESTC T107059
EC reel 2448: 01
comic

Hill, Aaron (1685–1750). Epitaph, on a young lady who died unmarried. 1753.
The Works of the Late Aaron Hill, 4 vols. (1753) 3: 344.
ESTC T107059
EC reel 2448: 01
elegiac

Hill, Aaron (1685–1750). To Miranda, after marriage; with Mr. Lock's Treatise on Education. 1753.
The Works of the Late Aaron Hill, 4 vols. (1753) 3: 343.
ESTC T107059
EC reel 2448: 01
advisory

Hill, Aaron (1685–1750). The wedding day. 1753.
The Works of the Late Aaron Hill, 4 vols. (1753) 3: 172–75.
ESTC T107059
EC reel 2448: 01
celebratory

Holmes, Ann (n.d.) An epic poem on Adam and Eve. Bedale, 1800.
An Epic Poem on Adam and Eve. With

Poetry, on Two Ladies in Disguise. A Short Pastoral: also the Soliloquy of a Young Lady; Together with a Poem, an Elegy, and a Vindication of Fate in Marriage: to Which Is Added Rules for Polite Behaviour (Bedale, 1800) 2–15.
ESTC T125699
celebratory

Howard, Edward (1624–c.1700). The wife. 1673.
Poems, and Essays: with a Paraphrase on Cicero's Laelius, or Of Friendship. Written in Heroick Verse by a Gentleman of Quality (1673) 22–23.
WNG H2973
exemplary/satiric

Ill news after marriage. To Miss E———ds. An ode. 1743.
Court Whispers: or, a Magazine of Wit. A Satyr for the Country (1743) 33–35.
witty

Irwin, Anne (1696–1764). An epistle to Mr. Pope occasioned by his Characters of Women. 1736.
The Gentleman's Magazine 6 (Dec. 1736): 745.
Fullard 303–5
satiric

Jackson, Samuel (n.d.). The duty of a wife. 1707.
FOX J12
ESTC N007566
exemplary

Jago, Richard (1715–81). Female empire. A true history. 1784.
Poems, Moral and Descriptive (1784) 174–76.
ESTC T126611
satiric

Jeffreys, George, Esq. (1678–1755) The happy pair; occasioned by the wedding of the Right Hon. the Lord and Lady Carnarvon, on the 22nd of March 1753. 1754.
Miscellanies in Verse and Prose (1754) 397–99.
ESTC N010051
EC reel 1285: 02
laudatory

Jemmat, Catherine (nee Yeo) (fl. 1752–71). The rural lass. 1750. 1766.
Miscellanies in Prose and Verse. By Mrs. Catherine Jemmat. Daughter of the Late Admiral Yeo, of Plymouth and Author of Her Own Memoirs (1766) 58–62.
Fullard 120–22
Lonsdale 235–37
ESTC T039452
EC reel 1541: 39
pastoral

Jemmat, Catherine (nee Yeo) (fl. 1752–71). An Epigram. 1766.
Miscellanies in Prose and Verse. By Mrs. Catherine Jemmat. Daughter of the Late Admiral Yeo, of Plymouth and Author of Her Own Memoirs (1766) 132.
Fullard 319
ESTC T039452
EC reel 1541: 39
comic/celebratory

Jemmat, Catherine (nee Yeo) (fl. 1752–71). On Lady Juverna's last marriage. 1766.
Miscellanies in Prose and Verse. By Mrs. Catherine Jemmat. Daughter of the Late Admiral Yeo, of Plymouth and Author of Her Own Memoirs (1766) 179–80.
ESTC T039452
EC reel 1541: 39
comic

Jemmat, Catherine (nee Yeo) (fl. 1752–71). On the marriage of a handsome couple. 1766.
Miscellanies in Prose and Verse. By Mrs. Catherine Jemmat. Daughter of the Late Admiral Yeo, of Plymouth and Author of Her Own Memoirs (1766) 191.
ESTC T039452
EC reel 1541: 39
comic

Jemmat, Catherine (nee Yeo) (fl. 1752–71). The reply. 1755.

The Gentleman's Magazine 25 (May 1755) 230.
Miscellanies in Prose and Verse. By Mrs. Catherine Jemmat. Daughter of the Late Admiral Yeo, of Plymouth and Author of Her Own Memoirs (1766) 82–83.
ESTC T039452
EC reel 1541: 39
comic

Jemmat, Catherine (nee Yeo) (fl. 1752–71). Verses, written to a friend on his marriage. 1755.
The Gentleman's Magazine 25 (May 1755) 230.
Miscellanies in Prose and Verse. By Mrs. Catherine Jemmat. Daughter of the Late Admiral Yeo, of Plymouth and Author of Her Own Memoirs (1766) 81.
ESTC T039452
EC reel 1541: 39
comic

Jenyns, Soame (1704–87). The modern fine lady. 1751.
Poems. by ***** (1751) 63–70.
Chalmers 17: 598. LEL 21796
ESTC T054035
EC reel 3413: 04
satiric

John & his mistris. n.d.
Samuel Pepys' Penny Merriments, ed. Roger Thompson (New York: Columbia UP, 1977) 277–79.
satiric

Jones, Mary (d. 1778). Ode on the Rt. Hon. Lady Henry Beauclerk on her marriage. 1757.
Poems by Eminent Ladies, 2 vols. (1755) 1: 311.
ESTC T042592
celebratory

K., Dr. Upon marriage. 1708.
Oxford and Cambridge Miscellany Poems, ed. Elijah Fenton (1708) 258–62.
ESTC T145730
celebratory

Kelly, Mrs. Isabella (nee Fordyce, later Hedgeland) (c. 1759?–1857). To a wandering husband, from a deserted wife. 1794.
A Collection of Poems and Fables (1794) 27–29.
ESTC T122123
EC reel 3984: 19
appellant

The ladies choice: A poem. 1702.*
FOX L9
ESTC T129669
exemplary/satiric

Langhorne, John (1735–79). Precepts of conjugal happiness addressed to a lady on her marriage. 1767 {1769}.
Chalmers 16: 437. LEL 21795
ESTC {T044180}
EC reel {1463: 09}
exemplary

Leapor, Mary (1722–46). An essay on woman. 1751 (1746).
Poems, 2nd ed. (1751) 64–67.
Lonsdale 207–8
ESTC T136743
EC reel 38411: 07
satiric

[Legh, George] (n.d.) *The clergyman's choice of a wife, delineated. In a letter to Dr. C. in England. Wherein are several important queries. by a foreign bishop, now residing and preaching in his diocese in Terra Incognita.* 1738.*
FOX L94
ESTC T084834
satiric

Leigh, Richard (c. 1649–1728). The union of friendship. 1675.
Poems upon Several Occasions (1675) 80–83.
Poems by Richard Leigh, rpr. and intro. by Hugh Macdonald (Oxford: Basil Blackwell, 1947) 49–51.
WNG 9
EC reel 605: 4
witty

Lewis, Esther (later Clark) (fl. 1747–89).
    Advice to a young lady lately married. 1752.
    The Gentleman's Magazine 22 (May 1752) 234–35.
    Poems Moral and Entertaining (1789) 83–87.
    ESTC N012302
    EC reel 1494:26
    didactic
The London ladies dressing-room: or, the shopkeepers wives inventory. A satyr. Written by the author of The True-born Englishman. 1705.
    FOX L238
    satiric
The lost maidenhead, or Sylvia's farewell to love; a new satyr against man. 1691.
    WNG L3081
    satiric
Love for love: or, a dialogue between a loving husband and a virtuous wife . . . [170?].*
    FOX L283
    ESTC N003064
    exemplary
Lovibond, Edward (1724–75). To lady F———, on her marriage. 1785.
    Poems on Several Occasions (1785) 114–16.
    Chalmers 16: 298. LEL 21795
    ESTC T025408
    exemplary
The maid's soliloquy. In imitation of Cato. 1798. *Gretna Green, or, Cupid's Introduction to the Temple of Hymen; Describing Many Curious Scenes, Love Anecdotes, and Characters, Prose and Verse. Calculated for the Entertainment of Both Sexes* (1798) 47.
    See also Single, Cupid and Hymen . . . (1746) 22–23.
    satiric
Mantovano, Giovanni Baptista Spagnoli (1448–1516). *Alphus: or, the fourth eclogue of Baptist Mantuan, a Carmelite; being a satyr against women. Done into English verse by William Bewick.* 1718.
    FOX B207
    ESTC N029873
    satiric
Mariott, Thomas (n.d.). *Female conduct: being an essay on the art of pleasing. To be practiced by the fair sex, before and after marriage. A poem, in two books. Humbly dedicated, to her Royal Highness the Princess of Wales. Inscribed to Plautilla.* 1759.
    ESTC N008154
    exemplary
Marriage a satire: with two satires on love and old age. 1728.
    ESTC T061540
    EC reel 2965: 12
    satiric
Marriage à la mode: an humorous tale, in six canto's, in hudibrastic verse; being an explanation of the six prints lately published by the ingenious Mr. Hogarth. 1746.
    ESTC T061540
    EC reel 2965: 12
    satiric
The marriage of the myrtle and the yew. A fable. To Delia, about to marry beneath herself. 1744. {1758}.
    A Collection of Poems in Six Volumes; By Several Hands (1758) 3: 265–68.
    ESTC T115893
    EC reel 1844: 04
    exemplary
Marriage. A warning poem. Addressed to those in humble life. Glasgow, 1797?*
    Poetry; Original and Selected (Glasgow, 1797) 2: 1–4.
    ESTC T042673
    EC reel 2592:08
    satiric
The married man's best portion. [1670–77].*
    Douce Ballads
    WNG M711
    celebratory
The married man's lament; or, fairly shot of her. To which are added, the butcher's daughter,

the roving young man, the complaint of the poor. [Newcastle? 1800?].
ESTC T039003
EC reel 871: 08
satiric

The married mans complaint who took a shrow instead of a saint. [1680].*
Douce Ballads
satiric

Marvell, Andrew (1622–78). The Garden. 1681.
Miscellaneous Poems (1681) 48–51.
The Poems and Letters of Andrew Marvell. Ed. H. M. Margoliouth. 2nd ed. 2 vols. (Oxford: Clarendon P, 1952) 1: 48–50.
WNG M872
pastoral/philosophic

Matrimonial advice. An epistle from Senex to his neice. 1736.
The Gentleman's Magazine 6 (July 1736): 418.
advisory

The matrimonial garland, containing several excellent new songs. [Newcastle? 1770?].
ESTC T039047
EC reel 897: 36
celebratory

Matrimony, pro and con: or, the resolve. 1745.*
FOX M138
satiric and anti-satiric

Mitchell, Joseph (1684–1738). A picture of Hymen, or matrimony à la mode: a tale. 1729.
Poems on Several Occasions, 2 vols. (1729) 2: 211–16.
ESTC T118847
exemplary/satiric

Mitchell, Joseph (1684–1738). To a young lady, on her marriage with an old gentleman. 1729.
Poems on Several Occasions, 2 vols. (1729) 1: 240–41.
ESTC T118847
elegiac

Mitchell, Joseph (1684–1738). To an humourist, who married a most ugly superannuated maid. 1729.
Poems on Several Occasions, 2 vols. (1729) 1: 299–302.
ESTC T118847
satiric

Mitchell, Joseph (1684–1738). Verses on a friend's marriage. 1729.
Poems on Several Occasions, 2 vols. (1729) 2: 296–98.
ESTC T118847
comic/celebratory

Mitchell, Joseph (1684–1738). Verses to the right honourable the Lady Sommerville, on her marriage. 1729.
Poems on Several Occasions, 2 vols. (1729) 1: 366–69.
ESTC T118847
celebratory

Modern matrimony. A satire to a young nobleman. 1737.*
FOX M376
ESTC N005005
satiric

Monck, Mary (nee Molesworth) (c. 1678–1715). Verses written on her death-bed at Bath, to her husband in London. 1755.
Poems by Eminent Ladies, 2 vols. (1755) 2: 195.
Fullard 102–3
ESTC T042592
elegiac

Moncreiff, John (fl. 1748–67). *Themistocles. A satire on modern marriage.* 1759.
ESTC T036871
EC reel 2766: 01
satiric

Montagu, Lady Mary Wortley (nee Pierrepont) (1689–1762). Friday: the toilette. Lydia. 1716. 1747.
Town Eclogues (1747).
Essays and Poems and Simplicity, a Comedy, ed. Robert Halsband and Isobel Grundy (Oxford: Clarendon P, 1977) 198–200.

Fullard 293–94
elegiac/satiric

Montagu, Lady Mary Wortley (nee Pierrepont) (1689–1762). Epithalamium. 1803 (before 1739).
Essays and Poems and Simplicity, a Comedy, ed. Robert Halsband and Isobel Grundy (Oxford: Clarendon P, 1977) 299.
satiric

Montagu, Lady Mary Wortley (nee Pierrepont) (1689–1762). Epistle from Mrs. Yonge to her husband. 1972 (1724).
Essays and Poems and Simplicity, a Comedy, ed. Robert Halsband and Isobel Grundy (Oxford: Clarendon P, 1977) 230–32.
The Norton Anthology of English Literature, 5th ed. (New York: Norton, 1986) 1: 1974–76.
pathetic/satiric

Montagu, Lady Mary Wortley (nee Pierrepont) (1689–1762). A satyr. 1977 (1718).
Essays and Poems and Simplicity, a Comedy, ed. Robert Halsband and Isobel Grundy (Oxford: Clarendon P, 1977) 210–14.
satiric

Moore, Edward (1712–57) and Henry Brooke (1703?–83). *Fables for the Female Sex*. 1744 {1754}.
ESTC T145050 {T078518}
EC reel {638:07}
didactic

Mysogynus, or a satyr upon women. 1682.
WNG M3178
EEB reel 1336: 16
satiric

[Newcomb, Thomas] (1682–1765). *The woman of taste. Occasioned by a late poem, entitled, The Man of Taste. By a friend of the author's. In two epistles, from Clelia in town to Sapho in the country*. 1733.
ESTC T003179
EC reel 1464: 09
satiric

Newman, Hugh (n.d.). A poem in praise of marrying for love. 1698.
WNG P2675
EEB reel 296: 6
laudatory

Of marriage. 1689.
The Parallel: an Essay on Friendship, Love and Marriage (1689) 11–13.
WNG P333
EEB reel 645: 2
satiric

Oldham, John (1653–83). A satyr upon a woman, who by her falshood and scorn was the death of my friend. 1686.
The Works of John Oldham. 1686. Repr. Ken Robinson (Delmar, N.Y.: Scholars' Facsimiles & Reprints, 1979). 1: 139–48.
satiric

Oldham, John (1653–83). Upon the marriage of the Prince of Orange with the Lady Mary. 1686.
The Works of John Oldham. 1686. Repr. Ken Robinson (Delmar, N.Y.: Scholars' Facsimiles & Reprints, 1979). Remains: 35–42.
satiric

On a Country Squire's Wedding. 1736.
The Gentleman's Magazine 6 (May 1736): 285.
satiric

On Infidelity. 1733.
The Gentleman's Magazine 3 (May 1733) 262.
satiric

Overbury, Sir Thomas (1581–1613). *The wife, a poem. Express'd in a compleat wife*. 1614 {1709}.
ESTC T052492
A Collection of the Best English Poetry, 2 vols. (1717).
FOX 0252

CASE 294
ESTC T000071
exemplary
[Overbury, Thomas] (1581–1613). *The husband, a poem expressed in a compleat man.* 1614 {1710}.
ESTC {T036871}
EC reel {1462: 29}
exemplary

A Paraphrase on part of the character of a good wife, as presented in the last chapter of the Book of Proverbs. 1736.
The Gentleman's Magazine 6 (June 1736): 349–50.
celebratory/advisory

Parker, Martin, trans. (d. 1656?) Wormwood lectures. 1682.
Samuel Pepys' Penny Merriments, ed. Roger Thompson (New York: Columbia UP, 1977) 264–65.
satiric

Parnell, Thomas (1679–1718), Archdeacon of Clogher. Hesiod: or, the rise of woman. 1722.
Poems on Several Occasions by Dr. Thomas Parnell (Dublin, 1722) {1726} 5–16.
ESTC T042653 {T042652}
EC reel {1875: 03}
satiric

Philips, Katherine (1631–64). To my dear sister, Mrs. C. P. on her nuptial. 1664.
Poems (1664) 52–53.
WNG P2032
EEB reel 268: 8
celebratory

Philips, Katherine (1631–64). Rosannia's private marriage. 1664.
Poems (1664) 106–8.
WNG P2032
EEB reel 268: 8
celebratory

Pilkington, Laetitia (nee Van Lewen) (c. 1708?–50). Consolatory verses to her husband. 1748.
Poems by Eminent Ladies, 2 vols. (1755) 2: 254.

ESTC T042592
advisory

Pilkington, Laetitia (nee Van Lewen) (c. 1708?–50). The happy pair: a ballad. 1748.
The Memoirs of Mrs. Laetitia Pilkington . . . Written by Herself. Wherein Are Occasionally Interspersed All Her Poems, with Anecdotes of Several Eminent Persons Living and Dead, 3 vols. (Dublin, repr. London, 1748–54; repr. London: Routledge, 1928) 1: 272–74.
Fullard 117–18
ESTC T141022
EC reel 951: 08
celebratory

[Plaxton, W.] (n.d.). Advice to new-married husbands, in hudibrastick verse. 1712.*
FOX P479
comic

The pleasures of a single life, or, the miseries of matrimony. Occasionally writ upon the many divorces lately granted by Parliament. 1701.*
ESTC T054238
EC reel 1640: 04
satiric

Poetical impertinence: or, advice unask'd. In two poems, the good wife and the good husband. 1752.
ESTC T011329
EC reel 3665: 02
exemplary

Pointon, Priscilla (later Pickering) (c. 1740–1801). Letter to a sister, giving an account of the author's wedding day. 1794 (c. 1788).
Poems (Birmingham, 1794) 1: 20–23.
Lonsdale 275–76
ESTC T125991
celebratory

Pomfret, John (1667–1702). On the marriage of the Earl of A—— with the Countess of S——. 1702.

Miscellany Poems on Several Occasions
[1702] {2nd ed. with additions (1707) 180–86}.
Chalmers 8: 233–34. LEL 21789
ESTC {N006151}
EC reel {1291: 04}
celebratory

Pomfret, John (1667–1702). To his friend inclined to marry. 1702.
Miscellany Poems on Several Occasions
[1702] {2nd ed. with additions (1707) 119–20}.
Chalmers 8: 319. LEL 21789
ESTC {N006151}
EC reel {1291: 04}
exemplary

Pope, Alexander (1688–1744). Epistle to Miss Blount, with the works of Voiture. 1712.
Poems 170, esp. lines 31–80.
satiric

Pope, Alexander (1688–1744). The rape of the lock. 1714.
Poems 230, esp. lines 157–58.
satiric

Pope, Alexander (1688–1744). A Roman Catholic version of the first psalm. For the use of a young lady. 1716.
Poems 300.
exemplary

Pope, Alexander (1688–1744). Eloisa to Abelard. 1717.
Poems 252–61, esp. 254, lines 73–98; 256, lines 151–54.
elegiac

Pope, Alexander (1688–1744). Epilogue to *Jane Shore*. Design'd for Mrs. Oldfield. 1717.
Poems 213–14.
witty/exemplary

Pope, Alexander (1688–1744). Two chorus's to *The Tragedy of Brutus*. ii. Chorus of youths and virgins. 1717.
Poems 297–98.
celebratory

Pope, Alexander (1688–1744). The happy life of a country parson. 1727.
Poems 15.
celebratory

Pope, Alexander (1688–1744). Verses on Gulliver's Travels. iv. Mary Gulliver to Captain Lemuel Gulliver. 1727.
Poems 486–88.
satiric

Pope, Alexander (1688–1744). Epistle iv. To Richard Boyle, Earl of Burlington. 1731.
Poems 588, lines 9–12.
satiric

Pope, Alexander (1688–1744). Verses to be placed under the picture of England's arch-poet. Containing a compleat catalogue of his works. 1732.
Poems 495, lines 25–34.
satiric

Pope, Alexander. Epistle iii. To Allen Lord Bathurst. 1733.
Poems 572, lines 21–28; 582, lines 275–82; 585, lines 375–401.
satiric

Pope, Alexander (1688–1744). An essay on man; Epistle iv. 1733–34.
Poems 541, lines 166–85.
satiric?

Pope, Alexander (1688–1744). The first satire of the second book of Horace imitated. 1733.
Poems 614, lines 15–18.
satiric

Pope, Alexander (1688–1744). The fourth satire of Dr. John Donne, Dean of St. Paul's, versifyed. 1733.
Poems 683–84, lines 148–57.
satiric

Pope, Alexander (1688–1744). The second satire of the second book of Horace paraphrased. 1734.
Poems 620, lines 45–60; 624, lines 161–64.
satiric

Pope, Alexander (1688–1744). Sober
advice from Horace, to the young
gentlemen about town. 1734.
Poems 667–73.
satiric

Pope, Alexander (1688–1744). Epistle ii.
To a lady. Of the characters of
women. 1735.
Poems 559–69.
satiric

Pope, Alexander (1688–1744). Epistle to
Dr. Arbuthnot. 1735.
Poems 598, lines 25–26; 611, lines 383–
405.
satiric

Pope, Alexander (1688–1744). Epitaph on
John Knight. 1736.
Poems 823, esp. line 4.
exemplary

Pope, Alexander (1688–1744). The first
epistle of the second book of Horace
imitated. To Augustus. 1737.
Poems 641, lines 161–74.
satiric

Pope, Alexander (1688–1744). Epilogue to
the satires: dialogue ii. 1738.
Poems 698, lines 105–9; 699, lines 133–
35.
satiric

Pope, Alexander (1688–1744). The first
epistle of the first book of Horace
imitated. 1738.
Poems 628–29, lines 134–60.
satiric

Pope, Alexander (1688–1744). The sixth
epistle of the first book of Horace
imitated. 1738.
Poems 632, lines 77–80.
satiric

Pope, Alexander (1688–1744). The
seventh epistle of the first book of
Horace. Imitated in the manner of
Dr. Swift. 1739.
Poems 666, lines 59–80.
satiric

Pope, Alexander (1688–1744). To Mr. C.
St. James's Palace. London, October 22. 1774 (1730?).
Poems 810, esp. lines 9–12.
witty

Portal, Abraham (n.d.). *Nuptial Elegies*. 3rd
ed. 1775.
celebratory

[Prior, Matthew] (1664–1721). To a young
gentleman in love. A tale. 1702.
The Literary Works of Matthew Prior, ed.
H. Bunker Wright and Monroe K.
Spears, 2nd ed., 2 vols. (Oxford:
Clarendon P, 1971) 1: 193–95.
FOX O1088
witty

Prior, Matthew (1664–1721). The wedding
night. 1704.
The Literary Works of Matthew Prior, ed.
H. Bunker Wright and Monroe K.
Spears, 2nd ed., 2 vols. (Oxford:
Clarendon P, 1971) 1: 213.
celebratory

Prior, Matthew (1664–1721). Paulo Purganti and his wife: an honest, but a
simple pair. 1709.
The Literary Works of Matthew Prior, ed.
H. Bunker Wright and Monroe K.
Spears, 2nd ed., 2 vols. (Oxford:
Clarendon P, 1971) 1: 259–64.
witty

Prior, Matthew (1664–1721). A hymn to
Venus, upon a marriage. 1907 (1690?).
The Literary Works of Matthew Prior, ed.
H. Bunker Wright and Monroe K.
Spears, 2nd ed., 2 vols. (Oxford:
Clarendon P, 1971) 1: 106–7.
celebratory

Prior, Matthew (1664–1721). To Mr.
Charles Montagu, on his marriage
with the Right Honorable the Countess of Manchester. 1907 (1688).
The Literary Works of Matthew Prior, ed.
H. Bunker Wright and Monroe K.
Spears, 2nd ed., 2 vols. (Oxford:

Clarendon P, 1971) 1: 61–63.
celebratory

Prior, Matthew (1664–1721). To the E of
D. upon his marriage. 1907 (1685).
The Literary Works of Matthew Prior, ed.
H. Bunker Wright and Monroe K.
Spears, 2nd ed., 2 vols. (Oxford:
Clarendon P, 1971) 1: 3–6.
celebratory

The progress of matrimony (in 4 cantos). 1733.
The Palace Miscellany (1733) 23–58.
CASE 385
comic

The rake in fetters or, the marriage mousetrap.
Edinburgh?, 17—.*
FOX R9
satiric

Ramsay, Allan (1686–1758). On the marriage of Urban and Bella. July 10th, 1721.
The Works of Allan Ramsay, ed. Alexander M. Kinghorn and Alexander Law, 3 vols. (1961; New York: Johnson, 1972) 3: 160–61.
celebratory

Ramsay, Allan (1686–1758). The Generous Gentlemen. 1724–29.
The Tea-Table Miscellany (1724–29).
The Works of Allan Ramsay, ed. Alexander M. Kinghorn and Alexander Law, 3 vols. (1961; New York: Johnson, 1972) 3: 64–65.
celebratory

Ramsay, Allan (1686–1758). My Dady forbad, my Minny forbad. 1724–29.
The Tea-Table Miscellany (1724–29).
The Works of Allan Ramsay, ed. Alexander M. Kinghorn and Alexander Law, 3 vols. (1961; New York: Johnson, 1972) 3: 44–45.
elegiac

Ramsay, Allan (1686–1758). On the marriage of the R. H. L. G——— and L. K——— C———. A song. 1724–29.

The Tea-Table Miscellany (1724–29).
The Works of Allan Ramsay, ed. Alexander M. Kinghorn and Alexander Law, 3 vols. (1961; New York: Johnson, 1972) 3: 59–61.
celebratory

Ramsay, Allan (1686–1758). Song ("Busk ye, busk ye, my bony bride"). 1724–29.
The Tea-Table Miscellany (1724–29).
The Works of Allan Ramsay, ed. Alexander M. Kinghorn and Alexander Law, 3 vols. (1961; New York: Johnson, 1972) 3: 55.
celebratory

Ramsay, Allan (1686–1758). Song ("O Mither dear, i 'gin to fear"). 1724–29.
The Tea-Table Miscellany (1724–29).
The Works of Allan Ramsay, ed. Alexander M. Kinghorn and Alexander Law, 3 vols. (1961; New York: Johnson, 1972) 3: 53–54.
elegiac

Ramsay, Allan (1686–1758). The young lass contra auld man. 1724–29.
The Tea-Table Miscellany (1724–29).
The Works of Allan Ramsay, ed. Alexander M. Kinghorn and Alexander Law, 3 vols. (1961; New York: Johnson, 1972) 3: 51–52.
satiric

Ramsay, Allan (1686–1758). Sang V. How can I be sad on my wedding-day. 1725–34.
Song inserted in *The Gentle Shepherd* (1725–34).
The Works of Allan Ramsay, ed. Alexander M. Kinghorn and Alexander Law, 3 vols. (1961; New York: Johnson, 1972) 3: 69.
celebratory

Ramsay, Allan (1686–1758). Advice to Mr. ——— on his Marriage. 1728.
The Works of Allan Ramsay, ed. Burns Martin and John W. Oliver, 3 vols. (1953; New York: Johnson, 1972) 2: 153–55.
advisory

Ramsay, Allan (1686–1758). Lass with a Lump of Land. 1728.
The Works of Allan Ramsay, ed. Burns Martin and John W. Oliver, 3 vols. (1953; New York: Johnson, 1972) 2: 282.
satiric

Ramsay, Allan (1686–1758). The Monk and the Miller's Wife. A Tale. 1728.
The Works of Allan Ramsay, ed. Burns Martin and John W. Oliver, 3 vols. (1953; New York: Johnson, 1972) 2: 146–53.
comic

Ramsay, Allan (1686–1758). The nuptials, a masque on the marriage of his Grace James Duke of Hamilton and Brandon. 1728.
The Works of Allan Ramsay, ed. Burns Martin and John W. Oliver, 3 vols. (1953; New York: Johnson, 1972) 2: 94–103.
celebratory

Ramsay, Allan (1686–1758). Ode on the marriage of the Right Honourable George Lord Ramsay and Lady Jean Maule. 1728.
The Works of Allan Ramsay, ed. Burns Martin and John W. Oliver, 3 vols. (1953; New York: Johnson, 1972) 2: 104–5.
celebratory

Ramsay, Allan (1686–1758). Ode to Alexander Murray of Brughton, Esq; on his marriage with Lady Euphemia, daughter of the Right Honourable Earl of Galloway. 1728.
The Works of Allan Ramsay, ed. Burns Martin and John W. Oliver, 3 vols. (1953; New York: Johnson, 1972) 2: 199–200.
celebratory

Ramsay, Allan (1686–1758). Ode to the Right Honourable Grace Countess of Aboyn, on her marriage day. 1728.
The Works of Allan Ramsay, ed. Burns Martin and John W. Oliver, 3 vols. (1953; New York: Johnson, 1972) 2: 113–14.
celebratory

Ramsay, Allan (1686–1758). An ode with a pastoral recitative on the marriage of the Right Honourable, James Earl of Wemyss and Mrs. Janet Charteris. 1728.
The Works of Allan Ramsay, ed. Burns Martin and John W. Oliver, 3 vols. (1953; New York: Johnson, 1972) 2: 85–87.
celebratory

Ramsay, Allan (1686–1758). On the marriage of Alexander Brodie of Brodie, Lord Lyon King of Arms, and Mrs. Mary Sleigh. 1728.
The Works of Allan Ramsay, ed. Burns Martin and John W. Oliver, 3 vols. (1953; New York: Johnson, 1972) 2: 115–16.
celebratory

Ramsay, Allan (1686–1758). The widow. 1728.
The Works of Allan Ramsay, ed. Burns Martin and John W. Oliver, 3 vols. (1953; New York: Johnson, 1972) 2: 287–88.
satiric

Ramsay, Allan (1686–1758). The man with twa wives. 1729.
The Works of Allan Ramsay, ed. Alexander M. Kinghorn and Alexander Law, 3 vols. (1961; New York: Johnson, 1972) 3: 106–7.
satiric

Ramsay, Allan (1686–1758). Address of thanks from the society of rakes. 1735.
The Works of Allan Ramsay, ed. Alexander M. Kinghorn and Alexander Law, 3 vols. (1961; New York: Johnson, 1972) 3: 128–34.
satiric

Ramsay, Allan (1686–1758). The miller

and his man: a counterpart to the monk and the millers wife. A tale. (c. 1728).
The Works of Allan Ramsay, ed. Alexander M. Kinghorn and Alexander Law, 3 vols. (1961; New York: Johnson, 1972) 3: 203–9.
comic

Ramsay, Allan (1686–1758). A pastoral epithalamium. n.d.
The Works of Allan Ramsay, ed. Alexander M. Kinghorn and Alexander Law, 3 vols. (1961; New York: Johnson, 1972) 3: 327–29.
celebratory

Ramsay, Allan (1686–1758). On the marriage of Mr. Bull Preacher and Mrs. Mary ———. n.d.
The Works of Allan Ramsay, ed. Alexander M. Kinghorn and Alexander Law, 3 vols. (1961; New York: Johnson, 1972) 3: 332–33.
comic

The rape of the bride; or, marriage and hanging go by destiny . . . a poem hudibrastick, in 4 canto's. With an epistle dedicatory to the fair sex. 1723.
FOX R119
ESTC T083022
comic

Relph, The Rev. Josiah (1712–43). On a wrangling couple. From martial. Glasgow, 1747.
A Miscellany of Poems. By the Late Josiah Relph of Sebergham, Cumberland (Glasgow, 1747) 51.
ESTC T109779
EC reel 2387: 07
comic

Robertson, James (fl. 1768–88). On Mr. D———'s marriage with Miss E———. 1770.
Poems, Consisting of Tales, Fables, Epigrams, &c. &c. By Nobody. (1770) 211–14.
ESTC N012185
EC reel 3053: 05
celebratory

Robertson, James (fl. 1768–88). To Mr. ——— Y———, on his marriage with a most joyous lady. 1770.
Poems, Consisting of Tales, Fables, Epigrams, &c. &c. By Nobody. (1770) 176.
ESTC N012185
EC reel 3053: 05
satiric

Robinson, Mary (1758–1800). Edmund's wedding. 1806 (1790s).
The Poetical Works of the Late Mrs. Mary Robinson, 3 vols. (1806) 3: 172–76.
pathetic

Rochester, John Wilmot, Second Earl of (1647–80). A letter from Artemisia in the town to Chloe in the country. 1679 (1675?).
The Complete Poems 104–12, esp. lines 24–31, 73–146, 209–51.
satiric

Rochester, John Wilmot, Second Earl of (1647–80). Tunbridge wells. 1697 (1674).
The Complete Poems 78–79, lines 114–48.
satiric

Rochester, John Wilmot, Second Earl of (1647–80). To my more than meritorious wife. 1747 (1666/7).
The Complete Poems 23.
witty

Rochester, John Wilmot, Second Earl of (1647–80). Fragment. 1935 (undated).
The Complete Poems 102–3.
satiric

Rochester, John Wilmot, Second Earl of (1647–80). Against marriage. 1968 (1675 or earlier).
The Complete Poems 159.
satiric

Rowe, Elizabeth (nee Singer) (1647–1737). An epistle from Alexias, a noble Roman to his wife, whom he left on his wedding-day, with a design to visit the eastern churches. 1739.

The Miscellaneous Works in Prose and Verse of Mrs. Elizabeth Rowe in Two Volumes (1739) 1: 1503.
ESTC T092685
EC reel 2553: 03
celebratory

Rowe, Elizabeth (nee Singer) (1647–1737). Upon the death of her husband. 1740 (1719).
A. Pope. *Eloisa to Abelard* (2nd ed., 1720 [for 1719]) 47–52.
The Gentleman's Magazine 10 (February 1740): 89.
Fullard 113–15
Lonsdale 49–51
elegiac

[S., M.]. *The great birth of man, or, the excellency of man's creation and endowments above the original of woman. A poem.* 1686. 1688.
WNG S114
EEB reel 1268: 14
satiric

A satyr against love. 1703. See Congreve.

A satyr against marriage. Directed to that inconsiderable animal, called husband. 1680.*
WNG S710A
EEB reel 1315: 8
satiric

A satyr against marriage. 1700.
WNG S710
EEB reel 1339: 33
satiric

A satyr against woman. 1679.
A Ternary of Satires, Containing 1. A Satyr against Man. 2. A Satyr against Woman. 3. A Satire against the Popish Clergy. Composed in French by an Exquisit Pen (1679) 16–40.
WNG T758
EEB reel 517: 10
satiric

Satyr upon woman's usurpation. 1679.
Female Excellence: or, Women Display'd in Several Satyrick Poems (1679) 4–5.
WNG R1749

EEB reel 777: 9
satiric

Savage, Mary (fl. 1763–77). Letter to Miss E. B. on marriage. 1777.
Poems on Various Subjects and Occasions (1777) 2: 8–12.
Lonsdale 348–49]
ESTC T125551
advisory

Sawyer, T. Antigamus; or a satire against marriage. 1714.*
The Oxford Packet. Containing 1. News from Magdalen College; Being an Inscription Written by Dr. Sacheverell . . . ii. Antigamus; or A Satire against Marriage . . . A Vindication of the Oxford Ladies, etc. (1714), repr. P. M. Hill (1949); (see NCBEL, ii, 348).
ESTC T126430
satiric

Scott of Amwell, John (1730–83). The author to his wife. 1782.
Poetical Works (1782) 322.
Chalmers 17: 498. LEL 21796
ESTC T084530
celebratory

Scott of Amwell, John (1730–83). Ode VI. To a friend, on his marriage and removal into the country. 1782.
Poetical Works (1782) 181–84.
Chalmers 17: 479. LEL 21796
ESTC T084530
celebratory

Sedley, Charles, 5th Bart. (1639–1701). The happy pair: or, a poem on matrimony. 1702.
The Miscellaneous Works of the Honourable Sir Charles Sedley, Bart. (1702) 153–73.
The Works of the Honourable Sir Charles Sedley, Bart., 2 vols. (1722) 1: 15–24.
ESTC T060073
EC reel 2264: 04
satiric

Sedley, Charles, 5th Bart. (1639–1701). To Bithinicus, lib. 2 ep. 12. 1702.
The Miscellaneous Works of the Honourable Sir Charles Sedley, Bart. (1702) 137.

The Works of the Honourable Sir Charles Sedley, Bart., 2 vols. (1722) 1: 97.
ESTC T060073
EC reel 2264: 04
satiric

Sedley, Charles, 5th Bart. (1639–1701). To Flavia. 1702.
The Miscellaneous Works of the Honourable Sir Charles Sedley, Bart. (1702) 141.
The Works of the Honourable Sir Charles Sedley, Bart., 2 vols. (1722) 1: 98.
ESTC T060073
EC reel 2264: 04
satiric

Selden, Amhurst. *Love and folly. A poem. In four cantos.* 1749.
FOX S198
ESTC T067056
EC reel 2125: 10
satiric

Shenstone, William (1714–63). A ballad. 1755. 1765.
The Works in Verse and Prose of Wm. Shenstone, Esq., 2 vols. (Edinburgh, 1765) {Edinburgh, 1770} 1: 191.
Chalmers 13: 302. LEL 21793
ESTC T161242 {T092454}
EC reel {897:01}
satiric

Shenstone, William (1714–63). To the memory of an agreeable lady bury'd in marriage to a person undeserving her. 1758.
A Collection of Poems in Six Volumes; By Several Hands (1758) 6: 265–68.
ESTC T115893
EC reel 1844: 05
The Works in Verse and Prose of Wm. Shenstone, Esq., 2 vols. (Edinburgh, 1765) 1: 178–79.
ESTC T161242
Chalmers 13: 300. LEL 21793
satiric

Shepherd, Richard (1732?–1809). *The nuptials. A didactick poem. In three books.* 1761.

ESTC T043214
exemplary

Shiells, Robert (d. 1753). *Marriage: a poetical essay.* 1748.*
FOX S422
ESTC T038995
celebratory

Simonides, tr. unacknowledged. *The creation of women; a poem.* 1725.
See *Spectator* No. 209 for prose version
ESTC N001202
EC reel 2504: 02
satiric

Single, John, of Grey's-Inn, Esq. The batchelor's estimate. 1746.
Cupid and Hymen: or a Voyage to the Isles of Love and Matrimony. Containing a Most Diverting Account of the Inhabitants of Those Two . . . Countries. Tr. from French. To Which is Added the Batchelor's Estimate of Expences Attending a Married Life. 6–8. [Only 6–8 are poetry—selections treating marriage by major figures].
satiric/comic

Smart, Christopher (1722–71). Epithalamium. 1752.
Miscellaneous Poems English and Latin, Vol. 4 of the *Poetical Works of Christopher Smart*, ed. Karina Williamson, 4 vols. to date (Oxford: Clarendon P, 1987) 4: 198–200.
celebratory

A song made for a wedding. 1708.
Oxford and Cambridge Miscellany Poems, ed. Elijah Fenton (1708) 118–19.
ESTC T145730
EC reel 3415: 12
celebratory

Stevenson, Matthew (d. 1684). The Quakers wedding. 1673.
Poems: or, a Miscellany of Sonnets, Satyrs, Drollery, Panegyrics, Elegies, &c. (1673) 78–80.
WNG S5508
EEB 991: 6
satiric

Stockdale, Mary R. (1769?–?). Song: conquest. 1798.
The Effusions of the Heart: Poems (1798) 143–44.
Fullard 143
ESTC T115875
EC reel 1875: 06
celebratory

Swift, Jonathan (1667–1745). Baucis and Philemon. Imitated, from the eighth book of Ovid. 1709.
The Poems of Jonathan Swift 1: 110–17.
satiric

Swift, Jonathan (1667–1745). The story of Baucis & Philemon. Ov. Met. i.8. 1711.
The Poems of Jonathan Swift 1: 88–95.
satiric

[Swift, Jonathan] (1667–1745). Oysters. 1712?
The Poems of Jonathan Swift 3: 952–53.
satiric

Swift, Jonathan (1667–1745). The journal. 1721?
The Poems of Jonathan Swift 1: 278–83.
satiric

Swift, Jonathan (1667–1745). Cadenus and Vanessa 1726 (1713).
The Poems of Jonathan Swift 2: 683–714, esp. lines 5–20.
satiric

Swift, Jonathan (1667–1745). Corinna. 1727 (1711).
The Poems of Jonathan Swift 1: 148–50, lines 25–28.
satiric

Swift, Jonathan (1667–1745). Epigram. 1727.
The Poems of Jonathan Swift 1: 327.
satiric

Swift, Jonathan (1667–1745). Phillis, or, the progress of love. 1727 (1719).
The Poems of Jonathan Swift 1: 221–25.
satiric

Swift, Jonathan (1667–1745). An elegy on Dicky and Dolly. 1732.
The Poems of Jonathan Swift 2: 429–31.
satiric

Swift, Jonathan (1667–1745). The grand question debated. Whether Hamilton's bawn should be turned into a barrack or a malt-house. 1732.
The Poems of Jonathan Swift 3: 863–73.
satiric

Swift, Jonathan (1667–1745). The journal of a modern lady. 1729.
The Poems of Jonathan Swift 2: 443–53.
satiric

[Swift, Jonathan] (1667–1745). The life and character of Dean Swift. Upon a maxim in Rouchefoucault. 1733.
The Poems of Jonathan Swift 2: 545, lines 15–22.
satiric

Swift, Jonathan (1667–1745). An epistle to a lady, who desired the author to make verses on her, in the heroic stile. 1734.
The Poems of Jonathan Swift 2: 633, lines 99–113.
satiric

Swift, Jonathan (1667–1745). Strephon and Chloe. 1734.
The Poems of Jonathan Swift 2: 584–93.
satiric

Swift, Jonathan (1667–1745). A quiet life, and a good name. To &c. Writ. A.D. 1719. 1735.
The Poems of Jonathan Swift 1: 219–21.
satiric

Swift, Jonathan (1667–1745). Verses made for women who cry apples, &c. 1746 (1712).
The Poems of Jonathan Swift 3: 951–52.
satiric

Swift, Jonathan (1667–1745). The progress of marriage. 1765 (1721–22).
The Poems of Jonathan Swift 1: 289–95.
satiric

Swift, Jonathan (1667–1745). The yahoo's overthrow; or, the Kevan Bayl's new ballad, upon Serjeant Kite's insulting the Dean. 1765 (1734).

The Poems of Jonathan Swift 3: 817, lines 71–75.
satiric

Swift, Jonathan (1667–1745). Sheridan at Cavan. 1937 (1736).
The Poems of Jonathan Swift 3: 1037–38.
satiric

Swift, Jonathan (1667–1745). An excellent new ballad: or, the true En——sh D——n to be hang'd for a r-pe. n.d. (1730).
The Poems of Jonathan Swift 2: 516–20.
satiric

Swift, Jonathan (1667–1745). The first of April: a poem. Inscrib'd to Mrs. E. C. n.d. (1723?).
The Poems of Jonathan Swift 1: 320–22.
comic

[Swift, Jonathan] (1667–1745). Verses written upon windows. 1735 (1726?).
The Poems of Jonathan Swift 2: 403–4.
satiric

Taylor, C. (n.d.) (author of *The Britannia*). *The scale, or, woman weigh'd with man a poem; in three canto's.* [Preston? 1750?].
FOX T102
ESTC T199875
anti-satiric

Thomas, Elizabeth (1677–1731). The forsaken wife. 1722.
Miscellany Poems upon Several Subjects (1722) 294–95.
Lonsdale 44
ESTC T053694
elegiac

Thomas, Elizabeth (1677–1731). The monkey dance. To a jealous wife. 1722.
Miscellany Poems upon Several Subjects (1722) 263–64.
ESTC T053694
satiric

Thomas, Elizabeth (1677–1731). A new litany, occasion'd by an invitation to a wedding. 1722.
Miscellany Poems upon Several Subjects (1722) 98.

Lonsdale 39
ESTC T053694
witty

Thomas, Elizabeth (1677–1731). A song. 1722.
Miscellany Poems upon Several Subjects (1722) 26–27.
ESTC T053694
satiric

Thomas, Elizabeth (1677–1731). To the Lady Chudleigh, the anonymous author of *The Lady's Defence*. 1722.
Miscellany Poems upon Several Subjects (1722) 145–50.
ESTC T053694
laudatory

Thompson, William (1712–67) (Late Fellow of Queen's College). The wedding morn: a dream. 1757.
Poems on Several Occasions, 2 vols. bound as one (Oxford, 1757) 149–52.
Chalmers 15: 31–32. LEL 21794.
ESTC T097631
EC reel 1427: 05
celebratory

Thompson, William (1712–67) (Late Fellow of Queen's College). Epithalamium on the royal nuptials. 1757.
Poems on Several Occasions, 2 vols. bound as one (Oxford, 1757) 1–13.
Chalmers 15: 11–13. LEL 21794.
ESTC T097631
EC reel 1427: 05
celebratory

Thompson, William (1712–67) (Late Fellow of Queen's College). To a friend on his marriage. An ode. 1757.
Poems on Several Occasions, 2 vols. bound as one (Oxford, 1757) 78–80.
Chalmers 15: 22. LEL 21794.
ESTC T097631
EC reel 1427: 05
celebratory

To a lady on her marriage. 1740.

The Gentleman's Magazine 10 (April 1740): 195.
hortatory celebration

Tollet, Elizabeth (1694–1754). Hypatia. 1724.
Poems on Several Occasions; With Ann Boleyn to King Henry VIII; An Epistle (1724) 62–63.
Lonsdale 99–100 (selection)
ESTC T075337
EC reel 3413: 05
satiric

Tollet, Elizabeth (1694–1754). To a lady lending me Heliodorus just before her marriage. 1724.
Poems on Several Occasions; With Ann Boleyn to King Henry VIII; An Epistle (1724) 43–44.
Poems on Several Occasions, 2nd ed. (c. 1760; probably a reissue of 1755 edition) 51.
ESTC T075337 (for 1st ed.)
EC reel 3413: 05
celebratory

Travers, Henry (d. 1754). Mrs. ****. 1731.
Miscellaneous Poems and Translations (1731) 76–82.
ESTC T090955
EC reel 2742: 02
laudatory

The unfortunate marriage; or, bigotry triumphant. A poem. Humbly dedicated to the Queen's most excellent Majesty. Birmingham, 1776.
ESTC T050417
EC reel 1188: 21
satiric

Verses by Mrs. M. E———ds. occasioned by a lampoon on L——d A——H——'s marriage. 1743.
Court Whispers: or, a Magazine of Wit. A Satyr for the Country (1743) 35–36.
ESTC N003743
witty

W., J. Vinegar and mustard: or, wormwood lectures for every day in the week; Being exercised and delivered in several parishes both of town and city, on several days. 1686.
Samuel Pepys' Penny Merriments, ed. Roger Thompson (New York: Columbia UP, 1977) 290–91.
satiric

Walsh, William (1663–1708). To his mistress, against marriage. 1692.
Letters and Poems, Amorous and Gallant (1692) 102–3.
WNG W647
EEB reel 522: 15
witty

[Ward, Edward] (1667–1731). *Marriage-dialogues; or, a poetical peep into the state of matrimony . . . with moral reflexions on every dialogue.* 1709 [1708].
FOX W113
ESTC T091568
satiric

Ward, Edward (1667–1731). *Nuptial dialogues and debates.* 2 vols. 1723—an expanded edition of *Marriage-dialogues.* 1709 [1708].

Ward, James (n.d.). Epithalamium on the marriage of Felim and Oonah. 1724.
Miscellaneous Poems, Original and Translated by Several Hands (1724) 328–36.
ESTC T25249
EC reel 1427: 10
celebratory

Warton (the Elder), Thomas (1688?–1745) (Vicar of Basinstoke). To a friend, on his marriage. 1748.
Poems on Several Occasions (1748) 119–21.
ESTC T125430
EC reel 1134: 43
celebratory

Wedlock a paradice; or, a defence of woman's liberty against man's tyranny. In opposition to a poem, entitul'd, the pleasures of a single life, &c. 1701.*
FOX W267

ESTC T112311
anti-satiric

Wedlock vindicated: or, the ladies answer to the (pretended) good advice to them, proving a married life, is the best way to support the reputation of both sexes and a single life scandalous, dangerous, and obnoxious both to men and women. With seasonable cautions to avoid it. By a young lady. 1702.
FOX W268
ESTC N025328
anti-satiric

Wesley (the Younger), Samuel (1691–1739). *The battle of the sexes: a poem.* 1723?
FOX W333
ESTC T058888
satiric

West, Jane (1758–1852). To a friend on her marriage, 1784. 1799.
Poems and Plays, 4 vols. (1799) 2: 169–72.
Lonsdale 380–82
ESTC N011804
EC reel 1291: 01
advisory

Wharton, Anne (c. 1659–85). Penelope to Ulysses. 1712 (before 1685).
Ovid's Epistles Translated by Several Hands; the Eighth Edition with a New Translation of Three Epistles and Several Cuts Never Before Published, 8th ed. (1712) 160–63.
Greer 291–92 (selection)
ESTC T061462
EC reel 2297: 10
elegiac

Whateley, Mary (later Darwall) (1738–1825). On the author's husband desiring her to write some verses. 1794 (c. 1780).
Poems on Several Occasions (1794) 2: 55–57.
Lonsdale 261–62
celebratory/satiric

The whores and bawd's answer to the fifteen comforts of whoring. 1706.
satiric

Williams, Anna (1706–83). Essays occasioned by the marriage of Miss ——— and Mr. ———. 1766.
Miscellanies in Prose and Verse (1766) 38–39.
ESTC T077856
celebratory

Winchilsea, Anne Finch (nee Kingsmill), Countess of (1661–1720). The following lines occasion'd by the marriage of Edward Herbert Esquire, and Mrs. Elizabeth Herbert. 1713.
Miscellany Poems, on Several Occasions. Written by a Lady. (1713) 102–3.
The Poems of Anne Countess of Winchilsea, ed. Myra Reynolds (1903; rpt. New York: AMS, 1974) 55.
laudatory

Winchilsea, Anne Finch (nee Kingsmill), Countess of (1661–1720). Reformation. 1713.
Miscellany Poems, on Several Occasions. Written by a Lady. (1713) 227–29.
The Poems of Anne Countess of Winchilsea, ed. Myra Reynolds (1903; rpt. New York: AMS, 1974) 202–3.
Lonsdale 21
ESTC T095540
satiric

Winchilsea, Anne Finch (nee Kingsmill) Countess of (1661–1720). The Unequal Fetters. 1903.
Folio MS
The Poems of Anne Countess of Winchilsea, ed. Myra Reynolds (1903; rpt. New York: AMS, 1974) 150–51.
satiric

Woman unmask'd and dissected; a satire. 1740.
FOX F89
ESTC N036129
satiric

Woodward, George (fl. 1717–27). A letter from a lady to her husband in Spain, in her last sickness. 1730.
Poems on Several Occasions (Oxford, 1730) 60–67.

ESTC T124981
EC reel 1575: 13
pathetic

Woty, William (1731?–91). The female advocate. 1771.
Poems on Several Occasions (1780) 42–80.
ESTC T035471
EC reel 1313: 43
laudatory

Wright, Mehetable (nee Wesley) (1697–1750). Address to her husband. 1823 (c. 1730).
A. Clarke, *Memoirs of the Wesley Family* (1823) 491–93.
Fullard 122–24
Lonsdale 111–14
pathetic/satiric

Wright, Mehetable (nee Wesley) (1697–1750). Wedlock. A satire. 1862 (c. 1730).
Samuel Wesley, *Poems on Several Occasions*, ed. J. Nichols (1862) 553–54.
Lonsdale 114
satiric

Wycherley, William (1641–1716). An epithalamium on the marriage of two very ill natur'd blacks, who were to have their liberty, in consideration of their match. 1704.
Miscellany Poems: as Satyrs, Epistles, Love-verses, Songs, Sonnets, etc. (1704) 430–32.
The Works of William Wycherley, ed. Montague Summers, 4 vols. (New York: Russell & Russell, 1964) 4: 53–54.
satiric

Wycherley, William (1641–1716). In answer to a mistress, who desired her lover to marry her . . . 1704.
Miscellany Poems: as Satyrs, Epistles, Love-verses, Songs, Sonnets, etc. (1704) 100–104.
The Works of William Wycherley, ed. Montague Summers, 4 vols. (New York: Russell & Russell, 1964) 3: 90–93.
satiric

Wycherley, William (1641–1716). Injustice out of honour. To the too honourable jilt, who to be true to her marriage-vow, and her husband, (whom she own'd she hated) was false to her love promise, and her lover, whom she confess'd she lov'd, and lov'd first. A song. 1704.
Miscellany Poems: as Satyrs, Epistles, Love-verses, Songs, Sonnets, etc. (1704) 39–41.
The Works of William Wycherley, ed. Montague Summers, 4 vols. (New York: Russell & Russell, 1964) 3: 45–46.
satiric

Wycherley, William (1641–1716). To a rich, mercenary, matrimonial mistress; who said, the most honourable match, was that, which was made for most money. 1704.
Miscellany Poems: as Satyrs, Epistles, Love-verses, Songs, Sonnets, etc. (1704) 401–3.
The Works of William Wycherley, ed. Montague Summers, 4 vols. (New York: Russell & Russell, 1964) 4: 31–33.
satiric

Wycherley, William (1641–1716). To a lady, an advocate for marriage. 1728.
Posthumous Works (1728) 157–60.
The Works of William Wycherley, ed. Montague Summers, 4 vols. (New York: Russell & Russell, 1964) 4: 215–17.
satiric

Young, Edward (1683–1765). *The universal passion. Satires v and vi.* 1727–28.
Chalmers 13: 391–99. LEL 21793
ESTC T050491 (V. 1727)
ESTC T050493 (VI. 1728)
satiric

INDEX

Abrams, Meyer, 288
Absalom and Achitophel (Dryden), 140
Abse, Dannie: "Portrait of a Marriage," 293
Account of Marriage, An, 34–35, 302 (n. 9)
"Ache of Marriage, The" (Levertov), 293
Adam and Eve: Adam as satirist, 25; as a companionate couple, 25–27, 214, 215–16, 231–32, 265; Eve as Adam's superior, 231–32, 265; fall of, responsibility for, 140–41, 223; as fornicators, 25, 303 (n. 3); in paradise, 202, 213, 271
"Address to Her Husband" (Mehetable Wright), 82–83
Advice to a Friend on His Marriage (Blyth), 112–13, 262
"Advice to a Young Lady Lately Married" (Esther Lewis), 116
Advice to New-Married Husbands (Plaxton), 206–7, 233–34
"Against Marriage" (Rochester), 58–59, 61, 82
Alphus: or, The Fourth Eclogue of Baptist Mantuan (Mantovano), 172–73
Alrick and Isabel (Duck), 148–49, 286
Ames, Richard: feminism of, suspect, 36–37; *The Folly of Love*, 248; as Grub Street formula poet, 304 (n. 14); as hostile group member, 75, 125–26, 304 (n. 14), 306 (n. 9); and modal alternation in poems, 238, 240; *The Pleasures of Love and Marriage*, 248–50, 253; as polemical poet, 280; *The Rake*, imputed author of, 67–68, 84, 118–19; and stock libertine argument, 68, 71; *Sylvia's Revenge*, 237–38
Amherst, Elizabeth Frances: "The Welford Wedding," 189
Amours de Voyage (Clough), 292
Angel in the House, The (Patmore), 285, 290–91
Anglican Church, 42, 222, 298 (n. 6)
Anstey, Christopher, 280
Answer to the Pleasures of a Single Life, An, 76, 197–98, 301 (n. 7), 304 (n. 11)
"Antigamus," 304 (n. 15)
Aquinas, Saint Thomas, 41, 270
Aristocracy, 10, 21, 147, 298 (n. 4). *See also* Upper classes
Armstrong, John: *The Oeconomy of Love*, 113–14, 216–17
Arthos, John, 310 (n. 4)
Astell, Mary, 49; *Some Reflections upon Marriage*, 20, 312 (n. 8)
Auburn, Mark, 303 (n. 4)
Auden, W. H., 314 (n. 8)

Aurora Leigh (Elizabeth Barrett Browning), 286
"Author to His Wife, The" (Scott), 274

Ballad, 119, 163, 169–72, 229, 235, 308 (n. 3)
"Ballad, A" (Shenstone), 98, 171–72
"Ballad upon a Wedding, A" (Suckling), 188
Barbauld, Letitia, 175–76, 269, 313 (n. 15); "Ovid to His Wife," 176; "The Rights of Woman," 264
Barber, Mary, 267–69; "The Conclusion of a Letter to the Rev. Mr. C——," 267–68; "On the Earl of Oxford and Mortimer's Giving His Daughter in Marriage," 309 (n. 10)
Barker, Jane, 75; "A Virgin Life," 73
Batchelars Banquet, The, 301 (n. 5)
Batchelors and Maids Answer, to the Fifteen Comforts of Matrimony, The, 37
Batchelor's Choice, The, 199–200
"Batchelor's Song, The" (Flatman), 65–66
Battle of the Sexes, The (Samuel Wesley the Younger), 261–62
"Baucis and Philemon" (Swift), 295
Behn, Aphra: criticism of, recent, ix; "The Disappointment," 303 (n. 7); and female libertine argument, 15, 27, 63–64, 80, 89; feminists' praise of, 15; "The Golden Age," 63–64; and libertine argument, 71, 140; "Song," 71, 139; "To Mrs. W. on Her Excellent Verses," 303 (n. 7)
"Belinda Waters" (Crabbe), 287
Berry, Wendell: "To Tanya," 315 (n. 8)
Betham, Matilda, 269; "[The Power of Women]," 264
Bewick, William, 172
Bible, 36; Canticles, 181; Genesis, 24, 34, 270; Pauline epistles, 23; Psalm 44 of Vulgate, 181
"Bithinicus, Lib. 2. Ep. 12" (Sedley), 167
Blake, William, 299 (n. 10), 314 (n. 5); *An Island in the Moon*, 281–83; "London," 154; *The Marriage of Heaven and Hell*, 288–89
Blamire, Susanna: "I've Gotten a Rock, I've Gotten a Reel," 308 (n. 8); "O Jenny Dear, The Word is Gane," 305 (n. 1); "The Siller Croun," 95

Blount, Martha, 106, 108, 305 (n. 2)
Blyth, Francis: *Advice to a Friend on His Marriage*, 112–13, 262
Book of Common Prayer, 223
Bothie of Tober-Na-Vuolich, The (Clough), 292
Boyd, Elizabeth: "To Mr. B—k on His Leaving His Mistress," 307 (n. 4)
Bride Woman's Counsellor, The (Sprint), 240–41, 242
"Broken Home, The" (Merrill), 314 (nn. 7, 8)
Brome, Alexander, 165, 174, 183, 307 (n. 2); "An Elegy on a Lady That Died before Her Intended Nuptials," 174; "The Wife" (attrib. to Brome), 307 (n. 2)
Brown, Laura, 106–7, 305 (n. 2)
Brown, N., 188–91, 208–9; "The North-Country Wedding," 188–89, 208
Brown, Tom, 66, 71, 233, 306 (n. 8), 307 (n. 3); "A Satire on Marriage," 233, 306 (n. 8), 307 (n. 3); "To a Lady, Whom He Refus'd to Marry," 66
Browne, Alice, 2
Browne, Moses, 175, 186, 271–72, 274, 308 (n. 11); "To Mr. Daniel Booth, Jun. on His Marriage," 186, 308 (n. 11); "Verses on the Death of a Dear and Most Lov'd Wife," 175, 271
Browning, Elizabeth Barrett, 286–87; *Aurora Leigh*, 286
Browning, Robert, 291–92; *Dramatis Personae*, 292; *Men and Women*, 292
Burns, Robert: "On Marriage," 313–14 (n. 3); "A Poet's Welcome to His Love-Begotten Daughter," 313–14 (n. 3)
Butler, Samuel: "The Licentious Age of Charles the 2D," 45; as polemical poet, 301 (n. 8); "Satyr upon Marriage," 134–35. See also *Hudibras*
Byrom, John, 213; "On the Marriage of Edward Greaves, Esq.," 212
Byron, Lord: *Don Juan*, 286

Cadenus and Vanessa (Swift), 47–49
Calvin, John, 27, 34, 41, 130, 192, 200, 224, 298 (n. 6)
Calvinism, 41–42
Cambridge, Richard Owen, 147, 280; *Verses Occasioned by the Marriage and the Game Act*, 150–51

Cambridge Group for the History of Population and Social Structure, 298 (n. 3)
Campion, Thomas, 181
Capellanus, Andreas, 54
Carew, Thomas, 55, 181
Carey, Henry: "The Happy Marriage," 310 (n. 1); "The True Woman's Man," 254–55
Cavalier poets, 55
Cawthorn, James: "The Temple of Hymen," 155–56
Celestial bed, 12
Centlivre, Susanna: *A Woman's Case: in an Epistle to Charles Joye*, 312 (n. 7)
"Character of a True-Born English-Woman, The," 121, 306 (n. 6)
Charles II, 55, 57, 139
Chatterton, Thomas: "The Happy Pair," 275
Chaucer, Geoffrey, 131
Chaucer: Sources and Backgrounds, 304 (n. 12)
Chudleigh, Lady Mary, 27, 43; "A Dialogue between Alexis and Astrea," 139–40; *The Ladies Defence*, 49–50, 240–43, 246, 312 (n. 11)
Churchill, Charles, 279
Church of England. *See* Anglican Church
Church of Ireland, 47
Civil divorce, 75, 135, 280. *See also* Divorce *a vinculo matrimonii;* Parliamentary divorce
Civil Wars, 129, 225, 227
Clancey, Richard, 249, 304 (n. 17)
Clarissa (Richardson), 67–68, 128, 306 (n. 10)
Cleland, John: *Memoirs of a Woman of Pleasure*, 310 (n. 4)
Cleveland, John, 307 (n. 3), 310 (n. 4); "On an Alderman Who Married a Very Young Wife," 142–43
Clough, Arthur Hugh: *Amours de Voyage*, 292; *The Bothie of Tober-Na-Vuolich*, 292; *Dipsychus*, 292
Coleridge, Samuel Taylor, 288, 314 (n. 5); *The Rime of the Ancient Mariner*, 289
Collier, Jeremy: *The Short View of the Immorality and Prophaneness of the English Stage*, 85

Collier, Mary, 50–52, 114, 150, 309 (n. 10); "The Happy Husband, and the Old Batchelor," 50–52; "Spectator Vol. the Fifth. Numb. 375," 149; *The Woman's Labour*, 113
Commonwealth, 130, 138, 225
"Composed on the Eve of the Marriage of a Friend" (Wordsworth), 314 (n. 4)
Concanen, Matthew, 188–89, 208
"Conclusion of a Letter to the Rev. Mr. C——, The," (Barber), 267–68
"Condition of Womankind, The," 313 (n. 12)
Conduct books: critical treatment of, ix, 305 (nn. 2, 3); debate about marriage in, ix; husband's dominion in, 23, 258, 261–63; prose, 100–101, 305 (n. 3); Puritan theological rationales in, 41
Conduct poems, 100–101, 112–17, 163, 266
Confessions of the New Married Couple, The (Marsh), 301 (n. 5)
Congreve, William: *A Satyr against Love* (attrib. to Congreve), 120, 306 (n. 6); *The Way of the World*, 238
Conjugal Lewdness (Defoe), 303 (n. 2)
Conjugal Love (Venette), 298–99 (n. 7)
Conjugium Conjurgium (Seymar), 35–36
Consistory courts, 24, 280, 299 (n. 12)
"Consolatory Epistle, A" (Gould), 119–20, 305 (n. 4), 306 (n. 8)
"Consolatory Verses to Her Husband" (Pilkington), 276
"Corinna" (Swift), 121–23, 306 (n. 7)
Corso, Gregory: "Marriage," 293–94
Cotton, Charles, 73, 75, 165; "The Joys of Marriage," 70–71; Martial's epigram 35 from his eighth book, 166
Cotton, Nathaniel, 272–74; "Marriage. Vision VII," 153, 272; *Visions in Verse*, 114, 153
Country retreat poem, 72
Courtly doctrine, 54
Courtly love, 38, 55–57, 65, 86, 175, 290; and eclipse of courtly myth, 149. *See also* Courtly doctrine; Romantic love
Court Whispers, 178
Cowley, Abraham, 177
Cowper, William, 50, 147, 308 (n. 10); epigram on *Thelyphthora*, 168; "Happy

Cowper, William (*continued*)
    the Man Whose Amorous Flame Has Found," 152–53; "If John Marries Mary, and Mary Alone," 94, 168–69; "Mutual Forbearance Necessary to the Happiness of the Married State," 50–51, 52–53, 278–79; "A New Ballad Intitled The Sorrowfull Husband's Garland," 170–71; "Ode. Supposed to be Written on the Marriage of a Friend," 179–80, 220–21
Crabbe, George, 314 (n. 3); "Belinda Waters," 287; "The Equal Marriage," 287; *The Parish Register*, 287; "The Wife and Widow," 287
Crashaw, Richard, 177
Creation of Woman, The (Simonides), 110
Criminal conversation suits, 24, 280–81, 299 (n. 12)
Crouch, Nathaniel: *Female Excellency, or The Ladies' Glory*, 312 (n. 6)
cummings, e. e.: "this little bride & groom are," 314–15 (n. 8)
Cupid and Hymen (Single), 308 (n. 1)
Curran, Stuart, 308 (n. 2)
Curtis, Laura A., 305 (n. 3)

Daly, Michael Joseph, 288, 314 (n. 5)
"Damages, Two Hundred Pounds" (Thackeray), 286
Davenant, William, 142; "Epithalamium. The Morning after," 184; "To Mistress E. S. Married to an Old Usurer," 307 (n. 3); "Upon the Nuptial of Charles Lord Herbert," 183
Davies, Kathleen M., 305 (n. 3)
Day-in-the-life convention, 119–20, 123–24
Debate format, 32–33, 36, 42–53, 56, 68–69, 173–74; and debates over sovereignty, 253, 266, 312 (n. 8); evolution in poets' handling of, 300 (n. 2); and *Hudibras* III.1., 43–47, 61–63, 134–37; and loaded debate, 97; and prose debates, 301 (n. 8), 313 (n. 2); and "Querelle des femmes," 301 (n. 8); Swift's use of, 47–49, 302 (n. 10)
"Debauchee, The" (Dorset), 304 (n. 16)
De Conscribendis Epistolis (Erasmus), 300 (n. 3)
Defoe, Daniel, ix, 305 (n. 3); *Conjugal Lewdness*, 303 (n. 2); *Good Advice to the Ladies* (attrib. to Defoe), 79, 102, 103; *Roxana*, 20
De La Motte, Antoine Houdar, 88
De La Salle, Antoine: *Les Quinze Joyes de Mariage* (attrib. to de La Salle), 301 (n. 5)
De Lauretis, Teresa, 2
Dello Ammogliarsi (Tasso), 302 (n. 8)
Denham, Sir John, 73, 75, 179; "Friendship and Single Life against Love and Marriage," 69–70
De Rougemont, Denis, 149
De Worde, Wynken: *The Fyfteene Joyes of Maryage*, 301 (n. 5)
"Dialogue between Alexis and Astrea, A" (Chudleigh), 139–40
Dialogue Concerning Women (Walsh), 301–2 (n. 8)
"Dialogue Song, A" (DuBois), 92–93
Dillon, Sir John, 304 (n. 11)
Dipsychus (Clough), 292
"Disappointment, The" (Behn), 303 (n. 7)
Diseases of the Times (Taylor), 226
Divorce, The, 280
Divorce Act of 1857, 23. See also Matrimonial Causes Act of 1857
Divorce *a vinculo matrimonii*, 23, 75, 300 (n. 3)
Dixon, Sarah, 94; "To Mrs. S—. An Epigram," 91
Dobbs, Francis, 214–15, 220; *Modern Matrimony*, 147, 158, 160–62, 214
Don Juan (Byron), 286
Dorman, Joseph: *The Female Rake*, 88–89
Dorset, Charles Sackville, Earl of: "The Debauchee," 304 (n. 16)
Double standard: domesticity's attack on, 6–9, 14–15, 298 (n. 5); Samuel Johnson's justification of, 299 (n. 8); strength of, in male ideology, 30; Victorian modification of, 290; women poets' attack on, 81, 131, 242, 245, 277
Douglas, F.: *Reflections on Celibacy and Marriage*, 302 (n. 8)
Dower rights, 17
Drake, James, 28
Drake, Judith: *An Essay in Defence of the Female Sex*, 28
Dramatis Personae (Robert Browning), 292

Drayton, Michael, 181
Dryden, John: *Absalom and Achitophel*, 140; *Eleonora: A Panegyrical Poem*, 201–2, 250–51; epithalamia of, 181; and his handling of marriage, criticism treating, ix; and Juvenal's sixth satire, translation of, 103–4; and libertine argument, 57–58, 63, 75; *MacFlecknoe*, 161; *Marriage à la Mode*, 57–58, 71, 303 (n. 4); "On the Marriage of . . . Mrs. Anastasia Stafford," 178–79, 197; and Pindarique odes, 178–79; as polemical poet, 280; "Prologue from *An Evening's Love*," 204–7; "Prologue to a New Play, Call'd, *The Disappointment*," 118, 303 (n. 6); and syntactical balance and antithesis, 179; "To my Honour'd Kinsman, John Driden, of Chesterton," 71–73
DuBois, Lady Dorothea, 91–94, 267; "A Dialogue Song," 92–93; "A True Tale," 266; "An Emblematic Tale," 92–93; "Ode on the Marriage and Coronation of . . . King George III and Queen Charlotte," 309 (n. 10)
Duck, Stephen: *Alrick and Isabel*, 148–49, 286; *The Thresher's Labour*, 113
Dugan, Alan: "Love Song: I and Thou," 314 (n. 7)
D'Urfey, Thomas, 142; *The Malecontent*, 138–40
Duty of a Husband, The, 112–13
Duty of a Wife, The (Jackson), 112, 252–53

Early Modern period, 8
Eclogue, 97, 163, 172–74, 177
Eddy, Donald, 309 (n. 11)
Eden, 24–26, 76, 202, 229, 233
Egerton, Sarah Fyge, 133, 143–47, 307 (n. 4); "The Emulation," 246; *The Female Advocate*, 300–301 (n. 4); "On My Wedding Day," 146–47; "The Repulse to Alcander," 303 (n. 8); "To Orabella," 143–44
Elegy, 163, 174–77, 310 (n. 5)
"Elegy on a Lady That Died before Her Intended Nuptials, An" (Brome), 174
"Elegy on Dicky and Dolly, An" (Swift), 174

Eleonora: A Panegyrical Poem (Dryden), 201–2, 250–51
Eloisa to Abelard (Pope), 86–87, 175
"Emblematic Tale, An" (DuBois), 92–93
Empiricism, Lockean and Humean, 288
"Emulation, The" (Egerton), 246
Enlightenment, 7, 8
Epic Poem on Adam and Eve, An (Holmes), 215–16, 265–66
Epigram, 94, 143, 163, 165–69, 177
Epigram on *Thelyphthora* (Cowper), 168
Epipsychidion (Shelley), 289–90
"Epistle from Alexias, An" (Rowe), 175, 219–20
"Epistle from Mrs. Yonge to Her Husband" (Montagu), 244–46
"Epistle to a Painter, An" (Travers), 185–86
Epistle to Cobham (Pope), 107
"Epistle to Miss Blount, with the Works of Voiture" (Pope), 258–60
Epistle II. To a Lady (Pope), 104, 106–10, 268, 305 (n. 2)
"Epitaph, An" (Prior), 295
Epithalamion (Spenser), 181, 184
Epithalamium: 111–12, 178–91, 196, 216; classical and Renaissance, 218, 293, 309 (n. 6); contemporary, 293, 314–15 (n. 8); development of, 165–66, 183, 288, 314–15 (n. 5); and emotional affirmation, 182–86; occasional, 309 (n. 8); 314–15 (n. 8); rusticated, 183, 188–90, 209–14, 310 (n. 12); satiric, 309 (n. 9), 314–15 (n. 8); Spenserian, 183, 190–91; as traditional genre, 177, 180; witty, 183, 186–87; and women poets, 189–90, 309 (n. 10)
"Epithalamium" (Smart), 310 (n. 11)
"Epithalamium, An," 89
"Epithalamium by Mr. D——," 186
"Epithalamium on the Marriage of Felim and Oonah" (James Ward), 189, 209
"Epithalamium on the Royal Nuptials" (William Thompson), 190–91
"Epithalamium. The Morning after" (Davenant), 184
"Equal Marriage, The" (Crabbe), 287
Erasmus, Desiderius: *De Conscribendis Epistolis*, 300 (n. 3)

"Espousal, The" (Gay), 173
Essay in Defence of the Female Sex, An (Judith Drake), 28
"Essay on Woman, An" (Leapor), 246
"Essays Occasioned by the Marriage of Miss —— and Mr ——," (Anna Williams), 309 (n. 10)
Essay upon Marriage, An (Forbes), 101, 103
Evangelical movement, 8, 9, 30
"Excellent New Ballad, An" (Swift), 308 (n. 3)

Fables for the Female Sex (Moore and Brooke), 114
Fair sex: and male gallantry, 85, 94; myth of, 30, 247, 249, 255, 263–66
Family: nuclear, 1, 6, 13, 297 (n. 1); traditional, 6, 7, 9–12
Fanny (Jong), 297 (n. 2)
Fawkes, Francis: "A Good Wife," 115
Female Advocate, The (Egerton), 300–301 (n. 4)
"Female Advocate, The" (Woty), 29
Female Apostacy, 121, 122, 233
Female Conduct (Mariott), 89, 114, 262–64
"Female Empire" (Jago), 257–58
Female Excellence, 230
Female Excellency, or The Ladies' Glory (Crouch), 312 (n. 6)
Female Rake, The (Dorman), 88–89
Female worthies, 239, 312 (n.6)
Feminist criticism, x, 2, 15, 20, 106, 297 (n. 1)
Feminization of marriage verse, 5, 27, 28
Fifteen Comforts of a Wanton Wife, The, 38, 233, 306 (n. 6)
Fifteen Comforts of Matrimony, The, 37, 104
XV Comforts of Rash and Inconsiderate Marriage, The, 301 (n. 5)
Fifteen Comforts of Whoring, The, 38
Fifteen-format: poems, 37–38, 233; prose pieces, 37–38
Fifteen Pleasures of a MaidenHead, The, 301 (n. 6)
Finch, Anne. *See* Winchilsea, Anne Finch, Countess of
Flatman, Thomas, 71; "The Batchelor's Song," 65–66; "The Second Part," 65, 304 (n. 10)

Fleet district, 32, 82; marriages in, 300 (n. 1)
Folly of Love, The (Ames), 248
Forbes, William, of Disblair: *An Essay upon Marriage*, 101, 103
"Forsaken Wife, The" (Elizabeth Thomas), 83
Foxon, David, 304 (n. 14)
"Fragment" (Rochester), 59–61
France, 9, 10, 12
Fraser, Antonia, 20, 311 (n. 3)
"Friday: The Toilette. Lydia" (Montagu), 305 (n. 5)
"Friendship and Single Life against Love and Marriage" (Denham), 69–70
Fyfteene Joyes of Maryage, The (De Worde), 301 (n. 5)

"Garden, The" (Marvell), 72
Gargantua and Pantagruel (Rabelais), 44, 301 (n. 8)
Gay, John, 172–73; "The Espousal," 173
Geneva Ordinances of 1561, 42
Gillis, John, 39, 130, 131, 271
G[lanvill], A[braham]: *The Rake Reform'd*, 84, 119, 305 (n. 4)
Glorious Revolution of 1688, 57, 303 (n. 5)
Glover, Jean: "O'er the Muir Amang the Heather," 313–14 (n. 3)
Golden age, 66, 95–96, 130, 133, 138–41, 226–27
"Golden Age, The" (Behn), 63–64
"Golden Garland," 169, 170
Goldsmith, Oliver, 188
Good Advice to Beaus and Batchelours, 102, 103, 304 (n. 11), 306 (n. 6)
Good Advice to the Ladies (attrib. to Defoe), 79, 102, 103
"Good Wife, A" (Fawkes), 115
Goreau, Angeline, 64
Gothic novel, 286, 308 (n. 8)
Gould, Robert, 75, 126, 237–38, 301 (n. 4), 304 (n. 14); "A Consolatory Epistle," 119–20, 305 (n. 4), 306 (n. 8); *Love Giv'n O're*, 36, 38, 237, 245
Graham, James, 12
"Grand Question Debated, The" (Swift), 302 (n. 10)
Graves, Richard, 279
Graves, Robert, 314 (n. 8)

Gray, Thomas, 175
Great Birth of Man, The (M. S.), 25, 231–33
Greene, Graham, 304 (n. 16)
Greene, Thomas, 309 (n. 6)
Griffith, Reginald Harvey, 117
Gubar, Susan, 311 (n. 1)

Habakkuk, Sir John, 129
Hagstrum, Jean, 127, 306 (n. 10)
Haller, William and Malleville, 251
"Happy Husband, and the Old Batchelor, The" (Mary Collier), 50–52
"Happy Marriage, The" (Carey), 310 (n. 1)
Happy Marriage: An Eclogue, The, 95–97, 173
"Happy Pair, The" (Chatterton), 275
"Happy Pair, The" (Jeffreys), 153–55
"Happy Pair, The" (Sedley), 140–42, 146, 275
"Happy Pair: A Ballad, The" (Pilkington), 310 (n. 13)
"Happy the Man Whose Amorous Flame Has Found" (Cowper), 152–53
Haraway, Donna, 2
Harding, Sandra, 2
Hardwicke's Marriage Act of 1753, Lord, 16, 130–31, 150
Harrington, Sir John, 165
Hartsock, Nancy, 2
Hawkins, Laetitia: *Letters on the Female Mind*, 21
Heliodorus, 28
Hemlow, Joyce, 305 (n. 3)
Henry VIII, 42, 130
Herbert, Hon. Nicholas: "Marriage à la Mode: or the Two Sparrows," 88
Herrick, Robert, 79, 188; "A Nuptial Song or Epithalamie," 181
"Hesiod" (Parnell), 95–96, 256
Higgins, Patricia, 311 (n. 2)
Hill, Bridget, 20, 312 (n. 8)
Holman, Hugh, 165
Holmes, Ann, 269; *An Epic Poem on Adam and Eve*, 215–16, 265–66
Homosocial relationships, 226, 271
Hopkins, Gerard Manley, 290
Horace: and country retreat poem, 72; and ode, 177, 179; personae of, 160
Horne, William: *Marriage Poems and Satires*, 304 (n. 15)

Hostile male satirists, 75, 120, 306 (n. 9)
Howard, Edward: *The Women's Conquest*, 238
Hudibras (Butler): domineering wife in skimmington in, 227–28; libertine argument of widow in, 60–63; marriage-as-trade satirized in, 134–37, 140–41; marriage debate in, 43–46, 134–36; Presbyterian knight in, 44, 46, 135, 227; Royalist satire in, 227, 311 (n. 4)
Huebner, Wayne, 304 (n. 12)
Hume, Robert, 303 (n. 1)
"Hymn to Venus, upon a Marriage, A" (Prior), 309 (n. 7)
"Hypatia" (Tollet), 246

Idler (Samuel Johnson), 182
Idylls (Theocritus), 172, 181, 291
Idylls of the King (Tennyson), 291
"If John Marries Mary, and Mary Alone" (Cowper), 94, 168–69
"Ill News after Marriage," 178–79
In Memoriam (Tennyson), 291
Instructions-to-painter formula, 186
Interregnum, 130, 225–27, 300 (n. 3), 311 (nn. 1, 2, 4)
Island in the Moon, An (Blake), 281–83
"I've Gotten a Rock, I've Gotten a Reel" (Blamire), 308 (n. 8)

Jackson, Samuel: *The Duty of a Wife*, 112, 252–53
Jago, Richard: "Female Empire," 257–58
James II, 139, 303 (n. 5)
Jeffreys, George, 308 (n. 11); "The Happy Pair," 153–55
Jemmat, Catherine, 167–68; "The Reply," 93–94, 210–11; "The Rural Lass," 310 (n. 13); "Verses, Written to a Friend on His Marriage," 93, 211
Jenyns, Soame: "The Modern Fine Lady," 126–28
Johnson, J. T. *See* Johnson, James Turner
Johnson, James Turner, 41, 112, 305 (n. 3), 313 (n. 2)
Johnson, Samuel, ix, 159, 160, 299 (n. 8); *Idler*, 182; *Rasselas*, 313 (n. 2)
Johnson, W. *See* Johnson, Wendell Stacy

Johnson, Wendell Stacy, 290–91, 314 (nn. 1, 2, 6)
Jointure, 9, 17, 44, 137
Jones, Mary: "Ode on the Rt. Hon. Lady Henry Beauclerk," 309 (n. 10)
Jong, Erica: *Fanny*, 297 (n. 2)
Jonson, Ben, 165, 181
"Journal of a Modern Lady, The" (Swift), 119
"Joys of Marriage, The" (Charles Cotton), 70–71
Juvenal, 25, 69, 78, 100, 102–6, 111, 119, 140, 226, 306 (n. 8)

Kavanagh, Patrick: "Tinker's Wife," 314 (n. 7)
Kunitz, Stanley: "River Road," 292

Ladies Choice, The, 106, 203, 251
Ladies Defence, The (Chudleigh), 49–50, 240–43, 246, 312 (n. 11)
Ladies Home Journal, 295
Langhorne, John: *Precepts of Conjugal Happiness*, 114–15, 273–74
Laslett, Peter, 298 (n. 3)
"Lass with a Lump of Land" (Ramsay), 307–8 (n. 5)
Leapor, Mary: "An Essay on Woman," 246
Leigh, Richard: "The Union of Friendship," 236–37
Leites, Edmund, 27, 29
Lennox, Charlotte, 91
Les Précieuses Ridicules (Molière), 90
Les Quinze Joyes de Mariage (attrib. to de La Salle), 301 (n. 5)
"Letter from a Lady to Her Husband in Spain, A" (Woodward), 175, 218–19
Letters on the Female Mind (Hawkins), 21
"Letter to a Sister" (Pointon), 189–90
"Letter to Miss E. B. on Marriage" (Savage), 277
Levertov, Denise: "The Ache of Marriage," 293
Lewis, C. S., 55; "Prelude to Space: An Epithalamium," 314–15 (n. 8)
Lewis, Esther: "Advice to a Young Lady Lately Married," 116
Libertine stance: domesticity's attack on, 30, 33, 93–95, 208, 212; on Enlightenment culture, 7; and fashionable aristocratic ideology, 33, 45–46, 135, 303 (n. 9); and female libertine argument, 44, 63–64, 86–87, 98, 175; on freedom, glorification of, 54–67, 69–75, 93–94, 247, 282, 289–90, 313–14 (n. 3); libertine argument, two forms of, 38–39, 54–56, 98, 192–93, 247; on pro-marriage ideology, 37, 45–46, 55, 128, 291; and Protestant antilibertine ideology, 34–35, 40–41, 44, 67–69, 118–19; Romanticism's rejection of, 8; on Stuart court, ethos of, 3, 15, 42, 56–57; women poets' attack on, 15, 56, 83–84, 93–94, 131; on women's traditional roles, 19, 35, 298 (n. 5)
Libertinism, x, 19, 88, 211; aristocratic, 35, 91; Enlightenment, 7; Restoration, 54. *See also* Libertine stance
"Licentious Age of Charles the 2D, The" (Butler), 45
Lind, L. R., 176
"Lines Occasion'd by the Marriage of Edward Herbert Esquire," (Winchilsea), 185
Lipking, Lawrence, 22, 245
"London" (Blake), 154
Love Giv'n O're (Gould), 36, 38, 237, 245
Love-in-a-cottage formula, 28, 111, 203–5, 310 (n. 13), 313 (n. 1); rose-covered cottage, 139, 193
Lovelace, Richard, 55, 67
"Love Song: I and Thou" (Dugan), 314 (n. 7)
Lovibond, Edward: "To Lady F——, on Her Marriage," 90
Lowell, Robert: "The Old Flame," 292

Macfarlane, Alan, 297–98 (n. 3)
MacFlecknoe (Dryden), 161
Madan, Martin, 168
Madonna-harlot syndrome, 314 (n. 2)
Malecontent, The (D'Urfey), 138–40
Mandeville, Bernard: *The Virgin Unmask'd*, 301–2 (n. 8)
Manley, Delarivier, Mrs., 123, 306 (n. 7)
Mantovano, Giovanni Battista Spagnoli:

Alphus: or, The Fourth Eclogue of Baptist Mantuan, 172–73
Mantuan. See Mantovano, Giovanni Battista Spagnoli
Mariott, Thomas: *Female Conduct*, 89, 114, 262–64
"Marriage" (Corso), 293–94
"Marriage, The" (Strand), 293
Marriage Act of 1753, 16, 130–31, 150
Marriage à la Mode (Dryden), 57–58, 71, 303 (n. 4)
Marriage à la Mode: An Humorous Tale, 147, 148
"Marriage à la Mode: or the Two Sparrows" (Herbert), 88
Marriage: A Poetical Essay (Shiells), 113–14, 159–60, 217–18, 298–99 (n. 7)
Marriage: A Satire, 104–5
Marriage Asserted, 35–36
"Marriage Ceremony, The" (Wordsworth), 314 (n. 4)
Marriage debates, 43–53, 301 (n. 8)
Marriage manual poems, 113, 208, 216–17, 298–99 (n. 7)
Marriage of Heaven and Hell, The (Blake), 288–89
"Marriage of the Myrtle and the Yew, The," 153
Marriage Poems and Satires (Horne), 304 (n. 15)
"Marriage. Vision VII" (Nathaniel Cotton), 153, 272
Married Mans Best Portion, The, 229, 230
Married Mans Complaint, The, 119, 169, 229, 234, 235
Marsh, A.: *The Confessions of the New Married Couple*, 301 (n. 5); *The Ten Pleasures of Marriage*, 301 (n. 5)
Martial's epigram 35 from his eighth book (Charles Cotton), 166
Martial's epigram 35 from his eighth book (Relph), 166
Marvell, Andrew, 181, 196; "The Garden," 72
Masefield, John, 314 (n. 8)
Matrimonial Causes Act of 1857, 284–85
Matrimony, Pro and Con, 50–51
"Matron of Jedborough and Her Husband, The" (Wordsworth), 314 (n. 4)

Maud (Tennyson), 291
Medieval era: antimatrimonial tradition in, 304 (n. 12); debate in prose and verse in, 43; epithalamium, tradition of in, 181, 309 (n. 6), 314 (n. 5); love vs. marriage in literature of, 131; marriage rite in, 42; and prose arguments against marriage, 300 (n. 3); satire in, 57, 69
Memoirs (Pilkington), 20
Memoirs of a Woman of Pleasure (Cleland), 310 (n. 4)
Men and Women (Robert Browning), 292
Meredith, George: *Modern Love*, 287
Merrill, James: "The Broken Home," 314 (nn. 7, 8)
Methodism, 8, 51
Middle Ages, 100. See also Medieval era
Middle class, 11, 39, 105–6, 150, 171, 226; defined, 298 (n. 6); and domesticity, 208; and ethos, 37–38, 56; lower, 6, 8, 13, 68; and middling sort, 39, 105; and propriety, 20–21, 85–86; and Protestantism, 9, 39, 41, 56–57, 68–69, 91, 201; upper, 6, 7, 13, 18, 131–32, 147–48, 284
Mill, John Stuart, 284; *The Subjection of Women*, 18
Milton, John, 73, 131, 300 (n. 3); and allegory, 273; and blank verse, 111, 114, 156, 159, 213, 216–17; and celebratory tradition, 76, 265, 273; and criticism, recent, of his treatment of marriage, ix; "L'Allegro," 304 (n. 15). See also *Paradise Lost*
Miltonic-Thomsonian tradition, 159
Miltonic tradition, 156, 213, 273, 275–76, 310 (n. 4); celebratory, 76; descriptive, 11, 113–14, 216
Mismatched hope, 132
Mismatches, 140–41, 146, 158, 165–66
Mitchell, Joseph, 143–46, 210, 211, 307 (n. 4); "To an Humorist," 144–45; "To a Young Lady," 145; "Verses to the Right Honourable the Lady Sommerville," 210
"Modern Fine Lady, The" (Jenyns), 126–28
Modern Love (Meredith), 287
Modern Matrimony (Dobbs), 147, 158, 160–62, 214
Modern Matrimony. A Satire, 110

Molière: *Les Précieuses Ridicules*, 90
Monck, Mary: "Verses Written on Her Death-Bed at Bath," 175
Moncreiff, John: *Themistocles, A Satire*, 308 (n. 6)
"Monkey Dance. To a Jealous Wife, The" (Elizabeth Thomas), 304 (n. 10)
Montagu, Lady Mary Wortley, 267, 269; "Epistle from Mrs. Yonge to Her Husband," 244–46; "Friday: The Toilette. Lydia," 305 (n. 5)
Montaigne, Michel de, 71
Moore, Edward and Henry Brooke: *Fables for the Female Sex*, 114
More, Hannah: *Strictures on the Modern System of Female Education*, 21
M. S.: *The Great Birth of Man*, 25, 231–33
"Mutual Forbearance Necessary to the Happiness of the Married State" (Cowper), 50–51, 52–53, 278–79
Mysogynus, 25

Nash, Ogden, 293
Neville, Henry: *Newes from the New Exchange*, 226–27
"New Ballad Intitled The Sorrowfull Husband's Garland, A" (Cowper), 170–71
Newes from the New Exchange (Neville), 226–27
"New Litany, A" (Elizabeth Thomas), 81–82
Newman, Hugh: *A Poem in Praise of Marrying for Love*, 118, 201–2, 250
Nonconformists, 8, 57, 304 (n. 14)
"North-Country Wedding, The" (N. Brown), 188–89, 208
Novak, Maximillian E., 303 (n. 1)
Noyes, Gertrude, 305 (n. 3), 312 (n. 6)
Nuptial Dialogues and Debates (Edward Ward), 47, 253
Nuptial Elegies (Portal), 176, 275
Nuptials, The (Shepherd), 111, 156–57, 213–14, 215
"Nuptial Song or Epithalamie, A" (Herrick), 181
Nussbaum, Felicity, 36–37, 238, 304 (n. 12), 305 (n. 2), 306 (nn. 8, 9), 311 (n. 1)

Ode, 177–80, 211, 288; Pindarique, 177, 178
"Ode on Solitude" (Pope), 308 (n. 10)
"Ode on the Marriage and Coronation of ... King George III and Queen Charlotte" (DuBois), 309 (n. 10)
"Ode on the Rt. Hon. Lady Henry Beauclerk" (Jones), 309 (n. 10)
"Ode. Supposed to be Written on the Marriage of a Friend" (Cowper), 179–80, 220–21
Oeconomy of Love, The (Armstrong), 113–14, 216–17
"O'er the Muir Amang the Heather" (Glover), 313–14 (n. 3)
Of Mariage and Wiving (Tasso), 301–2 (n. 8)
"O Jenny Dear, The Word is Gane" (Blamire), 305 (n. 1)
"Old Flame, The" (Lowell), 292
Oldham, John, 75, 126, 304 (n. 14); "A Satyr upon a Woman," 36
Old Maid; or; The History of Miss Ravensworth, The (Skinn), 306 (n. 10)
"On an Alderman Who Married a Very Young Wife" (Cleveland), 142–43
"On Marriage" (Burns), 313–14 (n. 3)
"On Mr. D——'s Marriage with Miss E——" (Robertson), 187
"On My Wedding Day" (Egerton), 146–47
"On the Author's Husband Desiring Her to Write Some Verses" (Whatley), 276
"On the Earl of Oxford and Mortimer's Giving His Daughter in Marriage" (Barber), 309 (n. 10)
"On the Marriage of Alexander Brodie of Brodie" (Ramsay), 185
"On the Marriage of Edward Greaves, Esq." (Byrom), 212
"On the Marriage of ... Mrs. Anastasia Stafford" (Dryden), 178–79, 197
"On the Marriage of the Earl of A——" (Pomfret), 184–85
Ovid, 91; *Tristia*, 175–76
"Ovid to His Wife" (Barbauld), 176
Oxford Packet, The, 304 (n. 15)

Pamela (Richardson), 150, 271
Paradise, 25–27, 30, 140–41, 214, 232; libertine, 63, 140; secular, 162, 202–4, 223

Paradise Lost (Milton): celebration of marital bliss, 202, 210, 282; companionate ideal in, 231–32, 271, 282; exegesis of Eden story in, 25–27, 29; feminized readings of, 27, 29, 30, 85; positive and negative attitudes toward marriage in, 25–27, 30, 228. *See also* Milton, John
Parish Register, The (Crabbe), 287
Parliament, 75, 88
Parliamentary divorce, 24, 280–81, 299 (n. 12)
Parnell, Thomas: "Hesiod," 95–96, 256
Pastoral, 215, 235, 274; comic, 150; dialogue, 91; eclogue, 172–74; elegies, 176–77; epithalamia, 181, 189–90; erotic mode of, 91–92, 265; as traditional genre, 175
"Pastoral Epithalamium, A" (Ramsay), 190
Patmore, Coventry: *The Angel in the House*, 285, 290–91
Patristic tradition: celibacy, arguments for, 38, 55, 57; satiric tradition, 25, 69, 72, 100
Paulson, Ronald, 308 (n. 7)
Peacham, Henry, 181
Perry, Ruth, 304 (n. 17), 306 (n. 10)
Philips, Katherine: "Rosannia's *Private Marriage*," 183, 195; "To My Dear Sister, Mrs. C. P. on Her Nuptial," 196–97
"Phillis, or, The Progress of Love" (Swift), 117, 120–24, 127
Pilkington, Laetitia, 279; "Consolatory Verses to Her Husband," 276; "The Happy Pair: A Ballad," 310 (n. 13); *Memoirs*, 20
Plaxton, W., 235; *Advice to New-Married Husbands*, 206–7, 233–34
Pleasures of a Single Life, The: Denham's poem finer than, 70; Gould/Ames poems of the 1680s and 1690s, affinity to, 304 (n. 14), 311 (n. 14); hyperbolic polarizations of, 73–76; initiates numerous replies, 68; list of replies to, 304 (n. 11); and pro- and antimarriage tract poems, 36; *The Rake Reform'd*, compared to, 84; *Wedlock a Paradice*, replies to, 240
Pleasures of Love and Marriage, The (Ames), 248–50, 253

Poem in Praise of Marrying for Love, A (Newman), 118, 201–2, 250
"Poet's Welcome to His Love-Begotten Daughter, A" (Burns), 313–14 (n. 3)
Pointon, Priscilla: "Letter to a Sister," 189–90
Pollak, Ellen: as feminist revisionist, ix, 3–4, 16; and myth of passive womanhood, 15, 30, 108, 249, 297 (n. 2), 311 (n. 1); and Pope as a reifier of sexist myth, 305 (n. 2); and woman as an "accessory to masculine desire," 18–19
Polwhele, Richard, 299 (n. 10)
Pomfret, John, 252, 304 (n. 11); "On the Marriage of the Earl of A——," 184–85; "To His Friend Inclined to Marry," 105–6
Poovey, Mary: as feminist revisionist, ix, 3–4, 17–18, 20; as feminist theorist, 2; ideology of, defined, 14, 297 (n. 2); on spiritualization of woman's role, 16; on woman's equality in marriage, 21
Pope, Alexander: courtly and anticourtly attitudes of, 86–88; *Eloisa to Abelard*, 86–87, 175; *Epistle to Cobham*, 107; "Epistle to Miss Blount, with the Works of Voiture," 258–60; *Epistle II. To a Lady*, 104, 106–10, 268, 305 (n. 2); and mock epic, 261; "Ode on Solitude," 308 (n. 10); and pastorals, singing match in, 172; patriarchal attitudes of, x, 286–87; and polite tradition, 32; *The Rape of the Lock*, 263; and sexist myth, reified, 297 (n. 2); style and tradition of, 110, 150, 160, 172, 179, 308 (n. 10); *Tragedy of Brutus*, 87–88; wit and intellectual vitality of, 280
Portal, Abraham: *Nuptial Elegies*, 176, 275
Porte, Joel, 310 (n. 2)
Porter, Roy, 7–8, 10, 298 (n. 5)
"Portrait of a Marriage" (Abse), 293
Poston, Carol, 299 (n. 10)
Pound, Ezra, 293
Powell, Chilton Latham, 300 (n. 3), 305 (n. 3)
"[Power of Women, The]" (Betham), 264
Precepts of Conjugal Happiness (Langhorne), 114–15, 273–74
"Prelude to Space: An Epithalamium" (C. S. Lewis), 314–15 (n. 8)

Princess, The (Tennyson), 291
Prior, Matthew, 181; "An Epitaph," 295; "A Hymn to Venus, upon a Marriage," 309 (n. 7); "To Mr. Charles Montagu, on His Marriage," 309 (n. 7); "To the E of D. upon His Marriage," 309 (n. 7); "The Wedding Night," 309 (n. 7)
Progressive historians: approaches of, ix; basic propositions of, 5; and companionate ideology, arguments concerning, 3–4, 7, 19, 284, 297–98 (n. 3); and double standard, attitude toward, 7; emphases and oversights of, 5; and emphasis on bliss in marriage, 11–13, 17–18; and husbandly dominion, attitude toward, 12–13, 19–20, 223; on patriarchal control over mating arrangements, 9–11, 17
"Progress of Marriage, The" (Swift), 117, 119–27, 306 (n. 9)
Progress of Matrimony, The, 117, 306 (n. 9)
Progress poems, 117–28; and grieving friend subtype, 119
"Prologue from *An Evening's Love*" (Dryden), 204–7
"Prologue to a New Play, Call'd, *The Disappointment*" (Dryden), 118, 303 (n. 6)
Protestant exegesis, 30
Prothalamion (Spenser), 181
Protofeminist poets, 27–28, 49, 113, 311 (n. 1)
Protofeminists: and domesticity, critique of, 18, 20, 22; and dominion, critique of, 18, 20, 22, 27; point of view of, 52, 113, 268–69, 284, 304–5 (nn. 17, 1); polemics of, 253–54; and rejection of marriage, 80; and writings, ideological basis of, 1, 85. *See also* Protofeminist poets
Provok'd Wife, The (Vanbrugh), 312–13 (n. 11)
Puritanism, 7, 9, 27

"Quaker's Wedding, The" (Stevenson), 183
Quarles, Francis, 181
"Querelle des femmes," 301 (n. 8)
"Quiet Life, and A Good Name, A" (Swift), 235

Rabelais, François, 26, 70; *Gargantua and Pantagruel*, 44, 301 (n. 8)

Rake, The (Ames), 67–68, 84, 118–19
Rake in Fetters, The, 54, 66–67
Rake Reform'd, The (G[lanvill]), 84, 119, 305 (n. 4)
Ramsay, Allan, 185, 190–91, 308 (n. 5); "A Pastoral Epithalamium," 190; "Lass with a Lump of Land," 307–8 (n. 5); "On the Marriage of Alexander Brodie of Brodie," 185
Rape of the Lock, The (Pope), 263
Rasselas (Johnson), 313 (n. 2)
Real, Hermann, 306 (n. 8)
Reflections on Celibacy and Marriage (Douglas), 302 (n. 8)
Reflexions on Marriage, 35
Relph, Rev. Josiah: Martial's epigram 35 from his eighth book, 166
Remarques on the Humours and Conversations of the Town, 35
Renaissance: and clerical tradition, 69; debate in prose and verse during, 43; early poets of, 70; and epithalamia, 181–82, 190–91, 218, 293, 309 (n. 6), 314 (n. 5); love vs. marriage in major poets of, 131; poetic genres during, 163–65; prose arguments against marriage during, 300 (n. 3); and satire, 57, 71, 100
Rendall, Jane, 2, 30, 299 (n. 10)
"Reply, The" (Jemmat), 93–94, 210–11
"Repulse to Alcander, The" (Egerton), 303 (n. 8)
Revisionist critics: and Christian conception of marriage, 23–24, 222; on companionate ideology and domesticity, 3–4, 13–14, 83–84, 85, 132, 267–69; on gender and social role, 2; identified, ix; ideology of, 17–18; and male superiority, 223, 269; on marriage as heaven, 24, 26–28, 30; and progressive arguments, challenges to, 13–23 passim, 28; and progressive/revisionist controversy, 4–5, 14; standards of, 170, 239–40
Reynolds, Myra, 304 (n. 17)
Richardson, Samuel, ix, 127, 149; *Clarissa*, 67–68, 128, 306 (n. 10); *Pamela*, 150, 271
"Rights of Woman, The" (Barbauld), 264
Rime of the Ancient Mariner, The (Coleridge), 289
Rivals, The (Sheridan), 89–90

"River Road" (Kunitz), 292
Robertson, James: "On Mr. D——'s Marriage with Miss E——," 187; "To Mr. Y——, on His Marriage," 187–88
Rochester, John Wilmot, Earl of: "Against Marriage," 58–59, 61, 82; as archrake of Charles II's court, 57; Behn's admiration for, 63, 303 (n. 7); "The Debauchee," imputed author of, 304 (n. 16); "Fragment," 59–61; and hostile tradition, 126, 306 (n. 9); and libertine argument, 57, 63, 68, 71; and libertine ethos of court wits, 55; "Satyr against Reason and Mankind," 70, 74; and Sedley, association with, 140; wit and intellectual vitality of, 280
Rogers, Katherine M., 299 (n. 9)
Rogers, Pat, 32, 300 (n. 1)
Romanticism, 8
Romantic love, 6, 8, 16–17, 87, 149, 297 (n. 2); in domesticity, 131; and love match, 154
Roos, Lord, 75
Root, Robert L., Jr., 303 (n. 5)
"Rosannia's *Private Marriage*" (Philips), 183, 195
Rossetti, Dante Gabriel, 314 (n. 2)
Rothstein, Eric: on poetry, evolving focus of, 33, 56, 99–101, 300 (n. 2); on poetry, schemata for, 83; on popular emotional efforts in later era poetry, 164–66; on power as theme in Restoration poetry, 80; on Restoration misogyny, causes of, 311 (n. 3); on traditional genres in later era poetry, 164
Rousseau, Jean Jacques, 20
Rowe, Elizabeth, 222; "An Epistle from Alexias," 175, 219–20; "Upon the Death of Her Husband," 175, 219
Roxana (Defoe), 20
Royalists, 70, 73, 174, 183, 307 (n. 2). *See also* Royalist satirists
Royalist satirists, 143, 183, 226, 227
"Rural Lass, The" (Jemmat), 310 (n. 13)

Saint Jerome, 72
Saint Pauls, 32, 300 (n. 1)
Sappho, 91, 181
Sarton, May, 293
Sarum Manual, 42

"Satire on Marriage, A" (Tom Brown), 233, 306 (n. 8), 307 (n. 3)
Satiric gallery, 100–111, 287, 305 (n. 1)
Satiric hostility: and prolonged-adolescence theory, 39–40; provident-warning explanation of, 39; psychosexual explanation of, 40
Satyr against Love, A (attrib. to Congreve), 120, 306 (n. 6)
Satyr against Marriage, A, 101, 104
"Satyr against Reason and Mankind" (Rochester), 70, 74
"Satyr against Woman, A," 230
"Satyr upon a Woman, A" (Oldham), 36
"Satyr upon Marriage" (Butler), 134–35
"Satyr upon Woman's Usurpation, A," 230, 231
Savage, Mary: "Letter to Miss E. B. on Marriage," 277
Schucking, Levin, 23
Scott, John, of Amwell, 271; "The Author to His Wife," 274
Scouten, Arthur, 312 (n. 11)
"Second Part, The" (Flatman), 65, 304 (n. 10)
Sedley, Sir Charles, 165, 280; "Bithinicus, Lib. 2. Ep. 12," 167; "The Happy Pair," 140–42, 146, 275; "To Flavia," 167
Separation *a mensa et thoro*, 42, 75
Settle, Elkanah, 182
Seymar, William: *Conjugium Conjurgium*, 35–36
Shakespeare, William, 131
Shearon, Forrest B., 314 (n. 3)
Shelley, Percy Bysshe, 177, 291; *Epipsychidion*, 289–90
Shenstone, William, 147, 279; "A Ballad," 98, 171–72; "To the Memory of an Agreeable Lady," 151–52
Shepherd, Richard, 158, 310 (n. 3); *The Nuptials*, 111, 156–57, 213–14, 215
Sheridan, Thomas: *The Rivals*, 89–90
Shiells, Robert: *Marriage: A Poetical Essay*, 113–14, 159–60, 217–18, 298–99 (n. 7)
Shorter, Edward, ix, 1, 4–6, 9–13
Short View of the Immorality and Prophaneness of the English Stage, The (Jeremy Collier), 85
"Siller Croun, The" (Blamire), 95
Simonides: *The Creation of Woman*, 110

372 INDEX

Single, John: *Cupid and Hymen,* 308 (n. 1)
Sitwell, Edith, 293, 314 (n. 8)
Skelton, John, 70
Skinn, Ann Masterman: *The Old Maid; or, The History of Miss Ravensworth,* 306 (n. 10)
Sloane, Eugene, 301 (n. 4)
Smart, Christopher, 182; "Epithalamium," 310 (n. 11)
Some Reflections upon Marriage (Astell), 20, 312 (n. 8)
"Song" (Behn), 71, 139
"Song: Conquest" (Stockdale), 313 (n. 1)
Spacks, Patricia Meyer, 298–99 (n. 7)
Spectator, The, 310 (n. 5)
"Spectator Vol. the Fifth. Numb. 375" (Mary Collier), 149
Spenser, Edmund: and epithalamia indebted to nature-centered tradition, 181–84, 188; epithalamia of, 181–84, 190–91, 261, 309 (n. 6); *Epithalamion,* 181, 184; and love and marriage, softening opposition between, 131; Protestant exegesis in marriage poetry of, 30; *Prothalamion,* 181
Sprint, Rev. John, 50, 244, 250, 312 (n. 8); *The Bride Woman's Counsellor,* 240–41, 242
Spufford, Margaret, 308–9 (n. 4)
Squirearchy, 6, 11
Stanford, Ann, 315 (n. 8)
Staves, Susan: and feminist revisionists, ix, 3–4; on heroine's revolt against male authority, 306 (n. 10); ideology of, 14; on jointure vs. dower rights of widows, 17; and male sovereignty, debate over, 312 (n. 8); and patriarchy in the Restoration, challenges to, 311 (n. 1); and sentimental ideology as reinforcement of patriarchy, 21
Stein, Gertrude, 313–14 (n. 8)
Stevenson, Matthew: "The Quaker's Wedding," 183
Stockdale, Mary R.: "Song: Conquest," 313 (n. 1)
Stone, Lawrence: and affective individualism, rise of, 6, 11, 13; on companionate model, emergence of, 6; on criminal conversation suits, 24; on divorce rate after World War II, 24; on double standard, 8–9, 14–15; on female adultery, frequency of, in late eighteenth century, 280; on kinship ties, weakening of, 13; on marital sexuality, mutual enjoyment of, 11; on marriage portions, amount paid in, 147; on normal authority patterns restored with Restoration, 311 (n. 1); on Parliamentary divorces, increase of, in late eighteenth century, 299 (n. 12); on patriarchy in sixteenth century, 13; and progressive historians, ix, 1; on romantic love, popularity of, 8; on sexual attraction as basis for marriage, 204; on traditional family, 9–10
Strand, Mark: "The Marriage," 293
Strictures on the Modern System of Female Education (More), 21
Stuart court: aristocratic and skeptical ethos of, 38; Frenchified culture and Catholicism of, 298 (n. 6); immorality of, 41, 68; libertine ethos of, 3, 15, 56–57
Suarez, Michael, 82, 246
Subjection of Women, The (Mill), 18
Suckling, Sir John, 55; "A Ballad upon a Wedding," 188
Swift, Jonathan: "Baucis and Philemon," 295; *Cadenus and Vanessa,* 47–49; "Corinna," 121–23, 306 (n. 7); "An Elegy on Dicky and Dolly," 174; and embedded debate, use of, 43; epigrams of, 167–68; "An Excellent New Ballad," 308 (n. 3); "The Grand Question Debated," 302 (n. 10); "The Journal of a Modern Lady," 119; judgmental morality of, 286; as mentor of Mary Barber, 267; patriarchal attitudes of, x, 43; "Phillis, or, The Progress of Love," 117, 120–24, 127; and polemical gusto, 280; "The Progress of Marriage," 117, 119–27, 306 (n. 9); and progress poem, use of, 117–19; "A Quiet Life, and A Good Name," 235; and satiric portrayal of the Fleet district, 32; and sexist myth, challenges to, 297 (n. 2)
Sylvia's Revenge (Ames), 237–38

Tasso, Torquato: *Dello Ammogliarsi,* 301–2 (n. 8); *Of Mariage and Wiving,* 301–2 (n. 8)

Taylor, John: *Diseases of the Times*, 226
"Temple of Hymen, The" (Cawthorn), 155–56
Tennyson, Alfred, Lord: *Idylls of the King*, 291; *In Memoriam*, 291; *Maud*, 291; *The Princess*, 291; *Two Voices*, 291
Ten Pleasures of Marriage, The (Marsh), 301 (n. 5)
Ternary of Satires, A, 230
Thackeray, William Makepeace: "Damages, Two Hundred Pounds," 286
Themistocles, A Satire (Moncreiff), 308 (n. 6)
Theocritus: *Idylls*, 172, 181, 291
Theology: Anglican, 23, 41–42, 130, 195, 224; Calvinist, 130, 224; Lutheran, 130, 224; Protestant, 13, 27, 47, 130, 138, 251; Puritan, 41; Roman Catholic, 41, 72, 193, 224
"this little bride & groom are" (cummings), 314–15 (n. 8)
Thomas, Dylan, 293
Thomas, Elizabeth, 81–83, 280, 306 (n. 7); "The Forsaken Wife," 83; "The Monkey Dance. To a Jealous Wife," 304 (n. 10); "A New Litany," 81–82; "To the Lady Chudleigh," 244
Thomas, Keith, 7, 311 (n. 2)
Thompson, Roger, 169, 309 (n. 4)
Thompson, William: "Epithalamium on the Royal Nuptials," 190–91; "To a Friend on His Marriage," 179
Thresher's Labour, The (Duck), 113
"Tinker's Wife" (Kavanagh), 314 (n. 7)
"To a Friend on Her Marriage, 1784" (West), 116–17, 266–67
"To a Friend, on His Marriage" (Warton), 212
"To a Friend on His Marriage" (William Thompson), 179
"To a Lady, an Advocate for Marriage" (Wycherley), 64–65
"To a Lady Lending Me Heliodorus" (Tollet), 28
"To a Lady, Whom He Refus'd to Marry" (Tom Brown), 66
"To an Humorist" (Mitchell), 144–45
"To a Young Lady" (Mitchell), 145
"To Flavia" (Sedley), 167
"To His Friend Inclined to Marry" (Pomfret), 105–6

"To His Mistress. Against Marriage" (Walsh), 303 (n. 9)
"To Lady F——, on Her Marriage" (Lovibond), 90
Tollet, Elizabeth, 28, 246, 313 (n. 12); "Hypatia," 246; "To a Lady Lending Me Heliodorus," 28
"To Mistress E. S. Married to an Old Usurer" (Davenant), 307 (n. 3)
"To Mr. B——k on His Leaving His Mistress" (Boyd), 307 (n. 4)
"To Mr. Charles Montagu, on His Marriage" (Prior), 309 (n. 7)
"To Mr. Daniel Booth, Jun. on His Marriage" (Moses Browne), 186, 308 (n. 11)
"To Mrs. S.——. An Epigram" (Dixon), 91
"To Mrs. W. on Her Excellent Verses" (Behn), 303 (n. 7)
"To Mr. Y——, on His Marriage" (Robertson), 187–88
"To My Dear Sister, Mrs. C. P. on Her Nuptial" (Philips), 196–97
"To my Honour'd Kinsman, John Driden, of Chesterton" (Dryden), 71–73
"To My Husband" ("Eliza"), 310–11 (n. 5)
"To One Married to an Old Man" (Waller), 143
"To Orabella" (Egerton), 143–44
Tory, 66, 130. *See also* Tory marriage satire
Tory marriage satire, 140
"To Tanya" (Berry), 315 (n. 8)
"To the E of D. upon His Marriage" (Prior), 309 (n. 7)
"To the Lady Chudleigh" (Elizabeth Thomas), 244
"To the Memory of an Agreeable Lady" (Shenstone), 151–52
Tragedy of Brutus (Pope), 87–88
Traugott, John, 303 (n. 1)
Travers, Henry: "An Epistle to a Painter," 185–86
Tristia (Ovid), 175–76
"True Tale, A" (DuBois), 266
"True Woman's Man, The" (Carey), 254–55
Trumbach, Randolph: on domesticity, ideal of, 297 (n. 1); on husbandly dominion, softening of, 13–14; on patriarchal control in mating arrange-

Trumbach, Randolph (*continued*) ments, 9–10, 16; on patrilinear vs. kinship ties, 298 (n. 4); as progressive historian, ix, 1, 7; on sexualization of woman's role in marriage, 19
Tufte, Virginia, 181–82, 309 (nn. 9, 11), 314–15 (nn. 5, 8)
Turner, James Grantham, 24–27
Two Voices (Tennyson), 291

"Unequal Fetters, The" (Winchilsea), 81
"Union of Friendship, The" (Leigh), 236–37
"Upon the Death of Her Husband" (Rowe), 175, 219
"Upon the Nuptial of Charles Lord Herbert" (Davenant), 183
Upper classes, 8, 15
Utley, Francis Lee, 301 (n. 8)

Vanbrugh, Sir John: *The Provok'd Wife*, 312–13 (n. 11)
Vanhomrigh, Esther, 48
Vaudracour and Julia (Wordsworth), 286, 314 (n. 4)
Vaughan, Thomas, 181
Venette, Nicholas: *Conjugal Love*, 298–99 (n. 7)
"Verses by Mrs. M. E——ds, Occasion'd by a Lampoon on L——d A—— H——'s Marriage," 309 (n. 5)
Verses Occasioned by the Marriage and the Game Act (Cambridge), 150–51
"Verses on the Death of a Dear and Most Lov'd Wife" (Moses Browne), 175, 271–72
"Verses to the Right Honourable the Lady Sommerville" (Mitchell), 210
"Verses Written on Her Death-Bed at Bath" (Monck), 175
"Verses, Written to a Friend on His Marriage" (Jemmat), 93, 211
Victorian era, 30, 285–87, 290–92
Vieth, David, 304 (n. 16)
Vindication of the Rights of Woman, A (Wollstonecraft), 264, 268; Barbauld's critique of, 18–20; contemporary debate over, 299 (n. 10)
Virgil, 97, 172, 173

"Virgin Life, A" (Barker), 73
Virgin Unmask'd, The (Mandeville), 301–2 (n. 8)
Visions in Verse (Nathaniel Cotton), 114, 153

Wagner, Peter, 7
Waller, Edmund, 142–43, 165–66; "To One Married to an Old Man," 143
Walsh, William, 71, 301–2 (n. 8), 303 (n. 9); *Dialogue Concerning Women*, 301–2 (n. 8); "To His Mistress. Against Marriage," 303 (n. 9)
Walton, Izaak, 71
Ward, Edward, 43, 49, 253–55; *Nuptial Dialogues and Debates*, 47, 253
Ward, James, 189–91, 209; "Epithalamium on the Marriage of Felim and Oonah," 189, 209
Ward, Ned. *See* Ward, Edward
Wardle, Ralph, 313 (n. 15)
Warton, Thomas, the Elder: "To a Friend, on His Marriage," 212
Watt, Ian, 239, 249
Way of the World, The (Congreve), 238
Weber, Harold, 303 (n. 1)
"Wedding Night, The" (Prior), 309 (n. 7)
Wedlock a Paradice, 78, 203, 238–40, 304 (n. 11)
"Wedlock: A Satire" (Mehetable Wright), 82
Wedlock Vindicated, 79, 198–99, 304 (n. 11)
"Welford Wedding, The" (Amherst), 189
Wesley, Charles, 82, 261
Wesley, John, 82, 261
Wesley, Samuel, the Younger: *The Battle of the Sexes*, 261–62
West, Jane: "To a Friend on Her Marriage, 1784," 116–17, 266–67
Whatley, Mary, 277, 279; "On the Author's Husband Desiring Her to Write Some Verses," 276
Wheeler, A. L., 176
Whig, 132, 298 (n. 6)
"Wife, The" (attrib. to Brome), 307 (n. 2)
"Wife and Widow, The" (Crabbe), 287
Wife beaters, 12, 236
Williams, Anna: "Essays Occasioned by the Marriage of Miss —— and Mr ——," 309 (n. 10)

Williams, Anne, 175
Williams, Harold, 306 (n. 7)
William III, 56–57, 303 (n. 5)
Winchilsea, Anne Finch, Countess of, 235; "Lines Occasion'd by the Marriage of Edward Herbert Esquire," 185; "The Unequal Fetters," 81
Windsor, 48
Winnett, A. R., 42, 306 (n. 1)
Winnett, Arthur R., 42, 306 (n. 1)
Winters, Ivor, 293
Wintle, Sarah, 61
Wittreich, Joseph, 27, 304 (n. 17)
Wollstonecraft, Mary: and domesticity, critique of, 18–20; on education of women, 23; feminism of, 314 (n. 1); and marriage-as-trade, attack on, 148; as protofeminist impetus, 284; and wifely subjection, protests against, 268. See also *Vindication of the Rights of Woman, A*
Woman's Advocate or Fifteen Real Comforts, The, 301 (n. 5)
Woman's Case: in an Epistle to Charles Joye, A (Centlivre), 312 (n. 7)
Woman's Labour, The (Mary Collier), 113
Women's Conquest, The (Howard), 238

Women Unmask'd and Dissected, 313 (n. 13)
Wonders of the Female World, The, 312 (n. 6)
Woodward, George, 165, 167, 222, 310 (n. 5); "A Letter from a Lady to Her Husband in Spain," 175, 218–19
Wordsworth, William, 177, 288–89; "Composed on the Eve of the Marriage of a Friend," 314 (n. 4); "The Marriage Ceremony," 314 (n. 4); "The Matron of Jedborough and Her Husband," 314 (n. 4); *Vaudracour and Julia*, 286, 314 (n. 4)
Woty, William: "The Female Advocate," 29
Wright, Hetty, 82–84, 267, 269
Wright, Louis B., 304 (n. 12)
Wright, Mehetable: "Address to Her Husband," 82–83; "Wedlock: A Satire," 82. *See also* Wright, Hetty
Wrigley, E. A., 298 (n. 3)
Wycherley, William, ix, 64–66, 71, 303 (n. 9); "To a Lady, an Advocate for Marriage," 64–65

Yonge, Mrs. Mary, 244–45
Yonge, William, 245